SCRIBAL MEMORY
AND WORD SELECTION

TEXT-CRITICAL STUDIES

Juan Hernández Jr., General Editor

Editorial Board:

Todd R. Hanneken
Roderic L. Mullen
W. Andrew Smith

Number 15

SCRIBAL MEMORY AND WORD SELECTION

Text Criticism of
the Hebrew Bible

Raymond F. Person Jr.

Atlanta

Copyright © 2023 by Raymond F. Person Jr.

All rights reserved. No part of this work may be reproduced or transmitted in any form or by any means, electronic or mechanical, including photocopying and recording, or by means of any information storage or retrieval system, except as may be expressly permitted by the 1976 Copyright Act or in writing from the publisher. Requests for permission should be addressed in writing to the Rights and Permissions Office, SBL Press, 825 Houston Mill Road, Atlanta, GA 30329 USA.

Library of Congress Control Number: 2023940981

Contents

Preface and Acknowledgments vii
Note on Transcription Conventions xiii
Abbreviations xv

Introduction 1
    Text Criticism of the Hebrew Bible   4
    Scribal Performance and Scribal Memory   28
    A New Cognitive-Linguistic Proposal   37

1. Word Selection in Conversation and Oral Traditions
    as a Lens to Understanding Text-Critical Variants 43
    Word Selection in Conversation   44
    Word Selection in Oral Traditions   57
    Word Selection and Text-Critical Variants   62

2. Category-Triggering and Text-Critical Variants 67
    Synonymous Readings   73
    Variants in Lists   96
    Harmonization   131
    Variants and Person Reference   167
    Category-Triggering and Variants: A Summary   195

3. Sound-Triggering and Text-Critical Variants 199
    Alliteration   203
    Wordplay   216
    Sound-Triggering and Variants: A Summary   230

4. Visual-Triggering and Text-Critical Variants 235
    Multimodality in Everyday Conversation   236
    Studies in Conversation Analysis That Include Written Data   238

    Visual-Triggering: An Analogous Practice   239
    Visual-Triggering and Variants: A Summary   271

5. Text-Critical Variants and Category-Triggering, Sound-Triggering,
    and Visual-Triggering: Conclusions and Implications 275
    Multimodality and Text-Critical Variants   277
    Methodological Reflections on Historical Criticism   304

Bibliography 311
Ancient Sources Index 339
Modern Authors Index 345

Preface and Acknowledgments

I began my exploration of the interdisciplinary work of applying insights from conversation analysis and the comparative study of oral traditions to the Hebrew Bible over thirty years ago as a doctoral student at Duke University. In conversations with English and history doctoral students, I enquired about professors outside of the religion program who could help me learn more about oral traditions; one of my peers suggested that I talk with William (Mack) O'Barr, a linguistic anthropologist. In our first conversation, Mack asserted that I must understand language at its most basic form, everyday conversation, if I wanted to know anything about how language worked in oral traditions or in literature. Trusting in Mack's insight was one of the most productive things I did as a doctoral student, because it started me down a path of research that has been especially productive in generating innovative solutions to interpretive problems. Mack also gave me advice to seek out postdoctoral opportunities to deepen my knowledge in these areas. Again trusting Mack's advice, in 1992 I participated in a National Endowment for the Humanities Summer Seminar directed by John Miles Foley entitled "Oral Traditions in Literature," which not only began a mentoring relationship with John, but John introduced me to the guest lecturer who visited the seminar for a week, some of whose publications I had already read, Werner Kelber. Werner continues to be one of my conversation partners. Then in 2001, I audited three doctoral seminars in the Conversation Analysis Sub-Institute of the Linguistic Summer Institute organized by the Linguistic Society of America, directed by Emanuel Schegloff, John Heritage, Gene Lerner, and Don Zimmerman, who are among the first generation of scholars in conversation analysis. These two summer opportunities directly led to some of my past publications and continue to influence my research, including through conversation partners I met while attending these events. Despite my past focus on drawing significant insights from conversation analysis and the comparative study of oral traditions to my work as a scholar of the Hebrew Bible, this is my first monograph that brings together these three research agendas, the culmination of thirty years of my trusting Mack's insight that he gave me in our first conversation at Duke, an insight that has also been encouraged by others outside of biblical studies, including especially John Foley, John Heritage, Rebecca Clift, Ilkka Arminen, Robin Wooffitt, and John Rae.

Even after almost thirty years of mulling over some of the ideas now developed in this monograph, I must give some significant credit to my friend and colleague, Ian Young. We have been conversation partners for some time, mostly at Annual Meetings of the Society of Biblical Literature. Ian often encouraged me to develop further the application of the comparative study of oral traditions to text criticism. When he recommended that we coauthor a popular book together, my response was that I thought that I needed to work out my ideas more fully in a more technical monograph before I could contribute much to such a project. Therefore, this project moved to the top of my list because of his encouragement. I sincerely thank Ian for his prodding me to complete this project and his comments on the manuscript. Ian was joined by Robert Rezetko, Jonathan Ready, and Shem Miller, all of whom have been among my close conversation partners, reading and commenting on my manuscripts and I on theirs. Werner Kelber and Ron Troxel have also offered encouraging comments on portions of this manuscript. This monograph is better because of the insightful input of all of these colleagues and any remaining deficiencies are mine alone. This monograph has also been enhanced by my gaining access to the work of the following colleagues who have shared offprints and more importantly graciously provided me with unpublished manuscripts of their forthcoming publications: Anneli Aejmelaeus, Lindsey Askin, Charlotte Hempel, Margaret Lee, Adina Moshavi, Daniel Pioske, Jonathan Vroom, Rebecca Schabach Wollenberg, and Molly Zahn. I have worked with many of these colleagues and others in The Bible in Ancient (and Modern) Media section of the Annual Meeting of the Society of Biblical Literature, which continues to nurture my work. Although he and I had interacted with each other for years concerning the Deuteronomistic History, after the publication of *Empirical Models Challenging Biblical Criticism*, Juha Pakkala and I have undertaken an intense but cordial and respectful discussion about our disagreements concerning the validity of source and redaction criticism as it is practiced today.[1] We

---

1. Raymond F. Person Jr. and Robert Rezetko, eds. *Empirical Models Challenging Biblical Criticism*, AIL 25 (Atlanta: SBL Press, 2016).

share a drive to carefully reassess the validity of historical-critical methods, and I have profited from our conversations, even though we continue to have different opinions about the efficacy of the standard criteria commonly used in source and redaction criticism. This volume continues that discussion in print; Juha's voice has been more present in its writing than the number of footnotes might suggest. He has often pushed me to be clearer concerning what a new model for historical criticism might look like, and this volume moves further in that direction. I look forward to the time when the pandemic has ended enough so that I can once again attend conferences and share meals with these and other colleagues as we continue the conversation concerning the future of biblical scholarship. Hopefully this happens before this monograph is in print.

I am pleased to be publishing with SBL Press again. Supporting a nonprofit press connected to a professional society is important in today's rapidly changing publishing environment, as many presses mostly abandon the scholarly monograph. Moreover, SBL Press has been forward-looking concerning e-publications, open access, and providing access to scholars in countries with lower GDPs than in the United States and European Union, who otherwise may have very limited access to scholarly publications. I want the thank members of the editorial boards for both the Ancient Israel and Its Literature series and the Text-Critical Studies series. I received helpful and encouraging comments from anonymous members of both groups. I want to especially thank Juan Hernández Jr., the series editor of Text-Critical Studies, whose careful editing strengthened the manuscript considerably.

Portions of chapter 2: "Category-Triggering and Text-Critical Variants" are revisions of chapters published in collections of essays as follows:

- "Formulas and Scribal Memory: A Case Study of Text-Critical Variants as Examples of Category-Triggering." Pages 147–72 in *Weathered Words: Formulaic Language and Verbal Art*. Edited by Frog and William Lamb. Milman Parry Collection of Oral Literature Series 6. Washington, DC: Center for Hellenic Studies, 2022. Reproduced by permission.
- "Harmonization in the Pentateuch and Synoptic Gospels: Repetition and Category-Triggering within Scribal Memory," Pages 318–57 in *Repetition, Communication, and Meaning in the Ancient World*. Edited by Deborah Beck. MnSup 442. Leiden: Brill, 2021. Reproduced by permission.

- "Poetics and List-Construction: A Study of Text-Critical Variants in Lists Found in the New Testament, Homer, and the Hebrew Bible," Pages 218–46 in *Bridging the Gap Between Conversation Analysis and Poetics: Studies in Talk-In-Interaction and Literature Twenty-Five Years after Jefferson*. Edited by Raymond F. Person Jr., Robin Wooffitt, and John P. Rae. Research in Language and Communication. London: Routledge, 2022. Reproduced by permission of Taylor & Francis Group.

In all three cases, I provided text-critical examples from both ancient Hebrew and ancient Greek (New Testament and, in two cases, Homeric epic). In this monograph I provide additional text-critical examples from ancient Hebrew, omitting all examples from the New Testament and Homer and some of the Hebrew examples. Therefore, readers of this monograph can find additional evidence for the sections of chapter 2 that are revisions of these chapters in these earlier publications. I thank the publishers of these chapters for the permission to reprint them in revised form and the editors of these three volumes for their helpful comments on these chapters and my methodology in general.

I began this project in earnest during my sabbatical granted by Ohio Northern University in the spring of 2019, for which I want to thank then provost Maria Cronley and then dean Holly Baumgartner for their generous support and Professor Doug Dowland for his covering my responsibilities as Director of Interdisciplinary Studies. The final stages of this project were significantly delayed due to the COVID-19 pandemic. My wife of over thirty years, Elizabeth Kelly, has supported my academic work for many years while she worked as a hospital chaplain and social worker. In March 2020, she took on the task of COVID coordinator for Mennonite Home Communities of Ohio, the local church-related nonprofit that has three skilled nursing facilities and a facility for assisted living and independent living for elders, as she continued in her role as president of the board. Since we live in a small town, we have had connections to the residents and staff for many years, so her work was full of grief and stress that wore on both of us and many others in our community, while at the same time the heroic efforts of many staff and volunteers continues to provide hope. As I finish the first full draft of this manuscript in January 2021, she is coordinating vaccinations for staff and residents and continues to help with testing. Fortunately, we can now begin to see light at the end of the tunnel—at least for those fully vaccinated—even though

I fear that there will continue to be significant tragedy for so many in the world for much too long a time to come. I dedicate this work of esoteric research to Elizabeth, my life partner, who helps keep me grounded.

Note on Transcription Conventions

The early practitioners of conversation analysis, especially Gail Jefferson, developed a transcription system with conventions to represent the sequential aspects of the audible elements of conversation. However, since the development of this early transcription system, conversation analysis has become increasingly sophisticated in its analysis of face-to-face talk-in-interaction, including a fuller examination of prosody and body movement, and, as a consequence, there is now increasingly variety among transcription conventions used in the literature. Since this study draws widely from conversation analysis, disparities exist among the studies concerning what elements in the talk-in-interaction to fully represent and how to represent them. For the benefit of my readers, I have standardized all of the transcribed examples used in this study. Although I may substitute one convention for another for the same features, I never add conventions for features not already represented in the studies used. Furthermore, for the purpose of ease of reading, I have occasionally eliminated the features found in the transcripts when they are not particularly relevant to the issue I am discussing. For those readers interested in learning more about the transcription system(s) used in conversation analysis, I highly recommend Schegloff's transcription module on his website: http://www.sscnet.ucla.edu/soc/faculty/schegloff/TranscriptionProject/index.html. There readers will find examples of transcription symbols with the audio excerpts illustrating each symbol.

Although these changes serve to aid the ease of reading this study, I realize that for some readers this simplification may have obscured other issues in which they might have an interest. These readers should refer to the secondary literature that is the source for the transcribed examples, where they will find not only fuller transcriptions but more examples.

The following transcription conventions are used in this book:

CAPS   indicates loud speech

underline	indicates higher pitch
° °	indicates that the items bracketed are spoken softer than normal
:	indicates that the previous sound is lengthened
[ ]	indicates that the items bracketed is overlapped by other speech; the first bracket of the second speaker's utterance will be indented
(1.2)	numerals within parentheses indicates the length of pauses in seconds, in this case a pause of 1.2 seconds
( )	verbal items within parentheses indicates that these words are uncertain
(*)	asterick within parentheses indicates that speech items were inaudible; each asterick indicates one syllable of the inaudible speech
,	indicates a pause
=	indicates no gap between the end of one speaker's utterance and the beginning of the next speaker's utterance
.	indicates falling intonation at the end of a word or phrase
?	indicates rising intonation at the end of a word or phrase
-	indicates an abrupt ending
wo(h)rd	laughter within a word
£	smile quality (tone of speech)
↓	indicates that the following syllable has falling intonation
↑	indicates that the following syllable has rising intonation
↑↓	upward arrow followed by downward arrow indicates that the following syllable has rising-falling intonation
(( ))	double parentheses are used to bracket comments made by the analysts within the examples

A few other transcription conventions are used that are specific to some of the examples discussed concerning a particular issue; in these cases, they will be explained just prior to those specific examples.

All examples from literature are given in the form of block quotations with the exact same spellings, punctuation, and font styles (e.g., capitals, italics) as in the text used. Paragraph indentation is also preserved, so that if an example begins in the middle of a paragraph it will not be indented. Also, since elipses are found in the original texts, all elipses that are added are placed in square brackets (i.e., [...]).

Abbreviations

AB	Anchor (Yale) Bible
ABD	Freedman, David Noel, ed. *Anchor Bible Dictionary*. 6 vols. New York: Doubleday, 1992.
ABR	*Australian Biblical Review*
AIL	Ancient Israel and Its Literature
ANEM	Ancient Near Eastern Monographs
AOAT	Alter Orient und Altes Testament
AOS	American Oriental Series
BETL	Bibliotheca Ephemeridum Theologicarum Lovaniensium
BHL	Blackwell Handbooks in Linguistics
BHQ	Biblia Hebraica Quinta
BHS	Biblia Hebraica Stuttgartensia
Bib	*Biblica*
BibInt	*Biblical Interpretation*
BJS	Brown Judaic Studies
BJSUCSD	Biblical and Judaic Studies from the University of California, San Diego
BKAT	Biblischer Kommentar, Altes Testament
BT	*The Bible Translator*
BZ	*Biblische Zeitschrift*
BZAW	Beihefte zur Zeitschrift für die alttestamentliche Wissenschaft
CBC	Cambridge Bible Commentary
CBET	Contributions to Biblical Exegesis and Theology
CBQ	*Catholic Biblical Quarterly*
CW	*Classical World*
DJD	Discoveries in the Judaean Desert
DSD	*Dead Sea Discoveries*
EJL	Early Judaism and Its Literature
ET	English text

ex(s).	example(s)
FAT	Forschungen zum Alten Testament
fem.	feminine
FRLANT	Forschungen zur Religion und Literatur des Alten und Neuen Testaments
Gen. Rab.	Genesis Rabbah
HBCE	Hebrew Bible Critical Edition
HS	*Hebrew Studies*
HSS	Harvard Semitic Studies
HUCA	*Hebrew Union College Annual*
Il.	Homer, *Iliad*
ISBL	Indiana Studies in Biblical Literature
JAJSup	Journal of Ancient Judaism Supplement
JBL	*Journal of Biblical Literature*
JHebS	*Journal of Hebrew Scriptures*
JJS	*Journal of Jewish Studies*
JNES	*Journal of Near Eastern Studies*
JSem	*Journal for Semitics*
JSJ	*Journal for the Study of Judaism*
JSJSup	Supplements to the Journal for the Study of Judaism
JSNTSup	Journal for the Study of the New Testament Supplement Series
JSOT	*Journal for the Study of the Old Testament*
JSOTSup	Journal for the Study of the Old Testament Supplement Series
JSPSup	Journal for the Study of the Pseudepigrapha Supplement Series
K	*ketiv*
LAI	Library of Ancient Israel
LHBOTS	Library of Hebrew Bible/Old Testament Studies
LNTS	Library of New Testament Studies
LSTS	Library of Second Temple Studies
LXX	Septuagint
m.	Mishnah
masc.	masculine
MnSup	Mnemosyne Supplements
MT	Masoretic Text
NETS	New English Translation of the Septuagint
NovTSup	Supplements to Novum Testamentum

NTTSD	New Testament Tools, Studies, and Documents
OBO	Orbis Biblicus et Orientalis
OG	Old Greek
OL	Old Latin
OTL	Old Testament Library
PFES	Publications of the Finnish Exegetical Society
pl.	plural
Q	*qere*
RBS	Resources for Biblical Studies
RevQ	*Revue de Qumrân*
SBLDS	Society of Biblical Literature Dissertation Series
ScrHier	Scripta Hierosolymitana
SDSS	Studies in the Dead Sea Scrolls and Related Literature
SemeiaSt	Semeia Studies
SFSHJ	South Florida Studies in the History of Judaism
SP	Samaritan Pentateuch
SSN	Studia Semitica Neerlandica
STDJ	Studies in the Texts of the Desert of Judah
SVTG	Septuaginta: Vetus Testamentum Graecum Auctoritate Academiae Scientiarum Gottingensis editum
TCS	Text Critical Studies
Text	*Text: Interdisciplinary Journal for the Study of Discourse*
TSAJ	Texts and Studies in Ancient Judaism
VT	*Vetus Testamentum*
VTSup	Supplements to Vetus Testamentum
ZAW	*Zeitschrift für die Alttestamentliche Wissenschaft*

Introduction

> But if we want to use the same method on the texts of the O.T., we meet with another difficulty. Here we have practically no divergent texts, for the only recension of the O.T. that has survived is the Masoretic Text.
> —Helmer Ringgren, "Oral and Written Transmission in the O.T.: Some Observations"

> It is time for us to stop thinking so much in terms of the *amount* of reworking in a given text and start looking for new conceptual tools that will provide new frameworks and vocabulary for discussing the various forms early Jewish scriptural rewriting could take.
> —Molly Zahn, *Rethinking Rewritten Scripture*

I begin with these two epigraphs—the first from Helmer Ringgren's 1950 essay and the second from Molly Zahn's 2011 monograph—because they represent a paradigm shift that is occurring.[1] Although he represents the dominant paradigm (what I will call the MT-priority paradigm), Ringgren was a part of the Scandinavian school that emphasized the importance of oral tradition on the biblical text, an approach that is beginning to have a significant influence on the now emerging paradigm (what I will call the text-critical paradigm). In his essay, he described the significant variation found between different copies of the same ancient Egyptian literary texts, pre-Islamic Arabic poetry, and the Quran that led him and others in the Scandinavian school to conclude that "oral and written transmission should not be played off against another: they do not exclude each other, but may be regarded as complementary."[2] Nevertheless, he concluded that

---

1. Helmer Ringgren, "Oral and Written Transmission in the O.T.: Some Observations," *Studia Theologica* 3 (1950): 34–59, here 35; Molly M. Zahn, *Rethinking Rewritten Scripture: Composition and Exegesis in the 4QReworded Pentateuch Manuscripts*, STDJ 95 (Leiden: Brill, 2011), 241, emphasis original.

2. Ringgren, "Oral and Written Transmission," 34.

MT is the "only recension of the O.T. that has survived." He was somewhat aware of the growing importance of the Dead Sea Scrolls; he mentioned 1QIsa[a] as "the Jerusalem Scroll," which provided him with "instances of oral variants" and "slips of memory."[3] But despite this awareness, Ringgren and others of his generation did not have the benefit of access to the wealth of information that the Dead Sea Scrolls have brought to the field, and as such he continued to work under the MT-priority paradigm. Nevertheless, he provided a careful study of numerous parallel texts in MT, especially Ps 18 // 2 Sam 22, as an empirical control somewhat analogous to the text-critical evidence he reviewed in other ancient Near Eastern literature.[4] Based on this analysis, he concluded as follows:

> I only want to state my opinion that it is probable that there existed an oral tradition along with the written one—concerning the correct way of reading the consonantal text—and that this oral tradition has survived up to the time of the Masoretes.[5]

Thus, although Ringgren clearly represents the MT-priority paradigm, we can also see hints in his insightful work that the text-critical evidence of the Dead Sea Scrolls combined with the comparative study of oral traditions will result in challenges to this paradigm made by those of us who are now advocating for the text-critical paradigm, including Zahn. In the epigraph from Zahn, we hear her appropriately complaining about others' arguments concerning "the *amount* of reworking" so that we can distinguish biblical from extrabiblical literature or Scripture from rewritten Scripture. Rather, she insisted that we need "new conceptual tools that will provide new frameworks and vocabulary," so that we can begin to make sense of text-critical variants but from the perspective of a new paradigm that takes text criticism seriously.[6]

---

3. Ringgren, "Oral and Written Transmission," 51, 54, 57–58.

4. Other parallel texts he analyzed are: Ps 14 // Ps 53; Ps 40:14–18 // Ps 70; Pss 57, 60 // Ps 108; Pss 105; 96; 106:1, 47 // 1 Chr 16:8–36; Isa 2:2–4 // Mic 4:1–3; Isa 16:6–12 // Jer 48:29–36; Isa 37:22–25 // 2 Kgs 19:21–34; Obad 1–6 // Jer 49:14–16, 9–10; Jer 6:12–15 // Jer 8:10–12; Jer 6:22–24; 49:19–21 // Jer 50:41–46; and Jer 10:12–16 // Jer 51:15–19.

5. Ringgren, "Oral and Written Transmission," 59.

6. See also Molly M. Zahn, *Genres of Rewriting in Second Temple Judaism: Scribal Composition and Transmission* (Cambridge: Cambridge University Press, 2020). This new monograph continues this line of argument in ways that are consistent with the

This volume is one attempt to provide such new conceptual tools. Below I will draw extensively from text criticism and the comparative study of oral traditions, building upon earlier work on scribal performance and scribal memory, in ways that are really an extension of the direction to which Ringgren's essay points, leading up to Zahn's call for new conceptual tools. In both text criticism and the comparative study of oral traditions, the following important questions have emerged: What is a word? and How are words selected? I will demonstrate that these questions can best be answered when we draw extensively from insights made in conversation analysis on how word selection works in everyday conversation and in institutional talk. That is, these questions—What is a word? and How are words selected?—are questions that require a cognitive-linguistic approach to finding answers. I contend that conversation analysis provides an excellent (if not the best) cognitive-linguistic approach to the question about word selection, because it is based on a rigorous methodology of studying naturally occurring linguistic data.[7] I will argue throughout the volume that many text-critical variants can be well explained from the perspective of word selection in everyday conversation, so that when scribes are copying manuscripts the same cognitive-linguistic processes of word selection are activated as they produce new manuscripts that have what we perceive as variants. To use Zahn's terminology, word selection as understood when we combine the insights of both the comparative study

---

text-critical paradigm advocated in this volume. Unfortunately, its publication came so late in my writing process that I have not drawn extensively from it. She discusses some of the same examples and I am certain that I could have found additional examples in her work that would have illustrated my conclusions as well.

7. I am aware that most recent applications of cognitive studies to biblical texts have not used conversation analysis, but draw more from cognitive psychology and other social science approaches. E.g., see the essays in István Czachesz and Risto Uro, eds., *Mind, Morality and Magic: Cognitive Science Approaches in Biblical Studies*, Bible World (Durham: Acumen, 2013). My limiting insights to conversation analysis is not meant to dismiss these other arguments; however, I have not engaged in a discussion of the value of these other applications of cognitive studies in this project because of the complexity of the argument in the volume due to my assumption that most of my readers will be completely unfamiliar with conversation analysis. That is, I am deliberately limiting my discussion primarily to conversation analysis for the sake of (1) illustrating its value to the discussion and (2) simplifying my argument so that my readers do not have to distinguish between conversation analysis and other approaches in my argument. However, in a few places I review how some of these other cognitive approaches have been used by text critics in my adaptation of their discussions.

of oral traditions and conversation analysis provides us with new conceptual tools, including new frameworks and vocabulary, for reimagining text-critical variants for the emerging text-critical paradigm.

Below I will elaborate on the emerging text-critical paradigm by discussing recent insights in the text criticism of the Hebrew Bible and how these insights relate to discussions of scribal performance and scribal memory, both within biblical studies and in the study of other ancient and medieval literature.[8] I will then state more explicitly my own proposal for a new cognitive-linguistic approach to reimagining text-critical variants.

Text Criticism of the Hebrew Bible

Above I asserted that a paradigm shift may be underway from what I am calling the MT-priority paradigm to the text-critical paradigm, adapting what Ian Young has labeled as a shift from "the MT-only paradigm" and

---

8. Although my primary interest is in the canonical Hebrew Bible, I am well aware that this term is anachronistic when applied even to the late Second Temple period. I also agree with those who assert that the distinction of *biblical* and *nonbiblical* for Second Temple literature is not only anachronistic but too often leads to assumptions about how biblical texts differ from the nonbiblical texts in ways that distort the evidence (e.g., Charlotte Hempel, "Pluralism and Authoritativeness: The Case of the S Tradition," in *Authoritative Scriptures in Ancient Judaism*, ed. Mladen Popović, JSJSup 141 [Leiden: Brill, 2010], 193–208; and Hempel, "The Social Matrix That Shaped the Hebrew Bible and Gave Us the Dead Sea Scrolls," in *Studies on the Text and Versions of the Hebrew Bible in Honour of Robert Gordon*, ed. Geoffrey Khan and Diana Lipton, VTSup 149 [Leiden: Brill, 2012], 221–37). Therefore, even though most of my examples come from canonical literature, I also include insights from those who specialize in the sectarian documents of the Dead Sea Scrolls. Therefore, in this monograph my use of *Hebrew Bible* should not be understood as limited to canonical literature, even though most of my examples come from canonical literature. In fact, I am confident that my conclusions in this volume generally apply well to all ancient and medieval literature. Nevertheless, this is one instance in which the language I continue to use reflects the difficulty of working in the midst of what is likely to be a paradigm shift. I agree with Hans Debel that (1) "it does not suffice, however, to merely switch terms" from "Bible"/"biblical" to "Scripture"/"scriptural" and that (2) "authoritativeness did not necessarily imply textual immutability" ("Anchoring Revelations in the Authority of Sinai: A Comparison of the Rewritings of 'Scripture' in *Jubilees* and in the P Stratum of Exodus," *JSJ* 45 [2014]: 473–74). That is, we need to rethink all of the terms that we are using in our effort to establish a new paradigm, including Hebrew Bible.

"the Text-Critical paradigm."⁹ Ironically, as I will argue below, even many text critics continue to operate under assumptions that are connected to what Young identified as the MT-only paradigm, even when they engage in discussions of other textual traditions. That is, as he is fully aware, even though Young labeled the reigning paradigm as "MT-only," this label does not mean that most biblical scholars completely ignore other textual traditions in their current research. It simply means that the methodological assumptions that they operate under continue to be informed by those same assumptions that arose when the vast majority of scholars did use only the MT as the biblical text. Thus, the text-critical paradigm is the challenging or emerging paradigm that significantly undercuts these long-held assumptions and advocates for a new set of methodological assumptions. Nevertheless, I will avoid Young's label of MT-only paradigm and use instead MT-priority paradigm to avoid giving the perception that scholars who continue to operate under the current paradigm completely ignore text-critical evidence. Like Young, however, I think that they have not yet

---

9. Ian Young, "Ancient Hebrew Without Authors," *JSem* 25 (2016): 972–1003; Young, "Starting at the Beginning with Archaic Biblical Hebrew," *HS* 58 (2017): 99–118. Other text critics have explicitly called for a paradigm shift. E.g., Eugene Ulrich wrote: "a paradigm shift is needed in the textual criticism and editing of the Hebrew Bible" ("The Evolutionary Production and Transmission of the Scriptural Books," in *Changes in Scripture: Rewriting and Interpreting Authoritative Traditions in the Second Temple Period*, ed. Hanne von Weissenberg, Juha Pakkala, and Marko Marttila, BZAW 419 [Berlin: de Gruyter, 2011], 48). I should note that any time that a paradigm shift is underway a lot of incommensurate language necessarily occurs in discussions. Sometimes the same scholar may be using the framework and vocabulary of one paradigm, while advocating for another, within the same publication. Furthermore, the same scholar may have publications that contain incommensurate frameworks when compared to each other. This is descriptively what happens when the reigning paradigm is being challenged significantly, but no new paradigm has (yet?) replaced it. Therefore, the illustrations I give in the introduction for these two paradigms in quotations by individual scholars should *not* be understood as an accurate characterization of an individual scholar's collective work, but simply an extract from that scholar's work that illustrates the point I am making at the time about biblical scholarship as a collective. This is especially the case when such a quotation comes from scholars' earlier work, when it is possible that they have changed their mind in later publications. Therefore, my quotation of an individual scholar's work is best understood as representing a paradigm shift that may be occurring within the guild understood collectively, rather than my assessment of an individual scholar's collective publications. This observation also applies to my own earlier work; i.e., I would nuance my own conclusions better now.

reimagined text criticism (and historical criticism in general) sufficiently on the basis of the extant text-critical evidence, remaining far too influenced by the past emphasis on only using MT. That is, they have not yet accepted that the text-critical evidence demands a new paradigm, the text-critical paradigm.

The title of Ronald Troxel's 2016 article, "What Is the 'Text' in Textual Criticism?," at first may appear to be an odd question, especially when one is working within the MT-priority paradigm that assumes that the original text divides the composition process from the transmission process.[10] Nevertheless, Troxel's question is critical to help us see that the foundational concepts associated with lexemes such as *word*, *text*, and *variant* are culturally constructed in ways to which text critics must be sensitive, so that their own cultural constructs do not adversely affect their analysis of literary texts and the variants they discern within them. As a needed corrective, Troxel concluded that "textual criticism must comprehend textual materiality and its sociological entailments."[11] Below I will explore the differing social constructs of text and variant between the MT-priority paradigm and the text-critical paradigm, including the various dichotomies that sustain the MT-priority paradigm.

Since the time of Karl Lachmann in the nineteenth century, most scholars of literature have understood text primarily as "original text" with the assumption that the original text should be equated with the literary text.[12] The task of text criticism was, then, to rediscover this original text of the literary text by stripping away the variants, that is, those readings that varied from the original text in its transmission history. Within the

---

10. Ronald L. Troxel, "What Is the 'Text' in Textual Criticism?," *VT* 66 (2016): 603–26. A similar question is raised in New Testament studies in Eldon Jay Epp, "The Multivalence of the Term 'Original Text' in New Testament Textual Criticism," in *Perspective on New Testament Criticism: Collected Essays, 1962–2004*, NovTSup 116 (Leiden: Brill, 2005), 551–93.

11. Troxel, "What Is the 'Text'?," 611.

12. For excellent reviews of the secondary literature on Lachmann and his influence, see Sebastiano Timpanaro, *The Genesis of Lachmann's Method*, ed. and trans. Glen W. Most (Chicago: University of Chicago Press, 2005); Bernard Cerquiglini, *In Praise of the Variant: A Critical History of Philology*, trans. Betsy Wing, Parallax (Baltimore: Johns Hopkins University Press, 1999). For an excellent review of the text-critical search for the original text especially in biblical studies, see Gary D. Martin, *Multiple Originals: New Approaches to Hebrew Bible Textual Criticism*, TCS 7 (Atlanta: Society of Biblical Literature, 2010), 12–61.

study of the Hebrew Bible, Lachmann's ideas became closely connected to the nineteenth-century scholar Paul de Lagarde. De Lagarde argued that the variety of evidence among manuscripts in the MT recension is the result of a long process that descended from one manuscript. Although de Lagarde's position was challenged in the early twentieth century by Karl Kahle, de Lagarde's arguments continued strongly among many text critics up to the present, including Emanuel Tov and Ronald Hendel.[13] As the general editor of *The Hebrew Bible: A Critical Edition* (hereafter HBCE), Hendel has significant influence in the text criticism of the Hebrew Bible. In his 2008 prologue to this project (previously announced as the Oxford Hebrew Bible [OHB]), Hendel quoted from the 2001 edition of Tov's widely influential *Textual Criticism of the Hebrew Bible*:

> Tov offers a cogent definition of the "original text" for the books of the Hebrew Bible which is compatible with the position of the OHB:
> At the end of the composition process of a biblical book stood a text which was considered authoritative (and hence also finished at the literary level), even if only by a limited group of people, and which at the same time stood at the beginning of a process of copying and textual transmission.[14]

This construction of the original text is closely connected to assumptions about how scribes operated once the composition process ended and the

---

13. For a good review of de Lagarde–Kahle debate, see Emanuel Tov, *Textual Criticism of the Hebrew Bible*, 3rd ed. (Minneapolis: Fortress, 2012), 169–74. Tov acknowledged his debt to de Lagarde (171). For an excellent discussion of the influence of Lachmann's idea of an original text on Tov and Hendel and text criticism more generally, see Hans Debel, "Rewritten Bible, Variant Literary Editions and Original Text(s): Exploring the Implications of a Pluriform Outlook on the Scriptural Tradition," in *Changes in Scripture: Rewriting and Interpreting Authoritative Traditions in the Second Temple Period*, ed. Hanne von Weissenberg, Juha Pakkala, and Marko Marttila, BZAW 419 (Berlin: de Gruyter, 2011), 65–91.

14. Ronald Hendel, "The Oxford Hebrew Bible: Prologue to a New Critical Edition," *VT* 58 (2008): 333, quoting Emanuel Tov, *Textual Criticism of the Hebrew Bible*, 2nd ed. (Minneapolis: Fortress, 2001), 177. Both Tov and Hendel may have softened their views to some degree in later works, but in my opinion they continue to work under the assumption of an original text, *even if* they have backed off on reconstructing the original text as a goal of text criticism. That is, even though I think that they represent the MT-priority paradigm better than many other contemporary text critics, I also see evidence that they too are struggling with the anomalies of that paradigm.

process of copying and textual transmission began. This construction of what scribes do as copyists extends beyond text criticism into many other approaches of historical-critical study of the Hebrew Bible, as is illustrated in this quotation from Aaron Hornkohl's work in historical linguistics:

> The scribes responsible for copying these DSS manuscripts, like those responsible for copying others, may have succeeded in doing exactly what copyists are generally supposed to have been capable of doing, i.e., producing a manuscript identical or at least very similar to its source text.[15]

What these two quotations illustrate is that some text critics (like Tov and Hendel) and other biblical scholars whose work is influenced to some degree by text criticism (like Hornkohl) too often are unaware of recent scholarship concerning what Troxel referred to as "sociological entailments" *or* for some reason have dismissed this scholarship, because of the assumptions they have based on the MT-priority paradigm. For example, although I can agree with Hornkohl that ancient scribes were supposed to copy texts that were considered authoritative in ways that produced "identical or at least very similar" texts, all of these terms must be clearly understood not on our own terms from the perspective of biblical scholars living after the Gutenberg press was invented (that is, as defined in the MT-priority paradigm), but on the terms of the ancient scribes themselves for whom everything was hand-written and remembered.[16] If we define these terms in ways that apply to our own modern standards as producers of academic literature, then the ancient scribes were regularly tremendous failures. Of course, we all know that such a conclusion is extremely anachronistic, so we must strive to better understand ancient texts and the scribes that copied them on their own terms, something a growing number of text critics and other biblical scholars have struggled with as they clearly see the failure of the MT-priority paradigm to address such sociological entailments.

---

15. Hornkohl, "Diachronic Exceptions in the Comparison of Tiberian and Qumran Hebrew: The Preservation of Early Linguistic Features in Dead Sea Scrolls Biblical Hebrew," in *The Reconfiguration of Hebrew in the Hellenistic Period*, ed. Jan Joosten, Daniel Machiela, and Jean-Sébastien Rey, STDJ 124 (Leiden: Brill, 2018), 68.

16. For an excellent discussion of the role that the invention of the printing press had on biblical studies, see Werner Kelber, "The 'Gutenberg Galaxy' and the Historical Study of the New Testament," *Oral History Journal of South Africa* 5 (2017): 1–16.

As noted above, Ringgren's insights and those of his Scandinavian colleagues hint at problems with the MT-priority paradigm as they insist on the importance of oral traditions to the composition of the Hebrew Bible. Furthermore, the influence of Lachmann and de Lagarde was challenged by Kahle, who argued that there was more variety behind the MT tradition, so that the MT recension represents a long process of reducing that variety. Although most Dead Sea Scrolls scholars and text critics of the twentieth century followed de Lagarde, an important exception was Shemaryahu Talmon, who more closely aligned with Kahle's ideas. As noted above, Zahn represents those contemporary Dead Sea Scroll scholars and text critics who are challenging the MT-priority paradigm in the tradition of Kahle and Talmon. Another contemporary text critic advocating for the text-critical paradigm is Young, who has expressed how scribal performance can enable us to understand the textual fluidity and textual plurality that is evident when we look at the text-critical evidence we now have:

> each manuscript of a biblical book in antiquity was a performance of a community tradition where the exact wording was not as important as the effective conveying of what was understood to be the meaning of the tradition. Thus, ancient literary manuscripts were not the repositories of fixed texts of compositions. Rather, each one of them contained a re-presentation of what was understood to be the essential meaning of the tradition as reflected in the written composition.[17]

When we abandon the idea of an original text that supposedly determined what future copies of the literary text should have been, then we can understand that a faithful copy depends less on verbatim reproduction and more on the transmission of the meaning of the tradition.

Below I will review how various dichotomies that are extensions of Lachmann's method—that is, they are closely based on the idea of an original text—are being challenged by text critics of the Hebrew Bible as they identify the failings of the MT-priority paradigm. However, before I do that I want to review how similar paradigm shifts are occurring in the study of other ancient and medieval literature.[18]

---

17. Ian Young, "Manuscripts and Authors of the Psalms," *Studia Biblica Slovaca* 8 (2016): 131.

18. For an excellent recent critique of the application of a literary paradigm focused on the *Urform* based on ethno-nationalist assumptions within folklore studies, see Dorian Jurić, "Back in the Foundation: Chauvinistic Scholarship and the

One of the most important voices in biblical studies for the application of media studies is Werner Kelber, whose work in gospel studies has earned him recognition beyond the guild of biblical scholarship so that he is widely respected in media studies in general.[19] Building upon the work of Elizabeth Eisenstein, Marshall McLuhan, Walter Ong, and other media critics, Kelber has concluded that "print was the medium in which modern biblical scholarship was born and from which it has acquired its formative methodological tools, exegetical conventions, and intellectual posture."[20] This print-based way of thinking led to Lachmann's method with its emphasis on the original text and the higher-critical methods that are dependent upon lower criticism's reconstruction of the original text. As Kelber states, "the historical-critical paradigm appears culture-bound and beholden to modern media dynamics that are many centuries removed from the ancient communications culture."[21] However, due to the easier availability of a much wider range of ancient and medieval manuscripts, such as the Dead Sea Scrolls, the Ptolemaic papyri of Homer, and Anglo-Saxon manuscripts, a growing number of scholars of ancient and medieval literature are questioning such distinctions.[22] This includes

---

Building Sacrifice Story-Pattern," *Oral Tradition* 34 (2020): 3–44. I.e., the emphasis on an original text within literature has also had a negative influence in the study of oral traditions and folklore.

19. E.g., Kelber was awarded the Walter J. Ong Award for Career Achievement in Scholarship by the Media Ecology Association in 2019 at their annual conference in Toronto. For a recent review of the secondary literature on media studies as applied to biblical literature (including Kelber's significant role), see Raymond F. Person Jr. and Chris Keith, "Media Studies and Biblical Studies: An Introduction," in *The Dictionary of the Bible and Ancient Media*, ed. Tom Thatcher et al. (London: Bloomsbury, 2017), 1–15.

20. Kelber, "'Gutenberg Galaxy' and the Historical Study of the New Testament," 3.

21. Werner H. Kelber, *Imprints, Voiceprints, and Footprints of Memory: Collected Essays of Werner Kelber*, RBS 74 (Atlanta: Society of Biblical Literature, 2013), 2.

22. On the Ptolemaic papyri of Homer, see Graeme D. Bird, *Multitextuality in the Homeric Iliad: The Witness of the Ptolemaic Papyri*, Hellenic Studies 43 (Washington, DC: Center for Hellenic Studies, 2010); and Jonathan Ready, *Orality, Textuality, and the Homeric Epics: An Interdisciplinary Study of Oral Texts, Dictated Texts, and Wild Texts* (Oxford: Oxford University Press, 2019). On Anglo-Saxon manuscripts, see Katherine O'Brien O'Keeffe, *Visible Song: Transitional Literacy in Old English Verse*, Cambridge Studies in Anglo-Saxon England (Cambridge: Cambridge University Press, 1990); and Joyce Tally Lionarons, ed. *Old English Literature in Its Manuscript Culture* (Morgantown: West Virginia University Press, 2004).

some biblical scholars whose work focuses on text criticism (especially influenced by the Dead Sea Scrolls). All of these challenges to the reigning paradigm of higher criticism come from a variety of approaches by scholars who study a variety of literary texts. When he surveys this variety of approaches, Kelber has labeled what he perceives as the emerging, challenging paradigm, "the oral-scribal-memorial-performative paradigm" to reflect the following various approaches: the comparative study of oral traditions, the new philology movement, memory studies, and performance studies.[23] Although this label is somewhat awkward, I nevertheless agree with Kelber that this combination of approaches has the possibility to establish a new paradigm, even though I think that has not yet been achieved, no matter how hard and long some of us have been working toward that goal. I also share Kelber's following concern: "My concern is … that the historical-critical paradigm is not historical enough. What is advocated here is a novel sense of sensibilities that seeks to come to terms with what Foley has called 'an inadequate theory of verbal art.'"[24] That is, what John Miles Foley labels as the "inadequate theory of verbal art" behind current models of historical criticism erroneously assumes the dichotomies that we will explore below that are depend on the anachronistic idea of an original text.[25] To return to Troxel's language, the inadequate theory of verbal art does not take seriously both "textual materiality and its sociological entailments," so that this inadequate theory has created sharp dichotomies that are deeply anachronistic in the context of the communications culture of the ancient world. In the study of the Hebrew Bible, the reigning historical-critical paradigm is the MT-priority paradigm and it is being challenged by the text-critical paradigm, which is certainly consistent with what Kelber called "the oral-scribal-memorial-performative paradigm."

One of the first dichotomies to be challenged remains ironically one of the most persistent—that is, the distinction between higher criticism and lower criticism. Although Dead Sea Scrolls scholars and text critics, who

---

23. Kelber, *Imprints, Voiceprints*, 2, 7; see also Werner H. Kelber, "The Work of Marcel Jousse in Context," in *The Forgotten Compass: Marcel Jousse and the Exploration of the Oral World*, ed. Werner H. Kelber and Bruce D. Chilton (Eugene, OR: Cascade, 2022), 1–53, esp. 43–49.

24. Kelber, *Imprints, Voiceprints*, 2–3.

25. John Miles Foley, *Immanent Art: From Structure to Meaning in Traditional Oral Epic* (Bloomington: Indiana University Press, 1991), 5.

have been relegated to lower criticism, have declared the demise of this distinction, many higher critics rely only or primarily on MT, still operating under the MT-priority paradigm.[26] Troxel's view is representative of most text critics:

> Even if the textual and compositional history of each book must be evaluated independently, the evidence of a more variegated origin for different forms of many biblical books creates problems for sustaining any rigid divide between "higher" and "lower" criticism.[27]

No longer is it acceptable to assume that higher critics simply take the results of lower criticism as published in a critical edition as the original text upon which they apply the higher-critical methods *or* that text critics have nothing to contribute beyond textual transmission.[28] Furthermore, as the quotation from Troxel also illustrates, we cannot easily divide composition and transmission, the first as the abode of higher criticism and the second as the abode of lower criticism. The composition-versus-transmission distinction is explicit in the MT-priority paradigm, as illustrated in the quotation I gave above from Hendel as he quoted Tov—"At the end of the composition process … the beginning of a process of copying and textual transmission"—and this dichotomy betrays the continuing influence of the higher criticism-versus-lower criticism dichotomy, even among many text critics.[29] That is, the original text as defined by Tov and accepted by Hendel is the text that defines the transition from compo-

---

26. E.g., George J. Brooke, "The Qumran Scrolls and the Demise of the Distinction between Higher and Lower Criticism," in *New Directions in Qumran Studies: Proceedings of the Bristol Colloquium on the Dead Sea Scrolls, 8–10 September 2003*, ed. Jonathan G. Campbell, William John Lyons, and Lloyd K. Pietersen, LSTS (London: T&T Clark, 2005), 26–42; Michael V. Fox, "Text Criticism and Literary Criticism," in *Built by Wisdom, Established by Understanding: Essays on Biblical and Near Eastern Literature in Honor of Adele Berlin*, ed. Maxine Grossman (Bethesda: University Press of Maryland, 2013), 341–56.

27. Ronald L. Troxel, "Writing Commentary on the Life of a Text," *VT* 67 (2017): 111–12.

28. Of course, some biblical scholars have abandoned the higher-critical methods altogether, only applying (at least they assume so) synchronic methods to a critical edition. Although I find real value in some such studies and some of my own publications reflect this method, I refuse to give up on historically informed research into the biblical text.

29. Hendel "Prologue," 333, quoting Tov, *Textual Criticism* (2nd ed.), 177.

sition to transmission and, therefore, justifies for Hendel, as the general editor, the need for HBCE. Nevertheless, HBCE includes text critics as editors of individual forthcoming volumes who distance themselves from this idea of an original text, including Troxel. Thus, the composition/transmission process is probably a better way of understanding that these are not necessarily successive, mutually exclusive stages in the literary history of books that became the Hebrew Bible (or at least the transmission-only phase must be understood to be very late).

Related to the composition-versus-transmission dichotomy that describes the literary process is a dichotomy that divides the tradents in the composition/transmission process into authors and copyists, a dichotomy evident in the above quotation from Hornkohl: copyists are those responsible for "producing a manuscript identical or at least very similar to its source text."[30] As early as 1975, Talmon challenged this distinction based on his study of the Dead Sea Scrolls, rabbinic literature, and apocrypha:

> in this sphere of biblical text transmission the possibility should be considered that the principle of "controlled variation" which was the legitimate right of biblical authors, editors, and likewise of transmitters and copyists, retained a lease on life also in the post-biblical period, and was utilized by writers who employed biblical quotations as building stones in their compositions.[31]

That is, Talmon observed that both authors and copyists employed the same literary techniques of controlled variations. Two more recent versions of this observation are found in the following quotations from Brennan Breed and JiSeong Kwon, respectively: "Scribes were always both copyists and authors, always changing and transmitting to various degrees" and "scribes were possibly the literati of oral-written texts who were equipped to transmit and produce literature."[32] I want to close my discussion of the

---

30. Hornkohl, "Diachronic Exceptions," 68.

31. Shemaryahu Talmon, "The Textual Study of the Bible: A New Outlook," in *Qumran and the History of the Biblical Text*, ed. Frank Moore Cross and Shemaryahu Talmon (Cambridge: Harvard University Press, 1975), 376.

32. Brennan W. Breed, *Nomadic Text: A Theory of Biblical Reception History*, ISBL (Bloomington: Indiana University Press, 2014), 21; JiSeong James Kwon, *Scribal Culture and Intertextuality: Literary and Historical Relationships between Job and Deutero-Isaiah*, FAT 2/85 (Tübingen: Mohr Siebeck, 2016), 139. In fact, Johann Cook has

author-versus-copyist dichotomy by quoting from the excellent work of Rebecca Scharbach Wollenberg, who demonstrated that in rabbinic literature there is a notion of continuing authorship that was also a collective project. This is illustrated in the following quotation:

> If Joshua added a portion to Moses' book and Joshua's own book was then added to first by Eleazar and then by Pinchas, and so on through the generations, we are left with a portrait of biblical composition as a progressive and collective project—an endeavor in which each generation completed the work of the previous generation, and individual contributions were transformed by the redactional activities of later recipients.[33]

That is, Wollenberg's conclusion illustrates how the author-versus-copyist dichotomy had no place even in late antiquity, supporting the assertion that this dichotomy is a post-Gutenberg invention.

The above quotation from Kwon introduces another dichotomy that continues, probably more than the others—oral-versus-written or oral-versus-textual—even though Kwon overcomes this dichotomy with "oral-written." In the traditional understanding of form criticism, oral traditions may have played an important role in the prehistory of biblical texts, providing oral sources for the biblical writers; however, the assumption tended to be that once a tradition was written down/composed by the author, that is, it became a literary text, the oral tradition ceased to influence the transmission of the text by the copyists. Therefore, oral and written were understood as successive stages in the composition/transmission process. However, this distinction has long been challenged by those who have studied oral traditions, as illustrated by the quotation I gave earlier from Ringgren: "oral and written transmission should not be played off against another: they do not exclude each other, but may be regarded as complementary."[34] Talmon made a similar observation: "In the milieu which engulfed all streams of Judaism at the turn of the era, a

---

made a strong argument that even translators can function much like an independent author. See Cook, "The Relationship between Textual Criticism, Literary Criticism, and Exegesis—An Interactive One?," *Textus* 24 (2009): 119–32.

33. Rebecca Scharbach Wollenberg, "A King and a Scribe Like Moses: The Reception of Deuteronomy 34:10 and a Rabbinic Theory of Collective Biblical Authorship," *HUCA* 90 (2019): 215.

34. Ringgren, "Oral and Written Transmission," 34.

text was by definition an aural text, a *spoken* piece of writing, a performed story."[35] Daniel Pioske has recently concluded similarly: "written and oral forms of discourse were continually intertwined throughout the centuries in which the Hebrew Bible was composed, with modes of textuality and orality shaping and being shaped by one another among societies in which writing was known but oral communication pervasive and persistent."[36] Despite how the oral-versus-written dichotomy persists, Gary Martin in his monograph *Multiple Originals* suggested that this dichotomy is being overcome, in ways that seem paradoxical from the MT-priority paradigm: "Textual criticism and oral studies are gradually evolving into a unified discipline.… We are moving away from thinking about textuality and orality as entirely separate disciplines toward examining their interconnections."[37]

After reviewing these problematic dichotomies within the MT-priority paradigm, I want to explore further three important interrelated questions: What is a text? What were scribes doing? and What is the role of textual plurality in the work of scribes copying manuscripts? First, what is a text? This is a question some text critics have explicitly asked recently. Troxel entitled an article "What Is the 'Text' in Textual Criticism?," and Hendel entitled a *Festschrift* chapter with a similar question, "What Is a Biblical Book?" In their answers to these questions, both Troxel and Hendel are clearly exploring what they are attempting to do in their participation in HBCE, that is, what is the text that they are attempting to produce in their respective text-critical volumes. Apparently still working out of the older paradigm even though here he avoided the term original text, Hendel used language from the work of philosopher Charles Peirce of "type" and "tokens" in such a way that hints at the original text as the type that is only represented by its tokens: "A literary work is, in this sense, a type, an abstract object. The physical instantiations of a literary work are its tokens."[38] When he applied this to HBCE, he concluded as follows: "the

---

35. Shemaryahu Talmon, "Oral Tradition and Written Transmission, or the Heard and the Seen Word in Judaism of the Second Temple Period," in *Jesus and the Oral Gospel Tradition*, ed. Henry Wansbrough, JSNTSup 64 (Sheffield: Sheffield Academic, 1991), 150.

36. Daniel Pioske, *Memory in the Time of Prose: Studies in Epistemology, Hebrew Scribalism, and the Biblical Past* (Oxford: Oxford University Press, 2018), 17–18.

37. Martin, *Multiple Originals*, 2.

38. Ronald Hendel, "What Is a Biblical Book?," in *From Author to Copyist: Essays on the Composition, Redaction, and Transmission of the Hebrew Bible in Honor of Zipi Talshir*, ed. Cana Werman (Winona Lake, IN: Eisenbrauns, 2015), 289.

concept of a book clarifies that one of the chief goals of a critical edition is to recover, to the extent feasible, the notation of the book at the point when it became a book, that is (in Kant's phrase) when 'someone delivers [it] to the public.'"[39] Here we can see that his formulation of book is essentially the same as the original text that defines the boundaries of the compositional process leading up to the book through the work of the author and the transmission process by copyists that follows the book's publication. In contrast, Troxel answers his question quite differently. First, he wrote "that the notion of an original text is illusory both epistemologically and, given what we know about the composition of biblical literature, ontologically."[40] Clearly Troxel is rejecting the original text as understood in the MT-priority paradigm. He then understood the critical edition of Isaiah that he is working on in a paradoxical manner—that is, his critical edition will be a text that "refers to a critically established verbal form … that entails analysis of meanings"; however, "speaking of 'the text of the Bible' is nonsensical, given its books' disparate origins and their early transmission in discrete scrolls."[41] One of Hendel's and Troxel's colleagues in HBCE who also addresses this question is Sidnie White Crawford. The following shows that for her the text that a text critic seeks is not the original text:

> The work of the text critic begins at the moment when a book reaches its recognizable shape. By "recognizable shape" I am referring to the arc of the book, its beginning, middle and end. Often this arc follows a narrative structure. Thus "Genesis" begins with the Priestly creation account followed by the primeval history, moves through the patriarchal narratives, and finishes with Joseph and the Israelites in Egypt. That is the "recognizable shape" of the book of Genesis. Within that recognizable shape, however, the text was still fluid and subject to change.[42]

That is, the recognizable shape of a book cannot be identified with any single manuscript as the original text, because "the text was still fluid and subject to change." Hendel, Troxel, and Crawford are fully aware that the results of their text-critical work will not reproduce the original text; how-

---

39. Hendel, "What Is a Biblical Book?," 301.
40. Troxel, "What Is the 'Text'?," 603–4.
41. Troxel, "What Is the 'Text'?," 622.
42. Sidnie White Crawford, *The Text of the Pentateuch: Textual Criticism and the Dead Sea Scrolls* (Berlin: de Gruyter, 2022), 147.

ever, Hendel seems to still think that there was an original text (even when he uses different terms for it), in contrast to Troxel who explicitly rejects the very idea of an original text and Crawford whose idea of a recognizable shape at least undercuts the idea of an original text. All three, however, understand that their task is to produce a critical edition that will provide a text of a biblical book that will be useful to other biblical scholars, especially those who are not text critics. As one who has profited much from my critical reading of the first (and, at the time of my writing, only) volume of HBCE—Michael Fox's *Proverbs: An Eclectic Edition with Introduction and Textual Commentary*—I look forward to using the future volumes of HBCE, including those edited by Hendel, Troxel, and Crawford.[43]

Despite some differences related to original text, Hendel, Troxel, and Crawford clearly do not equate any individual manuscript with the literary text of the books that they are editing for their critical editions, so I want to explore some other understandings of what individual manuscripts of biblical literature were in relationship to a literary text. Above we looked at Crawford's understanding of "the 'recognizable shape' of the book of Genesis"; here I want to complicate the relationship of an individual manuscript and its relationship to the book of Genesis by drawing from George Brooke's analysis of 4Q4 (4QGen^d). Brooke's study of 4Q4 led him to the conclusion that "not all of Genesis has to be included on every copy of the scriptural book."[44] Thus, by implication, both of the following observations can be true: on the one hand, no one manuscript that contains its full narrative structure (its beginning, middle, and end; Crawford's recognizable shape) can represent fully the book of Genesis, because of textual plurality and textual fluidity; on the other hand, a manuscript that contains only a portion of its recognizable shape can nevertheless represent metonymically the full narrative structure. This paradox underlines the fluidity of the very concept of literary text and book as they are related to individual manuscripts. No individual manuscript can fully represent the literary text or book, but every individual manuscript, no matter how incomplete, can nevertheless represent the

---

43. Michael V. Fox, *Proverbs: An Eclectic Edition with Introduction and Textual Commentary*, HBCE (Atlanta: SBL Press, 2015).

44. George J. Brooke, "4QGen^d Reconsidered," in *Textual Criticism and Dead Sea Scrolls Studies in Honour of Julio Trebolle Barrera: Florilegium Complutense*, ed. Andreés Piquer Otero and Pablo A. Torijano Morales, JSJSup 157 (Leiden: Brill, 2012), 60.

literary text or book sufficiently for the purpose of transmitting the text. We can complicate this even further. Based on their text-critical study of the Shema Yisrael (Deut 6:4–9), Armin Lange and Matthias Weigold concluded that "some key passages of individual books had in turn textual histories of their own which were mostly unaffected by their book's overall textual transmission."[45] From their analysis of phylacteries and mezuzot, they concluded that Deut 6:4–5 was transmitted in a stable form in contrast to Deut 6:6–9, which exhibits textual fluidity. They assumed, however, that together Deut 6:4–9 was transmitted primarily by memory in the making of phylacteries and mezuzot, especially since it had a prominent role in the liturgy. Therefore, the contrast between the textual stability of Deut 6:4–5 and the textual fluidity of Deut 6:6–9 raises another example of how transmission by memory can vary significantly from one passage to another or even within different sections of the same passage. Thus, Lange's and Weigold's conclusions suggest another paradox: on the one hand, no individual manuscript can fully contain the literary text or book; on the other hand, a manuscript may represent more than one literary text *or* a literary text may exist within a literary text.

So, what is a text? The answer to this question must be complex, allowing for the literary text to never be fully contained in any individual manuscript, but at the same time an individual manuscript may represent more than one literary text. Thus, there is a strong tension between literary text and written text/individual manuscript in ways that require the literary text to include oral texts based on memory as well as written texts. I want to end the exploration of What is a text? here with two quotations that further illustrate the complexity of the answer to this question in ways that broaden the discussion once again. In *Tracking the Master Scribe*, Sara Milstein drew extensively from her study of Mesopotamian literature and concluded the following: "Each tablet or fragment reflects a mere snapshot of a much larger tradition that surely had numerous oral and written expressions. Even when multiple versions of a text are available, it is unlikely that they are related directly."[46] In her discussion of rabbinic and early Christian literature, Wollenberg concluded, "The late antique thinkers quoted in these pages appear to have imagined the extant biblical text

---

45. Lange and Weigold, "The Text of the Shema Yisrael in Qumran Literature and Elsewhere," in Otero and Morale, *Textual Criticism and Dead Sea Scrolls Studies*, 177.

46. Sara Milstein, *Tracking the Master Scribe: Revision through Introduction in Biblical and Mesopotamian Literature* (Oxford: Oxford University Press, 2016), 12.

as a composite work that bore the literary scars of historical corruption and reconstruction."[47] Milstein drew from ancient Near Eastern literature that preceded the Hebrew Bible and Wollenberg drew from a variety of Jewish and Christian literature from the late antique period after the canonization of the Hebrew Bible; nevertheless, their conclusions demonstrate that, in the ancient world in which the Hebrew Bible was formed, individual manuscripts were understood as imperfect instantiations of literary texts preserved within the broader tradition that conceived of the composition/transmission process as a continuing, living, multigenerational project. As such, any answer to the question What is a text? must necessarily allow for a range of meanings from abstract literary texts held within scribal memory to specific manifestations of a literary text or a portion thereof in individual manuscripts with some manuscripts containing more than one literary text.

With this complex notion of text, the question What were scribes doing? must be also addressed with some complexity. Adrian Schenker asked this question in his chapter "What Do Scribes, and What Do Editors Do?" Later he refined his question in a way that clearly struggles with the implications of some of the dichotomies described above: "Did some copyists take the initiative to intervene literarily in the text they were supposed to reproduce faithfully?"[48] That is, intervening literarily seems to be the realm of authors, since copyists should reproduce the text faithfully, so did some copyists cross this boundary? Although he answered affirmatively that some copyists were "creative scribes" (borrowing a term from Eugene Ulrich), Schenker nevertheless asserted that "textual variants are mainly due to scribes and copyists."[49] Here we can see that the language

---

47. Rebecca Scharbach Wollenberg, "The Book That Changed: Narratives of Ezran Authorship as Late Antique Biblical Criticism," *JBL* 138 (2019): 159.

48. Adrian Schenker, "What Do Scribes, and What Do Editors Do? The Hebrew Text of the Masoretes, the Old Greek Bible and the Alexandrian Philological *Ekdoseis* of the Fourth and Third Centuries B.C., Illustrated by the Example of 2 Kings 1," in *After Qumran: Old and Modern Editions of the Biblical Texts—The Historical Books*, ed. Hans Ausloos, Bénédicte Lemmelijn, and Julio Trebolle Barrera, BETL 246 (Leuven: Peeters, 2012), 298, 275.

49. Schenker, "What Do Scribes, and What Do Editors Do?," 298. See Eugene Ulrich, "The Canonical Process, Textual Criticism and Latter Stages in the Composition of the Bible," in *Sha'arei Talmon: Studies in the Bible, Qumran, and the Ancient Near East Presented to Shemaryahu Talmon*, ed. Michael Fishbane and Emanuel Tov (Winona Lake, IN: Eisenbrauns, 1992), 276–87.

of the author-versus-copyist dichotomy continues its influence, even as Schenker is struggling with the implications of text-critical variants that undercut this assumption. We see a similar tension, when Brooke concluded, "Few, if any, copyists were just scribal automata," although in contrast to Schenker the tension here is used by Brooke to uncut this dichotomy well.[50] Before addressing this question further, I want to back up and look at the definition of scribe. *Scribe* can have a broader meaning, as illustrated in the following quotation from Eibert Tigchelaar:

> depending on text and context, a "scribe" (*sofer/safar/grammateus*) could be an administrative official; a person who drafts and sometimes also physically writes records and documents; a person who composes or edits literary texts; a sage who studies and teaches wisdom and ancient literature; a scholar who studies torah and legal interpretation of texts; or someone who copies existing texts by hand.[51]

Tigchelaar also noted that "individual scribes may have been involved in multiple activities."[52] Although I agree with his broader definition in general, in this work I am only interested in scribes according to a narrower definition, one more often assumed in text-critical studies, such as that of Lindsey Askin: "A scribe can be defined as a person engaged professionally in tasks of written activity. Although education served to make both literate people and scribes, scribes can be said to be engaged professionally in tasks such as copying and accounting."[53] My narrower

---

50. Brooke, "Demise," 37. See also Brooke, "What Is Editing? What Is an Edition? Towards a Taxonomy for Late Second Temple Jewish Literature," in *Insights into Editing in the Hebrew Bible and the Ancient Near East: What Does Documented Evidence Tell Us about the Transmission of Authoritative Texts?*, ed. Reinhard Müller and Juha Pakkala, CBET 84 (Leuven: Peeters, 2017), 23–39; Brooke, "Hot at Qumran, Cold in Jerusalem: A Reconsideration of Some Late Second Temple Period Attitudes to the Scriptures and Their Interpretation," in *Hā-'îsh Mōshe: Studies in Scriptural Interpretation in the Dead Sea Scrolls and Related Literature in Honor of Moshe J. Bernstein*, ed. Binyamin Y. Goldstein, Michael Segal, and George J. Brooke, STDJ 122 (Leiden: Brill, 2018), 64–77.

51. Tigchelaar, "The Scribes of the Scrolls," in *T&T Clark Companion to the Dead Sea Scrolls*, ed. George J. Brooke and Charlotte Hempel (London: T&T Clark, 2018), 524. See similarly, Leo G. Perdue, ed. *Scribes, Sages, and Seers: The Sage in the Eastern Mediterranean World*, FRLANT 219 (Göttingen: Vandenhoeck & Ruprecht, 2008).

52. Tigchelaar, "Scribes of the Scrolls," 524.

53. Askin, *Scribal Culture in Ben Sira*, JSJSup 184 (Leiden: Brill, 2018), 15.

focus in no way minimizes the multiple activities that scribes performed in the ancient world; I am simply interested in this monograph in their professional activity of copying and transmitting previously existing manuscripts.[54] Therefore, the real question I am interested in is What were scribes doing in their act of copying texts? This question is also asked by Crawford: "Did he feel free to edit, expand, and otherwise make changes to his received text, or was he attempting to copy his *Vorlage* as faithfully as possible?"[55] However, the way Crawford asked the question seems to assume some division between composition by authors and transmission by copyists—that is, like Schenker's question above, Crawford's question itself necessarily draws from the framework and language of the MT-priority paradigm with its anachronistic dichotomies. I should note that to some degree we all are trapped in the use of these dichotomies, because they are so integral to our way of understanding ancient literature. In fact, throughout the volume I continue to use some terms connected to these dichotomies, even as I strive to overcome these dichotomies. For example, I will continue to use "author" and "copyist," even though I prefer simply "scribes," because the use of even anachronistic terminology may prove helpful in my advocating for a different way of thinking about, in this case, those who write.

As just noted, the question What were scribes doing? needs further clarification, so I now want to turn to what I identified above as my third question: What is the role of textual plurality in the work of a scribe copying a manuscript? This is really a guiding question for this volume— that is, the answer demands, in my opinion, insights from the ideas of scribal performance and scribal memory combined with insights of word selection drawn from both the comparative study of oral traditions and conversation analysis. Furthermore, the previous two questions cannot be answered well without a clear answer to this question, because all three

---

54. For my discussion of this broader understanding of scribes, see Raymond F. Person Jr., "Education and Transmission of Tradition," in *Companion to Ancient Israel*, ed. Susan Niditch (Oxford: Blackwell, 2016), 366–78.

55. Sidnie White Crawford, "Interpreting the Pentateuch through Scribal Processes: The Evidence from the Qumran Manuscripts," in Müller and Pakkala, *Insights into Editing*, 63. Here I should note that with Crawford and most other scholars, I assume that the vast majority of scribes were male, so that the use of masculine pronouns is acceptable in the historical description of what was likely a male-biased profession in the ancient world.

questions are so interrelated. That is, What is a text? is a question that must be asked when we consider scribal activity within the textual plurality present throughout the composition/transmission process.[56] Moreover, if scribes are not copying a text that is supposed to be closely connected to the original text (or even the *Vorlage* physically present), the question of What were scribes doing? becomes more important. Below I will give my preliminary answer to this third question that implies an answer to the other two questions, but before I do so I want to be more specific on the cognitive processes involved in the scribal act of copying manuscripts. I will explore two models proposed by Hendel and Jonathan Vroom, but I will adapt them further, including drawing from some important insights in Askin's recent work.

In his introduction to HBCE, *Steps to a New Edition of the Hebrew Bible*, Hendel constructed "a plausible typology that addresses how scribal errors happen" based significantly on the typology of Eugene Vinaver published in 1939 on his text-critical work on medieval English and French literature.[57] Vinaver's typology has four stages under which Hendel discussed the typology of scribal variants in the text criticism of the Hebrew Bible as follows, all of which will be noted in the text-critical apparatus of volumes in HBCE and which Hendel illustrated with examples from Fox's *Proverbs* volume in HBCE:

(A) The Reading of the Text
    Graphic Confusion
    Metathesis
    Dittography with Graphic Confusion
    Word Misdivision
    Aural Error
    Synonym with Graphic or Aural Trigger
(B) The Passage of the Eye from the Text to the Copy
(C) The Writing of the Copy
    Forgetting

---

56. For an excellent discussion of the history of scholarship concerning textual plurality and the Hebrew Bible, see David Andrew Teeter, *Scribal Laws: Exegetical Variation in the Textual Transmission of Biblical Law in the Late Second Temple Period*, FAT 92 (Tübingen: Mohr Siebeck, 2014), 210–39.

57. Ronald Hendel, *Steps to a New Edition of the Hebrew Bible*, TCS 10 (Atlanta: SBL Press, 2016), 151.

Dittography
Distorted Dittography
Haplography
Synonym
(D) The Passage of the Eye from the Copy Back to the Text
Eye-Skip: homoioteleuton, homoioarchton, homoiomeson[58]

In this typology, Hendel explicitly discussed forgetting and memory slips. For example, he noted that he did not include any text-critical variants in "(B) The Passage of the Eye from the Text to the Copy" for the following reason: "Since slips of memory only show up in slips of the pen, the errors of memory that occur in this movement are only instantiated in the writing of the copy."[59] Then the first category of scribal errors in (C) is "forgetting," and the last category is "synonyms," which he described as follows: "synonymous variants are memory variants, because their generation relies on a lapse or misprision in the scribe's act of reading or in his short-term memory. But such memory slips are wholly at home in the setting of literary transcription."[60] Here we can clearly see how Hendel assumes that short-term memory plays an important role in the transmission process. Hendel then provided a further typology of scribal revisions, which he understood as exegetical changes (which usually expanded the text). From my perspective, Hendel's typology of scribal errors/transcriptional errors and scribal revisions/exegetical changes seems to be based too much on the composition-versus-transmission dichotomy and the author-versus-copyist dichotomy—that is, scribal errors are accidental variants from the

---

58. Hendel, *Steps to a New Edition*, 153–62.
59. Hendel, *Steps to a New Edition*, 158.
60. Hendel, *Steps to a New Edition*, 167. I should simply note here that, in his long excursus (164–69), Hendel mostly rejected Carr's conclusions concerning memory variants with the exception of synonymous readings, something hinted at in this quotation ("wholly at home in the setting of literary transcript"). See David M. Carr, *The Formation of the Hebrew Bible: A New Reconstruction* (Oxford: Oxford University Press, 2011), 17–18. However, in my opinion, Hendel misunderstood Carr's argument significantly. Below I will discuss Carr's work in the section concerning scribal memory, so I will not engage in a thorough critique of Hendel's misreading of Carr here. As is clear in this section, Hendel is still operating under an assumption of the original text and variants, most of which are scribal errors; therefore, I think he misses important nuances in Carr's understanding of memory variants, especially in his narrow focus on short-term memory.

original text made by copyists and scribal revisions are intentional variants from the original text made by copyists who have abandoned their task of copying during the transmission process.

Drawing from cognitive psychology, Vroom described the copying process in more elaborate terms than Hendel. He first noted that there are two facts to any copying process: "(1) copying involves constant alternation between reading and writing; [and] (2) human eyes cannot simultaneously focus on two spatially distinct objects."[61] He then identified the following steps of the copying process.

Scribes had to:
1. Identify the appropriate place on their *Vorlage* (where they last left off)
2. Select the next unit of text to be transferred to the new copy (a transfer unit).
3. Hold that unit of text to their short-term memory.
4. Turn their eyes from the *Vorlage* to the new copy while retaining the memory of that transfer unit.
5. Convert the transfer unit from memory to writing on the new copy.
6. Turn their eyes back to the *Vorlage* while still retaining the memory of that text unit.
7. Repeat (locate that transfer unit on the *Vorlage*—the place they left off).[62]

Vroom insisted that these steps are "essential to all manner of *Vorlage*-based copying (i.e., they do not apply to dictation-based copying)" and provided references to similar observations by scholars in New Testament, classical Greek and Latin texts, and medieval literature.[63] Like

---

61. Jonathan Vroom, "A Cognitive Approach to Copying Errors: Haplography and Textual Transmission of the Hebrew Bible," *JSOT* 40 (2016): 267. Here I should note that Vroom's use of "transfer unit" from cognitive psychology may have close connections to Foley's use of "word" (see pp. 57–62 below). E.g., the English lexeme "the" by itself is unlikely to be a transfer unit, because a transfer unit will be a unit of meaning and "the" would be selected as part of the noun phrase in which it is located pragmatically. In fact, we cannot know how to pronounce "the" without the following lexeme.

62. Vroom, "Cognitive Approach to Copying Errors," 267–68.

63. Vroom, "Cognitive Approach to Copying Errors," 268.

Hendel, Vroom understood the importance of short-term memory in the copying process.

Both Hendel and Vroom assumed that their typologies apply to *Vorlage*-based copying and Vroom explicitly stated that the steps he identified do not apply to dictation-based copying. In *Scribal Culture in Ben Sira*, Askin engaged in an excellent critique of the widely held assumption made by text critics that most (if not all) manuscript transmission was conducted by *Vorlage*-based copying—that is, a solitary activity in which a scribe has both a physical existing manuscript and the new manuscript-in-progress before him. Her critique included an excellent survey of ancient descriptions of reading and writing throughout the ancient Near East, especially focused on furniture that may have accompanied writing as well as bodily positions. In light of her survey of the material culture of reading and writing, Askin concluded as follows:

> The question of "simultaneous use" of scrolls for textual transmission, copying or translation as a solitary activity becomes rather difficult to maintain. The major issue of textual variants in manuscripts also becomes one of transmission through oral recitation, and visual mistakes in reading would be caused by the scribe reading aloud to a copyist.[64]

She also observed that "the solitary scribe, as we imagine it, quietly copying out a text without assistance, seems to be a product of the Middle Ages."[65]

Although I find Askin's conclusions quite convincing and a much needed corrective to an assumption that most (if not all) textual transmission occurred according to a *Vorlage*-based copying process, I am not yet ready to agree with her wholeheartedly that textual transmission rarely occurred in this way, but occurred primarily through dictation or memory.[66] Furthermore, for the purposes of this study, I do not think that I must come down firmly on one side or the other, because it seems to me that the copying process described by Hendel and Vroom would equally apply to a dictation-based copying process, despite Vroom's assertion to the

---

64. Askin, *Scribal Culture*, 26.
65. Askin, *Scribal Culture*, 26.
66. See esp. my discussion of stichography below, which implies some likelihood of some cases of the same scribe visually copying a *Vorlage* physically present before him. Although stichography would not have necessarily required the narrower understanding of *Vorlage*-based copying (as understood by Vroom), it is a practice that might have been complicated by dictation of the *Vorlage*.

contrary. In fact, the following quotation from Askin illustrates my own assertion, in that she implicitly located some of the same scribal errors within the steps described by Vroom:

> It is not possible to be certain of whether a scribal mistake is due to visual or oral error, regardless of whether the scribe dictating is reading aloud or reciting from memory. Scribal errors and variants can be the result of hearing incorrectly (oral error), from a scribe disagreeing with the dictated manuscript, or from reading aloud incorrectly (visual error such as parablepsis).[67]

In fact, I will go a step further and argue that the phrase "*Vorlage*-based copying" can refer not only to what Hendel and Vroom imagine but also to Askin's dictation-based copying, because the scribe dictating the text may have a physical *Vorlage* before him. Therefore, when I apply Vroom's steps given above, I will adapt his wording by interpreting his use of the plural scribes to include not only solitary scribes, each of whom have both a *Vorlage* and a new manuscript before them (as he intended), but also at least two scribes, one with the *Vorlage* before him dictating to a scribe (or more) who has the new manuscript before him (as in Askin's work). For example, in the latter case, the scribe with the *Vorlage* would have to select a transfer unit to dictate and then wait for the copying scribe(s) to write that transfer unit before returning his gaze to the *Vorlage* to select the next transfer unit to dictate. That is, the process of moving from *Vorlage* to new manuscript does not differ that significantly whether there is one or more than one scribe involved in the copying process.

Even my reinterpretation of Vroom's steps for the copying process on the basis of Askin's work needs further refinement. Hendel and Vroom both assume that memory can contribute to scribal errors in the copying process, but they limit that influence to slips of memory based on short-term memory.[68] However, if no one manuscript can fully represent

---

67. Lindsey A. Askin, "Scribal Production and Literacy at Qumran: Consideration of Page Layout and Style," *Material Aspects of Reading in Ancient and Medieval Cultures: Materiality, Presence, and Performance*, ed. Jonas Leipziger, Anna Krauß, and Friederike Schücking-Jungblut, Materiale Textkulturen 26 (Berlin: de Gruyter, 2020), 31. See similarly, Askin, *Scribal Culture*, 26.

68. In a later publication, Vroom drew more widely from memory studies, including both short-term and long-term memory. See Jonathan Vroom, "The Role of Memory in *Vorlage*-Based Transmission," *Textus* 27 (2018): 258–73. In this publica-

a literary text, then in a real sense any *Vorlage* that is physically present in its written form may not be the only text present in the copying process. If it is possible (no matter how unusual) that the production of a new manuscript can occur based strictly on memory, that is, with no written *Vorlage* present, then we certainly should consider that more than one *Vorlage* may be present during *Vorlage*-based copying. That is, the *Vorlage* that is physically present in its written form may be joined by other *Vorlagen* that reside in scribal memory.[69] In this sense, short-term memory may influence scribes' copying of the *Vorlage* physically present before them, but the other *Vorlagen*, those not physically present in written form but stored in long-term memory, may nevertheless influence the scribes' new manuscripts; therefore, the new manuscripts may be more than copies of even the one *Vorlage* that is physically present in written form. Therefore, it seems likely to me that the scribes' physical libraries (no matter how large or small; public or private) not only included different recensions or editions of literary texts, but these physical libraries were representations of the libraries of literary texts preserved in the collective memory of the scribes. Although access to physical libraries likely was greatly limited to a few resident scribes, the libraries held in scribal memory would have been libraries that the scribes could carry with them in all times and places; and even if they had access to the physical libraries, the mechanics of handling scrolls would have meant that the libraries stored in scribal memory would have been more often accessed for quotations in composition as well as corrections in transmission or, better, throughout the entire composition/transmission process.

What is the role of textual plurality in the work of a scribe copying a manuscript? *Even if* a scribe's act of producing a new manuscript includes *Vorlage*-based copying, textual plurality and textual fluidity remain a distinct possibility, because any physically present *Vorlage* in written form, that is, a manuscript, cannot adequately represent the textual plurality in

---

tion, Vroom explicitly drew from my work on scribal memory in one of my book chapters directly connected to this project: Raymond F. Person Jr., "Formulas and Scribal Memory: A Case Study of Text-Critical Variants as Examples of Category-Triggering," in *Weathered Words: Formulaic Language and Verbal Art*, ed. Frog and William Lamb, Publications of the Milman Parry Collection of Oral Literature 6 (Washington, DC: Center for Hellenic Studies, 2022). Thus, I am confident that Vroom has accepted some of what I now argue in this work.

69. For a fuller discussion of scribal memory, see below.

which the literary text exists, of which the *Vorlage* is but one instantiation; therefore, any scribe may access the full textual plurality of the literary text that exists within scribal memory, even when he may not have access to other physical manuscripts of the literary text. Before I explicate further the ideas of scribal performance and scribal memory that are critical to my answer, I want to reflect on the following from Tov's essay, "Some Reflections on Consistency in the Activity of Scribes and Translators":

> I suggest that consistency was not part of their world. These persons sometimes display *tendencies* towards consistency, but no more than that. The absence of consistency did not disturb the ancients, since the aspiration for consistency is an invention of later centuries. Consistency is probably a product of schools, universities, and other frameworks that did not exist in the world of the ancient biblical scribes and translators and to the extent that such frameworks did exist, the ancients did not try to adhere to them.[70]

Consistency may not have been part of the scribes' world, but note that Tov cleverly does not conclude that inconsistency was. Something else must have been going on. When I apply this important insight to *Vorlage*-based copying, I explicitly note that much of the time scribes adhered closely to the *Vorlage*. However, their inconsistency (as we tend to perceive it) suggests that this verbal adherence to the *Vorlage* was *not* something that was ideologically required of copyists who were supposed to copy and expected themselves to copy the text of the *Vorlage* verbatim. Rather, they faithfully performed the literary texts in their very act of copying them within the composition/transmission process for their continued use in the communities that they served.

Scribal Performance and Scribal Memory

Above I have referred to both scribal performance and scribal memory in my preliminary answer to the question What were scribes doing? Here I will elaborate on these concepts that are so critical to my argument by

---

70. Emanuel Tov, "Some Reflections on Consistency in the Activity of Scribes and Translators," in *Textual Criticism of the Hebrew Bible, Qumran, Septuagint: Collected Essays*, vol. 3, VTSup 167 (Leiden: Brill, 2015), 36, emphasis original. Here we see Tov undercutting the MT-priority paradigm significantly by implying that historical-critical assumptions are post-Gutenberg inventions.

reviewing the secondary literature and explicating further my own adaptation of these concepts.

The argument of scribes as performers coalesced most clearly in the work of Alger Doane, especially in his 1994 article, "The Ethnography of Scribal Writing and Anglo-Saxon Poetry: Scribe as Performer."[71] Doane applied insights from both the comparative study of oral traditions (especially by Foley) and performance studies (especially by Dell Hymes and Richard Bauman) to text-critical evidence in Anglo-Saxon literature, specifically two versions of the poem *Soul and Body* as one example of the type of textual plurality found in those rare cases in which a literary work in Anglo-Saxon is preserved in two or more manuscripts.[72] He concluded:

> performance ... is to be understood as centering on the scribe as transmitter of traditional vernacular messages. Such a scribe differs in his behavior from a scribe preserving authoritative messages in Latin; the performing scribe transmits a tradition gist to an audience for present use, not for future generations. As such, the scribe is part of an emergent tradition, and he is responsible to that tradition, not to an unknown "author" or to a dead piece of sheepskin, as he exercises his memory and competence to produce the tradition for a particular audience on a particular occasion. The tradition itself is the dynamic but unrealized amalgam of lore and story frameworks, of linguistic and cultural competences that were stored in the heads of people linked with that tradition. The performing scribe produced the text in an act of writing that evoked the tradition by a combination of eye and ear, script and memory.[73]

---

71. Doane, "The Ethnography of Scribal Writing and Anglo-Saxon Poetry: Scribe as Performer," *Oral Tradition* 9 (1994): 420–39.

72. See also, Alger N. Doane, "Oral Texts, Intertexts, and Intratexts: Editing Old English," in *Influence and Intertextuality in Literary History*, ed. Jay Clayton and Eric Rubinstein (Madison: University of Wisconsin Press, 1991), 75–113; Doane, "Spacing, Placing and Effacing: Scribal Textuality and Exeter Riddle 30 a/b," in *New Approaches to Editing Old English Verse*, ed. Sarah Larratt Keefer and Kathleen O'Brien O'Keeffe (Rochester, NY: Brewer, 1998), 45–64; Doane, "Beowulf and Scribal Performance," in *Unlocking the Wordhord: Anglo-Saxon Studies in Memory of Edward B. Irving*, ed. Mark Amodio and Kathleen O'Brien O'Keeffe (Toronto: University of Toronto Press, 2003), 62–75.

73. Doane, "Scribe as Performer," 435–36.

I provided this lengthy quotation because within it are various insights that may apply to the study of the Hebrew Bible, beyond the idea of scribal performance itself. For example, the contrast between Anglo-Saxon scribes writing in their vernacular language and writing in an ancient language associated with sacred texts (Latin) may prove insightful for the difference between scribes of Hebrew texts in the Second Temple period and the Masoretes of the medieval period—that is, a contrast between textual plurality and scribal performance found in the Dead Sea Scrolls and the (relative) stability found in MT. Furthermore, Doane's conclusion implies scribal memory, even though he does not use the exact term.

Doane's idea of scribal performance has been influential beyond his own area of expertise in Old English literature, including in biblical studies. In my 1998 article "The Ancient Israelite Scribe as Performer," I applied Doane's arguments to text-critical evidence in the Hebrew Bible.[74] Other biblical scholars who have cited him include Susan Niditch, David Carr, Richard Horsley, Alan Kirk, and Shem Miller.[75] Since I will discuss Carr, Kirk, and Miller further below when I discuss scribal memory, here I will only summarize the work of the Homerist, Jonathan Ready, whose monograph *Orality, Textuality, and the Homeric Epics* is exemplary in its use of scribal performance. He provided an excellent survey of the secondary literature on scribal performance from Doane to the present, including the work of numerous biblical scholars.[76] He then applied scribal performance

---

74. Raymond F. Person Jr., "Ancient Israelite Scribes as Performer," *JBL* 117 (1998): 601–9.

75. Susan Niditch, *Oral World and Written Word: Ancient Israelite Literature*, LAI (Louisville: Westminster John Knox Press, 1996), 74–75; David M. Carr, "Torah on the Heart: Literary Jewish Textuality within Its Ancient Nar Eastern Context," *Oral Tradition* 25 (2010): 27; Richard A. Horsley, "Oral and Written Aspects of the Emergence of the Gospel of Mark as Scripture," *Oral Tradition* 25 (2010): 95; Alan Kirk, *Q in Matthew: Ancient Media, Memory, and Early Scribal Transmission of the Jesus Tradition*, LNTS (London: T&T Clark, 2016), 115, 146; Kirk, *Memory and the Jesus Tradition* (London: T&T Clark, 2018), 100, 114–17, 121, 123, 127–28, 132, 138–43; Shem Miller, *Dead Sea Media: Orality, Textuality, and Memory in the Scrolls from the Judean Desert*, STDJ 129 (Leiden: Brill, 2019), 16, 32, 143–44, 232–33, 235; Marvin Miller, *Performances of Ancient Jewish Letters: From Elephantine to MMT*, JAJSup 20 (Göttingen: Vandenhoeck & Ruprecht, 2015), 158; and Pioske, *Memory in a Time of Prose*, 50.

76. Ready, *Orality, Textuality, and the Homeric Epics*, esp. 192–215. The following are a selection of biblical scholars whose work he referred to in his chapter on scribal performance: David M. Carr, *Writing on the Tablet of the Heart: Origins of Scripture and Literature* (Oxford: Oxford University Press, 2005); Carr, *Formation of the Hebrew*

to the Ptolemaic papyri of the Homeric epics, which are often viewed as containing wild variants from the received text. Ready concluded, "A scribe never stops performing; he never disclaims responsibility. He performs both when he sticks to his exemplar and when he departs from it."[77] He also stated, "I find it preferable not to restrict the use of the term '(re)performance' to a particular kind of scribal act."[78] Although this study concerns a particular kind of scribal act—*Vorlage*-based copying—I nevertheless agree with Ready that scribal performance should be understood as active in all scribal acts. In fact, in other publications I have explicitly included scribal activities like public readings and recitations of literary texts, so that scribal performance can relate to each of these (and other) activities.[79] However, this study is more narrowly focused on scribal performance in *Vorlage*-based copying as I have defined it above.

Although the application of memory studies is now getting more attention in biblical scholarship, memory has been understood as important in textual transmission for some time.[80] For example, in his 1957 formulation of his "law of scribes," Moshe Goshen-Gottstein insisted that for most text-critical variants "we have to suspect spontaneous creation"—that is, he assumed that most scribes intended to copy their *Vorlagen* verbatim, so that, whenever we cannot detect an ideologically motivated exegetical revision, the variants were so unintentional (i.e., scribal errors) as to "have

---

Bible; Horsley, "Oral and Written Aspects"; Alan Kirk, "Manuscript Tradition as a Tertium Quid: Orality and Memory in Scribal Practices," in *Jesus, the Voice, and the Text: Beyond the Oral and Written Gospel*, ed. Tom Thatcher (Waco, TX: Baylor University Press, 2008); Shem Miller, "Oral-Written Textuality of Stichtographic Poetry in the Dead Sea Scrolls," *DSD* 22 (2015): 162–88; Eva Mroczek, *The Literary Imagination in Jewish Antiquity* (Oxford: Oxford University Press, 2016); Person, "Ancient Israelite Scribe as Performer," 601–9; Person, "Formulas and Scribal Memory"; Ian Young, "The Original Problem: The Old Greek and the Masoretic Text of Daniel 5," in Person and Rezetko, *Empirical Models*, 271–301; Young, "The Dead Sea Scrolls and the Bible: The View from Qumran Samuel," *ABR* 62 (2014): 14–30.

77. Ready, *Orality, Textuality, and the Homeric Epics*, 213.
78. Ready, *Orality, Textuality, and the Homeric Epics*, 214.
79. E.g., Raymond F. Person Jr., "Character in Narrative Depictions of Composing Oral Epics and Reading Historiographies," in *Voice and Voices in Antiquity*, vol. 11 of *Orality and Literacy in the Ancient World*, ed. Niall W. Slater, MnSup 396 (Leiden: Brill, 2016), 277–94.
80. For a fuller review of the combination of memory studies and biblical studies, see Person and Keith, "Media Studies and Biblical Studies."

arisen spontaneously" in the copying process as new readings.[81] Furthermore, many of these new spontaneously created readings "rest solely on the memory and power of association of the copyist, who conflates the readings of different verses."[82] This possibility was so common that Goshen-Gottstein concluded, "Any copyist is liable to invent his share, and the better he knows his Bible, the better he knows its grammar—the more numerous may his inventions become."[83] That is, when a scribe has internalized passages and biblical grammar so well in his memory, he is more likely to depend somewhat less on the exact wording of a *Vorlage* and more on his memory during *Vorlage*-based copying. Goshen-Gottstein's colleague, Talmon, reached a similar conclusion in 1991, "In the biblical milieu, and presumably also at Qumran, memory and manuscript were not conceived as alternatives, but rather as complementary means for the preservation of revered teachings. The two media existed one next to the other throughout the biblical era."[84] Although Goshen-Gottstein and Talmon wrote these insights before Doane's work on scribal performance, we can nevertheless see how Doane's terminology would apply to their insights, especially since Doane's understanding of scribal performance included "a combination of eye and ear, script and memory."[85]

Although Doane did not use the exact term "scribal memory," his understanding of scribal performance assumes scribal memory. Scribal memory refers to the knowledge of traditional texts (oral and/or written) held in the collective memory of scribes. Thus, scribal memory of traditional texts is what underlies the scribal performance of texts, including during *Vorlage*-based copying of manuscripts that imperfectly represent the traditional literature as it exists in the collective memory of the tradition, as it is embodied within the memory of individual scribes and the memory of all of the readers and hearers of the scribes' texts, whether they were written, read aloud, or recited. Scribal memory may influence how an individual scribe copied a physical manuscript before him, producing readings that may have differed from the *Vorlage* (variants) but were not necessarily new, because the so-called variants simply reflected the scribe's conscious or subconscious reappropriation of other versions

---

81. Goshen-Gottstein, "Biblical Philology and the Concordance," *JJS* 8 (1957): 7.
82. Goshen-Gottstein, "Biblical Philology and the Concordance," 8.
83. Goshen-Gottstein, "Biblical Philology and the Concordance," 10.
84. Talmon, "Oral Tradition and Written Transmission," 148–49.
85. Doane, "Scribe as Performer," 436.

of the same text, other texts, or the broader tradition. Thus far, the term scribal memory has rarely been used by biblical scholars and most of those who have used it have done so infrequently.[86] Two important exceptions are Kirk and Miller, both of whom have emphasized the role of scribal memory in recent works. Before discussing their work, however, I should begin with Carr's contribution concerning memory as applied to biblical texts, especially since his work influenced both Kirk and Miller.

Although he infrequently used the term scribal memory, Carr's influence has been significant, especially on the basis of his 2005 monograph, *Writing on the Tablet of the Heart*, and his coining of the term "memory variants," which is most fully developed in his 2011 monograph, *The Formation of the Hebrew Bible*.[87] In *Writing on the Tablet of the Heart*, he surveyed comparative data from ancient Mesopotamia, Egypt, and Greece and concluded that "many ancient texts were not written in such a way that they could be read easily by someone who did not already know them well."[88] Mesopotamian cuneiform, Egyptian hieratic script, and the consonant-only Semitic alphabets are limited in their representation of how the texts should be pronounced, thereby requiring a high degree of familiarity with their content to facilitate reading. Thus, he concluded,

> this element of visual presentation of texts is but one indicator of the distinctive function of written copies of long-duration texts like the Bible, Gilgamesh, or Homer's works. The visual presentation of such texts presupposed that the reader already knew the given text and had probably memorized it to some extent.[89]

Carr located the primary social location for many ancient literary texts within educational settings in which they were used as mnemonic aids for the internalization of the tradition, what he labeled as "the process of

---

86. Carr, *Writing on the Tablet of the Heart*, 38; April D. DeConick, *The Original Gospel of Thomas in Translation with a Commentary and New English Translation of the Complete Gospel*, LNTS (London: T&T Clark, 2006), 24; George J. Brooke, *Reading the Dead Sea Scrolls: Essays in Method*, EJL 39 (Atlanta: Society of Biblical Literature, 2013), 57.

87. In these two works, scribal memory occurs only once. See Carr, *Writing on the Tablet of the Heart*, 38.

88. Carr, *Writing on the Tablet of the Heart*, 4.

89. Carr, *Writing on the Tablet of the Heart*, 5.

indoctrination/education/enculturation."[90] His understanding of memorization within the educational process significantly influenced his notion of both composition and transmission of literary texts:

> Rather than juggling multiple scrolls or having one scribe take dictation from two or three others, this model suggests that Israelite scribes most likely would have drawn on their verbatim memory of other texts in quoting, borrowing from, or significantly revising them. Of course, as in other cultures, Israelite scribes probably visually copied certain texts that they wished to reproduce precisely. Yet, as in other cultures, Israelite scribes probably did not work with cumbersome scrolls when they needed to produce something new, something not bearing the claim of being a precise visual copy of an earlier document.[91]

As the above quotation from *Writing on the Tablet of the Heart* suggests, Carr may have been assuming to some degree verbatim transmission not only when "they wished to reproduce [their *Vorlagen*] precisely" but also drawing from their verbatim memory. However, explicitly drawing from scribal performance, Carr made more explicit how his understanding of memory in the composition/transmission process moves us further from the idea of verbatim transmission when he later coined the term "memory variant."[92] He defined memory variants as follows: "the sort of variants that happen when a tradent modifies elements of texts in the process of citing or otherwise reproducing it from memory," such as "exchange of synonymous words, word order variation, [and] presence and absence of conjunctions and minor modifers."[93] The following clearly demonstrates that Carr understood memory variants as something that occurred even in the process of *Vorlage*-based copying:

---

90. Carr, *Writing on the Tablet of the Heart*, 5.
91. Carr, *Writing on the Tablet of the Heart*, 161.
92. Carr, "Torah on the Heart"; Carr, *Formation of the Hebrew Bible*, 13–101. He referred to Person, "Ancient Israelite Scribe as Performer" as a predecessor of his work on memory variants in the Hebrew Bible (Carr, *Formation of the Hebrew Bible*, 24).
93. Carr, *Formation of the Hebrew Bible*, 17, 33. Below, I discuss the relationship between Talmon's influential idea of synonymous readings and Carr's memory variants, before applying scribal memory to some of their examples and examples from other scholars. See Shemaryahu Talmon, "Synonymous Readings in the Textual Traditions of the Old Testament," *Studies in the Bible 1*, ed. Chaim Rabin, ScrHier 8 (Jerusalem: Magnes, 1961): 335–83.

Introduction
35

the massive verbatim agreement between different recensions testifies to the probable use of writing to support the transmission of these traditions, since the transmission of textual tradition through exclusively oral means produces wider forms of variety than most examples seen here. Yet the presence of memory variants testifies to the use of memory—at least at times—to reproduce traditions as well. In some cases, such memory variants may have been produced when scribes reproduced an entire text from memory, having mastered it as students or teachers.[94]

Although I agree with Carr that sometimes scribes may have reproduced texts based exclusively upon scribal memory—that is, without a *physical Vorlage*—in this work I am interested in *Vorlage*-based copying. However, as Carr concluded, even in *Vorlage*-based copying, memory variants occurred; therefore, even though he infrequently used the term scribal memory, his work continues to influence my own.[95]

Referring to both Doane and Carr in his 2008 essay, Kirk provided what appears to be the first sustained discussion of scribal memory.[96] He wrote that "scribal memory was the interfacial zone where writing and oral-traditional practices converged and interacted," "scribal memory was not a rote but a performative competence," and "scribal memory practices were not evidence of a special precocity but an acquired set of skills that marshaled the ordinary cognitive resources of the brain."[97] His understanding of scribal memory relativized the importance of manuscripts, presumably even in *Vorlage*-based copying. "As an unformatted, undifferentiated stream of letters, the manuscript text has only a weak representational correspondence to the composition that it recorded."[98] In this quotation, we can see the influence of Carr's work; in the following, Kirk quoted from Carr: "The manuscript was ancillary, it was the visual, material support—and external 'reference point'—for the primary existence and transmission of the text in the medium of memory."[99] If this is true, then the type of memory variants that occurs in the act of scribal performance in *Vorlage*-

---

94. Carr, *Formation of the Hebrew Bible*, 98.
95. In fact, in ch. 2 I provide some examples taken from Carr's work.
96. Kirk, "Manuscript Tradition as a Tertium Quid," 218–20.
97. Kirk, "Manuscript Tradition as a Tertium Quid," 219. See also Kirk, *Q in Matthew*, 146.
98. Kirk, "Manuscript Tradition as a Tertium Quid," 219.
99. Kirk, "Manuscript Tradition as a Tertium Quid," 219. Quoting Carr, *Writing on the Tablet of the Heart*, 160.

based copying depends on scribal memory. "Manuscript tradition and oral tradition interfaced in scribal memory."[100] In his 2016 monograph, Kirk explored how scribal memory brings a new perspective to source-critical conclusions concerning the author of the Gospel of Matthew's use of Q, not as a loose collection of early Christian traditions in a manuscript, "but an intelligible sequence of composite deliberative speeches organized in accordance with conventional moral *topoi*."[101]

In his 2019 monograph *Dead Sea Media*, Miller drew extensively from Doane, Carr, and Kirk. Miller's important contribution is making the elements of performance and tradition in scribal memory even more explicit:

> Scribal memory includes texts, performance, and tradition. In ancient Judaism, scrolls were not the primary medium of texts; rather, texts chiefly existed in the human mind. Orbiting around the texts themselves, performance is also part of scribal memory—that is, the specific ways of reading or writing texts, as well as variations in a text's performance, also constituted scribal memory. Finally, scribal memory includes traditional associations of words and traditional interpretations of texts. A written text, a traditional text, and a performed text all interfaced with one another in the mind of the scribe during the copying process.[102]

When he applied scribal memory to the Dead Sea Scrolls, he concluded, "The Dead Sea Scrolls were mediums for scribal memory, and they functioned as reference points for performance, memorization, and recall."[103] In the following chapters, I draw significantly from Millers' work, using some of his examples as my own.

I will close with the following answer to the question What were scribes doing? by closely paraphrasing and combining quotations I have given above by Doane, Ready, Kirk, and Miller as follows: Performing scribes transmitted a living tradition to their contemporary audience as they exercised their scribal memory while copying their *Vorlagen*. Scribes never stopped performing. Whether they were sticking to their *Vorlagen* or departing from them, their *Vorlagen* were ancillary—that is, visual, material supports for the primary existence and transmission of the literary texts in the medium of memory. When performing their texts, they

---

100. Kirk, *Q in Matthew*, 114.
101. Kirk, *Q in Matthew*, 183.
102. Miller, *Dead Sea Media*, 265.
103. Miller, *Dead Sea Media*, 30.

drew not only from the *Vorlagen* physically present before them, but also from those *Vorlagen* that existed within scribal memory, which included traditional associations of words and traditional interpretations of literary texts. When scribes copied their *Vorlagen* into new manuscripts, written texts, traditional texts, and performed texts all interfaced with one another in the mind of the scribes in ways that often produced what we understand as variants, but for them are simply alternative attestations of tradition and performance.

A New Cognitive-Linguistic Proposal

Above I asked three closely interrelated questions taken from text criticism—What is a text? What were scribes doing? and What is the role of textual plurality in the work of a scribe copying a manuscript?—and my preliminary answers drew significantly from recent studies that draw from scribal performance and scribal memory. However, I should note that, even though my answers to these questions remain in the minority, they are answers that have been given in previous recent scholarship, even though they are somewhat formulated on my own terms. In other words, the MT-priority paradigm continues to hold its own, despite what I and others who are also challenging it understand to be evidence to the contrary. These three questions all suggest that their answers must have some cognitive-linguistic basis, because literary texts participate in, what Troxel called, "sociological entailments," including cultural notions of what word, text, and variant mean in the ancient contexts. What is a word? and How are words selected in texts? remain important questions, because a text is understood as participating in textual plurality because the new text is somehow the same-but-different because the scribe may have selected different words. Therefore, I want to propose a unique cognitive-linguistic approach to these questions that is based on my combination of how word selection is understood in conversation analysis and the comparative approach to oral traditions, two disciplines that I will argue provide us with insightful lenses for reimagining what scribes were doing when they engaged in *Vorlage*-based copying that nevertheless resulted in textual plurality, not simply as an accident but as a characteristic of the literary tradition in which they performed/composed their texts in their very act of transmitting them. A literary text is more than any manuscript or combination of manuscripts, because it resides in scribal memory, so that, when scribes were performing their tradition in the act of copying

Vorlagen, they depended not solely on the *Vorlagen* that were physically present before them as they selected words, but also all of the *Vorlagen* as well as traditional words, phrases, and interpretations, all of which were held in scribal memory. Thus, we have a cognitive-linguistic process that requires further exploration in order to understand scribal memory and its effect on *Vorlage*-based copying and, as I will argue more fully in the next chapter, conversation analysis and the comparative study of oral traditions provide excellent (if not the best) observations that, when combined together, will provide us with a new conceptual tool for understanding how word selection functioned in scribal memory, including the production of variants that are much too often understood as scribal errors, but should be understood as alternative readings within the literary texts in their multiformity, textual fluidity, and textual plurality. In *From Conversation to Oral Tradition* I argued that the same process of word selection that occurs in everyday conversation (as described in conversation analysis) is adapted into the special grammar and traditional register of living oral traditions and literature with roots in oral tradition (as described in the comparative study of oral traditions) and I illustrated this observation with discussions of the living oral tradition of Serbo-Croatian epic as well as literature with roots in oral tradition, including Homeric epic, *Beowulf*, the *Arabian Nights*, and the Bible.[104] That is, both the poetics of oral performance and the composition of traditional literature were derived and adapted from cognitive-linguistic practices present in everyday conversation. In other publications, I have applied conversation analysis to literature to demonstrate close relationships between everyday conversation and literary discourse in works as varied as Shakespeare, American short stories, and the book of Jonah.[105] In these publications, my focus has been on composition and reception, generally ignoring transmission. However, in three forthcoming publications, I began my exploration of the application of these insights to scribal transmission based on the concepts

---

104. Raymond F. Person Jr., *From Conversation to Oral Tradition: A Simplest Systematics for Oral Traditions*, Routledge Studies in Rhetoric and Stylistics (London: Routledge, 2016).

105. Raymond F. Person Jr., "'Oh' in Shakespeare: A Conversation Analytic Approach," *Journal for Historical Pragmatics* 10 (2009): 84–107; Person, *Structure and Meaning in Conversation and Literature* (Lanham, MD: University Press of America, 1999); Person, *In Conversation with Jonah: Conversation Analysis, Literary Criticism, and the Book of Jonah*, JSOTSup 220 (Sheffield: Sheffield Academic, 1996).

of scribal performance and scribal memory combined with word selection in conversation analysis, discussing synonymous readings, harmonization, and variants in lists in ancient Hebrew and ancient Greek literature.[106] This monograph is the first devoted to a systematic application of this approach to text-critical variants in any literary tradition. Here I limit my exploration to the Hebrew Bible (broadly understood), but, as these forthcoming publications demonstrate, this approach can be easily applied to other literary traditions, including the New Testament and Homer. With this approach, I am confident in the conclusion that scribal performance and scribal memory draw from the same cognitive-linguistic approaches found in word selection in everyday conversation. In the first chapter, I will discuss word selection in everyday conversation and oral traditions by introducing to my readers relevant insights from conversation analysis and the comparative study of oral traditions. The following chapters will be organized according to my adaptation of conversation analyst Gail Jefferson's "poetics of ordinary talk" as applied to text-critical categories—that is, chapter 2 will concern category-triggering with a discussion of synonymous readings, harmonization, variants within lists, and variants related to person reference and chapter 3 will concern sound-triggering with discussion of variants containing alliteration and wordplay.[107] Chapter 4 will be my extension of Jefferson's poetics to visual variants in what I will call analogously visual-triggering with a discussion of homographs, confusion of similar letters, division of words, metathesis, haplography, and stichography. Chapter 5 will serve as the conclusion in which I demonstrate how what I discussed separately in the previous three chapters—category-triggering, sound-triggering, and visual-triggering—can occur together in a discussion of four passages with text-critical variants that illustrate the complexity and interaction of these gross-selection mechanisms.

---

106. Person, "Formulas and Scribal Memory"; Person, "Harmonization in the Pentateuch and Synoptic Gospels: Repetition and Category-Triggering within Scribal Memory," in *Repetition, Communication, and Meaning in the Ancient World*, ed. Deborah Beck, MnSup 442 (Leiden: Brill, 2021); and Person, "Poetics and List Formation: A Study of Text-Critical Variants in Lists Found in the New Testament, Homer, and the Hebrew Bible," in *Bridging the Gap between Conversation Analysis and Poetics: Studies in Talk-in-Interaction and Literature Twenty-Five Years after Jefferson*, ed. Raymond F. Person Jr., Robin Wooffitt, and John P. Rae, Research in Language and Communication (London: Routledge, 2022).

107. Gail Jefferson, "On the Poetics of Ordinary Talk," *Text and Performance Quarterly* 16 (1996): 11–61.

Thus, I will demonstrate how word selection in everyday conversation and word selection in the composition/transmission process of *Vorlage*-based copying operate using the same gross-selection mechanisms in ways that suggest that what we identify as variant readings are better understood as same-but-different alternative readings in ways that the identification of the original reading should be abandoned and even the identification of earlier readings becomes extremely problematic methodologically.

Before turning to the next chapter concerning word selection, I want to explicitly identify some shortcomings and limitations of this study in relationship to my selective use of text criticism and biblical poetics. Concerning text criticism, the emphasis is on Hebrew manuscripts with secondary attention to LXX (especially when retroversion is more certain). I rarely refer to the Latin and Syriac traditions. I generally avoid discussions of orthography and different vocalizations of the consonantal text. In some cases, I have done my own limited search of variants, but most of my examples come from secondary sources and are somewhat skewed because of that—for example, the only volume of HBCE to be published at this writing is Fox's *Proverbs*, so Proverbs is overrepresented. When I make reference to LXX, I generally depart from common practice in LXX studies—that is, translating the Greek literally rather than the purported *Vorlage*—because I generally use LXX for the purpose of reconstructing a *Vorlage* different from the Hebrew manuscript traditions. That is, *in this study* I am more interested with what LXX can tell us about the transmission history of the Hebrew *Vorlage* than with how it was interpreted into the Old Greek and its transmission in the Greek. Therefore, I sometimes vary from the secondary sources in this way. Furthermore, despite acknowledging the bias in reconstructions of lacuna in the Dead Sea Scrolls based on the MT-priority paradigm, I nevertheless continue to use the published reconstructions; even if the reconstructions are problematic, the reconstructions nevertheless fit within the broader literary tradition of the manuscripts.[108]

Although my work is informed by biblical poetics, this is not a study in biblical poetics in general, because it is limited to selective passages with

---

108. For an excellent discussion of the problem of reconstructing lacuna, see Corrado Martone, "Textual Plurality and Textual Reconstructions: A Cautionary Tale," *RevQ* 30 (2018): 131–41. Because of this, I focus on variants which are not reconstructed, but nevertheless use the published text (including reconstructions) for my discussion of the larger literary context.

text-critical variants in the Hebrew manuscript tradition (and in the LXX-*Vorlage* as reconstructed in the secondary literature). As noted further below in chapter 3 concerning sound-triggering, few text-critical studies pay much attention to poetics and few studies in biblical poetics pay much attention to text criticism, reflecting the higher criticism-versus-lower criticism dichotomy. Therefore, the examples for this chapter were not only harder to find, but often required my own combination of insights from text criticism and biblical poetics.

Despite these limitations, I am confident that my conclusions are highly suggestive concerning the cognitive-linguistic processes that were operative throughout the composition/transmission process, including when scribes engaged in *Vorlage*-based copying.

1

Word Selection in Conversation and Oral Traditions as a Lens to Understanding Text-Critical Variants

As generally understood, text-critical variants concern scribes selecting (consciously or unconsciously) different words or phrases and then changing the text (intentionally or not) on the basis of this selection, whether the change involved additions, omissions, substitutions, or transpositions. For the purpose of understanding better the cognitive-linguistic processes behind the scribes' word selection, I am convinced that the disciplinary perspectives on word selection in conversation analysis and the comparative study of oral traditions can contribute significantly to our understanding of the role that scribal memory plays in the creation of variants.[1] Thus, in this chapter, we will explore these questions: What is a word? and How are words selected? The combined insights of conversation analysis and the comparative study of oral traditions suggest the following answers: A word, the smallest unit of meaning, can be less than a lexeme (e.g., "hm") or more than a lexeme (e.g., a phrase or full line of poetry); therefore, words are selected within the particular linguistic registers and pragmatic contexts in which they occur based on a variety of factors, including the

---

1. For my readers who are unfamiliar with conversation analysis, an excellent introductory textbook is Ian Hutchby and Robin Wooffitt, *Conversation Analysis: Principles, Practices and Applications* (Cambridge: Polity, 1998). Also helpful but more technical is Jack Sidnell and Tanya Stivers, eds. *The Handbook of Conversation Analysis*, BHL (Oxford: Wiley-Blackwell, 2013). For those unfamiliar with the comparative study of oral traditions, I recommend Niditch's excellent application to the Hebrew Bible (*Oral World and Written Word*). The only combination of these two approaches with any depth is in Person, *From Conversation to Oral Tradition*, which includes good summaries of both disciplines for literary scholars and draws much more widely from insights in these two disciplines than I do in this project.

meanings that each word may carry, the sounds of the spoken word, and the relationship of the word to other words that occur within the larger pragmatic context. I will support this conclusion below by demonstrating how word selection works in everyday conversation and in oral traditions before I apply these insights to text-critical variants and how word selection works within scribal memory.

Word Selection in Conversation

The vernacular understanding of word as a single lexeme as found in standard dictionaries certainly occurs in the study of naturally occurring data in conversation analysis, but that does not exhaust the meaning of word, *if* by the term we mean the smallest unit of meaning in talk-in-interaction. Conversation analysts not only strive to understand lexemes in the context of talk-in-interaction, but have a broader understanding of word, including only the beginning sounds of a lexeme that is cut off, nonlexicals (e.g., "huh" and "mm-hmm"), and even nonverbal forms of communication (e.g., gaze and gestures). Furthermore, some of the units of meaning that conversation analysts have examined at first appear to be lexemes (or combinations of lexemes), but their use in specific conversational contexts is often lacking in the definitions of standard dictionaries—for example, "oh" and "you know" (especially when voiced "y'know") have more complex meanings in everyday conversation than standard dictionary entries suggest.[2] Admittedly, conversation analysts generally do not use the term word for things such as "uh-huh" and head nods, but these items are nevertheless considered to be some of the smallest units of meaning that are important in conversational practices, especially in the multimodal

---

2. On "oh," see John Heritage, "A Change-of-State Token and Aspects of Its Sequential Placement," in *Structure of Social Action: Studies in Conversation Analysis*, ed. J. Maxwell Atkinson and John Heritage, Studies in Emotion and Social Interaction (Cambridge: Cambridge University Press, 1984), 299–345; Heritage, "*Oh*-Prefaced Response to Inquiry," *Language in Society* 27 (1998): 291–334; Heritage, "*Oh*-Prefaced Responses to Assessments: A Method of Modifying Agreement/Disagreement," in *The Language of Turn and Sequence*, ed. Cecilia Ford, Barbara Fox, and Sandra Thompson, Oxford Studies in Sociolinguistics (Oxford: Oxford University Press, 2002), 196–224. For "you know," see Janet Holmes, "Functions of *You Know* in Women's and Men's Speech," *Language in Society* 15 (1986): 1–21. For my application of these studies of "oh" and "you know" to modern English literature, see Person, *Structure and Meaning in Conversation and Literature*, 56–67. See also, Person, "'Oh' in Shakespeare."

environments of face-to-face talk-in-interaction.[3] Thus, in contrast to vernacular understandings, conversation analysts understand that sometimes a word is less than a word ("hmm") and sometimes is more than a word ("you know"), at least in their analysis of the smallest units of meaning within a turn at talk.

In conversation analysis, word selection is closely connected to the social action that is being performed in the conversation-in-progress. This is most obvious in cases in which speakers are producing word searches within the conversation itself as well as within contexts in which words are repaired in the context of the conversation itself. Below I provide a discussion of examples of word searches within everyday conversation.[4] I will then discuss what Jefferson in her article "On the Poetics of Ordinary Talk" identified as a "gross selection-mechanism" that "may well be systematic," that is, a second-level mechanism (beyond the necessity of the pragmatic context) "by which words are selected in the course of an utterance."[5] Jefferson's poetics provides us with an explanation for why certain words may be selected within a pragmatic context when there are numerous synonymous words and phrases that would have communicated the same meaning; however, something poetic is occurring that aids in word selection in ways for which we are most often completely unaware, unless maybe if we have the ear of a poet. These two observations from conversation analysis, word searches and poetics, combine to give us a helpful understanding of word selection in everyday conversation.

Word Searches in Conversation

Speakers choose words whenever they are speaking and these words are closely connected to the social action being performed in the talk-in-progress. Although this happens so quickly that it often goes unnoticed,

---

3. My use of *word* here is dependent on the work of Foley from the comparative study of oral traditions as discussed below. Its application to conversation analysis is my own, and I acknowledge that few conversation analysts may accept how I am using the term here. Nevertheless, when understood as "the smallest unit of meaning," I think that my application to conversation analysis, though idiosyncratic, remains valid for the purpose of my argument comparing these two disparate academic disciplines concerning word selection.

4. In the following chapter on category-triggering, I will discuss more examples that illustrate word searches in the context of repairs.

5. Jefferson, "On the Poetics of Ordinary Talk," 9, 12, 48, 5.

there are cases in which word searches are evident in the conversation itself, such as in example 1.1.

Example 1.1[6]

> An: 'e took the inside out 'n found it 'uz full of- full of- uh:- calcium deposits.

In this example, the speaker is overtly doing a word search for the right word to describe what something was full of by (1) repeating "full of" twice, each time with a cut-off (denoted by the -) and (2) using the particle "uh" with both lengthening of the sound (denoted by the :) and a cut-off (denoted by the -). That is, instead of producing "full of calcium deposits" fluidly in the talk, there is a certain amount of disruption and delay, which communicates that the speaker is seeking the correct word, especially when combined with "uh." This is also illustrated in the following example:

Example 1.2[7]

> I don' know. The school- school uh, (1.0) bookstore doesn't carry anything anymo(h)uh,

Here we see again the use of repetition, a cut-off, and "uh" to mark an overt word search with an additional delay (denoted by (1.0)). The next two examples illustrate a common form of word searches, that is, word searches for names.

Example 1.3[8]

> Yihknow Mary uh::::: (0.3) oh:: what was it. Uh:: Tho:mpson.

---

6. Emanuel Schegloff, "The Relevance of Repair to Syntax-For-Conversation," in *Discourse and Syntax*, ed. Talmy Givon, Syntax and Semantics 12 (New York: Academic Press, 1979), 279.
7. Schegloff, "Relevance of Repair to Syntax-For-Conversation," 279.
8. Emanuel Schegloff, Gail Jefferson, and Harvey Sacks, "The Preference for Self-Correction in the Organization of Repair in Conversation," *Language* 53 (1977): 363.

Example 1.4[9]

> B't, a-another one theh wentuh school with me wa:s a girl na:med uh,
> (0.7)
> ° W't th' hell wz er name. ° Karen. Right Karen.

As with examples 1.1 and 1.2 we see similar delaying tactics (including "uh"), but in these two examples we also see the speaker stating a question to denote a word-search-in-progress, respectively, "what was it" and "W't the hell wz er name" (note that in the second case the inserted question is spoken softly with lower volume, denoted by the bracketing use of °…°).[10]

The use of specific inserted questions that signal a word search can be used to invite the hearer to help the speaker with the word search. This may have been the case in example 1.3 above, especially since it begins "Yih-know Mary"—that is, presumably they both know Mary Thompson. Of course, even if a word search is overtly marked, the speaker may find the word before someone else presents a candidate; however, in other cases, a speaker's word search may be resolved by the participation of another speaker, as in the following. Emanuel Schegloff introduced this example with some background information on what occurred before this excerpt from the conversation as follows: "Mark has called to complain about not being invited to a party Bob is involved in planning. Lengthy discussion transpires. Near the end of the conversation," the following occurs:

Example 1.5[11]

> Mark: Okay well Bo:b? ah hhmhh Ah'll see yuh Friday.
> (0.2)
> Bob: t'hhh Okay Mark en uh:::: yihknow, a (.) thous'n pard'ns.=
> =fer yer- the oversight.
> (0.2)

---

9. Schegloff, Jefferson, and Sacks, "Preference for Self-Correction," 363.

10. Other practices may be used in word searches. E.g., gaze and demonstrative pronouns can be used to invite collaboration and to suggest particular domains of words. See Makoto Hayashi, "Language and the Body as Resources for Collaborative Action: A Study of Word Searches in Japanese Conversation," *Research on Language and Social Interaction* 36 (2003): 109–41.

11. Schegloff, "Relevance of Repair to Syntax-For-Conversation," 265 n. 2.

Mark: 't'hhhh=
Bob: (Or // is it)
Mark: Oh: .uh no:. Well I wasn't I didn't fee:l like I wu:z::
ah.hh wt's the wo:rd. uhm=
Bob: =rebu:ffed?=
Mark: ='hh-'hh rebuffed,h

.
.
.

Mark: Uh::mhh I didn't feel rebu:ffed.

In this example, we see how a word search itself can be used in certain contexts to collaboratively perform a social action, in this case managing the delicate case of an oversight or being rebuffed. As the conversation is potentially coming to an ending with Mark's "Ah'll see yuh Friday," Bob returns to the topic of the conversation as a way of summarizing it—that is, he apologizes again, but how he refers to what he is apologizing for is so important as to be negotiated between them. He cuts off "fer yer-," possibly because the problematic social action was not Mark's doing, and then selected "the oversight." Then he pauses. When Mark does not immediately accept Bob's word selection, Bob restarts the word search with "Or, is it." Now Mark responds and searches for the right word ("wt's the word") and Bob hesitantly suggests "rebuffed." Mark accepts "rebuffed" with some laughter (denoted by the h's before and after "rebuffed"). Later in the conversation, Mark repeats the phrase, this time with the word that they collaboratively selected. Thus, this is a good example of how word selection is not necessarily simply looking for the right word, but may also be a social action that performs some other function than simply word selection—in this case, cooperatively reestablishing a relationship that may have been somewhat strained by collaboratively negotiating the proper word selection for what Mark's feelings may have been prior to the conversation.

Although word searches are something found in everyday conversation, they are more frequent in conversations with those who have some type of cognitive impairment. Example 1.6 is taken from a study of naturally occurring conversation of Ed, an elderly man with aphasia, and his wife, M, in their home. In this conversation, another visitor has asked Ed about his occupation and he is having difficulty with his answer:

Example 1.6[12]

> Ed: Well, I was a (1.0) I'm the- uhm how should I say it? (2.1) I'm::: (1.7) can't think of the name of it.
> M: Draftsman?
> Ed: Draftsman.

Again, we can see here how word searches that are resolved collaboratively can serve other social actions. In this case, Ed's wife waits for him to find the word for himself, but, when he may be giving up on the word search, she offers a candidate with the intonation of a question to Ed, rather than simply providing the answer to their friend. Ed can then accept her offer and answer the friend's question himself. What this example illustrates so well is how those close to people with aphasia can learn how to adapt everyday conversational practices to the new circumstances of communicating with someone whose cognitive-linguistic abilities have been somehow diminished and do so in a way that shows care and concern.[13]

All of these examples of word searches are exceptional in that word selection generally occurs so naturally that it is rarely noticed in conversation, much less becoming an overt topic within a conversation. However, these cases of overt word searches give us a glimpse into how word selection works within the cognitive-linguistic processes of everyday conversation. Some of these overt word searches may help us see how

---

12. Mary L. Oelschaeger and Jack S. Damico, "Word Searches in Aphasia: A Study of Collaborative Responses of Communicative Partners," in *Conversation and Brain Damage*, ed. Charles Goodwin (Oxford: Oxford University Press, 2003), 216.

13. On word searches in conversations with speakers with aphasia, see also Marja-Liisa Helasvuo, Minna Laakso, and Marja-Leena Sorjonen, "Searching for Words: Syntactic and Sequential Construction of Word Search in Conversations of Finnish Speakers with Aphasia," *Research on Language and Social Interaction* 37 (2004): 1–37; Minna Laakso, "Collaborative Participation in Aphasia Word Searching: Comparison between Significant Others and Speech and Language Therapists," *Aphasiology* 29 (2015): 269–90. Word searches in language instruction between native speakers and nonnative speakers play similar roles. See Catherine E. Brouwer, "Word Searches in NNS-NS Interaction: Opportunities for Language Learning?," *Modern Language Journal* 87 (2003): 534–45; Tim Greer, "Word Search Sequences in Bilingual Interaction: Codeswitching and Embodied Orientation toward Shifting Participant Constellations," *Journal of Pragmatics* 57 (2013): 100–117.

sometimes word selection operates in such a way that selecting the precise word becomes a collaborative effort for the purpose of maintaining social harmony. However, as we will see below in the discussion of poetics and word selection, some conversational situations do not require such precision. This will especially be the case in the discussions in the next chapter concerning category-triggering in the formation of lists.

Jefferson's Poetics: Sound-Triggering and Category-Triggering

In her 1996 article "On the Poetics of Ordinary Talk," Jefferson identified a second-level process for word selection, what she described as a "gross selection-mechanism."[14] Even though she remained somewhat dismissive of her own conclusions based on the wild evidence she analyzed, Jefferson's poetics is widely accepted in the secondary literature in conversation analysis. The gross selection-mechanism that Jefferson identified relates to word selection and her data include numerous examples of errors, Freudian slips, and puns; however, it is not restricted to such data. Jefferson began by making two observations about conversation: "(1) The objects (words, phrases, etc.) out of which people build their talk are made up of *sounds*. (2) A lot of these words and phrases belong to more than one *category*."[15] On the basis of these two observations and her review of the data, Jefferson argued that "triggering mechanisms are not something inevitable and irresistible," but nevertheless they may function within word selection in talk-in-interaction.[16] She identified two phenomena for word selection, what she called sound-triggering and category-triggering. In sound-triggering, there is a "a tendency for sounds-in-progress to locate particular next words."[17] In category-triggering, speakers choose among various options as they select their next word based on some category created by a preceding word or words. Below I will discuss both sound-triggering and category-triggering further, including a few examples of each from errors that were repaired in the conversation in ways that clearly demonstrate how the errors were selected according to sound-triggering or category-triggering. Here I will provide only a few examples to illustrate how poetics works in word selection in general. In the fol-

---

14. Jefferson, "On the Poetics of Ordinary Talk," 9, 12, 48.
15. Jefferson, "On the Poetics of Ordinary Talk," 3, emphasis original.
16. Jefferson, "On the Poetics of Ordinary Talk," 39.
17. Jefferson, "On the Poetics of Ordinary Talk," 3.

lowing chapters I will begin with additional examples and discussion as I apply sound-triggering and category-triggering to text-critical variants in order to explore what the cognitive-linguistic processes are in the word selection of ancient scribes within scribal memory as they transmitted their literary texts in writing.

Sound-triggering occurs when the sound of words earlier in a conversation seems to influence the selection of words in the conversation-in-progress. This is most obvious in cases in which the sound-triggering produced an error that was quickly repaired by the speaker as in the following two examples. In example 1.7, the speaker, Audrey, appears to have selected "Wednesday" as the day of the week due to the alliterative pattern of the "w" (marked by Jefferson with brackets) in the preceding words, but cuts off the word, so as to select "Thursday."

Example 1.7[18]

> Audrey: 'hhh en I: I: [w]ill uh be: up that [w]ay [w]'n- (.) uh Thurs:dee.

That is, the phrase "be up that way [day of the week]" was influenced so much by the preceding [w]-sounds that Audrey initially selected "Wednesday" as the day of the week, even though that was not the day she was planning on traveling; therefore, sound-triggering influenced her word selection, thereby producing an error that she quickly corrected with "Thursday," the day she was planning on traveling. This is just one of the many similar examples Jefferson provided, some of which are entertaining, including the following in which a radio talk show host is reading a commercial for men's suits from Bond's Blue Chips:

Example 1.8[19]

> [B]ig, [b]eautifu[l] savings from America's [l]argest c[l]othier.
> [Bl]oh- Bond's. Blondes, my goodness.
> Wuh that's a Freudian Slip.

---

18. Jefferson, "On the Poetics of Ordinary Talk," 5.
19. Jefferson, "On the Poetics of Ordinary Talk," 6.

Jefferson noted that [b] and [l] are repeated often enough to explain the sound error [bl]; however, the talk show host quickly caught his mistake, corrected it, and then went on to comment on his Freudian slip. These two examples represent many of Jefferson's examples, illustrating the sound-triggering that is related to what literary scholars would refer to as alliteration. In chapter 3 below, I will look more closely at not only sound-triggering that concerns alliteration, but also wordplay or what Jefferson calls "co-class puns," providing additional examples from her article.

Category-triggering refers to when a word suggests a category containing other words that are then selected in the following discourse. Jefferson described category as a loose term involving "objects that very strongly belong together, sometimes as contrasts, sometimes as co-members, very often as pairs. Up-down, right-left, young-old, husband-wife."[20] Many of Jefferson's examples of category-triggering concern coclass errors. Example 1.7 above also illustrates category-triggering, in that both Wednesday and Thursday belong to the same category, a day of the week, but Wednesday was mistakenly chosen because of the sound-triggering repetition of the [w]-sound influenced the selection of the word in that category with a [w]-sound. That is, both the error and the correction are coclass members of the same category. The following two examples also illustrate category-triggering; however, in these cases sound-triggering may not be present and they illustrate contrasting pairs.

Example 1.9[21]

A:n:d, (.) the last we hea:rd they were coming sou:th < uh north.

Example 1.10[22]

The men'll start wearing dresses, and the men'll- and the women'll start wearing pants?

The examples I have given above (and many below) could erroneously give the impression that such sound-triggering or category-triggering occurs in only short spurts of talk and are produced only by one speaker;

---

20. Jefferson, "On the Poetics of Ordinary Talk," 9.
21. Jefferson, "On the Poetics of Ordinary Talk," 10.
22. Jefferson, "On the Poetics of Ordinary Talk," 12.

however, Jefferson discussed some examples that are "terribly long and cumbersome" that she labeled "flurries" in which two or more participants are clearly being influenced by sound-triggering or category-triggering.[23] She discussed two sound-flurries, one involving alliteration and the other assonance. The sound-flurry that included alliteration was sixty-nine lines long in which [k]- and [g]-sounds occur throughout. She noted that "up to about line 44 the talk is liberally sprinkled with [k]s and [g]s, which more than occasionally form [g]-[k] or [k]-[g] clumps," which she illustrated by repeating selective lines in this format:[24]

Example 1.11[25]

- "[G]OOD [C]LOTHES" (line 7)
- "the [k]ind of [g]uy who" (line 10)
- "[k]i[ck]s," "[g]uidance," ... "from [K]ieretz" (lines 21–25)
- "[c]ause my father said now there's [g]oing to be a bunch of [k]ids in here" (lines 32–33)
- "[K]eep your [g]uard up" (line 37)

I should note that Jefferson's selection here does not exhaust the cases of [k]- and [g]-sounds in the first forty-four lines and they occur after line 44 as well—for example, the last line of the transcript is "[C]uz YOU LOO[K] LI[K]E A ↑HOO:D."[26] In addition, she provided an example of a specific type of category-flurry, what she labeled a "body-part flurry," in which words that are homophones or have homophonous syllable(s) to body parts reoccur. In one body-part flurry of thirty-six transcribed lines the following phrases occur in the speech of the two female participants: "[back] from Europe," "never come [back]," "that I [faced]," "any[body]," "thirty six square [feet]," "on my [neck]," "don't har[ass] me," "go right a[head]," and "here's my [body]."[27] This body-part flurry is a complaint story about returning from a trip to Europe and having to find things that coworkers or employees hid or misplaced in her store and as such only the last body-part reference is the least bit literal in meaning, that is,

---

23. Jefferson, "On the Poetics of Ordinary Talk," 30.
24. Jefferson, "On the Poetics of Ordinary Talk," 32.
25. Jefferson, "On the Poetics of Ordinary Talk," 32.
26. Jefferson, "On the Poetics of Ordinary Talk," 32.
27. Jefferson, "On the Poetics of Ordinary Talk," 35.

"here's my [body] go look it over," which seems to be a metaphor to martyrdom, especially since the other participant's response includes "good Christ" (as another example of category-triggering). What these flurries suggest is that once sound-triggering or category-triggering occurs, all of the participants in a conversation may become influenced, quite unintentionally, by these gross selection-mechanisms and therefore in some real sense they collaboratively contribute to the poetics of the conversation, often unaware of the poetics that they have coproduced and how the poetics is influencing their word selection as a second-level mechanism in the cognitive-linguistic processes involved.

Word Selection in Conversation: A Summary

Word selection obviously occurs in the cognitive-linguistic processes that precede talk and sometimes word selection is evident in overt word searches within the conversation-in-progress in ways that can even become a collaborative social action of finding just the right word. Since our vocabularies include numerous options of words that may fit well in any particular pragmatic context for a conversation, an interesting question is Why was the specific word chosen for this context when there were synonyms available to the speaker? Jefferson's observations about the poetics of everyday conversation provide us with one answer in her identification of sound-triggering and category-triggering as gross selection-mechanisms: The poetics of ordinary talk influences (at least some of the time) word selection, so that a particular word may be chosen for such poetic reasons from a category of other potential possible words. This occurs so naturally that in the vast majority of cases it goes unnoticed and therefore should be understood as unintentional. However, Jefferson noted a range of expertise in terms of the poetics of ordinary talk. On the one end of the spectrum, she referred to the work of a physician who studied the talk of his patients with psychosis and how he described the disfluencies in their talk: "The patient progresses from one ... word to another by associations determined by similarities in sound, category or phrase."[28] That is, sound-triggering and category-trigging are driving the word selection so often as

---

28. Jefferson, "On the Poetics of Ordinary Talk," 4; quoting William L. Woods, "Language Study in Schizophrenia," *Journal of Nervous and Mental Disease* 87 (1938): 295.

to produce incomprehensible talk. At the other end of the spectrum, she described the work of poets:

> It's pretty much figured out that all these wonderful mixtures of sounds and meanings are the provenance of poets who make it their business to work out, to seek, to really endeavor to find just the right word.... That's the poet's job. The *arrangement* of sounds and categories.[29]

In contrast to those with some disfluencies and to those with heightened poetic expertise, most of us are in the middle: "Ordinary people neither reject the task nor make it their life work. They just get it done."[30]

Like most of us, conversation analysts have not made poetics their life work; however, based on Jefferson's observations, conversation analysts must pay some attention to the poetics of ordinary talk in their research, especially since it sometimes asserts itself in the study of their conversational data. Thus, Jefferson provided some advice to her colleagues. Jefferson reported the following concerning how one of her students identified a case of poetics in ordinary talk and the advice she gave the student. Note, however, that Jefferson suggests that the student may have discovered the method herself, implying that the method itself is somewhat naturally occurring.

Example 1.12 (transcript, lines 824–831)[31]

>> and <u>how</u> she found it was a system some of us h've discovered by our<u>selves</u>
> o:r I told <u>her</u> about it
> it's simply <u>this</u>
> the word shows up and it strikes you as
> a little bit funny
> just something special
> or interesting

---

29. Jefferson, "On the Poetics of Ordinary Talk," 4, emphasis original.
30. Jefferson, "On the Poetics of Ordinary Talk," 4.
31. A digitized version of the video of Jefferson's conference presentation and a draft transcript (from which the above quotation is taken) are available at: https://tinyurl.com/SBLPress7015a1.

track back through the data and you're gonna find out where it came from
and lots of times it works.

At the end of her article in appendix B, Jefferson provided a sample of working with poetics from her own teacher, Harvey Sacks, which includes related sounds circled with lines connecting these sounds in the transcript. That is, the advice that Jefferson gave about analyzing poetics in everyday conversation is very similar to how scholars of literature have analyzed literary poetics for a long time, probably because Sacks and his students adapted literary poetics to the study of conversation.[32] Therefore, the connections between conversational poetics and literary poetics were explicit in Jefferson's work from the beginning, even though this connection has rarely been pursued by either conversation analysts or literary scholars.[33]

---

32. I once had a personal conversation at a conference with Gene Lerner, one of Sacks's earliest students with Jefferson and someone with whom I had studied conversation analysis, about my work combining conversation analysis and the comparative study of oral traditions. He told me that I had uncovered a connection that had been mostly forgotten, but that he now recalled. When the first group of Sacks's students started their doctoral programs at University of California-Irvine, Sacks had a problem with the curriculum, that is, what could he possibly assign to his students to read, since they were creating a new discipline. One of the books that Sacks told Lerner to read was Albert B. Lord, *Singer of Tales*, Harvard Studies in Comparative Literature 24 (Cambridge: Harvard University Press, 1960). Lord's research involved recording living oral traditions and then paying close attention to how those oral traditions functioned, so that it provided a model for doing the kind of ethnographic work that became the basis of conversation analysis. Based on this conversation, I am quite confident that Sacks was influenced by the study of literary poetics and that he shared this with his earliest doctoral students.

33. For a fuller discussion of the influence of Jefferson's poetics in conversation analysis and its relatively sparse influence in literary studies, see John P. Rae, Robin Wooffitt, and Raymond F. Person Jr., "Bridging the Gap: Conversation Analysis and Poetics from Jefferson to Now," in Person, Wooffitt, and Rae, *Bridging the Gap*, 1–22. Furthermore, this volume contains four chapters written by conversation analysts who argue that Jefferson's initial insights point to a much greater role of poetics in ordinary talk than Jefferson suggested and four chapters written by scholars of literature who demonstrate how Jefferson's insights illuminate literary issues extremely well. Thus, Rae, Wooffitt, and Person conclude that the study of everyday conversation and literary discourse can only be undertaken fully by seriously taking into account the role of poetics as suggested by Jefferson.

Nevertheless, this connection sets us up for turning to word selection in oral traditions, which have their own poetic systems.

Word Selection in Oral Traditions

Jefferson noted the following: "It may be that the triggering mechanisms are not something inevitable and irresistible, something that we're just not in control of. It's possible that you can have *selective* triggering."[34] In *From Conversation to Oral Tradition*, I applied Jefferson's poetics to the comparative study of oral traditions, arguing that oral performers use a traditional register in which certain poetic practices in conversation are selected, adapted, and exaggerated for aesthetic purposes, including how both traditional phraseology and thematic structures are such adaptations. For example, the alliterative line of Old English poetry is an exaggeration of sound-triggering and the formulaic system in Serbo-Croatian epic is an exaggeration of category-triggering. Moreover, even what are often mistakenly understood as elaborate literary (therefore, necessarily written) structures, such as ring composition, can be understood as exaggerations of conversational practices. That is, since poets do not have to navigate the complex turn-taking system of everyday conversation, the communicative economy has changed in such a way that generations of oral poets can produce a poetic system that emphasizes aesthetic qualities that are adaptations of practices in conversation—for example, prosody in conversation can become meter in poetry. In this section I expand on earlier observations about what is a word in oral traditional literature and when one word is understood to be the same word or a different word.

Studies in oral traditions demonstrate that the understanding of word in oral literature differs from our own highly literate understanding—that is, a unit of meaning in a primarily oral culture may be equivalent to what we would call a line, a stanza, or even the entire epic rather than a lexeme. This general observation has been emphasized throughout the work of Foley and is illustrated in his translation of the interview between Milman Parry's Yugloslavian assistant Nikola Vujnovic (N) and the Serbo-Croatian oral poet (*guslar*) Mujo Kukuruzovic (M) in which they are discussing the Serbo-Croatian word *reč* that is translated here as "word":[35]

---

34. Jefferson, "On the Poetics of Ordinary Talk," 39, emphasis original.
35. See esp. John Miles Foley, "Editing Oral Epic Texts: Theory and Practice," *Text Transactions of the Society of Textual Scholarship* 1 (1981): 77–78; Foley, *Tradi-*

Example 1.13[36]

> N: Let's consider this: "Vino pije licki Mustajbeze" ("Mustajbeg of Lika was drinking wine"). Is this a single word?
> M: Yes.
> N: But how? It can't be *one*: "Vino pije licki Mustajbeze"
> M: In writing it can't be one.
> N: There are four words here.
> M: It can't be one in writing. But here, let's say we're at my house and I pick up the *gusle* [a traditional single-stringed instrument]—"Pije vino licki Mustajbeze"—that's a single word on the *gusle* for me.
> N: And the second word?
> M: And the second word—"Na Ribniku u pjanoj mehani" ("At Ribnik in a drinking tavern")—there.

In this interview, we can see a clash of cultures as the literate Yugoslav insists that "Vino pije licki Mustajbeze" is not one word but four, while the oral poet insists that it is only one word. In fact, the oral poet's conception of the entire phrase being one word even allows for some variation. Notice that Nikola is discussing the phrase "Vino pije licki Mustajbeze," but, when Kukuruzovic imagines playing his *gusle* (a one-string instrument) and singing this phrase, he says what from a highly literate viewpoint might be considered a different phrase because of the inversion of the first two words, that is, "Pije vino licki Mustajbeze." For Kukuruzovic, the oral poet, both "Vino pije licki Mustajbeze" and "Pije vino licki Mustajbeze" are not only one word but the *same* word.

Foley's understanding of word is now widely accepted in the comparative study of oral traditions. For example, the volume *Weathered Words: Formulaic Language and Verbal Art* demonstrates the value of this understanding of word in Turkic oral epics, Old English epic, South Slavic epic, Old Norse epic, Homeric epic, Gaelic traditional narratives, Rotenese (Indonesian) oral poetry, Kalevalaic poetry, Icelandic epic, Latin poetry, Ifugao (Filipino) poetry, Russian folktales, English folk-

---

tional Oral Epic: The Odyssey, Beowulf, and the Serbo-Croatian Return Song (Berkeley: University of California Press, 1990), 121–239; Foley, "Comparative Oral Traditions," in *Voicing the Moment: Improvised Oral Poetry and Basque Tradition*, ed. Samuel G. Armistead and Joseba Zulaika (Reno: University of Nevada at Reno Press), 67–68.

36. Foley, "Editing Oral Epic Texts," 92 n. 11; his translation.

1. Word Selection in Conversation and Oral Traditions

tales, stand-up comedy, and radio commentary of rugby games as well as my own study of text-critical variants classified as synonymous readings in the Hebrew Bible, New Testament, and Homeric epic. In their preface to the volume, the editors, the folklorist Frog and the linguist William Lamb, noted their dependence on Foley when they wrote that "a formula is a 'word' of the register describable 'as an integer of traditional meaning.'"[37] This understanding of a word that can be more than a lexeme has influenced biblical scholarship. In fact, the semantic range of the Hebrew word דבר includes not only word, but can also mean utterance, speech, or message.[38] In her *Beyond Orality*, Jacqueline Vayntrub compared Foley's understanding of the Serbo-Croatian word *reč* with the Biblical Hebrew word משל as follows:

> In the case of the *reč*, as in the case of the biblical *mashal*, length makes no difference. Both terms can refer to what the modern, literary mind would understand as utterances that fall anywhere on the spectrum of very short and very long. This is because both Serbo-Croatian *reč* and Biblical Hebrew *mashal* refer to an "irreducible atom of performance, a speech act."[39]

David Carr also referred to Foley's idea of word in his discussion of memory and transmission.[40]

---

37. Frog and Lamb, *Weathered Words: Formulaic Language and Verbal Art*, Publications of the Milman Parry Collection of Oral Literature 6 (Cambridge: Harvard University Press, 2022), 5, quoting from John Miles Foley and Peter Ramey, "Oral Theory and Medieval Studies," in *Medieval Oral Literature*, ed. Karl Reichl (Berlin: de Gruyter, 2012), 80.

38. For my first discussion of this insight by Foley, see Person, "Ancient Israelite Scribe as Performer." For further discussion of the meaning of word דבר, see Natalie Mylonas, Stephen Llewelyn, and Gareth Wearne, "Speaking to One's Heart: דבר and Its Semantic Extension," *JHS* 16 (2016), https://doi.org/10.5508/jhs.2016.v16.a7; and Raymond F. Person Jr., "Self-Referential Phrases in Deuteronomy: A Reassessment Based on Recent Studies concerning Scribal Performance and Memory," in *Collective Memory and Collective Identity*, ed. Johannes Unsok Ro and Diana Edelman, BZAW 534 (Berlin: de Gruyter, 2021), 217–42.

39. Vayntrub, *Beyond Orality: Biblical Poetry on Its Own Terms* (London: Routledge, 2019), 82; quoting John Miles Foley, *How to Read an Oral Poem* (Urbana: University of Illinois Press, 2002), 13.

40. Carr, *Writing on the Tablet of the Heart*, 7, 44, 299; Carr, *Formation of the Hebrew Bible*, 18.

As noted above in example 1.13, what we might consider to be two different words—that is, "Vino pije licki Mustajbeze" and "Pije vino licki Mustajbeze"—are clearly understood by the oral poet as the same word. That is, with word understood as the smallest unit of meaning, it is possible that the lexemes that combine to make up the word can be different (from our perspective) and the word can still be understood to be the same (from their perspective). In *Homeric Similes in Comparative Perspectives*, Ready provided a table of "Investigators of oral traditions on sameness" that includes twenty-one different oral traditions, including an Uzbek epic poet, an Igbo (Nigerian) singer, a Korean singer, Iroquois longhouse speakers, and a northern Irish storyteller.[41] Ready concluded, "Investigators of numerous traditions attest to the idea that for performances to be considered the same they do not have to be shown to be verbatim the same."[42] He also provided another quotation from Parry and Lord's fieldwork, this time a conversation between Parry's Yugloslavian assistant Nikola Vujnovic (N) and another Serbo-Croatian oral poet (*guslar*), Avdo Međedović (A):

A: They sang it exactly alike.
N: You mean everything exactly alike?
A: Everything. Not more than ten words' difference in the whole thing.
N: But I'll bet the decoration of the song was different, now wasn't it—the things they dressed up in the song?
A: That's just what I mean—it wasn't.
N: Nothing different at all?
A: Nothing so help me, no more, no less.[43]

Once again Vujnovic, the literate Yugoslav, challenges the oral poet's understanding, in this case concerning what must be different in various performances of the same Muslim epic. However, Međedović, the illiterate poet, insists that they were exactly alike, even though it is possible that there might be "ten words' difference." Thus, Ready concluded:

---

41. Jonathan Ready, *Homeric Simile in Comparative Perspective: Oral Traditions from Saudi Arabia to Indonesia* (Oxford: Oxford University Press, 2018), 75.
42. Ready, *Homeric Simile*, 74.
43. Ready, *Homeric Simile*, 74.

the same song or tale reproduces the same plot line, but as important "the recognizability of its building blocks," of "its composite elements," enables oral performers and audience members to judge the presentation the same as previous ones. There must be a good number of familiar lines, and every stretch of familiar lines must be taken to be the same as previous iterations of those lines: every familiar part of a performance must be taken to be the same as previous presentations of that part.[44]

Thus, we need to pay attention to our own cultural notions of what a word is, because sometimes a word may be more than a word. Furthermore, based on our cultural notions of what is the same and what is different, we might erroneously identify what appears to us to be two different words, when we should understand them to be the same word. We should remember Albert Lord's observation concerning oral traditions: "we cannot correctly speak of a 'variant,' since there is no 'original' to be varied."[45]

When we apply our culturally determined notions of same and different, we can easily let our assumptions distort our understanding of ancient texts. In his work on Akkadian *šuila*-prayers, Alan Lenzi asked the question, "How do we know two tablets represent the same text?"[46] Reflecting on this question, he concluded that

> it admonishes us to own up to the fact that we are the ones who decide what counts as evidence of revision and what does not by deciding which texts to compare because they are *similar* enough to each other—despite some differences—to catch our eye and which to leave aside because they are *dissimilar* enough—despite some similarities—that we do not consider them relevant for our purposes.[47]

Similarly, based on her study of the Dead Sea Scrolls, Maxine Grossman observed:

---

44. Ready, *Homeric Simile*, 74; quoting Lauri Honko, *Textualizing the Siri Epic* (Helsinki: Suomalainen Tiedeakatemia, Academia Scientiarum Fennica, 1998), 144–45.

45. Lord, *Singer of Tales*, 101.

46. Alan Lenzi, "Scribal Revision and Textual Variation in Akkadian Šuila-Prayers: Two Case Studies in Ritual Adaptation," in Person and Rezetko, *Empirical Models*, 68.

47. Lenzi, "Scribal Revision and Textual Variation in Akkadian Šuila-Prayers," 65–66.

To the extent that a variety of very diverse manuscripts—with different wording, content, and character—can be recognized not only as examples of the same *textual tradition* but in fact as copies of the same *literary text*, it becomes necessary to rethink our larger understanding of original texts and text formation in an ancient Jewish setting.[48]

For example, are 1QSa and 1QSb independent from or a part of the literary text of the Community Rule (best preserved in 1QS)? In my earlier work, these kinds of questions have led me to question the relationship between Samuel–Kings and Chronicles as representing different literary texts that contain significantly different theologies, not unlike the relationship between MT Samuel and LXX Samuel.[49] In sum, when we think of the books that became the Hebrew Bible as traditional texts (whether oral, written, or better oral/written), it might be helpful to consider understandings of what is the same and what is different based on what we can learn from the comparative study of oral traditions.

Word Selection and Text-Critical Variants

Before discussing text-critical variants, I will synthesize the conclusions from the previous two sections. A word should not simply be understood as a standard lexeme found in dictionaries, because a word can be less than a lexeme (e.g., "hm" in conversation) or more than a lexeme (e.g., "you know" in conversation or "Vino pije licki Mustajbeze" in an oral tradition). If we understand word with this broader meaning, then how word selection functions must be reimagined as well: word selection should not be limited to a discussion of how individual lexemes are selected, because sometimes a word is more or less than a lexeme. In this sense, we should not only understand that Kukuruzovic selected "Vino pije licki

---

48. Maxine Grossman, "Community Rule or Community Rules: Examining a Supplementary Approach in Light of the Sectarian Dead Sea Scrolls," in Person and Rezetko, *Empirical Models*, 329–30, emphasis original.

49. Raymond F. Person Jr., *The Deuteronomic History and the Book of Chronicles: Scribal Works in an Oral World*, AIL 6 (Atlanta: Society of Biblical Literature, 2010); Person, "Text Criticism as a Lens for Understanding the Transmission of Ancient Texts in Their Oral Environments," in *Contextualizing Israel's Sacred Writings: Ancient Literary, Orality, and Literary Production*, ed. Brian Schmidt, AIL 22 (Atlanta: SBL Press, 2015); Person, "The Problem of 'Literary Unity' from the Perspective of the Study of Oral Traditions," in Person and Rezetko, *Empirical Models*, 217–37.

Mustajbeze"/"Mustajbeg of Lika was drinking wine" as one word with "Na Ribniku u pjanoj mehani"/"At Ribnik in a drinking tavern" selected as the next word in his epic singing (in example 1.13), but maybe we should also consider "Mary Thompson" is the word in the word search in example 1.3—that is, here Mary is insufficient as a word because it does not function well enough as the smallest unit of meaning in the pragmatic context of that particular conversation; it may not provide adequate representivity for the recognition of Mary Thompson as the proper character in the story.

In conversation, speakers select their words to fit within the pragmatic context of the social action being performed in the talk-in-progress. For the vast majority of the time, word selection goes unnoticed, but it is performed overtly in conversation when word searches become a part of the conversation itself and when speakers repair errors, that is, select the correct words after first selecting the wrong words. Furthermore, overt word searches may serve social functions other than simply word selection, especially when they are collaborative projects—for example, in example 1.5 the word search ("oversight" or "rebuffed"?) plays an important role in negotiating an apology and in example 1.6 the word search ("Draftsman?") provides caring support to a spouse with aphasia. Thus, word selection naturally occurs in all conversation and in some cases selecting the precise word becomes a collaborative effort for the purpose of maintaining social harmony, but in other times word selection does not require such precision. Furthermore, word selection is influenced by a second-level process, the gross-selection mechanism of poetics in ordinary talk in the form of sound-triggering and category-triggering. Speakers have a treasure trove of words from which to select that would fit well into the pragmatic context and sometimes the word selection is influenced by the preceding sounds and/or categories that have been established in the earlier turns at talk. This too can be collaborative as demonstrated by the sound-flurries and category-flurries identified by Jefferson, so that together conversational participants can coproduce stretches of talk based on this second-level process of word selection.

My use of word as the smallest unit of meaning comes from the comparative study of oral tradition, especially the work of Foley. In living oral traditions we have substantial comparative evidence that a word—that is, a unit of meaning in a primarily oral culture—may be equivalent to what we would call a poetic line, a stanza, or even an entire epic. For example, not only is "Vino pije licki Mustajbeze" one word for Kukuruzovic, but "Vino pije licki Mustajbeze" and "Pije vino licki Mustajbeze" are the same word. Moreover, Međedović can insist that oral epics are sung exactly alike, despite empirical evidence that suggests otherwise. Thus, we must be careful with our own culturally limited understanding of word when we study oral traditions, because sometimes what we insist on being two or more different words is really the same word, whether that word is a poetic line or maybe even the entire piece of literature.

How does this understanding of word and word selection help us understand text-critical variants? Before directly addressing this question, we should consider Jefferson's continuum concerning the use of poetics with psychotic patients as those who are the most inept and poets as those who are the most skilled with most of us somewhere in the middle. Jefferson noted that poetics in ordinary talk includes "*selective triggering.*"[50] By implication, then, poets engage in selective triggering more often, so that sound-triggering and category-triggering become embodied in standard poetic features of the tradition, such as the hexameter poetic line of Homer or the alliterative verse in *Beowulf*.[51] In these traditions and others, word selection performs social actions in a collaborative project that involves generations of poets—that is, much like the collaborative projects of sound-flurries and category-flurries in conversation, these traditional poets have learned what Lord called the "special grammar" of the tradition and Foley called the "traditional register" that includes specific adaptations of the poetics of ordinary talk in a system that values more highly the aesthetics of sound-triggering and category-triggering to produce literature that serves as a source of social cohesion and social identity. Although in oral traditions poetics may remain a second-level process of word selection that is in some sense naturally occurring, poetics have become far more significant to the collaborative project of traditional literature, so that these poetic practices can be playfully manipulated.

When we combine these insights from conversation analysis and the comparative study of oral traditions with new insights in text criticism, we must caution ourselves that poets are not simply authors but may also be copyists. That is, the effect of poetics on word selection through sound-triggering and category-triggering is not confined to composition but is also found in transmission. Or put even better, sound-triggering

---

50. Jefferson, "On the Poetics of Ordinary Talk," 39, emphasis original.
51. Person, *From Conversation to Oral Tradition*.

and category-triggering occur throughout the composition/transmission process of literature. Therefore, when we speak of text-critical variants, we must not limit our understanding of variants to single lexemes, because sometimes a word is less than or more than a lexeme. In the next chapter this will be especially evident in the discussion of synonymous readings, including formulaic phrases. Moreover, although this volume is concerned with variants that are words limited to lexemes and phrases, we can imagine the scribes of the Dead Sea Scrolls insisting somewhat like Međedović that the different versions of the Community Rule or the book of Psalms are the same, maybe even exactly alike. Therefore, we must be vigilant not to let our own culturally determined notions of word as well as what is the same versus what is different too easily influence our assessment of the text-critical variants in the Hebrew Bible. When we understand better how word selection works in everyday conversation and in living oral traditions, we may also understand better the cognitive-linguistic processes within scribal memory as the ancient scribes (both authors and copyists) performed their literary texts. Their performances of these living traditions took place within a community in a collaborative project of transmitting authoritative literature by drawing from a scribal memory that included the special grammar and traditional register of their shared ancient literature.

2
Category-Triggering and Text-Critical Variants

The classification of text-critical variants into categories has been undertaken since antiquity, and in the introduction I discussed Hendel's "Typology of Scribal Error," which is representative of text criticism and is the basis of the typology used in the critical apparatus of HBCE.[1] In this and following chapters, I will continue to use text-critical terminology from such typologies; for example, in this chapter I discuss synonymous readings and harmonizations, which fit in Hendel's typology, respectively, as a form of scribal error and an exegetical form of a scribal revision. Although I think that such typologies can be helpful in my analysis of the cognitive processes involved in *Vorlage*-based copying and the resulting text-critical variants (at least for the purpose of organizing my argument), I nevertheless have some criticisms of the specifics of most typologies and consider even the best typologies as having dangerous implications when it comes to identifying individual cases of text-critical variants as belonging in only one category. For example, I am critical of Hendel's typology because his discussion of the copying process assumes that only two texts are present, the physical *Vorlage* and the new copy, so that any variation from the *Vorlage* is necessarily a scribal error or a scribal revision. The role of textual plurality and scribal memory is lacking in his discussion; in fact, in his "Excursus: 'Memory Variants'" at the end of his typology chapter, Hendel rejects Carr's understanding of memory variants because "a typological contrast between memory variants and transcriptional variants does not hold."[2] Since this entire volume can be understood as a response to such misunderstandings of memory variants and the role of scribal memory, here I will simply note

---

1. Hendel, *Steps to a New Edition*, 149–72.
2. Hendel, *Steps to a New Edition*, 169.

that I think that Hendel misunderstood Carr, in that I do not think that Carr ever stated that there was such a typological contrast. Rather, Carr was not discounting the possibility of transcriptional errors or scribal revisions, but was reimagining how they could occur in the transmission process from a cognitive perspective; that is, the memory of the text(s) was involved during transcription, so that the new manuscript was not simply based on the physical *Vorlage* before the scribe. The difference of opinion between Hendel and Carr can be understood as based on short-term memory in *Vorlage*-based copying (Hendel and Carr) and the effect of long-term memory in transmission, including *Vorlage*-based copying (Carr, not Hendel). Similarly, below I will demonstrate how a strict division between transcriptional errors and scribal revisions itself is problematic based on the text-critical evidence—for example, I will conclude that (at least most) harmonizations can also be classified as synonymous readings, even though I discuss these separately based on the typology generally accepted in the secondary literature. Thus, even though I accept that such classification systems provide us with some helpful perspectives for the purpose of our categorization of text-critical evidence, they may also lead us down a path of distortion by artificially dividing text-critical variants into categories that mask the bigger picture of the role of scribal memory in the composition/transmission process. Another way of stating this is that the same text-critical variant may fit within multiple categories—for example, both synonymous readings and harmonizations—from the perspective of how scribal memory works. Nevertheless, I will continue to structure the organization of text-critical variants according to the widely accepted typologies, even though I will attempt to demonstrate how scribal memory helps us see the broader cognitive-linguistic processes behind all of these various types that I discuss in this and the following chapters. Furthermore, I must add the following, so as to not give a false impression of my criticism of typologies by Hendel and others: I am *not* discounting that sometimes scribes made unintentional errors or that sometimes scribes made theologically motivated revisions. Both of these are possible in the transmission of ancient texts. However, given the characteristics of textual fluidity and textual plurality of ancient texts, I assert that it is methodologically difficult (often impossible) to distinguish between scribal error and scribal revision, especially when I have a linguistic explanation for how variants—that is, readings that we tend to understand as different in meaning—can nevertheless be understood as the same not only from the perspective of the ancients who lived

2. Category-Triggering and Text-Critical Variants 69

in a primarily oral culture, but even from the perspective of how word selection works in everyday conversation today.

In this chapter I explore the possibility that some of the categories used in text-critical typologies correspond well to Jefferson's understanding of category in conversation analysis, especially as comembers. For example, Hendel gave the following two examples in his discussion of "Synonym with Graphic or Aural Trigger": (1) in Prov 5:3, the MT reading (זרה; "strange woman") and the LXX reading (γυναικὸς πόρνης; זנה; "harlot") are (near-)synonyms and (2) in Prov 23:27, these two synonymous readings are reversed with זרה; ἀλλότριος; "strange woman" in LXX and זנה; "harlot" in MT.[3] Both nouns in Proverbs clearly refer to what we can describe as comembers of the category of dangerous women who should be avoided by the male audience. Since he could conclude that this "interchange is motivated by either visual or aural cues or a combination of both," Hendel included this type of synonym as an error in the scribe's reading of the *Vorlage* in his confusion of two synonyms with the same first and last consonants and a similar middle consonant.[4] However, he also understood that synonyms could be errors of copying on the new manuscript, when they "have no graphic trigger and are therefore more likely to be caused by misremembering."[5] For example, Hendel provided the following synonyms as two examples of this category: (1) in Prov 3:1, the MT reading (מצותי; "my commands") and the LXX reading (τὰ ῥήματά μου; אמרי; "my words") and (2) in Prov 5:1 the MT reading (תבונתי; "my understanding") and the LXX reading (ἐμοῖς λόγοις; אמרי; "my words").[6] Hendel argued in both cases that the LXX reading is secondary, because it uses the "commonplace אמרי."[7] From the perspective of Jefferson's poetics, all three of these synonyms (מצותי, תבונתי, and אמרי) can be understood as comembers of the category of first-person speech.[8]

---

3. Hendel, *Steps to a New Edition*, 157–58. See also Fox, *Proverbs*, 114–15, 316.
4. Hendel, *Steps to a New Edition*, 157.
5. Hendel, *Steps to a New Edition*, 160.
6. Hendel, *Steps to a New Edition*, 160. See also Fox, *Proverbs*, 97, 113–14.
7. Hendel, *Steps to a New Edition*, 160.
8. Although Hendel noted Talmon's arguments concerning synonymous readings, he argued that they do not apply to these synonyms. See Hendel, *Steps to a New Edition*, 158. However, it appears that Fox understood these as synonymous readings when he wrote: "there is much variation in the treatment of words for 'words,' 'commandments,' and 'teachings,' since they are functional synonyms, and variations can occur in Hebrew or in translation" (Fox, *Proverbs*, 97, see also 113–14). This illustrates

Although I introduced poetics in conversation analysis in the previous chapter, here I provide two additional examples of category-triggering from Jefferson's article to help my readers understand better how word selection works in everyday conversation as a basis for my argument applying her insights to text-critical variants, especially in preparation for my discussion of synonymous readings in the next section. Specifically, I will provide two examples of what Jefferson labeled as topical puns, that is, puns that are based on words selected from the same category. These two examples need little introduction to be understood, especially since Jefferson placed brackets around the words/phrases that are comembers of the same category that are the basis of the pun.

Example 2.1[9]

> Russia's the worst. We went twenty four hours once without [eating] a thing. I just got [fed] up waiting.

Example 2.2[10]

> HHH: … somebody's gonna fall on a [portion of their anatomy], and you know what I mean! The short leg of the Federal Reserve Bank has got everyone in a (0.3) [tail]spin.

Both examples illustrate how a word or phrase earlier in the utterance influenced the selection of a word later in the utterance by its selection being from the same category, but its meaning in the context of this utterance was not directly related to what the term means as a comember. In example 2.1, "eating" suggested a category related to food, so that "fed up" is selected by category-triggering as a metaphorical way of expressing frustration rather than simply eating. In example 2.2, "portion of their anatomy" was presumably a polite way of referring to what can euphemistically be called one's "tail," so that "tailspin" is selected to refer metaphorically to an economic crash. In this case, the pause before the pun ("a [3.0] tailspin") may indicate that the speaker was aware of the pun

---

the different understandings between Fox and Hendel, since Fox distances himself from an original text in ways that conflict with Hendel.

9. Jefferson, "On the Poetics of Ordinary Talk," 17.
10. Jefferson, "On the Poetics of Ordinary Talk," 18.

2. Category-Triggering and Text-Critical Variants 71

and thereby drawing some attention to how witty it is. However, Jefferson noted that such word selection often occurs without any recognition by any of the participants in the conversation, so that topical puns cannot be understood as necessarily intentional.

Before applying category-triggering to text-critical variants, I probably should provide further examples of how category-triggering functions within literature more at the composition level of the composition/transmission process. In *From Conversation to Oral Tradition*, I demonstrated how both sound-triggering and category-triggering can help us understand better what Lord called the "special grammar" of oral traditions and what Foley called the "traditional oral register."[11] That is, I used Jefferson's poetics to answer the pressing question of how can oral poets compose poetry during the demands of the performance arena when it is clear that they are not simply repeating verbatim the traditional oral literature. For example, I showed how the oral-formulaic system in Serbo-Croatian oral epics combines the sound-triggering of meter to preserve the decameter of the poetic line with a form of category-triggering in its formulaic system. For example, one particular formulaic system combines (1) verbs meaning "mounted" with (2) nouns referring to a horse, so that whatever combination is used from these two closely related categories nevertheless meet the metrical requirements of the second colon in the poetic line.[12] For another example of an oral-traditional formula using category-triggering, I discussed the Anglo-Saxon formulaic system of "if X did not wish it," in which X refers to a category of persons ("the ruler," "the earl," and "the youth") and noted that in some cases the half-lines themselves can be swapped from first half-line to second half-line of the alliterative Anglo-Saxon verse.[13] That is, both of these oral formulaic systems, Serbo-Croatian epic poetry and Anglo-Saxon epic poetry, can be understood as adapting category-triggering from everyday conversation not only for aesthetic purposes but as compositional (and receptional) techniques within the linguistic register of the traditional poetry.

---

11. Person, *From Conversation to Oral Tradition*, esp. 4–7. See also Lord, *Singer of Tales*, 35–36; Foley, *Traditional Oral Epic*.
12. Person, *From Conversation to Oral Tradition*, 74–79. See also Lord, *Singer of Tales*, 48; Foley, *Traditional Oral Epic*, 160.
13. Person, *From Conversation to Oral Tradition*, 79–87. See also Foley, *Traditional Oral Epic*, 213.

In the study of poetry in the Hebrew Bible, parallelism continues to be understood as an (if not the most) important characteristic of Hebrew poetry.[14] For example, Ps 24:3 has two (near-)synonymous phrases: מִי יַעֲלֶה בְהַר יְהוָה וּמִי יָקוּם בִּמְקוֹם קָדְשׁוֹ; "Who shall ascend the hill of the LORD? And who shall stand in his holy place?" The parallel construction is quite obvious in that the same question is essentially being asked, that is, Who is capable of going up Mount Zion to the Jerusalem temple and standing in God's presence? Thus, the characteristic of parallelism in Hebrew poetry can be understood as an adaptation of category-triggering for meaningful word selection applied to aesthetic purposes.[15] The Hebrew poet selects from a range of words and phrases within the same category, such as phrases referring to the Jerusalem temple cult, and uses these words or phrases together so as to present a fuller picture of what the poet is describing. If category-triggering works at the level of composition within the Hebrew Bible, then we should not be surprised that it can also be found at the level of transmission. In fact, in his discussion of synonymous readings, Talmon explicitly made this connection within the composition/transmission process: "I propose to refer to such variants as *synonymous readings*, on the analogy of the term *synonymous parallelism* which is a basic feature of biblical stylistics."[16] Talmon argued that "the diverse practitioners involved in the process, viz., author, redactors, and scribes, employed the same or similar literary tenets and techniques."[17] I am simply extending Talmon's argument by noting that these "diverse practitioners … [not only] employed the same or similar literary tenets and techniques," but these very "literary tenets and techniques" are rooted in conversational structures and practices that can be selected and exaggerated for aesthetic purposes, thereby becoming "literary tenets and

---

14. For an excellent review of recent discussions concerning parallelism, see Andreas Wagner, "Der Parallelismus Membrorum zwischen Poetischer Form und Denkfigur," in *Parallelismus Membrorum*, ed. Andreas Wagner, OBO 224 (Fribourg: Presses Universitaires; Göttingen: Vandenhoeck & Ruprecht, 2007), 1–26. For an excellent analysis, see Shem Miller's discussion of how stichography in the Dead Sea Scrolls graphically represents parallelism (*Dead Sea Media*, 132–37).

15. For a systematic discussion of category-triggering and synonymous parallelism in a variety of poetic traditions, see Frog, "Repetition, Parallelism, and Non-Repetition: From Ordinary Talk to Ritual Poetry and Back Again," in Person, Wooffitt, and Rae, *Bridging the Gap*, 180–217.

16. Talmon, *Text and Canon*, 171, emphasis original.

17. Talmon, *Text and Canon*, 83.

techniques." Therefore, category-triggering occurs in everyday conversation, in the oral composition of epics, and in the composition/transmission process of ancient literature in various but analogous ways, including in the word selection in scribal memory that explains how what we consider to be variants from our cultural perspective may be nevertheless understood as the same by the ancients who produced these variants from their cultural perspective. That is, I am asserting that category-triggering (and sound-triggering) are cognitive-linguistic practices that occur throughout the many various linguistic registers that we, both ancient and modern humans, use unconsciously and sometimes, especially by poets, intentionally for aesthetic purposes.

Below I will explore this idea in four major sections relating to categories of text-critical variants that are discussed in text-criticism: synonymous readings, variants in lists, harmonizations, and variants related to person reference. Before analyzing specific text-critical examples, I review the relevant secondary literature, including further discussion of the important role of category-triggering from the perspective of conversation analysis in list-construction and person reference. That is, the above review of category-triggering should be sufficient for my discussion of synonymous readings and harmonizations, but conversation analysis has a more sophisticated understanding of how category-triggering relates to list-construction and person reference that proves especially helpful to the application of category-triggering to variants in lists and variants related to person reference. Therefore, I will review this secondary literature to explicate further the importance of category-triggering in these specific conversational practices as analogues to the text-critical variants I will discuss in the later sections below.

Synonymous Readings

In "Synonymous Readings in the Masoretic Text," Talmon laid out what became an extremely influential argument for a class of text-critical variants he labeled "synonymous readings."[18] Even some of the most traditional

---

18. Talmon, "Synonymous Readings." See also Talmon, "Textual Study of the Bible." Although most of Talmon's influence has been within the study of the Hebrew Bible, see also Paul Delnero, "Memorization and the Transmission of Sumerian Literary Compositions," *JNES* 71 (2012): 189–208. This section is a major revision of Person, "Formulas and Scribal Memory," which includes not only examples from the

text critics—those who continue to publish what they confidently reconstruct as the original text—understand that the Hebrew Bible exists in a state of textual plurality and textual fluidity as late as the Second Temple period and that some classes of text-critical variants, especially synonymous readings, simply require text critics to make their best guess for what the original reading was. From their perspective, this problem is reflected in Talmon's definition:

1. The variant resulted from the substitution of a word or phrase by a lexeme that is used interchangeably with it in the text of the Hebrew Bible.
2. The variant does not adversely affect the structure of the verse, nor its meaning or rhythm, and therefore cannot have been caused by scribal error.
3. No sign of systematic or tendentious emendation characterizes such a variant, which must be taken at face value. Synonymous readings are not marked by a clearly definable ideological purpose, but rather are characterized by the absence of any difference between them in content or meaning.
4. As far as we can tell, synonymous readings do not stem from chronologically or geographically distinct literary sources.[19]

That is, methodologically the original cannot possibly be determined in these cases. Explicitly building upon the work of Talmon and others, Carr introduced the term "memory variants," which he defined as follows: "the sort of variants that happen when a tradent modifies elements of texts in the process of citing or otherwise reproducing it from memory."[20] With

---

Hebrew Bible but also from Homer and the New Testament. Thus, although much of the argument remains the same, this section includes additional examples from ancient Hebrew literature.

19. Talmon, "Synonymous Readings," 336.

20. Carr, *Formation of the Hebrew Bible*, 17. Talmon's and Carr's examples differ somewhat. Talmon's examples are exclusively from the Hebrew Bible, often from different manuscripts of the same literary text. Carr's examples not only come from the Hebrew Bible, but also from other literature from the ancient Near East and the Mediterranean basin. Both use examples from parallel biblical texts, e.g., Chronicles is generally understood to be a later revision of the books of Samuel–Kings. Although in previous works I have focused on parallel biblical texts (see esp. Person, *Deuteronomic History and the Book of Chronicles*), in this chapter I will generally limit my discussion to examples from different manuscripts of the same literary text, unless

such text-critical variants as synonymous readings and memory variants, some of the standard explanations of these variants (such as scribal error or ideologically motivated revisions) simply do not apply, so that the question Why would a scribe make such a change in the process of copying an existing text? and the related question Why would a culture accept different versions of literary texts with such changes? become more pressing. However, when we consider Lord's insight that "in oral tradition the idea of an original is illogical" and apply this to the notion that there was no original text in the transmission history of some ancient literary works as well, then "we cannot correctly speak of a 'variant,' since there is no 'original' to be varied."[21] Rather, we need to consider the characteristic of multiformity in oral traditions and how it may inform textual transmission.[22] Lord's insights apply to those ancient and medieval texts that exist in textual plurality, so that in a real sense we should consider ancient and medieval scribes as performers of literary texts in ways that are somewhat analogous to oral performers, thereby explaining what we often perceive as variants under the influence of scribal memory.

As argued above, category-triggering is not only a phenomenon in everyday conversation, but can also occur in the special grammar of oral traditions, thereby preparing the way further for an argument that category-triggering may also occur when scribes as performers draw from their memory of the tradition, allowing them to substitute words, phrases, and formulas (all of which in some sense are traditional words/units of meaning) that occur in the same category, *even when* they are copying a *Vorlage* to produce a new manuscript. In this section, I will provide examples of synonymous readings, including the following types: (1) different, single lexemes, (2) the same words in a different order, (3) different formulas, and (4) double readings, in which a manuscript preserves two synonymous readings found singly in other manuscripts. Furthermore, in some cases passages have so many of these types of synonymous readings that the passages themselves can be considered synonymous, despite differences in wording (see also below the section on harmonization). We

---

a parallel text provides additional insight into the textual variation. See also Shemaryahu Talmon, "Observations on Variant Readings in the Isaiah Scroll (1QIsa[a])," in *The World of Qumran from Within: Collected Studies* (Jerusalem: Magnes; Leiden: Brill, 1989), 71–116.

21. Lord, *Singer of Tales*, 101.
22. Lord, *Singer of Tales*, 102.

will see that these various types of synonymous readings (all of which are memory variants) are evidence that category-triggering is a phenomenon in scribal memory in the process of the transmission of texts.

Different, Single Lexemes

Although his definition of synonymous readings includes words and phrases, Talmon's examples are primarily phrases in which only one lexeme differs.[23] Below I give a few examples from Talmon that occur often in the manuscript evidence. Examples 2.3–2.4 concern the synonyms of the verbs דבר/אמר ("say"/"speak"), which occur often together within the same verse (e.g., Lev 1:2; Isa 40:27).

Example 2.3: Exod 7:26; 9:1[24]

> MT 7:26
>
> ויאמר יהוה אל משה בא אל פרעה ואמרת אליו כה אמר יהוה
> And the Lord said to Moses, "Go to Pharaoh and **say** to him, 'Thus says the Lord'"
>
> SP 7:26
>
> ויאמר יהוה אל משה בא אל פרעה ודברת אליו כה אמר יהוה
> And the Lord said to Moses, "Go to Pharaoh and **speak** to him, 'Thus says the Lord'"
>
> MT 9:1
>
> ויאמר יהוה אל משה בא אל פרעה ודברת אליו כה אמר יהוה
> And the Lord said to Moses, "Go to Pharaoh and **speak** to him, 'Thus says the Lord'"
>
> SP 9:1
>
> ויאמר יהוה אל משה בא אל פרעה ואמרת אליו כה אמר יהוה
> And the Lord said to Moses, "Go to Pharaoh and **say** to him, 'Thus says the Lord'"

---

23. Talmon, "Synonymous Readings," 336.
24. Talmon, "Synonymous Readings," 345.

2. Category-Triggering and Text-Critical Variants

Example 2.4: Deut 5:27[25]

> MT
>
> כל אשר יאמר יהוה אלהינו
>
> all that the Lord our God **will say**
>
> 4QDeut[n]
>
> כול אשר ידבר יהוה אלוהינו
>
> all that the Lord our God **will speak**

Talmon also provided examples of the substitution of two sets of nouns, ארץ/אדמה ("ground"/"land") and שדה/ארץ ("land"/"field").[26] He gave example 2.5, which illustrates how all three of these synonyms are interchangeable. Note that all three variants are within the MT tradition:

Example 2.5: Jer 9:21[27]

> MT[Occ]
>
> כדמן על פני השדה
>
> like dung on the face of the **field**
>
> MT[Or]
>
> כדמן על פני הארץ
>
> like dung on the face of the **land**
>
> MT[mss]
>
> כדמן על פני האדמה
>
> like dung on the face of the **ground**

Since Talmon's article is often referred to in discussions of similar examples, I will provide example 2.6 from another scholar, one that demonstrates the substitution of the verbs עבר/בוא ("enter"/"cross over").

---

25. Esther Eshel, "4QDeut[n]—A Text That Has Undergone Harmonistic Editing," *HUCA* 62 (1991): 117–54.

26. Talmon, "Synonymous Readings," 348–51.

27. Talmon, *Text and Canon*, 187. Cf. Talmon, "Synonymous Readings," 350.

Example 2.6: Deut 6:1[28]

MT

בארץ אשר אתם עברים שמה לרשתה

in the land which you are **crossing over** into it to possess it

4Q22 (4QpaleoExod^m)

בארץ אשר אתמה באים שמה לרשתה

in the land which you are **entering** into it to possess it

Note that in all of these examples, the synonyms belong in what Jefferson would refer to as a coclass category. Therefore, the substitution of a synonymous reading for another can be understood as the scribe being influenced by category-triggering in scribal memory, so that the *Vorlage* provides the scribe access to the category from which the scribe copies the *Vorlage* verbatim or sometimes selects a synonym as a coclass member of the same category. Thus, what we may perceive as a variation can nevertheless be understood as authentic or original from the traditional perspective of the ancient scribes and their audiences.

Same Words, Different Order

Talmon noted the following: "the order of the synonymous expression in the parallel members of a verse can be inverted ... without causing any distorting of the author's original intention or any disturbance of the syntax and rhythm of the verse."[29] Below I will provide two examples of the same words given in a different order as synonymous readings. The first compares the MT and 4Q22 and involves a simple change in word order.

---

28. George J. Brooke, "Deuteronomy 5–6 in the Phylacteries from Qumran Cave 4," in *Emanuel: Studies in Hebrew Bible, Septuagint, and the Dead Sea Scrolls in Honor of Emanuel Tov*, ed. Shalom M. Paul, Robert A. Kraft, Lawrence H. Schiffman, and Weston W. Fields, VTSup 94 (Leiden: Brill 2003), 65.

29. Talmon, "Synonymous Readings," 336–37.

2. Category-Triggering and Text-Critical Variants

Example 2.7: Exod 26:10³⁰

MT

ועשית המשים ללאת

You shall make **fifty loops**

4Q22

[ועש׳ת ללא]ות המשים

[You shall make **lo]ops fifty**

The difference here ("fifty loops" // "loops fifty") is grammatically permissible and insignificant in meaning. The second example compares a reading in MT with 1QIsaᵃ. This is a clear example of what Talmon described as "the order of the synonymous expression in the parallel members of a verse can be inverted."³¹

Example 2.8: Isa 49:6³²

MT

להקים את שבטי יעקב ונצירי ישראל

to raise up the tribes of **Jacob** and the survivors of **Israel**

1QIsaᵃ

להקים את שבטי ישראל ונצירי יעקוב

to raise up the tribes of **Israel** and the survivors of **Jacob**

According to the tradition (e.g., see Gen 32:28), "Jacob" and "Israel" are two names for the same individual; therefore, this exchange of proper names does not change the meaning of either noun phrase in this parallel construction. That is, "tribes of Jacob," "tribes of Israel," "survivors of Israel," and "survivors of Jacob" are synonymous readings, all referring to

---

30. Judith E. Sanderson, *An Exodus Scroll from Qumran: 4QpaleoExodᵐ and the Samaritan Tradition*, HSS 30 (Atlanta: Scholars Press, 1986), 115.

31. Talmon, "Synonymous Readings," 336.

32. Talmon, "Synonymous Readings," 340; Paulson Pulikottil, *Transmission of Biblical Texts at Qumran: The Case of the Large Isaiah Scroll 1QIsaᵃ*, JSPSup 34 (Sheffield: Sheffield Academic, 2001), 68.

the descendants of Jacob/Israel in the surviving tribes as coclass members of the same category.

Different Phrases

As already noted, most of Talmon's examples really concerned single lexemes.[33] However, many studies that apply his insights to other texts include more examples of phrases, including formulas. The following examples come from studies that are drawing from Talmon's works or other works explicitly influenced by Talmon. The first three examples come from the work of Ian Young in his comparison of MT Daniel and LXX Daniel. Concerning example 2.9, the immediately preceding phrase in both texts describes King Belshazzar as drinking wine, so that the two synonymous readings here refer to his mood under the influence of the alcohol.

Example 2.9: Dan 5:2[34]

> MT
> בלשאצר אמר בטעם חמרא להיתיה
> **Belshazzar said, under the influence of the wine,** to bring
>
> LXX[OG]
> καὶ ἀνυψώθη ἡ καρδία αὐτοῦ, καὶ εἶπεν ἐνέγκαι
> ורם לבבה ואמר להיתיה
> **And his heart was exalted and he said** to bring

That is, "under the influence of the wine" "his heart was exalted" are two descriptions that access the category of possible alcohol-induced moods.

In the following example, we see different ways of referring to the category of idols or false gods.

---

33. Talmon, "Synonymous Readings," 336.
34. Young, "Original Problem," 273. The translations of the Aramaic are Young's. For the Greek translations, Young used *New English Translation of the Septuagint* (NETS), which is available online at http://ccat.sas.upenn.edu/nets/edition/. In some cases, he adapted NETS to provide a better comparison with the Aramaic. See Young, "Original Problem," 273 n. 8. The retroversion of the Greek into Aramaic is my own based on Dan 5:20; 11:12.

Example 2.10: Dan 5:4, 23[35]

5:4 MT

לאלהי דהבא וכספא נחשא פרזלא אעא ואבנא

the gods of **gold** and **silver**, bronze, iron, wood, and stone

5:23 MT

לאלהי כספא ודהבא נחשא פרזלא אעא ואבנא די לא חזין ולא שמעין ולא ידעין

the gods of **silver** and **gold**, bronze, iron, wood, and stone **who do not see and do not hear and do not know**

First, we should note that we have a transposition of "gold" and "silver" between these two phrases, thereby providing us with another example of a synonymous reading of the same words in different orders. Second, the description of the gods of metal, wood, and stone found in Dan 5:4 is repeated in Dan 5:23, but with the additional phrase of "who do not see … hear … know." That is, gods made of inanimate objects do not have perception and knowledge. Looking at the parallel verses of Dan 5:4 and 5:23 in the LXX, we find two other synonymous phrases for the category of false gods/idols.

Example 2.11[36]

Dan 5:4
LXX[OG] τὰ εἴδωλα τὰ χειροποίητα αὐτῶν

אלהיהון עובדי בידיהין

idols made by **their** hands

Dan 5:23
LXX[OG] τὰ εἴδωλα τὰ χειροποίητα τῶν ἀνθρώπων

אלהיהין עובדי אנשא

the idols made by **human** hands

---

35. Young, "Original Problem," 274, 281, his translation.
36. Young, "Original Problem," 274, 281, his translation; my retroversion.

These phrases are clearly synonymous, simply substituting the pronoun "their" for "human" (or vice versa). When we combine examples 2.10–2.11—that is, we compare Dan 5:4 in the MT and LXX and Dan 5:23 in the MT and LXX—we see how the way I have presented these synonymous readings above is somewhat misleading, in that the comparison between the MT and LXX of the two passages has what appears to be (from our modern perspective) phrases that contain more variation, in that the lexical variation is greater. That is, "the gods of gold and silver, bronze, iron, wood, and stone" in MT Dan 5:4 and "the idols made of their hand" in LXX Dan 5:4 differ more significantly as do "the gods of silver and gold, bronze, iron, wood, and stone who do not see and do not hear and do not know" in MT Dan 5:23 and "the idols made by human hands" in LXX Dan 5:23. However, if the two phrases in the MT of Dan 5:4 and Dan 5:23 are synonymous and the two phrases in the LXX of Dan 5:4 and Dan 5:23 are synonymous, then we must consider all four phrases synonymous. In other words, the description of "the gods of gold and silver, bronze, iron, wood, and stone" is explicitly a reference to the observation that these gods/"idols made by their/human hands" cannot see, hear, or know anything. Therefore, these are four synonymous readings that access the category of false gods/idols.

Examples 2.12–2.13 come from different versions of the Community Rule, one in 1QS and one in 4Q256 (4QS[b]). In example 2.12, this section of these two manuscripts of the Community Rule begins with a different line introducing what follows.

Example 2.12: Community Rule[37]

1QS V, 1

זה הסרך לאנשי היחד

This is the rule for the men of the community

4Q256 IX,1

מדרש למשכיל [על אנשי התורה

A midrash for the wise leader [over the men of the Torah

---

37. Carr, *Formation of the Hebrew Bible*, 86, his translation. See also Sarianna Metso, *The Textual Development of the Qumran Community Rule*, STDJ 21 (Leiden: Brill, 1997), 27–28.

Although the first lines of these two versions differ, they can nevertheless be understood as synonymous, because "the wise leader" is charged in both documents to oversee the application of "the rule" within the life of the community. In example 2.13, the two synonymous readings explain under whose authority interpretation of the community's rules fall, in the first this is quite explicit but in the second the single lexeme must have been understood within the community to refer to the list of individuals in the first.

Example 2.13: Community Rule[38]

> 1QS V, 2–3
> על פי בני צדוק הכוהנים שומרי הברית ועל פי רוב אנשי היחד המחזקים בברית
> under the authority of **the Zadokites, the priests, who keep the covenant and under the authority of the majority of the men of community who hold fast to the covenant**
>
> 4Q256, 258 (4QS[d]) IX, 3
> ועל פי הרבים
> under the authority of **the many**

Although the reading from 1QS is certainly more specific, these two phrases could have been understood as synonymous within the community; that is, members of the community already knew who "the many" were in their communal structure, so the specification given in 1QS was not necessary to repeat in every reference to "the many" but could nevertheless be substituted easily in the process of copying due to scribal memory. In Jefferson's terminology, both phrases refer to the same category, that is, the leaders who have the authority in the community.

Example 2.14 comes from Jean-Sébastien Rey's study of the medieval manuscripts of Ben Sira from the Cairo Genizah.

---

38. Carr, *Formation of the Hebrew Bible*, 86, his translation. See also Metso, *Textual Development of the Qumran Community Rule*, 27–28; Metso, *The Community Rule: A Critical Edition with Translation*, EJL 51 (Atlanta: SBL Press, 2019), 26.

Example 2.14: Sir 4:30[39]

> MS A
>
> אל תהי ככלב בביתך ומוזר ומתירא במלאכתך
> Do not be like a **dog** in your house **and oppressed and fearful** in your **acts**.

> MS C
>
> אל תהי כאריה בביתך ומתפחז בעבודתך
> Do not be like a **lion** in your house **and arrogant** in your **works**.

Although "dog" (כלב) and "lion" (אריה) are not synonyms, they belong to the same category of animals that are unclean and in the biblical tradition they are often understood as threats to human safety (for "dog," see Exod 11:7; Ps 22:21; for "lion," see Num 23:24; Deut 33:20; Judg 14:5; 1 Sam 17:34). In that sense, they may be understood as near-synonyms. However, because of their differences, the attitude connected with each of them differs; that is, the dog (sometimes a domesticated household member) is "oppressed and fearful," and the lion is "arrogant." Nevertheless, the attitude in both versions is connected to words that are synonymous for behaviors ("in your acts"/"in your works"). Therefore, even though many scholars are confident that they can reconstruct the earliest inferable text state, Rey nevertheless concluded that the "Hebrew texts of MSS A and C make perfect sense and generate new proverbs."[40] It seems to me that these two versions of this proverb (as well as others in the extant texts not discussed here by Rey) are *either* (near-)synonymous proverbs, that is, coclass members of the same category, *or*, if we understand them as collectively giving contrasting advice ("Do not be … oppressed and fearful" versus "Do not be … arrogant"), they belong to a different type of category, that is, "sometimes as contrasts … very often as pairs."[41] In other words, as is common in wisdom literature, moderation is a virtue that is best achieved by avoiding two extremes, in this case being "arrogant" or "oppressed and fearful" and therefore advice concerning one may open up within scribal

---

39. Rey, "Reflections on the Critical Edition of the Hebrew Text of Ben Sira: Between Eclecticisim and Pragmatism," *Textus* 27 (2018): 191, his translation.

40. Rey, "Reflections," 192.

41. Jefferson, "On the Poetics of Ordinary Talk," 9.

memory access to the other, much like "Up-down, right-left, young-old, husband-wife."[42]

Double Readings

Talmon extended his identification of synonymous readings with his discussion of double readings.[43] Talmon described double readings as a scribal technique of "preserving equally valid readings" and "the conflation of alternative readings" that are synonymous readings within the same manuscript.[44] In Jefferson's terminology, the scribes simply provided two synonymous readings from the broader tradition that are accessing the same category. Below I provide five examples of double readings.

Example 2.15 comes from a comparison of the parallel biblical passages of 2 Kgs 18–20 and Isa 36–39, in which the double reading is found in 1QIsa^a. In this case, the double reading is simply preserving the two synonymous readings based on the substitution of only one lexeme.

Example 2.15: Isa 37:9 // 2 Kgs 19:9[45]

MT Isa 37:9

וישמע וישלח מלאכים

and he heard and he sent messengers

MT 2 Kgs 19:9

וישב וישלח מלאכים

and he returned and he sent messengers

1QIsa^a 37:9

וישמע וישוב וישלח מלאכים

and he heard and he returned and he sent messengers

The readings in the two MT texts contain synonymous readings in which "he heard" and "he returned" are substituted. The 1QIsa^a reading simply

---

42. Jefferson, "On the Poetics of Ordinary Talk," 9.
43. Shemaryahu Talmon, "Double Readings in the Masoretic Text," *Textus* 1 (1960): 144–84. See also Talmon, "Synonymous Readings," 343, 345.
44. Talmon, "Double Readings," 150.
45. Talmon, "Variant Readings in the Isaiah Scroll," 86.

conflates the two synonymous readings into a double reading, a third synonymous reading.

The second example is similar to example 2.15 in that the two readings using synonymous verbs are conflated.

Example 2.16: 2 Sam 12:16[46]

LXX[B]
καὶ εἰσῆλθεν καὶ ηὐθλίσθη ἐπὶ τῆς γῆς

ויבוא וילן ארצה

and he came **and spent the night** on the ground

4Q51 (4QSam[a])

ויב[ו]א וישכב בשק ארצה

and he came **and lay down in sackcloth** on the ground

MT

ובא ולן ושכב ארצה

and he was coming and **spending the night and lying down** on the ground

LXX[LMN]
καὶ εἰσῆλθεν καὶ ηὐθλίσθη καὶ ἐκάθεθδεν ἐν σάκκῳ ἐπὶ τῆς γῆς

ויבוא וילן וישכב בשק ארצה

and he came and **spent the night and lay down in sackcloth** on the ground

As in the previous example, here we have two versions with two verbs—"he came and spent the night" and "he came and lay down"—that are conflated in other versions ("he came and spent the night and lay down" with the variant verb tenses) with the variant plus of "in sackcloth" occurring in one of the shorter versions and in one of the longer versions.

The third example, the first one of a double reading containing obvious formulaic phrases, comes from a comparison of the parallel passages of 2 Kgs 24:18–25:30 and Jer 52 in the MT with the LXX reading of Jeremiah.

---

46. Young, "Dead Sea Scrolls and the Bible," 23, his translation.

2. Category-Triggering and Text-Critical Variants

Example 2.17: 2 Kgs 25:30 // Jer 52:34[47]

    MT 2 Kgs 25:30

                                                                               כל ימי חיו

    all the days of his life

    LXX Jer 52:34
    ἕως ἡμέρας, ἧς ἀπέθανεν

                                                                               עד יום מותו

    until the day of his death

    MT Jer 52:34

                                                    עד יום מותו כל ימי חיו

    until the day of his death, all the days of his life

The MT Kings and LXX Jeremiah contain two synonymous formulas referring to the length of the king's life that are conflated in MT Jeremiah.

    Example 2.18 comes from Rey's study of Ben Sira from the Cairo Genizah; as with his example 2.14 above, it contains synonymous proverbs.

Example 2.18: Sir 11:3[48]

    MS A

                                 אליל בעוף דברה וראש תנובות פריה

    Insignificant among birds is the bee,
    but its fruit is the chief of products.

    LXX
    μικρὰ ἐν πετεινοῖς μέλισσα, καὶ ἀρχὴ γλυκασμάτων ὁ καρπὸς αὐτῆς
                                 קטנה בעוף דברה וראש תנובות פריה
    Small among birds is the bee,
    but its fruit is the chief of products.

    MS B

                                 קטנה בעוף דברה וראש תנובות פריה

---

    47. Person, "Ancient Israelite Scribe as Performer," 605; Tov, *Textual Criticism* (3rd ed.), 225–26.

    48. Rey, "Reflections," 192–93, his translation.

אליל בעוף דברה וראש תנובות פריה
Small among birds is the bee,
but its fruit is the chief of products.
Insignificant among birds is the bee,
but its fruit is the chief of products.

Since the only variation between these two versions of this proverb are the first words, קטנה ("small") and אליל ("insignificant"), we clearly have synonymous proverbs. Manuscript B contains a double reading preserving the two versions found separately in MS A and the LXX *Vorlage*.

The last example of double readings comes from Judith Sanderson's study of 4Q22. This example shows the flexibility that can occur within a formulaic system in that she showed how the text-critical evidence of Exod 32:11, Deut 9:26, and Deut 9:29 is especially illuminating concerning the formulaic phrases referring to the people of Israel as those whom God brought out of Egypt.[49] Sanderson's analysis included evidence from MT, the SP, 4Q22, and LXX, including in one case an important variation within LXX tradition itself.

Example 2.19: Exod 32:11 // Deut 9:26 // Deut 9:29[50]

MT Exod 32:11

אשר הוצאת מארץ מצרים בכח גדול וביד חזקה
whom you brought out of the land of Egypt with great power and with a mighty hand

SP Exod 32:11

אשר הוצאת ממצרים בכוח גדול ובזרוע נטויה

---

49. For an excellent collection of essays on formulas and formulaic systems from a comparative perspective, see Frog and Lamb, *Weathered Words*, in which an earlier version of this section appeared.

50. See Eugene Ulrich, *The Biblical Qumran Scrolls: Transcriptions and Textual Variants*, VTSup 134 (Leiden: Brill, 2010), 99. Ulrich noted a large lacuna in the middle of this verse that is not reflected in Sanderson's analysis; therefore, a reconstruction of this reading would need to include additional words here. This would also make it likely that this reading is no longer the shortest, even though it would be among the shortest. This is another reminder of how precarious working with reconstructions can be.

2. Category-Triggering and Text-Critical Variants

whom you brought out of Egypt with great power and with a raised arm

4Q22

אשר הוצ[את ו]בזרוע חזק[ה

whom you brought [out *lacuna* with] a strong arm

LXX Exod 32:11

οὓς ἐξήγαγες ἐκ γῆς Αἰγύπτου ἐν ἰσχύι μεγάλῃ καὶ ἐν τῷ βραχίονί σου τῷ ὑψηλῷ

אשר הוצאת מארץ מצרים בכח גדול ובזרוע נטויה

whom you brought out of the land of Egypt with great power and with a raised arm

MT Deut 9:26

אשר הוצאת ממצרים ביד חזקה

whom you brought out of Egypt with a mighty hand

SP Deut 9:26

אשר הוצאת ממצרים בידך החזקה

whom you brought out of Egypt with your mighty hand

LXX Deut 9:26

οὓς ἐξήγαγες ἐκ γῆς Αἰγύπτου ἐν τῇ ἰσχύι σου τῇ μεγάλῃ καὶ ἐν τῇ χειρί σου τῇ κραταιᾷ καὶ ἐν τῷ βραχίονί σου τῷ ὑψηλῷ

אשר הוצאת מארץ מצרים בכחך גדול ובידך החזקה ובזרעך הנטויה

whom you brought out of the land of Egypt with your great power, with your mighty hand, and with your raised arm

MT Deut 9:29

אשר הוצאת בכחך הגדל ובזרעך הנטויה

whom you brought out with your great power and with your raised arm

SP Deut 9:29

אשר הוצאת ממצרים בכחך הגדול ובזרועך הנטויה

whom you brought out of Egypt with your great power and with your raised arm

LXX Deut 9:29
οὕς ἐξήγαγες ἐκ γῆς Αἰγύπτου ἐν τῇ ἰσχύι σου τῇ μεγάλῃ καὶ ἐν τῷ βραχίονί σου τῷ ὑψηλῷ

אשר הוצאת מארץ מצרים בכחך הגדל ובזרעך הנטויה

whom you brought out of the land of Egypt with your great power and with your raised arm

LXX[B] Deut 9:29
οὕς ἐξήγαγες ἐκ γῆς Αἰγύπτου ἐν τῇ ἰσχύι σου τῇ μεγάλῃ καὶ ἐν τῇ χειρί σου τῇ κραταιᾷ καὶ ἐν τῷ βραχίονί σου τῷ ὑψηλῷ

אשר הוצאת מארץ מצרים בכחך הגדל ובידך החזקה ובזרעך הנטויה

whom you brought out of the land of Egypt with your great power, with your mighty hand, and with your raised arm[51]

All of these phrases—from the shortest (Exod 32:11 in 4Q22; "whom you brought out with a raised arm") to the longest (Deut 9:26 in LXX, Deut 9:29 in LXX[B]: "whom you brought out of the land of Egypt with your great power, with your mighty hand, and with your raised arm")—are synonymous and are made up of various possible options that can be represented in the following table, so that every instantiation begins with the phrase in the first column, selects a phrase (or not) from the second column, and then selects one or more of the phrases in the last column, but nevertheless keeping those selected from the third column in the same order as given in the table. Note that each column can be understood as a coclass category in Jefferson's terminology.

	[lacking]	with [your] great power
whom you brought out	of Egypt	with [a/your] mighty hand
	of the land of Egypt	with [a/your] raised/strong arm

All of the readings begin with "whom you brought out," a phrase that even by itself implicitly denotes "out of Egypt/the land of Egypt" (the category of the place of enslavement) and is then followed by a phrase referring to God's "power"/"hand"/"arm" (the category of "power" sometimes represented by body parts). Sanderson noted that all of these synonymous readings are "possible and defensible."[52] Furthermore, since the variation

---

51. Sanderson, *Exodus Scroll from Qumran*, 146.
52. Sanderson, *Exodus Scroll from Qumran*, 147.

occurs within the textual traditions of each of the three verses as well as among the three verses, we can conclude that this formulaic system worked within the scribal memory of the tradents of each of these texts, so that in one sense the substitution of one particular instantiation for another has not changed the text at all, because it maintains the same meaning contained within the formulaic system itself. Furthermore, since this variation occurs within the same manuscript traditions as well as among them, the flexibility of this formulaic system works throughout the composition/transmission process, thereby breaking down the distinction between authors and copyists.

Complex Example from the Community Rule

The following example from Miller's *Dead Sea Media* is more complex than those discussed above in that, within this one passage from the Community Rule, there are multiple synonymous readings, so that in effect the entire passage can be understood collectively as three synonymous readings. I will begin by giving the three parallel texts in a table and then discuss the individual variants within the passage, in order to show how all of them together create three synonymous readings of the passage.

Example 2.20: 1QS V, 22–23 // 4Q258 // 4Q261 (4QSᵍ)[53]

1QS V, 22–23	4Q258 II, 2–3	4Q261 1a–b 2–4
לשוב ביחד לבריתו	לשוב ביחד	לשבת יחד
וכתבם	ולהכתב	ולכת[ב
בסרכ איש לפני רעהו	איש לפני רעה בסרך	איש לפנ[י רע]הו בסרך
לפי שכלו	איש לפי שכלו	לפי] שכלו
ומעשיו	ומעשיו בתורה	ומעשו בתור]ה
להשמע הכול איש לרעהו	להשמע הכול איש לרעה[ו]	[להשמע
הקטן לגדול	הקטן לגדול	הקטן [לגדול]

---

53. Miller, *Dead Sea Media*, 260–61. I have reformatted Miller's chart and adapted his translation, in order to facilitate my discussion of the individual synonymous readings in the passage.

to return together to his covenant.	to return together	to dwell together,
And they shall inscribe them	and to be inscribed	and to be inscrib[ed
by rank, each before his fellow	each before a fellow by rank	each befor]e [his] fell[ow, by rank
according to his understanding	each according to his understanding	according to] his understanding
and his works,	and his works in the law,	and his works in the la[w,
so that all may be obedient,	so that all may be obedient,	so that] the junior [may be obedient to the senior.]
each to his fellow,	each to [his] fellow,	
the junior to the senior.	the junior to the senior.	

I will briefly discuss the variants in each of the lines in the tables above, combining my discussion of the last two lines as necessary. The first line begins with an infinitive, continuing the sentence from the previous lines. The infinitive phrases "to return together" (לשוב ביחד) and "to dwell together" (לשבת יחד) refer to the same action, that is, returning to dwell together. The plus, "to return together *to his covenant*," simply emphasizes that the community to which he is returning to dwell is a covenant-community, which is the self-understanding of the *yaḥad* (יחד). In the second line, we have two variations of the verb כתב ("inscribe")—the infinitive connected to the preceding one ("to return ... and to be inscribed") and a finite verb with a pronominal suffix ("and they inscribed them") presumably beginning another sentence—both of which, as Miller noted, refers to the enrolling of initiates into the community. The third line contains a change in word order—"by rank, each before his fellow" or "each before his fellow, by rank"—as well as the addition/omission of the pronoun ("fellow"/"his fellow"). The fourth line in 4Q258 includes a plus of איש ("*each* according to his understanding"), which occurs in the previous line and therefore is not necessary to carry forward the meaning.[54] The fifth line of both 4Q258 and 4Q261 includes a plus of בתורה ("[and his

---

54. Metso has a slightly different reconstruction here: her reconstruction of the lacuna in 4Q261 5:22 is שכלו [איש לפי, containing the same plus as 4Q258 5:22. See Metso, *Community Rule*, 30.

works] *in the law*"), which simply makes explicit what is implicit. The sixth and seventh lines in 1QS and 4Q258 simply make more explicit what is implied in the reading in 4Q261; that is, the reason that "the junior [should] be obedient to the senior" is that "all [should] be obedient, each man to his fellow" according to the hierarchy established within the community. Thus, when all of these synonymous readings are taken together, we can see that this passage exists in three synonymous versions. Thus, Miller concluded: "Because the majority of variations between these parallel versions are textually ambiguous and grammatically acceptable, it is extremely difficult for editors to identify so-called original readings."[55] Furthermore, when we consider the complexity of the formulaic system above in example 2.19 and how various other options were possibly available within scribal memory, we should not assume that these are the only synonymous readings of this passage that existed. The flexibility inherent within the tradition would suggest the possibility of other variations of this passage that are nevertheless synonymous.

Synonymous Readings and Double Readings: A Summary

I began my discussion of reimagining text-critical variants with synonymous readings, because, since Talmon's influential studies, even the most conservative text critics recognize that this is a class of variants for which we often have no methodological basis for determining the original reading, because, as Talmon wrote, "there is no justification for terming these readings early and late, primary and secondary, original and copy."[56] Talmon described the early period of written transmission as follows:

> When the variants in question were purely stylistic, without any ideological significance, and the number of books supporting each of the parallel readings was equal, there was not even any formal justification, let alone any considerations of intrinsic value, for rejecting one reading and upholding another. It was this recensional dilemma that gave rise to the preservation of synonymous readings, because "these and these alike are the words of the living God."[57]

---

55. Miller, *Dead Sea Media*, 261.
56. Talmon, "Synonymous Readings," 337.
57. Talmon, "Double Readings," 148.

Therefore, synonymous readings provide us with the most obvious starting point for our understanding of textual fluidity and textual plurality, because the tradition valued having manuscripts with these different readings in them. Then double readings are simply an extension, "a kind of modification of *synonymous readings*, which made it possible for alternative wordings of the same time to be incorporated in a single verse."[58]

Although Talmon does not use the term "scribal memory" or make reference to Jefferson's idea of category-triggering, his understanding of how synonymous readings occurs is certainly consistent with these later ideas. Because of the common feature of parallelism in Hebrew literature, he understood that synonymous readings were simply an adaptation of this characteristic of the composition of the literature that carried over into the transmission of the literature. Note the similarity in the following quotation from Talmon to Jefferson's definition of category:

> pairs of words came into being which were pragmatically used as synonyms, even if, etymologically speaking, they actually expressed different shades of meaning. Such lexemes became so closely wedded to each other that the mention of one of the pair automatically evoked the mention of the other. This development may have come about unconsciously, or it may have resulted from deliberate scribal practice.[59]

In Jefferson's terms, one of the pair triggers the other, because synonymous readings are "co-members, very often as pairs."[60] Category-triggering works unconsciously in terms of word selection; however, once it occurs it may become conscious, so that it may become a deliberate scribal practice or in Jefferson's words, "That's the poet's job."[61]

Talmon's influence is especially obvious in the recent work of both Rey and Miller. Based on his text-critical study of Ben Sira, including his identification of numerous synonymous readings and double readings, Rey concluded as follows: "This reconstructed process shows that scribes involved in the transmission of this text were not simply copyists

---

58. Talmon, "Double Readings," 150, emphasis original.
59. Talmon, "Synonymous Readings," 335.
60. Jefferson, "On the Poetics of Ordinary Talk," 9.
61. Jefferson, "On the Poetics of Ordinary Talk," 4.

but were actively involved in the creation of the text as learned authors."[62] Therefore, Rey rejected the typical distinctions between redaction criticism and text criticism and reconstructing the original text as a goal for text criticism. The last example I gave above from Miller's *Dead Sea Media* (example 2.20) was selected because it alone illustrates evidence of the different kinds of memory variants that occur within scribal memory. Miller concluded:

> Overall, this passage [1QS V, 22–23, 4Q258 2 2–3, and 4Q261 1a–b 2–4] displays four types of changes that are typical of texts transmitted by scribal working memory in an oral-written context. First, the passage above exhibits differences in morphology…. Second, the passage above displays substitutions of words with similar or different meanings…. Third, the passage above exhibits additions or omissions…. Fourth, the passage above displays reordering.[63]

Although in this study I have mostly ignored morphological differences in my comments, I nevertheless provided the evidence above that shows that morphological differences are common under the influence of scribal memory and, therefore, I certainly agree with Miller on this point. The other three types of variants Miller identified in this one passage in the Community Rule include what Talmon identified as synonymous readings and what Carr identified as memory variants. Like Miller's study, this study builds upon Talmon's important insights as combined with media studies, so that what may be understood as a synonymous reading is expanded to include other types of text-critical variants and to move beyond single lexemes and even phrases to include, in some cases, entire passages and even variant literary editions. Thus, in one sense, most of the following examples in this chapter and the next can be understood as (near-)synonymous readings. What is most obviously added to these recent studies in this study is how Jefferson's poetics can begin to explain the cognitive-linguistic mechanisms behind synonymous readings (even when defined more broadly than Talmon's original notion). In the following section we will see how Jefferson's poetics opens up new possibilities to understand how lists are constructed and how they function, as we

---

62. Rey, "Reflections," 198.
63. Miller, *Dead Sea Media*, 261–64.

continue to explore category-triggering and expand what can be understood as synonymous readings.

Variants in Lists

List Formation in Conversation

"On the Poetics of Ordinary Talk" is not the first publication in which Jefferson discussed "the 'poetics' of natural talk," because poetics was an important part of her discussion of list-construction in everyday conversation.[64] The poetics article is based on a lecture Jefferson gave at a conference in 1977 drawing from "stuff which we'd [Harvey Sacks and some of his students, including Jefferson] pretty much kept to ourselves and played with as a hobby" and was only published in 1996 at Robert Hopper's prodding of Jefferson, including his giving to her his draft transcript of her lecture based on the video.[65] However, the fact that poetics was a significant aspect of her discussion of list-construction suggests that Jefferson herself took the observations about poetics more seriously than some of her dismissive hedges and the excesses in the poetics article may suggest. What follows is my summary of Jefferson's discussion of poetics within the context of list-construction. Note, however, that in my summary I will often use terms from Jefferson's poetics article that she did not use in her list-construction article; careful reading shows the close connections in her development of the terms she used in her 1996 article that differ from both her 1977 lecture on poetics and her discussion of poetics

---

64. Gail Jefferson, "List-Construction as a Task and Resource," in *Interaction Competence*, ed. George Psathas, Studies in Ethnomethodology and Conversation Analysis (Washington, DC: University Press of America, 1990), 63–92, esp. 68–73. This section is a major revision of Person, "Poetics and List Formation," which includes not only examples from the Hebrew Bible but also one from Homer (The Catalog of Ships in *Il.* 2.494–877) and one from the New Testament (Paul's list of vices in Gal 5:19–21). Thus, although much of the argument remains the same, this section includes additional examples from the Hebrew Bible.

65. Jefferson, "On the Poetics of Ordinary Talk," 2. For an excellent discussion of the poetics exhibited in Jefferson's 1977 lecture based on the application of an extension to her poetics, see Robin Wooffitt, Darren Reed, Jessica A. Young, and Clare Jackson, "The Poetics in Jefferson's Poetics Lecture," in Person, Wooffitt, and Rae, *Bridging the Gap*, 97–116. A video of Jefferson's conference presentation and a draft transcript are available at: https://tinyurl.com/SBLPress7015a1.

in her 1990 article on list-construction. For example, although in her lecture Jefferson referred generally to "mechanisms" (lines 1385, 1386, 1407, 1427), she does not use the more precise word phrases such as "sound-productional mechanisms," "gross selection-mechanism," or "triggering mechanisms" until its publication.[66] In fact, these terms do not show up in her 1990 article on lists, where she simply refers to "acoustic consonance and punlike relationships."[67] However, these relationships are obvious to the careful reader, so I will tend to use her more developed terms from the 1996 poetics article, even when I am summarizing her discussion of poetics in list-construction in her 1990 article. My discussion is also influenced by other studies that build upon Jefferson's, especially Gene Lerner, "Responsive List Constructions."[68] Furthermore, the summary below of list-construction as understood by Jefferson and Lerner is selective: I am emphasizing parts of the argument that most directly apply to my discussion of the literary examples below, so that some observations I am mostly overlooking. For example, I do not adequately discuss the important role that list-construction plays in the turn-taking system in conversation, since turn-taking is (mostly) irrelevant to the transmission process of scribes copying manuscripts.

Jefferson gave a loose definition of category as "objects that very strongly belong together; sometimes as contrasts, sometimes as co-members, very often as pairs."[69] As is the case throughout this chapter, I am only concerned here with category-triggering that includes comembers, since this type of category-triggering is an important aspect of list-construction.

Jefferson identified the "list-constructional principle of adequate representivity"—that is, in any list-in-progress the participants orient to the task of "the 'adequate representivity' of prior for subsequent list member(s)."[70] In other words, it is possible that even one item may suggest a category from which additional coclass items may be drawn in the formation of a list, but this suggestion may not be precise enough to represent the category accurately. Participants in a conversation need enough clues

---

66. Jefferson, "On the Poetics of Ordinary Talk," 8–9, 39.
67. Jefferson, "List-Construction," 71.
68. Lerner, "Responsive List Constructions: A Conversation Resource for Accomplishing Multifacted Social Action," *Journal of Language and Social Psychology* 13 (1994): 20–33.
69. Jefferson, "On the Poetics of Ordinary Talk," 9.
70. Jefferson, "List-Construction," 78, 77.

to adequately identify the category that the list-in-progress represents. Moreover, since "a list can be constructed by more than one speaker," exactly which category is being represented can be negotiated between the participants, so that it is possible that a list-in-progress may be produced at the end of the list-construction process in a way that might not have been projected at its beginning (see further below).[71]

An important practice that helps participants solve this potential problem of adequate representivity is a preference for three-part lists. Jefferson observed that "many lists occur in three parts" and that "three-partedness appears to have 'programmatic relevance' for the construction of lists."[72] In Lerner's words, "Lists require no more than three parts to establish that a class of items is being invoked."[73] One piece of evidence for three-partedness is that speakers who are constructing lists-in-progress can be observed to search for the final third item and/or use what Jefferson labeled a "generalized list completer." Example 2.21 illustrates a word search for the third item. Note that Jefferson placed brackets around the list items.

Example 2.21[74]

>   Mr. B: It's not in the same league with [adultery, and murder, and— and—thievery]

The first two items in this list ("adultery" and "murder") suggest a category of serious moral wrongs or vices and the delay in producing the third item ("thievery") suggests that Mr. B is searching for the right final coclass item in his list—that is, something that is also a serious moral wrong in contrast to whatever (from earlier in the conversation) is "not in the same league" (i.e., not in the same category) as the items in the list. Sometimes the third item in the list is occupied by a generalized list completer, thereby producing what Jefferson described as belonging to "less-than-three-*item* three-part *lists*."[75] In example 2.22, Jefferson used brackets to indicate repeating sounds, including in the list itself ("cakes and candy and crap"):

---

71. Jefferson, "List-Construction," 81.
72. Jefferson, "List-Construction," 63, 66.
73. Lerner, "Responsive List Construction," 24.
74. Jefferson, "List-Construction," 67.
75. Jefferson, "List-Construction," 66, emphasis original.

Example 2.22[76]

> Nora: there's only one on the Ways'n Means [C]ommittee. And I [c]annot serve on two: be[c]ause ˙hhhh all these [c]a[k]es and [c]a:ndy and [c]rap…

Jefferson identified "and crap" as a generalized list completer "selected from among such candidates as 'and stuff,' 'and junk,' 'and things,' etc."[77] That is, this format (two items + generalized list completer) makes explicit that the list represents a broader category—"not only do the named items not exhaust the possible array of nameables, but a third item would not do such work; i.e., there are 'many more' relevant nameables which will not, and need not, be specified."[78] I chose this example from the many Jefferson provided—and copied it from her poetics article rather than the lists article—to illustrate that sound-triggering may also occur in list-construction. In this case, "and crap" is selected from a range of possible generalized list completers, because it "is acoustically consonant with a series of prior words, including the two just-prior list items," that is, the repeated k-sound marked with brackets.[79] This is just one example Jefferson provides of how sound-triggering may influence the selection of generalized list completers and should serve as a reminder that category-triggering and sound-triggering often occur together, even though I have decided to focus on category-triggering in this chapter and sound-triggering in the next.[80]

As noted above, lists can be constructed by multiple participants in a conversation.[81] Lists are context-sensitive in that they are constructed in ways that are consistent with the topic of the conversation and as such they can be the locus of both collaborative social action and disputes. Because the first two items of a list project a category and therefore a range of possible third (or otherwise final) items in a list, a list begun by one speaker can

---

76. Jefferson, "On the Poetics of Ordinary Talk," 13. See also Jefferson, "List-Construction," 69.
77. Jefferson, "List-Construction," 69.
78. Jefferson, "List-Construction," 68.
79. Jefferson, "List-Construction," 69.
80. Jefferson, "List-Construction," 68–73.
81. Jefferson, "List-Construction," 81–89; Lerner, "Responsive List Constructions."

be completed by another participant in the talk. If the first two items have produced adequate representivity, another speaker can produce a final coclass item in the list-in-progress that is readily accepted by the participant who began the list, as is often the case. However, it is also possible that the other speaker produces a final item as a way of moving the category in another direction in an uncollaborative manner, so that the participant who began the list rejects the proposed third item. Below are some examples to illustrate some of the range of these possibilities. In example 2.23, Louise begins a list about bad weather that Ken cooperatively completes with an appropriate third item.

Example 2.23[82]

> Louise: first of all they hit rain.
> Ken: Mm hm
> Louise: then they hit hail.
> Ken: and then they hit snow.

Thus, Louise and Ken collaboratively create a list of bad weather—"rain," "hail," and "snow." In example 2.24, Sally completes the list begun by Sheila with the use of a generalized list completer. Lerner noted that sometimes the generalized list completer does not only complete the list, but also identifies the category that is represented by the list as in this example:

Example 2.24[83]

> Sheila: then I turn on the tee vee:, (0.2)
> an' I wanna watch (.) Cheers
> Sally: mm hm
> Sheila: or (0.7) Bill Cosby=or
> (0.2)
> Sally: some show thatcha wanna watch

Lerner observed that such a use of generalized list completers can occur in a list produced completely by one speaker, but this example shows how

---

82. Lerner, "Responsive List Constructions," 24.
83. Lerner, "Responsive List Constructions," 24.

recipients also can orient to this practice and can collaboratively complete the three-part list with a generalized list completer that demonstrates the speaker's understanding that the first two items have adequate representivity. "The first two items are needed to establish the dimensions or range of class membership, and the generalized list completer transforms the list from being merely a collection of items to a reference to the class."[84] That is, the "range of class membership" is the category of coclass items (in this case, TV shows that Sheila enjoys watching regularly). Example 2.25 is taken from a conversation in which Jessie has reported the death of a mutual friend to Goldie, who had no recent contact with the deceased prior to her death. Jefferson suggested that Jessie had entitled speakership as the bearer of the news, but this excerpt from the conversation can be seen as somewhat argumentative in that there is a lot of overlapping talk, so that Jessie and Goldie appear to be competing with each other for the turns at talk and maybe who knows the friend best. Goldie interrupts Jessie. Then Jessie interrupts Goldie and takes Goldie's utterance and reuses it to begin a list by supplying another two items and a generalized list completer:

Example 2.25[85]

Jessie: I, I-I jis couldn' take the constant repetition of [uh:::[:::
Goldie: [of- [of the same story. Oh don' I kno:w=
Jessie: =or how enla:rged it was or why huhr artery wz: five times larger or this that,=
Goldie: =en [e v r y b o d y o]wes me a livi[ng 'n,]
Jessie: [the othuh thing,]   [ˈhhhhh]hhhhhh k-
Jessie: Well uh- (.) uhhhh this is something that uh:: yihknow uh evrybody owes huhr.

Jessie turns Goldie's first utterance ("the same story") into the beginning of a list of things about the dead friend that he "couldn't take" anymore, claiming his entitled speakership, by producing what could have been by itself a complete list with two items plus a generalized list completer ("or how enla:rged it was or why huhr artery wz: five times larger or this that,

---

84. Lerner, "Responsive List Constructions," 24.
85. Jefferson, "List-Construction," 85.

the othuh thing"). However, Goldie challenges Jessie's speakership again by interrupting and adding another item to the list ("en evrybody owes me a living"). The excerpt ends with Jessie producing the final item of the list by repeating, after some delay, what Goldie had proposed as the final item ("evrybody owes huhr"), thereby coproducing the final item in the list with Goldie.

With these examples we can see how recipients of a list-in-progress can produce a range of items that can be understood as a (co)listing or a counterposed response and, in Jessie's repetition of Goldie's final item, how "a potentially 'counterposed response' can be reformulated as an 'equivalent list co-member.'"[86] Participants in conversation actively interpret the list items in order to achieve adequate representivity, that is, in order to identify the category represented by the coclass members in the list.

Lists in the Hebrew Bible

Before turning to my text-critical examples below, I want to emphasize some of the observations above concerning list-construction in conversation as I transition to lists in the Hebrew Bible. That is, I want to make explicit what may be implicit in the above summary concerning how lists may be adapted into literature. Lists function by establishing categories of coclass members in the social interaction between participants. Because of this function, the same category can be represented by other lists containing coclass members and, therefore, the actual items in a list can be replaced with other coclass members and the list could continue to serve much the same purpose: representing the same category of coclass members. Once adequate representivity of the category of coclass members has been reached, often after the first two items in a list, those participants who are other than the one who initiated the list-in-progress can contribute to the list-construction in a collaborative way. In contrast, sometimes the responsive coproduction of lists in conversation occurs in what appear to be competitive disputes, so that it is possible that the list-in-progress as projected by the speaker who initiated the list-construction can be hijacked in another direction. However, since this section concerns text-critical variants in lists that may have entered the transmission process when a scribe was copying a manuscript of traditional (sacred?) litera-

---

86. Jefferson, "List-Construction," 87, 90.

ture, I strongly suspect that ideological manipulation of the lengthy lists I am examining was extremely difficult to achieve, *even if* a scribe was so inclined to do so (which I seriously doubt was generally the case). Therefore, at least in the cases I have selected, I suspect that the variants should be understood as collaborative list-construction—that is, the addition, omission, or substitution of coclass members in the same category that does not change the function of the list in its literary context. In this sense then the various versions of a list can be understood collectively as synonymous readings, because despite some variation they nevertheless serve the same function of identifying the category by using selected coclass members for adequate representivity.

As is widely noted in the secondary literature, the Hebrew Bible contains many lists of different types of items. In *Theme and Context in Biblical Lists*, Benjamin Scolnic provided a "Master List of Lists Proper" that contained 101 items.[87] He summarized the various types of lists in the Hebrew Bible in outlined form, which I have abbreviated by omitting his third and fourth levels in the outline (e.g., I.A.1.a: Genealogies on the Israelite Tribes [1 Chr 8:1–40]) and providing only one of his examples as follows:

I. Name Lists
   A. Genealogies (Ruth 4:18–22)
   B. Personnel Lists (military personnel: 2 Sam 23:8–39)
   C. Participant Lists (returnees: Ezra 2)

II. Geographical Lists
   A. Boundaries (Num 34:1–15)
   B. Itineraries (Num 33:1–49)
   C. Allotments of Territories by Tribe (Ezek 48)
   D. Cities (foreign: Jer 48:21–24)

III. Lists of Israel's Tribes and Clans
   A. Census (Num 1:20–46)
   B. Camp and Marching Arrangements (Num 10:11–28)
   C. Participation of Tribes/Clans in Special Events (1 Chr 12:24–39)
   D. Divisions/Duties/Camp Arrangements of Special Tribes/Clans (Num 3:14–39)

---

87. Benjamin Edidin Scolnic, *Theme and Context in Biblical Lists*, SFSHJ (Atlanta: Scholars Press, 1995), 15–17.

IV. Materials
   A. Temple Objects (Ezra 1:8–11)
   B. Merchandise (Ezek 7:25a)
   C. Booty (Num 31:32–40)
V. Ritual
   A. Offerings (Num 7)
   B. Permitted/Forbidden Animals (Lev 11:1–47)[88]

Scolnic's lists clearly suggests a multiplicity of lists proper in the Hebrew Bible, but nevertheless we should note that his selection of what belonged on his master list was "suggestive rather than definitive" and tended to favor length.[89] For example, shorter lists such as "the pan, or kettle, or caldron, or pot" (1 Sam 2:14; NRSV; example 2.26 below) were excluded.

Many studies of biblical lists begin with an assumption that, although common, is unfounded—that is, that lists tend to be fixed, written genres independent of their literary context. Scolnic wrote, "To understand the importance of lists in the development of written forms, we must first recognize that lists had to be written down; inventories were a necessary precaution against theft."[90] Similarly, Zecharia Kallai concluded as follows:

> The fundamental characteristic observed is the preeminent position of established formalized records that have attained normative status. Any variations due to changes of territorial or habitational circumstances are formulated on the basis of these underlying records, introducing modifications only. To this end certain segments are exchanged, added or eliminated, all within the basic structure that is otherwise maintained in its primary form.[91]

That is, many biblical scholars assume that authors accurately copied "established formalized records" as sources in the composition of their literary works "in order to convey completeness, comprehensiveness" and "to give a text the impression of factuality."[92] Based on this assumption, many biblical scholars further assume that these records can be used

---

88. Scolnic, *Theme and Context in Biblical Lists*, 17–18.
89. Scolnic, *Theme and Context in Biblical Lists*, 14.
90. Scolnic, *Theme and Context in Biblical Lists*, 5.
91. Kallai, "Simeon's Town List: Scribal Rules and Geographical Patterns," *VT* 53 (2003): 95.
92. Scolnic, *Theme and Context in Biblical Lists*, 12.

for accurate historical reconstructions. Of course, they often recognize that there are discrepancies between the same list, whether in different passages within the same manuscript tradition (e.g., the Benjaminite genealogies in Gen 46:21; Num 26:38–40; 1 Chr 7:6–12; 1 Chr 8:1–40 in the MT) or differences among manuscripts for the same passage (e.g., the difference between the MT and LXX of the list of Jerusalem's residents in Neh 11:3–19); however, as illustrated by the above quotation from Kallai, many still assume that the "basic structure" of the "established formalized records" remains, so that, with the application of standard historical-critical principles (such as *lectio brevior potior*), the records can be recovered in their original form.[93] For example, concerning the above list of vessels in 1 Sam 2:14, Donald Parry wrote the following: "Lists tend to inflate in the course of their transmission."[94] Therefore, if one seeks the lowest common denominator by applying the principle of *lectio brevior potior*, one has presumably reconstructed the original list with some degree of certainty.

A few biblical scholars, however, have started questioning this assumption. Yigal Levin argued that the genealogies in 1 Chr 1–9 reveal "a large degree of *fluidity*," so that "the resemblance to oral genealogies seems unmistakable."[95] James Watts wrote the following, which compares well with my own assumptions about how lists function based on conversation analysis: "Lists, by their nature, invite readers and listeners to choose items relevant to themselves and ignore the rest."[96] If we translate Watts's insight into Jefferson's terminology we get the following: due to the principle of adequate representivity, lists give readers and listeners access to the category of coclass items from which they may choose the most familiar or relevant ones. Below I will discuss examples of text-critical variants in lists,

---

93. For good examples of discussions of variations between genealogical lists and town lists, see, e.g., respectively, Levin, "From Lists to History," 601–36; and Gary N. Knoppers, "Projected Age Comparisons of Levitical Townlists: Divergent Theories and Their Significance," *Textus* 22 (2005): 21–63.

94. Donald W. Parry, "'How Many Vessels'?: An Examination of MT 1 Sam 2:14/4QSam[a] 1 Sam 2:16," in *Studies in the Hebrew Bible, Qumran, and the Septuagint Presented to Eugene Ulrich*, ed. Peter W. Flint, Emanuel Tov, and James C. VanderKam, VTSup 101 (Leiden: Brill, 2006), 84.

95. Levin, "From Lists to History," 607.

96. Watts, "Narratives, Lists, Rhetoric, Ritual, and the Pentateuch as a Scripture," in *The Formation of the Pentateuch: Bridging the Academic Cultures of Europe, Israel, and North America*, ed. Jan C. Gertz et al., FAT 111 (Tübingen: Mohr Siebeck, 2016), 1143.

in which it seems that the scribes chose different list items, but that the lists themselves continue to serve the same literary function of representing the intended category. I will discuss four examples of lists: (1) a list of vessels in 1 Sam 2:14, 16 (mentioned briefly above); (2) a proverb that uses the three-four structure (Prov 30:15b–16); (3) an excerpt from the list(s) of Levitical cities (Josh 21:13–26 // 1 Chr 6:57–60, 67–70); and (4) selective examples of the list(s) of "seven nations" (Gen 15:19–21; Exod 3:8; 3:17; 23:23, 28; 33:2; 34:11; Num 13:29; Deut 20:17; Josh 11:3). As previously, I will give the MT reading first simply as a base text and then I will note pluses compared to MT with **bold** print and variants in which the same items are given in a different order than MT with *italics*.

Example 2.26: 1 Sam 2:14[97]

MT

והכה בכיור או בדוד או בקלחת או בפרור

and he would thrust it into the wash-basin or small pot or cauldron or pot

4Q51

והכה] בסיר או בפרור

and he would thrust] it into **the large pot** or pot

LXX

καὶ ἐπάταξεν αὐτὴν εἰς τὸν λέβητα τὸν μέγαν ἢ εἰς τὸ χαλκίον ἢ εἰς τὴν κύθραν

---

97. Parry, "How Many Vessels?," 87–88, his translation and retroversions. Although Parry did not provide the Greek, I have supplied it from the text-critical apparatus of the Cambridge Septuagint. See Alan England Brooke, Norman McLean, and Henry St. John Thackeray, eds., *The Later Historical Books: I and II Samuel*, vol. 2.1 of *The Old Testament in Greek according to the Text of Codex Vaticanus, Supplemented from Other Uncial Manuscripts, with a Critical Apparatus containing the Variants of the Chief Ancient Authorities for the Text of the Septuagint*, (Cambridge: Cambridge University Press, 1927), 7. I have followed Parry's selection of boc$_2$e$_2$ with one exception; I omitted o because it had a spelling of one word that differed from e$_2$, which Parry had combined. That is, since I have provided the Greek, I did not provide a separate Greek text for both e$_2$ and o, since they are so similar in the Greek and I agree with Parry that they represent the same Hebrew *Vorlage*.

2. Category-Triggering and Text-Critical Variants

והכה בסיר הגדולה או בקלחת או בפרור
and he would thrust it into **the large pot** or cauldron or pot

LXX[b]
καὶ κάθιει αὐτὴν εἰς τῷ λουτηρι ἢ εἰς τὴν χύθραν ἢ εἰς τὸ χαλκίον
והכה בכיור או בפרור או בקלחת
and he would thrust it into the wash-basin or *pot* or *cauldron*

LXX[c2]
καὶ κάθιει αὐτὴν εἰς τῷ λουτηρα ἢ εἰς τὸν λέβητα τὸν μέγαν ἢ εἰς τὴν χύτραν ἢ εἰς τὸ χαλκίον
והכה בכיור או בסיר הגדולה או בפרור או בקלחת
and he would thrust it into the wash-basin or **large pot** or *pot* or *cauldron*

LXX[e2]
καὶ κάθιει αὐτὴν εἰς τὸν λέβητα τὸν μέγαν ἢ εἰς τὴν χύτραν ἢ εἰς τὸ χαλκίον
והכה בסיר הגדולה או בפרור או בקלחת
and he would thrust it into **the large pot** or *pot* or *cauldron*

After providing a discussion of what he understood as five different vessels—כיור, דוד, קלחת, פרור, and סיר—based on his knowledge of the material culture and biblical texts, including their various uses in daily life and/or the cult, Parry concluded that "סיר ('large pot') was likely the only one identified in the primitive literary unit delineated as 1 Sam 2:12–17."[98] Rather than reading this as a list of different cultic items, Parry assumed that this list in all of its extant versions is the result of scribal errors, such as the confusion of ס/כ in כיור/סיר, or as scribal attempts "to modernize the reading for contemporary readers."[99] That is, Parry assumed a linear progression of textual development from the original text, which in his opinion must have been only one vessel, to the various extant texts, all of which have experienced some corruption through expansion in their transmission history as later scribes struggled to identify the vessel. Although I do not disagree necessarily with his discussion of the mate-

---

98. Parry, "How Many Vessels?," 93.
99. Parry, "How Many Vessels?," 94.

rial culture related to these vessels—for example, "דוד infrequently refers to a cooking pot"—it seems to me that he does not take seriously enough the textual fluidity of the tradition he studied and the implications of this fluidity.[100] Although I do not rule out the possibility of scribal error in the process of copying a *Vorlage*, I also think that list-construction allows for a certain degree of fluidity in the items, so that what we might understand as an error is in some ways encouraged; that is, if there are two similar items (in spelling and/or in form/function), including both items simply expands the representivity of the list (unless the added items really do not belong in the same category). Nevertheless, even such presumed errors tell us something about the influence of category-triggering in list-construction. Even if the list triggers something in the scribal memory that maybe should not be in the list, the error is a categorical error that can continue in the textual tradition, because even later scribes understand that the new item is a (near-)match for whichever category the list represents.

Example 2.27: Prov 30:15b–16[101]

MT

שלוש הנה לא תשבענה ארבע לא אמרו הון
שאול ועצר רחם ארץ לא שבעה מים ואש לא אמרה הון

Three things are never satisfied; four never say, "Enough":
Sheol, the barren womb, the earth ever thirsty for water,
and the fire that never says, "Enough."

LXX

καὶ αἱ τρεῖς αὗται οὐκ ἐνεπίμπλασαν αὐτήν,
καὶ ἡ τετάρτη οὐκ ἠρκέσθη εἰπεῖν Ἱκανόν·
ᾅδης καὶ ἔρως γυναικὸς
καὶ τάρταρος καὶ γῆ οὐκ ἐμπιπλαμένη ὕδατος
καὶ ὕδωρ καὶ πῦρ οὐ μὴ εἴπωσιν Ἀρκεῖ

---

100. Parry, "How Many Vessels?," 91.
101. Fox, *Proverbs*, 383–84. Note that here I am varying from my normal practice of translating the Hebrew *Vorlage* of the LXX. Rather I am providing Fox's translation of the Greek, because it illustrates the double translation of Sheol as "Hades" and "Tartarus." If I had followed my normal practice, the only variation in the English translation from the NRSV for MT to the Hebrew *Vorlage* for LXX would have been as follows: "the earth ever thirsty for water, and water and the fire that never says."

2. Category-Triggering and Text-Critical Variants

שלוש הנה לא תשבענה ארבע לא אמרו הון
שאול ועצר רחם ארץ לא שבעה מים מים ואש לא אמרה הון
And these three did not sate her,
and the fourth was not satisfied, so as to say, "Enough!"
Hades and the love of a woman,
and Tartarus, and the earth, which is not filled with water,
and water and fire do not say, "It is enough."

In his retroversion of the Greek, Fox suggested only one variant in the Hebrew: the dittography of מים מים; however, he concluded that the translator "makes the four insatiables into six" by translating the dittography in his Hebrew source text ("water and fire") and by giving a "double translation" of Sheol (as "Hades" and "Tartarus").[102] Thus, in Fox's interpretation, despite the explicit three-four pattern, the list in the LXX reading has six items, by repeating one and translating one Hebrew word with two (near-) synonyms. Of course, it is possible that, because of this repetition, the translator and later LXX scribes understood that the three-four pattern remained in the Greek. However, either interpretation suggests that the list-construction in the Hebrew *Vorlage* and the Greek translation allows for some flexibility in the number of items as represented by individual lexemes. Furthermore, Fox often noted that the MT reading and the LXX reading of individual proverbs often "make equal good sense," whether they are based on different Hebrew *Vorlage* or are simply a variation at the stage of translation.[103] In my estimation, that is the case here, since both lists (whether four items or six items) present adequate representivity to the readers/hearers.

Example 2.28: Josh 21:13–26

MT

[13]ולבני אהרן הכהן נתנו את עיר מקלט הרצח את חברון ואת מגרשה ואת לבנה ואת מגרשה [14]ואת יתר ואת מגרשה ואת אשתמע ואת מגרשה [15]ואת חלן ואת מגרשה ואת דבר ואת מגרשה [16]ואת עין ואת מגרשה ואת יטה ואת מגרשה את בית שמש ואת מגרשה ערים תשע מאת שני השבטים האלה

---

102. Fox, *Proverbs*, 384.
103. Fox, *Proverbs*, 59.

17וממטה בנימן את גבעון ואת מגרשה את גבע ואת מגרשה 18את ענתות ואת מגרשה ואת עלמון ואת מגרשה ערים ארבע 19כל ערי בני אהרן הכהנים שלש עשרה ערים ומגרשיהן
20ולמשפחות בני קהת הלוים הנותרים מבני קהת ויהי ערי גורלם ממטה אפרים 21ויתנו להם את עיר מקלט הרצח את שכם ואת מגרשה בהר אפרים ואת גזר ואת מגרשה 22ואת קבצים ואת מגרשה ואת בית חורן ואת מגרשה ערים ארבע
23וממטה דן את אלתקא ואת מגרשה את גבתון ואת מגרשה 24את אילון ואת מגרשה את גת רמון ואת מגרשה ערים ארבע
25וממחצית מטה מנשה את תענך ואת מגרשה ואת גת רמון ואת מגרשה ערים שתים 26כל ערים עשר ומגרשיהן למשפחות בני קהת הנותרים

NRSV

[13]To the descendants of Aaron the priest they gave Hebron, the city of refuge for the slayer, with its pasture lands, Libnah with its pasture lands, [14]Jattir with its pasture lands, Eshtemoa with its pasture lands, [15]Holon with its pasture lands, Debir with its pasture lands, [16]Ain with its pasture lands, Juttah with its pasture lands, and Beth-shemesh with its pasture lands—nine towns out of these two tribes.

[17]Out of the tribe of Benjamin: Gibeon with its pasture lands, Geba with its pasture lands, [18]Anathoth with its pasture lands, and Almon with its pasture lands—four towns. [19]The towns of the descendants of Aaron—the priests—were thirteen in all, with their pasture lands.

[20]As to the rest of the Kohathites belonging to the Kohathite families of the Levites, the towns allotted to them were out of the tribe of Ephraim. [21]To them were given Shechem, the city of refuge for the slayer, with its pasture lands in the hill country of Ephraim, Gezer with its pasture lands, [22]Kibzaim with its pasture lands, and Beth-horon with its pasture lands—four towns.

[23]Out of the tribe of Dan: Elteke with its pasture lands, Gibbethon with its pasture lands, [24]Aijalon with its pasture lands, Gath-rimmon with its pasture lands—four towns.

[25]Out of the half-tribe of Manasseh: Taanach with its pasture lands, and Gath-rimmon with its pasture lands—two towns. [26]The towns of the families of the rest of the Kohathites were ten in all, with their pasture lands.

LXX^B

¹³καὶ τοῖς υἱοῖς Ααρων ἔδωκεν τὴν πόλιν φυγαδευτήριον τῷ φονεύσαντι, τὴν Χεβρων καὶ τὰ ἀφωρισμένα τὰ σὺν αὐτῇ, καὶ τὴν Λεμνα καὶ τὰ ἀφωρισμένα τὰ πρὸς αὐτῇ, ¹⁴καὶ τὴν Αιλωμ καὶ τὰ ἀφωρισμένα αὐτῇ, καὶ τὴν Τεμα καὶ τὰ ἀφωρισμένα αὐτῇ, ¹⁵καὶ τὴν Γελλα καὶ τὰ ἀφωρισμένα αὐτῇ, καὶ τὴν Δαβειρ καὶ τὰ ἀφωρισμένα αὐτῇ, ¹⁶καὶ Ασα καὶ τὰ ἀφωρισμένα αὐτῇ, καὶ Τανυ καὶ τὰ ἀφωρισμένα αὐτῇ, καὶ Βαιθσαμυς καὶ τὰ ἀφωρισμένα αὐτῇ· πόλεις ἐννέα παρὰ τῶν δύο φυλῶν τούτων. ¹⁷καὶ παρὰ τῆς φυλῆς Βενιαμειν τὴν Γαβαων καὶ τὰ ἀφωρισμένα αὐτῇ, καὶ Γαθεθ καὶ τὰ ἀφωρισμένα αὐτῇ, ¹⁸καὶ Αναθωθ καὶ τὰ ἀφωρισμένα αὐτῇ, καὶ Γαμαλα καὶ τὰ ἀφωρισμένα αὐτῇ, πόλεις τέσσαρες. ¹⁹πᾶσαι αἱ πόλεις υἱῶν Ααρων τῶν ἱερέων δέκα τρεῖς. ²⁰Καὶ τοῖς δήμοις υἱοῖς Κααθ τοῖς Λευείταις τοῖς καταλελιμμένοις ἀπὸ τῶν υἱῶν Κααθ, καὶ ἐγενήθη πόλις τῶν ἱερέων αὐτῶν ἀπὸ φυλῆς Εφραιμ, ²¹καὶ ἔδωκαν αὐτοῖς τὴν πόλιν τοῦ φυγαδευτηρίου τὴν τοῦ φονεύσαντος, τὴν Συχεμ καὶ τὰ ἀφωρισμένα αὐτῇ, καὶ Γαζαρα καὶ τὰ πρὸς αὐτὴν καὶ τὰ ἀφωρισμένα αὐτῇ, ²²καὶ Βαιθωρων καὶ τὰ ἀφωρισμένα αὐτῇ, πόλεις τέσσαρες. ²³καὶ ἐκ τῆς φυλῆς Δαν τὴν Ελκωθαιμ καὶ τὰ ἀφωρισμένα αὐτῇ, καὶ τὴν Γεθεδαν καὶ τὰ ἀφωρισμένα αὐτῇ, ²⁴καὶ Αιλων καὶ τὰ ἀφωρισμένα αὐτῇ, καὶ Γεθερεμμων καὶ τὰ ἀφωρισμένα αὐτῇ, πόλεις τέσσαρες. ²⁵καὶ ἀπὸ τοῦ ἡμίσους φυλῆς Μανασση τὴν Ταναχ καὶ τὰ ἀφωρισμένα αὐτῇ, καὶ τὴν Ιεβαθα καὶ τὰ ἀφωρισμένα αὐτῇ, πόλεις δύο. ²⁶πᾶσαι πόλεις δέκα καὶ τὰ ἀφωρισμένα τὰ πρὸς αὐταῖς τοῖς δήμοις υἱῶν Κααθ τοῖς ὑπολελειμμένοις.

¹³To the descendants of Aaron they gave Hebron, the city of refuge for the slayer, with its pasture lands, Libnah with its pasture lands, ¹⁴**Ailom** with its pasture lands, Tema with its pasture lands, ¹⁵**Gella** with its pasture lands, Debir with its pasture lands, ¹⁶**Asa** with its pasture lands, **Tany** with its pasture lands, and Beth-shemesh with its pasture lands—nine towns out of these two tribes.

¹⁷Out of the tribe of Benjamin: Gibeon with its pasture lands, **Gatheth** with its pasture lands, ¹⁸Anathoth with its pasture lands, and **Gamala** with its pasture lands—four towns. ¹⁹The towns of the descendants of Aaron—the priests—were thirteen in all.

²⁰As to the rest of the Kohathites belonging to the Kohathite families of the Levites, the town of their priests was out of the tribe of Ephraim. ²¹To them were given Shechem, the city of refuge for

the slayer, with its pasture lands, Gezer with its lands with its pasture lands, ²²Beth-horon with its pasture lands—four towns.

²³Out of the tribe of Dan: Elteke with its pasture lands, **Gethe-dan** with its pasture lands, ²⁴**Ailon** with its pasture lands, Gath-rimmon with its pasture lands—four towns.

²⁵Out of the half-tribe of Manasseh: Taanach with its pasture lands, and **Jebatha** with its pasture lands—two towns. ²⁶The towns of the families of the rest of the Kohathites were ten in all, with their pasture lands.

The lists of Levitical towns in Josh 21:1–43 // 1 Chr 6:39–66 (ET 6:54–81) have been the object of much study. Despite some debate about the historicity of the lists, most commentators assume that these two versions of the lists descend from one original list that had some connection to the historical reality of the period in which the original list was compiled.[104] Variations between the lists are then understood as some combination of textual corruption and adjustment of the lists to new historical realities (such as new toponyms for the same city). William Albright confidently reconstructed the original list, which he dated to the reign of David, and concluded as follows: "A comparison of the lists in Joshua and Chronicles shows clearly that the latter derived from a form of Joshua which is slightly earlier than our present Hebrew and Greek text."[105] Against the majority position concerning the relationship of the Deuteronomistic History and the book of Chronicles (influenced by Albright), Graeme Auld concluded that the Chronicler used the list as a source and then the author of Joshua used Chronicles, with LXX[B] Joshua being earlier than MT Joshua and therefore closer to the Chronicler's source.[106] Defending the majority position against Auld, Gary Knoppers agreed with most scholars since Max Margolis that LXX[B] Joshua is an important witness to the early text of Joshua, so that the Chronicler's source for the lists was an early form of

---

104. For a good argument concerning the difficulties of connecting Josh 21 to the monarchic period or earlier, see Ehud Ben Zvi, "The List of the Levitical Cities," *JSOT* 17.54 (1992): 77–106.

105. Albright, "The List of Levitic Cities," in *Louis Ginzberg: Jubilee Volume on the Occasion of His Seventieth Birthday* (New York: American Academy for Jewish Research, 1945), 51.

106. Auld, "The 'Levitical Cities': Texts and History," *ZAW* 91 (1979): 194–207.

2. Category-Triggering and Text-Critical Variants   113

Joshua, closer to LXX[B] than MT. He concluded with two possible explanations for the differences between the lists in Joshua and Chronicles:

> The text of Joshua may have continued to grow (and change) after the Chronicler used it in the Persian period.... Alternatively, there may have been multiple editions of Joshua already in existence, when the author of Chronicles began his work. In this case, the Chronicler happened to employ an edition of Joshua that was somewhat different from and briefer than the editions of the work that were to make their appearance in the LXX and the MT.[107]

What Albright, Auld, and Knoppers all have in common—despite their significant disagreements about when to date the lists as well as the priority of Joshua or Chronicles—is an assumption that there was an original text with some relationship to the historical reality behind the text. Furthermore, all of the extant texts descended unilinearly from that original list, even if we do not have the tools or methods to fully trace the details of the combination of scribal errors and historical updating made to the lists.[108]

What I have given above is a simplified version of the text-critical evidence for Josh 21:13–26, that is, only MT and LXX[B], because of the length of these texts. I have chosen only this section of Josh 21:1–43 as well for the same reason. Nevertheless, I think that this excerpt from the longer list will illustrate my approach, especially since I have chosen the portion of the longer list that has the most comparative material with Chronicles, since in other portions the material is mostly lacking in Chronicles. I have not, however, given the MT Chronicles above or LXX Chronicles anywhere in my analysis, again because of issues of space. Therefore, below I supply a table of MT Josh 21:13–26, LXX[B] Josh 21:13–26, and MT 1 Chr 6:57–60, 67–70 that simply lists the toponyms in the three versions.[109] I have bolded selected toponyms in LXX[B] Joshua

---

107. Knoppers, "Levitical Townlists," 63.
108. For my earlier critique of such unilinear assumptions related to Samuel–Kings // Chronicles, see Person, *Deuteronomic History and the Book of Chronicles*, esp. 93, 101–3, 108–9, 127–29; Person, "The Role of Memory in the Tradition Represented by the Deuteronomic History and the Book of Chronicles," *Oral Tradition* 26 (2011): 537–50; and Person, "Text Criticism as a Lens," 197–215.
109. See Albright, "List of Levitic Cities," 61–65. Albright's chart exhibits the fuller complexity, including both LXX[A]-Joshua and LXX Chronicles.

and MT Chronicles that differ from MT Joshua for the ease of locating them in the table, but this should not be understood as giving preference to MT Joshua as more original. I am simply using MT Joshua here as the arbitrary base text for discussion. The toponyms I have selected are those that are most likely representing a different Hebrew *Vorlage* for either a different town or a different toponym for the same town; I am generally ignoring some possible variants that may simply represent linguistic variants of the toponyms (e.g., Τεμα ["Tema"] may be a shortened form of אשתמע ["Eshtemoa"]). I am not following the standard practice of transliterating the Greek toponyms (see NETS); rather, I am repeating the same English spelling as used in the NRSV for Joshua throughout the table, when appropriate—for example, I use "Gibeon" for גבעון ("Gibeon" in NRSV) and Γαβαων ("Gabaon" in NETS). Furthermore, I ignore some variations between Joshua and Chronicles as insignificant—for example, חלן ("Holon") in Josh 21:15 and חילן ("Hilen") in 1 Chr 6:58—because they can easily be explained linguistically. I may have overlooked such explanations for some of those variants I selected. Nevertheless, the three versions of the list clearly differ from each other in ways that fit with my observations concerning lists in general and I will focus on those that I have selected and bolded. It is also possible that some of the variants in LXX[B] Joshua occurred during the transmission of the Greek text; however, as is generally assumed now in LXX studies, LXX[B] Joshua mostly closely represents the Old Greek and LXX[A] has been assimilated in various cases toward MT. However, no matter which direction such changes may have occurred, it appears that scribal performance of this list occurred during the transmission of both the Hebrew text and the Greek text, as scribal memory of the text(s) and/or the actual cities influenced the list-construction for the Levitical cities.

MT Josh 21		LXX[B] Josh 21		MT 1 Chr 6	
v. 13:	Hebron	v. 13:	Hebron	v. 42:	Hebron
	Libnah		Libnah		Libnah
v. 14:	Jattir	v. 14:	**Ailom**		Jattir
	Eshtemoa		Tema		Eshtemoa
v. 15:	Holon	v. 15:	**Gella**	v. 43:	Hilen
	Debir		Debir		Debir
v. 16:	Ain	v. 16:	**Asa**	v. 44:	**Ashan**
	Juttah		**Tany**		**lacking**
	Beth-shemesh		Beth-shemesh		Beth-shemesh

v. 17:	Gibeon	v. 17:	Gibeon	v. 45:	**lacking**
	Geba		**Gatheth**		Geba
	lacking		lacking		**Alemeth**
v. 18:	Anathoth	v. 18:	Anathoth		Anathoth
	Almon		**Gamala**		**lacking**
v. 21:	Shechem	v. 21:	Shechem	v. 52:	Shechem
	Gezer		Gezer		Gezer
v. 22:	Kibzaim	v. 22:	**lacking**	v. 53	**Jokmeam**
	Beth-horon		Beth-horon		Beth-horon
v. 23:	Elteke	v. 23:	Elteke		**lacking**
	Gibbethon		**Gethedan**		**lacking**
v. 24:	Aijalon	v. 24:	Ailon	v. 54:	Aijalon
	Gath-rimmon		Gath-rimmon		Gath-rimmon
v. 25:	Taanach	v. 25:	Taanach	v. 55:	**Aner**
	Gath-rimmon		**Jebatha**		**Bileam**

There is little variation in this list related to the larger cities that are mentioned most often throughout the Hebrew Bible. Most of the variation occurs in relationship to what could be understood as minor cities, at least from the perspective of the ancient scribes who transmitted the Hebrew Bible. Below I will briefly discuss the selected variants in which there is a different toponym; that is, for the sake of brevity, I will not discuss all of those variants in which the only variant is where a toponym is lacking. When referring to other passages in which a specific toponym occurs, I will also note when that toponym is associated in that passage with other toponyms given in this table.

Jattir (יתר)/Ailom (Αιλωμ)/Jattir (יתר): In MT Josh 15:48, Jattir is in the list of towns in the hill country allotted to Judah (with Debir, Eshtemoa, Holon, Hebron, and Juttah in 15:48–60) and, in MT Josh 21:14 and MT 1 Chr 6:42, Judah gave Jattir to the Levites. Jattir is also mentioned in David's campaign against the Amalekites in Judah's territory in 1 Sam 30:27 (with Eshtemoa and Hebron in 30:28, 31). Jattir is usually associated with modern Khirbet ʿAttir, which is northeast of Beersheba, which was not occupied during the purported time of Joshua and David.[110] Ailom (Αιλωμ), the variant reading in LXX[B] Josh 21:14, is probably also mentioned (with variant spellings) in LXX[A] Judg 12:11 (Ailon/Αιλων) and LXX[B] Judg 12:11 (Ailom/

---

110. John L. Peterson, "Jattir," *ABD* 3:650.

Αιλωμ), where MT Judg 12:11 reads Elon/Aijalon (אילון); in each of these versions the town is "in the land of Zebulun." In 2 Chr 11:10, Aijalon (אילון/ Αιαλων) is one of the walled cities of Judah and Benjamin during the time of Rehoboam (with Hebron).[111] Note that, Aijalon (MT Josh 21:24; 1 Chr 6:54) and Ailon (LXX[B] Josh 21:24) occur later in the list of Levitical cities and for my purposes in that location in the list I have not selected them as variants (thus, they are not bolded). Nevertheless, it is quite possible that the lists have some repetition, given the similarities of these toponyms.

Holon (חלן)/Gella (Γελλα)/Hilen (חילן): In MT Josh 15:51, Holon is in the list of towns in the hill country allotted to Judah (with Jattir, Debir, Eshtemoa, Hebron, and Juttah in 15:48–60) and, in MT Josh 21:15 and MT 1 Chr 6:43, Judah gave Holon/Hilen to the Levites. Holon is also mentioned in the oracle against Moab in Jer 48:21 (חלון; in LXX Jer 31:21 Χαιλων). Holon/Hilen is usually associated with modern Khirbet 'Alîn, which "was an obscure town, very difficult to visit."[112] Gella (Γελλα) occurs only in LXX[B] Josh 21:15, so it is difficult, if not impossible, to draw conclusions concerning whether or not it is a different toponym for the same site or a toponym for a different site.

Ain (עין)/Asa (Ασα)/Ashan (עשן): In MT Josh 15:32 (lacking in LXX[B]), Ain is in the list of Judahite towns "in the extreme south, toward the boundary of Edom" (15:21) (with Rimmon [Gath-rimmon?]) and, in MT Josh 21:16 and LXX[A] Josh 21:16, Judah gave Ain (עין/Αιν) to the Levites. In MT Josh 19:7, LXX[A] Josh 19:7, and MT 1 Chr 4:32, both Ain (עין/Αιν) and Ashan (עשן/Ασαν) are in the list of cities for the tribe of Simeon "until David became king" (MT 1 Chr 4:31) and that "lay within the inheritance of the tribe of Judah" (MT Josh 19:1). (Ain is lacking in LXX[B] Josh 19:7.) In MT Josh 21:16, Ain is in the list of Judahite cities given to the Levites. In LXX[B] Josh 21:16, Asa is in the list of Judahite cities given to the Levites. In MT 1 Chr 6:44, Ashan is in the list of Judahite cities given to the Levites. Thus, it appears that within scribal memory there is an association between Ain and Asa/Ashan, so that they were two cities in the extreme south that are considered closely related. Interestingly, there also appears to be an association between Ain and Asa within scribal memory that placed them in the extreme north. In a passage defining the boundaries of the promised land (MT Num 34:1–29), Ain (עין; 34:11) is referred to

---

111. John L. Peterson, "Aijalon," *ABD* 1:131.
112. John L. Peterson, "Holon," *ABD* 3:258.

as in the northernmost part of the promised land, in what is present-day Syria, and, therefore, is possibly a reference to a different town named after a different spring (עין). Also, in LXX[B] Josh 19:41, Asa (Ασα) is in the list of cities allotted to the northern tribe of Dan. Therefore, it seems as if scribal memory associates these two obscure cities, Ain and Asa/Ashan, as closely related on the extreme edge of the promised land; however, the extreme edge is specified as a contrasting pair, north-south, that is, a different type of category-triggering than comembers. In other words, Ain and Asa/Ashan are comembers of a category consisting of closely related cities on the extreme edge of the promised land, but the identification of that extreme edge can be north or south, a category consisting of a contrasting pair. The southern Ain/Asa/Ashan is generally identified with either modern Khirbet Anim and/or Khirbet Asan, but this identification remains uncertain.[113] However, we should also note that Ain is not found at all in LXX[B] Joshua (Asa is in 19:7, 41; 21:16), so this close connection is not necessarily the case in scribal memory with all scribes.

Juttah (יטה)/Tany (Τανυ)/lacking: In MT Josh 15:55, Juttah is in the list of towns in the hill country allotted to Judah (with Jattir, Debir, Eshtemoa, Holon, and Hebron in 15:48–60) and, in MT Josh 21:16, Judah gave Juttah to the Levites. Juttah is generally identified with modern Yatta, which is east of Hebron on the road connecting Hebron, Jerusalem, Shechem, Eshtemoa, Arad, and Mormah.[114] Since Tany is mentioned only in LXX[B] Josh 21:16, the relationship between Juttah and Tany cannot be determined, but they probably belong within the same category.

Geba (גבע)/Gatheth (Γαθεθ)/Geba (גבע): In MT Josh 18:24, Geba is in the list of towns allotted to the tribe of Benjamin (with Gibeon in 18:28) and, in MT Josh 21:17 and MT 1 Chr 6:45, Benjamin gave Geba to the Levites (with Alemeth in MT 1 Chr 6:45 and with Anathoth in MT Josh 21:18, LXX[B] Josh 21:18, and MT 1 Chr 6:45). Geba is mentioned more often than the other towns in the variants in this list. "Geba is mentioned in such close connection with Gibeah in Judg 20:10, 33; 1 Sam 13:3, 16; and 14:5, and Isa 10:29 that textual emendations in the commentaries are legion; uncertainty exists as to whether the two toponyms refer to separate sites or are linguistic variants of the same site name."[115] Since

---

113. John L. Peterson, "Ain," *ABD* 1:132; Jeffries M. Hamilton, "Ashan," *ABD* 1:476.
114. John L. Peterson, "Juttah," *ABD* 3:1135.
115. Patrick M. Arnold, "Geba," *ABD* 2:921.

Gatheth (Γαθεθ) is mentioned only in LXX^B Josh 21:17, the uncertainty concerning the relationship of Geba and Gatheth is even greater. Geba is generally identified with the modern Jaba', which is 9 kilometers northeast of Jerusalem.[116]

Lacking/lacking/Alemeth (עלמת): In this list, Alemeth occurs only in MT 1 Chr 6:45 in the list of towns allotted to Benjamin. Anathoth is found in all three versions of the list of Levitical towns. In the Benjaminite genealogy in MT 1 Chr 7:8, both Anathoth and Alemeth are sons of Becher.[117] Therefore, we can conclude that "the creator of this section of the genealogy was defining a relationship between various Benjaminite cities by positing an ancient kinship relation between ancestors with city names."[118] That is, within scribal memory, the category of the siblings of Anathoth and Alemeth triggered the inclusion of both towns named after these siblings (whether both towns existed or both toponyms refer to the same city).

Almon (עלמון)/Gamala (Γαμαλα)/lacking: Almon is found only here in Josh 21:18 (including MT and LXX^A) and Gamala only in LXX^B Josh 21:18. The obscurity of these terms has led to speculation that Almon and Gamala are variant toponyms for Alemeth, since Alemeth is a plus in MT 1 Chr 6:45 and Almon and Gamala are lacking in MT 1 Chr 6:45.[119] I prefer to remain agnostic on the specific relationship between Anathoth, Alemeth, Almon, and Gamala, given the obscurity of the terms and what I understand of the function of such lists within scribal memory. That is, I am skeptical of the assumption that there is a one-to-one relationship between these diverse variants, leading back by to an original text that was corrupted during its transmission.

Kibzaim (קבצים)/lacking/Jokmeam (יקמעם): Kibzaim is found only in Josh 21:22 (including in MT and LXX^A) and Jokmeam is found only in 1 Chr 6:53 (including MT and LXX) and in 1 Kgs 4:12 (MT but not LXX). In MT Josh 21:22, Kibzaim is in the list of towns allotted to the tribe of Ephraim and then given to the Levites. In MT 1 Chr 6:52, Jokmeam (a variant of Jokneam?) is in the list of towns allotted to the tribe of Ephraim and then given to the Levites. In MT 1 Kgs 4:12, Jokmeam (with Taanach) is in the list of cities associated with Baana, one of Solomon's twelve offi-

---

116. Arnold, "Geba," 921.
117. A different Alemeth is mentioned in the Benjaminite genealogy in MT 1 Chr 8:36, who is the son of Jehoaddah.
118. Marc Z. Brettler, "Alemeth," *ABD* 1:146.
119. Henry O. Thompson, "Almon," *ABD* 1:161.

cials who is responsible for providing Solomon with provisions from cities in his administrative area. Although there continues to be some debate about whether Kibzaim and Jokmeam (Jokneam?) refer to the same city or two cities, "these two cities are so obscure, any identification becomes speculative."[120]

Gibbethon (גבתון)/Gethedan (Γεθεδαν)/lacking: In MT Josh 19:44, Gibbethon is in the list of cities allotted to the tribe of Dan (with Aijalon, Eltekeh, Gath-rimmon) and, in MT Josh 21:23 and LXX[A] Josh 21:23, the Danites gave Gibbethon to the Levites. In MT 1 Kgs 15:27; 16:15, 17 Gibbethon is mentioned as a Philistine city. Gibbethon is also mentioned in campaign lists by Thutmose III (1468 BCE) and two by Sargon II (713 BCE and 712 BCE) and is generally identified with modern Tell Malat.[121] Gethedan is found only in LXX[B] Josh 21:23 and may be another toponym for Gibbethon, but this cannot be certain. Both Gibbethon and Gethedan are lacking in 1 Chr 6:53.

Taanach (תַּעְנָךְ)/Taanach (Τανάχ)/Aner (עָנֵר): In MT Josh 12:21, Taanach is in the list of "kings of the land" that Joshua and the Israelites defeated (with Hebron, Gezer, Debir, Libnah, and Jokneam [Jokmeam?]). In MT Josh 17:11 (lacking in LXX[B]) and MT Judg 1:27, Taanach is included in the territory of Manasseh (with Ibleam/Bileam), but the Canaanites were not completely forced out, so that they did not have full control of their territory. Taanach is mentioned in various contemporary sources, both Egyptian and Mesopotamian, and is identified with modern Tell Ti'innik, one of the Canaanite fortresses associated with the Jezreel Valley.[122] Aner is only mentioned in MT 1 Chr 6:55 and is generally understood as a variant of Taanach through scribal corruption.[123] Although this explanation is possible, there are other possibilities. For example, in Gen 14:13, 24, Aner is a brother of Mamre the Amorite, who with their brother Eshcol are allies of Abram when he rescues Lot. Since the description of these events occurs in the same or nearby geographical area, it is possible that the toponym Aner is related to Aner the Amorite. However, it is probably best to remain agnostic concerning the relationship between Taanach and

---

120. John L. Peterson, "Kibzaim," *ABD* 4:36. See also, Wesley I. Toews, "Jokmeam," *ABD* 3:933.
121. John L. Peterson, "Gibbethon," *ABD* 2:1007.
122. A. E. Glock, "Taanach," *ABD* 6:287–90.
123. Melvin Hunt, "Aner," *ABD* 1:248.

Aner, other than to note that within scribal memory they appear to be somehow related.

Gath-rimmon (גת רמון)/Jebatha (Ιεβαθα)/Bileam (בלעם): Earlier in the list, MT Josh 21:25, LXX^B Josh 21:24, and MT 1 Chr 6:54 include Gath-rimmon in the list of Ephraimite cities given to the Levites. In MT Josh 19:45, Gath-rimmon is in the list of cities allotted to Dan (with Aijalon, Eltekeh, and Gibbethon in 19:40–48). Only in MT Josh 21:25 is Gath-rimmon repeated in this list, this time in the list of cities that the tribe of Manasseh gave to the Levites. Although it is mentioned in only these passages, Gath-rimmon is mentioned in the list of cities in Thutmose III's campaign and in the Amarna letters and is generally identified with modern Tell Abu Zeitun or Tell Jerishe.[124] LXX^B Josh 21:25 reads Jebatha here and it is uncertain what (if any) the relationship may be to Gath-rimmon. In 1 Chr 6:55, Bileam is probably a variant of Ibleam, which was one of the Canaanites fortress cities (with Megiddo and Jokneam [Jokmeam?]) guarding the southern Jezreel Valley. In MT Josh 17:11 (lacking in LXX^B) and MT Judg 1:27, Ibleam is included in the territory of Manasseh (with Taanach), but the Canaanites were not completely forced out, so that they did not have full control of their territory. Ibleam is also mentioned in the list of cities in the report of Thutmose III's campaign.[125] In MT 2 Kgs 9:27, Ibleam is associated with Gur and Megiddo, places near the Jezreel Valley where Ahaziah was shot and then died. Thus, it appears that Gath-rimmon and Bileam (presumably Jebatha) are associated closely with the Jezreel Valley within scribal memory.

Although I have been quite limited in my selection of both the specific passage within Josh 21:1–43 and in terms of which manuscripts to consistently discuss, we nevertheless can see significant variation within this selection. Thirteen of twenty-four lines of the above table of toponyms have at least one variant, and this ignores some of what appear to be variant spellings (e.g., Eshtemoa/Tema). The list in MT Josh 21:13–25 contains twenty-three items (lacking Alemeth in 21:17); the list in LXX^B Josh 21:13–25 contains twenty-two items (lacking Alemeth in 21:17 and Kibzaim/Jokmeam in 21:22); MT 1 Chr 6:42–55 contains nineteen items (lacking Juttah/Tany in 6:44, Gibeon and Almon/Gamala in 6:45, and Elteke and Gibbethon/Gethedan in 6:53). MT Joshua includes Gath-

---

124. John L. Peterson, "Gath-rimmon," *ABD* 2:910.
125. "Bileam," *ABD* 1:742; Melvin Hunt, "Ibleam," *ABD* 3:355.

rimmon as two items (21:24, 25), LXX^B Joshua may include Ailom/Ailon twice (21:14, 24). *If* arguments that the Ailom, Alemeth, Almon, Aijalon, and Ailon are all variations for the same city are valid, all three versions include it twice. However, rather than making firm conclusions about the relationships among these toponyms and between the toponyms and historical sites (sometimes a valid endeavor), I want to emphasize the fluidity of this list. The list clearly represents geographical spaces, but without the kind of precision we hope for, when we read the list for historical information based on the assumption that there was a list (or maybe lists) at some point in the literary history of the texts that had an accurate one-to-one relationship with some historical reality. Rather, it seems to me that the list more accurately represents that geographical space through scribal memory, not in relationship to the scribe's present geographical knowledge, but to the scribe's traditional knowledge of the past. There clearly is a close relationship between this list and the lists in MT Josh 12–19, which include the list of the cities Joshua and the Israelites conquered from "the kings of the land" (12:9–24) as well as the allotments to each of the tribes (13–19); that is, these cities were first allotted to one of the tribes (excluding the Levites), and then in MT Josh 21:1–43 the various tribes gave cities to the Levites. In other words, during the transmission of Josh 21:1–43, scribal memory included not only the possible knowledge of variant versions of this list but also knowledge of the lists in Josh 12–19 in various versions; therefore, scribal memory influenced the copying of a physical manuscript of Josh 21:13–25 in ways that allowed the scribe to copy the list with variant items, but the list nevertheless represented the same (imagined) geographical area(s); that is, despite what we may view anachronistically as variants, the lists provided sufficient representivity so that readers/hearers could locate the geographical area(s) in their own memories.[126] When we consider the relationship between Josh 21:13–25 and 1 Chr 6:42–55, scribal memory was also at work, no matter which

---

126. Although he does not interact with the text-critical evidence significantly, Daniel Pioske has published various studies with a methodologically sophisticated approach to applying memory studies to history and place. See Pioske, *David's Jerusalem: Between Memory and History*, Routledge Studies in Religion (London: Routledge, 2015); Pioske, "Memory and Its Materiality: The Case of Early Iron Age Khirbet Queyafa and Jerusalem," *ZAW* 127 (2015): 78–95; and Pioske, "Retracing a Remembered Past: Methodological Remarks on Memory, History, and the Hebrew Bible," *BibInt* 23 (2015): 291–315.

direction one prefers to give priority of literary influence at the level of composition. However, since we cannot easily separate composition from transmission, I prefer to think that the literary influence of these texts possibly ran in both directions over the long composition/transmission history.[127]

Examples 2.29–38: Seven Nations

Below I will focus on the lists of the "seven nations": the foreign nations that Israel must avoid contact with at all costs, including commandments of genocide toward them. These lists occur in various biblical passages and exhibit some variation in the text-critical evidence as well. The starting point for my research was the thorough work done by Kevin O'Connell.[128] O'Connell fits the traditional approach to text criticism, in that he assumes that behind the multiplicity in the biblical texts he can reconstruct the original list of seven nations that had historical facticity. Nevertheless, his collection of the evidence remains a helpful beginning and is referred to as such in subsequent studies as well.[129] However, with one exception, I have selected those examples in O'Connell's study for which we have text-critical variants in Hebrew manuscripts (eliminating many of his examples from LXX), thereby reducing the number of passages to analyze from twenty-eight to ten. This should be understood in no way as to deny the credibility of the Greek evidence of the LXX to the question, rather it is simply a way of reducing the number of examples I will discuss within my emphasis on Hebrew texts. However, since all of the Hebrew evidence that differs from MT comes from SP, I will include one example from LXX outside of the Pentateuch (Josh 11:3) to point to the additional complexity that would occur if I had included all of O'Connell's examples. Also, some of the evidence from the Dead Sea Scrolls was unavailable to O'Connell,

---

127. For my fuller discussion of the relationship of Samuel–Kings // Chronicles, see Person, *Deuteronomic History and the Book of Chronicles*.

128. O'Connell, "The List of Seven Peoples in Canaan: A Fresh Approach," in *The Answers Lie Below: Essays in Honor of Lawrence Edmund Toombs*, ed. Henry O. Thompson (Lanham, MD: University Press of America, 1984), 221–41.

129. E.g., David Noel Freedman and Shawna Polansky Overton, "Omitting the Omissions: The Case for Haplography in the Transmission of the Biblical Text," in *"Imagining" Biblical Worlds: Studies in Spatial, Social and Historical Constructs in Honor of James W. Flanagan*, ed. David M. Gunn and Paula M. McNutt, JSOTSup 359 (Sheffield: Sheffield Academic, 2002), 99–116.

2. Category-Triggering and Text-Critical Variants

so I have updated his work in relationship to new text-critical evidence. Despite this significant reduction in the number of passages, the examples I have chosen illustrate the textual fluidity of this list; therefore, I think it will sufficiently serve my purposes. Although above I discussed each example in turn, here I will simply provide examples 2.29–2.38, which I have given in their canonical order (Gen 15:19–21; Exod 3:8; 3:17; 23:23; 23:28; 33:2; 34:11; Num 13:29; Deut 20:17; Josh 11:3) and then discuss them as a collective. As above, I will **bold** those readings that are not in MT and *italicize* those list items in different orders from MT.

Example 2.29: Gen 15:19–21

MT

את הקיני ואת הקנזי ואת הקדמני ואת החתי ואת הפרזי ואת הרפאים ואת האמרי ואת הכנעני ואת הגרגשי ואת היבוסי ואת האמרי ואת הכנעני ואת הגרגשי ואת היבוסי

the Kenites, the Kenizzites, the Kadmonites, the Hittites, the Perizzites, the Rephaim, the Amorites, the Canaanites, the Girgashites, and the Jebusites.

SP

את הקיני ואת הקנזי ואת הקדמון ואת החתי ואת הפרזי ואת הרפאים ואת האמרי ואת הכנעני ואת הגרגשי ואת החוי ואת היבוסי

the Kenites, the Kenizzites, the Kadmonites, the Hittites, the Perizzites, the Rephaim, the Amorites, the Canaanites, the Girgashites, **the Hivites,** and the Jebusites.

Example 2.30: Exod 3:8

MT

הכנעני והחתי והאמרי והפרזי והחוי והיבוסי

the Canaanites, the Hittites, the Amorites, the Perizzites, the Hivites, and the Jebusites.

SP

הכנעני והחתי והאמרי והפרזי והגרגשי והחוי והיבוסי

the Canaanites, the Hittites, the Amorites, the Perizzites, **the Girgashites**, the Hivites, and the Jebusites.

4QGen-Exod^a

הכ]נעני והחתי והפ[ר]זי והאמרי החוי הגרגשי והיבוסי

the Canaanites, the Hittites, *the Perizzites, the Amorites, the Hivites,* the Girgashites, and the Jebusites.

Example 2.31: Exod 3:17

MT

הכנעני והחתי והאמרי והפרזי והחוי והיבוסי

the Canaanites, the Hittites, the Amorites, the Perizzites, the Hivites, and the Jebusites

SP

הכנעני והחתי והאמרי והפרזי והגרגשי והחוי והיבוסי

the Canaanites, the Hittites, the Amorites, the Perizzites, **the Girgashites,** the Hivites, and the Jebusites

Example 2.32: Exod 23:23

MT

והאמרי והחתי והפרזי הכנעני והחוי והיבוסי

the Amorites, the Hittites, the Perizzites, the Canaanites, the Hivites, and the Jebusites

SP

הכנעני והאמרי והחתי והגרגשי והפרזי והחוי והיבוסי

the Canaanites, the Amorites, the Hittites, **the Girgashites,** the Perizzites, the Hivites, and the Jebusites

Example 2.33: Exod 23:28

MT

את החוי את הכעני ואת החתי

the Hivites, the Canaanites, and the Hittites

SP

את הכנעני ואת האמרי ואת החתי ואת הגרגשי ואת הפרזי ואת החוי ואת היבוסי

2. Category-Triggering and Text-Critical Variants

the Canaanites, the Amorites, *the Hittites,* the Girgashites, the Perizzites, *the Hivites, and* the Jebusites

SP manuscripts

את הכנעני ואת האמרי ואת החתי ואת הגרגשי ואת החוי ואת היבוסי
the Canaanites, the Amorites, *the Hittites,* the Girgashites, *the Hivites, and* the Jebusites

Example 2.34: Exod 33:2

MT

את הכנעני האמרי והחתי והפרזי והחוי והיבוסי
the Canaanites, the Amorites, the Hittites, the Perizzites, the Hivites, and the Jebusites

SP

את הכנעני האמרי והחתי והגרגשי והפרזי והחוי והיבוסי
the Canaanites, the Amorites, the Hittites, **the Girgashites,** the Perizzites, the Hivites, and the Jebusites

Example 2.35: Exod 34:11

MT

ואת האמרי והכנעני והחתי והפרזי והחוי והיבוסי
the Amorites, the Canaanites, the Hittites, the Perizzites, the Hivites, and the Jebusites

SP

ואת הכנעני והאמרי והחתי והגרגשי והפרזי והחוי והיבוסי
the Canaanites, the Amorites, the Hittites, **the Girgashites,** the Perizzites, the Hivites, and the Jebusites

Example 2.36: Num 13:29

MT

והחתי והיבוסי והאמרי יושב בהר והכנעני ישב על הים ועל יד הירדן
the Hittites, the Jebusites, and the Amorites, who live in the hill country; and the Canaanites, who live by the sea and along the Jordan

SP

והחתי והחוי והיבוסי והאמרי יושב בהר והכנעני ישב על הים ועל יד הירדן

the Hittites, **the Hivites,** the Jebusites, and the Amorites, who live in the hill country; and the Canaanites, who live by the sea and along the Jordan

Example 2.37: Deut 20:17

MT

החתי והאמרי והכנעני והפרזי והחוי והיבוסי

the Hittites and the Amorites, the Canaanites and the Perizzites, the Hivites and the Jebusites

SP

הכנעני והאמרי והחתי והגרגשי והפרזי והחוי והיבוסי

the Canaanites, the Amorites, *the Hittites,* **the Girgashites,** the Perizzites, the Hivites, and the Jebusites

Example 2.38: Josh 11:3

MT

הכנעני ממזרח ומים והאמרי והחתי והפרזי והיבוסי בהר והחוי תחת חרמון בארץ המצפה

to the Canaanites in the east and in the west, the Amorites, the Hittites, the Perizzites, and the Jebusites who are in the hill country, and the Hivites who are under Hermon in the land of Mizpah.

LXX[B]

καὶ εἰς τοὺς παραλίους Χαναναίους ἀπὸ ἀνατολῶν καὶ εἰς τοὺς παραλίους Αμορραίους καὶ Ευαίους καὶ Ιεβουσαίους καὶ Φερεζαίους τοὺς ἐν τῷ ὄρει καὶ τοὺς Χετταίους τοὺς ὑπὸ τὴν ἔρημον εἰς τὴν Μασευμαν

to the coastal Canaanites in the east, the coastal Amorites, *the Hivites, the Jebusites, the Perizzites* who are in the hill country, and *the Hittites* who are under the wilderness of Maseuman.

LXXˢ
καὶ εἰς τοὺς παραλίους Χορραίους καὶ Αμορραίους καὶ τοὺς Χετταίους καὶ Φερεζαίους καὶ Ιεβουσαίους τοὺς ἐν τῷ ὄρει καὶ τοὺς Ευαίους τοὺς ὑπὸ τὴν ἔρημον εἰς τὴν Μασευμαν
to the coastal **Horites** in the east, Amorites, the Hittites, the Perizzites, the Jebusites who are in the hill country, and the Hivites who are under the wilderness in the land of Masemmath.

LXXᵖᵗ
καὶ εἰς τοὺς παραλίους Χαναναίους ἀπὸ ἀνατολῶν καὶ εἰς τοὺς παραλίους Χορραίους καὶ εἰς τοὺς παραλίους Αμορραίους καὶ τοὺς Χετταίους τοὺς ὑπὸ τὴν ἔρημον εἰς τὴν μασφου καὶ Φερεζαίους τοὺς ἐν τῷ ὄρει καὶ Ιεβουσαίους τοὺς ἐν τῷ ὄρει καὶ τοὺς Ευαίους τοὺς ὑπὸ τὴν ἀερμων εἰς τὴν Μασσηφαθ
to the coastal Canaanites in the east, the coastal **Horites**, the coastal Amorites, the Hittites who in the wilderness of Mizpah, the Perizzites who are in the hill country, the Jebusites who are in the hill country, and the Hivites who are under Hermon in the land of Massephath.

All of these lists clearly refer to the foreign peoples who were imagined to have lived in the area of the promised land, most generally referred to as the land of Canaan. Although according to tradition there are seven nations (based on Deut 7:1), the number of peoples mentioned in these lists spans from three (MT Exod 23:28) to eleven (SP Gen 15:19–21). We see variation within the same manuscript tradition (e.g., three peoples in MT Exod 23:28 to ten in MT Gen 15:19–21 as well as five peoples in SP Num 13:29 to eleven in SP Gen 15:19–21) and between different manuscripts of the same passage (e.g., six peoples in MT Exod 3:8; 3:17; 23:23; 33:2; 34:11; MT Deut 20:17 versus seven in SP Exod 3:8; 3:17; 23:23; 33:2; 34:11; SP Deut 20:17). In one case, the variation between manuscripts of the same passage differs significantly in terms of numbers: MT Exod 23:28 lists three peoples; SP Exod 23:28 lists seven. When we look only at those Hebrew manuscripts that have the traditional number of seven peoples, we find that, although they contain the same set of seven, there are nevertheless four different orders to the list of seven: (1) "the Canaanites, the Hittites, the Amorites, the Perizzites, the Girgashites, the Hivites, and the Jebusites" (SP Exod 3:8; 3:17), (2) "the Canaanites, the Amorites, the Hittites, the Girgashites, the Perizzites, the Hivites, and the Jebusites"

(SP Exod 23:23; 23:28; 33:2; 34:11; Deut 20:17), (3) "the Canaanites, the Hittites, the Perizzites, the Amorites, the Hivites, the Girgashites, and the Jebusites" (4Q1 [4QGen-Exod^a] Exod 3:8), and (4) "the Hittites, the Girgashites, the Amorites, the Canaanites, the Perizzites, the Hivites, and the Jebusites, seven nations" (MT Deut 7:1). However, we should note that LXX^{pt}-Josh 11:3 also has seven nations, but, in comparison to the Hebrew manuscripts, it differs in that, instead of the Girgashites, it has the Horites. Thus, I find it difficult to imagine (with O'Connell and others) that this tremendous variety began with one list from which modifications were made sparingly in the composition/transmission process.

Despite this tremendous diversity, O'Connell still concluded that he could establish which were the original seven nations (those in Deut 7:1), even though he could not determine the original order with certainty. He criticized most scholars who ignored the text-critical evidence. For example, he noted that "MT has all seven names only three times," due to its tendency toward haplography, especially the omission of "the Girgashites" from the list.[130] Nevertheless, he could describe the list behind the literature as having a "closed formulaic character of the original seven-name list" that "was already fixed formula and symbol" before the earliest written source of the Pentateuch (his "Yahwist") was written, reflecting "experiences of the settlement (or at least of the pre-monarchical period)."[131] In these quotations, we can clearly see the desire for lists to be able to take us back to the earliest period of ancient Israel, before the written texts of the canonical books, in order to recover historical data for the reconstruction of ancient Israelite history.

Variants in Lists: A Summary

I began this section by noting how the assumptions often made by biblical scholars about lists are unfounded, especially concerning the fixity and historicity of lists. I also included an insightful quotation from Watts that I repeat here: "Lists, by their nature, invite readers and listeners to choose items relevant to themselves and ignore the rest."[132] Watts's insight conforms to what we know about list-construction in everyday conversation.

---

130. O'Connell, "List of Seven Peoples," 224, 226. See also Freedman and Overton, "Omitting the Omissions," 109.

131. O'Connell, "List of Seven Peoples," 227.

132. Watts, "Narratives, Lists, Rhetoric, Ritual," 1143.

That is, a three-part list in conversation (sometimes with a generalized list completer as the third part) establishes a category of comembers, so that the items in the list when taken together necessarily suggest other comembers of that category. Although there are practices that can override such suggestions (something like "nothing more, nothing less"), the fact that these practices exist suggests their need.[133] Thus, as Watts suggests, readers and listeners, including scribes copying a *Vorlage*, have access to more than the individual items in a given list; they have access to other items that are comembers in the category that the list represents.

Each example discussed above illustrates not only how, because of scribal memory, scribes have access to other items that are comembers in the category of a particular list but also how that very access may lead scribes to produce the same list with different items in ways such that in some sense the list has not changed at all from the perspective of the scribes copying the *Vorlage*. Of course, from other perspectives, it is certainly possible that these changes have introduced different understandings of what the list represents; however, our difficulty in distinguishing between the same and the different is methodological, hindered by millennia between then, when textual fluidity was the norm, and now, when we too often erroneously assume a fixed text. In 1 Sam 2:12–17, whatever is in the list of vessels used by the "scoundrels," "the sons of Eli," the list represents the vessel(s) that they could have used each time in their scandalous cultic activity, so much so that one could easily make opposing conclusions concerning the theological tendency of the scribal changes: either (1) later pious scribes could change the list by adding/substituting vessels approved by the law and/or omitting vessels not approved by the law, because this is the way it should have been and should continue to be or (2) later pious scribes could change the list so that the vessels are even more aberrant as a way of making the sons of Eli look more scandalous. Rather than choosing one of these theological tendencies (both of which may have existed during the text's long transmission history), we should rather

---

133. We find similar phrases in the biblical text, such as "do not add to it or take anything from it" (Deut 12:32) and "nothing can be added or taken away" (Sir 42:21); however, although these phrases are often assumed to refer to written texts, their literary contexts imply that they are referring to the words/works of God, which can only imperfectly be represented in writing. For my discussion of Deut 12:32 in the context of the book of Deuteronomy, see Person, "Self-Referential Phrases in Deuteronomy," 217–42.

accept that the list creates a category of vessels that could have been used (appropriately and/or inappropriately) throughout the (imagined) history of the sacrificial cult, no matter where the actual location and time. In Prov 30:15b–16, we can accept that, despite the explicit three-four pattern, the actual list can expand or contract to represent the insatiables. In Josh 21:13–26 // 1 Chr 6:57–60, 67–70, the list of toponyms for the Levitical cities represented geopolitical boundaries in the imagined past, regardless of the specific toponyms given in the list, especially with regard to lesser-known cities. In the various passages that contain lists of foreign nations (the "seven nations"), the point of the list is not to provide an exact list of seven nations, implying that all of the other foreign nations are perfectly acceptable; rather, the seven nations is a list of foreign nations/peoples that can expand and contract, representing the category of foreign peoples who are to be avoided in the texts' xenophobic attitude of the ethnic/religious other.[134] Therefore, scribal memory could influence the copying of these lists by allowing them to contract or expand as the scribe composed a new piece of literature (as author) or transmitted an existing literary work (as copyist). The list in scribal memory gave the scribes access to the category of coclass members (e.g., vessels, insatiables, Levitical cities within tribal boundaries, or foreign peoples), so that even in their *Vorlage*-based copying the scribes were not constrained to copy the list verbatim, even when they do copy it that way. A list with a different number of items in whatever order (typically three or more) could nevertheless adequately represent the same category of coclass members. If this interpretation is correct, then these lists probably should not be understood as representing a historical reality behind the literature as much as representing the traditional past. This does not require us to assume that the actual past (during different stages of the composition/transmission process) had no influence on the narrative past; however, it seems that the narrative past that connects the (imagined) past with the present of the readers/hearers is what is primary.[135]

---

134. For my discussion of the theme of the annihilation of everything related to the "seven nations" (Deut 7:1) and related secondary literature, see Raymond F. Person Jr., *Deuteronomy and Environmental Amnesia*, Earth Bible Commentary 3 (Sheffield: Sheffield Phoenix, 2014), 45–55, 93–98. This is certainly one of the most ethically problematic themes in the Bible; unfortunately, it continues to influence xenophobia in today's society.

135. For my discussion of traditional history, see Raymond F. Person Jr., "Biblical

Harmonization

I begin this section with a quotation from Jerome (347–420 CE), who complained about harmonization in the transmission of the gospels in his preface to his Latin translation of the gospels:

> Error has sunk into our books, while concerning the same thing one Evangelist has said more, in another, because they thought he had said less, they added; or while another has differently expressed the same sense, whichever one of the four he had read first, he will decide to enumerate the remaining ones according to that version.[136]

Although harmonization is a modern term for this type of text-critical variant, Jerome provides us with evidence that even the ancients understood that sometimes variations occur when scribes remembered another text (especially when reading a parallel passage) and harmonized (intentionally or not) the *Vorlage* they were copying, so that the two versions became closer in wording. As Wollenberg argued so well, some Jewish and Christian scholars in late antiquity recognized similar issues with regard to the text of the Hebrew Bible.[137]

Although other modern scholars discuss harmonization, my summary will be primarily based on the work of Tov, who has focused on harmonization in the Pentateuch in multiple recent studies and has provided the most thorough theoretical discussion of harmonization.[138] Tov defined harmonization as follows:

Historiography as Traditional History," in *Oxford Handbook of Biblical Narrative*, ed. Danna Nolan Fewell (Oxford: Oxford University Press, 2016), 73–83.

136. Cited in Cambry G. Pardee, *Scribal Harmonization in the Synoptic Gospels*, NTTSD 60 (Leiden: Brill, 2019), 22, his translation. See also Bruce M. Metzger, "St. Jerome's Explicit References to Variant Readings in Manuscript of the New Testament," in *Text and Interpretation: Studies in the New Testament Presented to Matthew Black*, ed. Ernest Best and R. McLachan Wilson (Cambridge: Cambridge University Press, 1979), 179–90.

137. Wollenberg, "Book That Changed"; Wollenberg, "King and a Scribe like Moses."

138. Here I give the titles of individual works. In later references to those reprinted in his collected works, I will generally simply provide references to the volume title: Emanuel Tov, "The Nature and Background of Harmonizations in Biblical Manuscripts," *JSOT* 10.31 (1985): 3–29; Tov, "Textual Harmonizations in the Ancient Texts of Deuteronomy," in *Hebrew Bible, Greek Bible, and Qumran: Collected Essays*, TSAJ

> Harmonization is recognized when a detail in source A is changed to align with another detail in source A or source B because they differ. Scribes adapted many elements in the text to other details in the same verse, the immediate or a similar context, the same book, or parallel sections elsewhere in Scripture.[139]

Tov's definition allows for three different types of harmonization: "(a) within the same context; (b) within the same book; [and] (c) between different books"; that is, types (a) and (b) concern "another detail in source A," and type (c) concerns "another detail ... in source B."[140] Although Tov's definition allows for these three different types, his primary interest is clearly in his type (c), specifically, harmonizations between different books of the Torah.

Tov argued that "the Torah was rewritten and changed more extensively than the other biblical books in the Second Temple period," because

---

121 (Tübingen: Mohr Siebeck, 2008), 271–82; Tov, "The Coincidental Textual Nature of the Collections of Ancient Scriptures," in *Collected Essays 3*, 20–35; Tov, "Some Reflection on Consistency," 36–44; Tov, "The Scribal and Textual Transmission of the Torah Analyzed in Light of Its Sanctity," in *Collected Essays 3*, 154–65; Tov, "Textual Harmonization in the Stories of the Patriarchs," in *Collected Essays 3*, 166–88; Tov, "The Harmonizing Character of the Septuagint of Genesis 1–11," in *Collected Essays 3*, 470–89; Tov, "The Development of the Text of the Torah in Two Major Text Blocks," *Textus* 26 (2016): 1–27; and Tov, "Textual Harmonization in Exodus 1–24," *TC* 22 (2017); https://tinyurl.com/SBL7015a. Below I will also refer to some other secondary literature on harmonization, especially when I discuss specific examples not discussed by Tov. This section draws significantly from Person, "Harmonization in the Pentateuch and Synoptic Gospels," in which all of my pentateuchal examples were taken from Tov's work; however, I repeat only one of the examples (Exod 20:10–12; Deut 5:14–16; Lev 16:29; example 2.44), so that here I can discuss examples provided by other scholars and examples outside of the Torah. Although I will not engage in a discussion of the secondary literature that I referred to in this earlier work on the Synoptic Gospels, their influence remains: Martin Hengel, "The Four Gospels and the One Gospel of Jesus Christ," in *The Earliest Gospels: The Origins and Transmission of the Earliest Christian Gospels—The Contribution of the Chester Beatty Gospel Codex P*[45], ed. Charles Horton, JSNTSup 258 (London: T&T Clark, 2010), 13–26; William L. Petersen, "The Diatessaron and the Fourfold Gospel," in Horton, *Earliest Gospels*, 50–68; Nicolas Perrin, "Hermeneutical Factors in the Harmonization of the Gospels and the Question of Textual Authority," in *The Biblical Canons*, ed. Jean-Marie Auwers and H. J. de Jonge, BETL 163 (Leuven: Peeters, 2003), 599–605; and esp. Pardee, *Scribal Harmonization*.

139. Tov, "Textual Harmonization in Exodus 1–24," 2.
140. Tov, "Nature and Background of Harmonizations," 5.

of its popularity and sacred status.[141] Thus, harmonization is "the most prominent feature" of the Torah's transmission history.[142] However, Tov concluded that "there is no overall guiding principle behind these harmonizing additions."[143] This implies a more haphazard pattern to harmonization, even within the same manuscript. "Harmonizing additions reflect an aspect of scribal activity that, as with all other such activities, is inconsistent. Items that were harmonized once were not necessarily harmonized on another occasion."[144] This haphazard pattern means that one scribe may have a tendency to harmonize more than another and yet that tendency may differ according to what sections of the manuscript that the scribe has are parallel to passages with which the scribe is especially familiar. The tendency to harmonize can also differ within textual families and scribal traditions. Thus, Tov stated that harmonization is more frequent in LXX and SP than MT.[145] This conclusion is based on Tov's (and others) tendency to emphasize harmonizing additions/harmonizing pluses based on the widely held principle of *lectio brevior potior*, despite the fact that their definitions of harmonization allows for additions, omissions, substitutions, and transpositions. Thus, Tov can assert: "By definition, all harmonizating additions are secondary. They were made in order to adapt one context to another one."[146] Although I agree with this statement itself, in practice Tov seems to minimize the role of omission in harmonization and assume, therefore, that every plus is an addition, unless there is substantial evidence to the contrary. That is, I agree that this statement may be true, *whenever* we can identify a harmonizing addition with certainty; however, I question the presumption that harmonization occurs primarily in the form of additions, a presumption that is at least implicit in his analysis. It seems to me that the texts are more fluid than his general assumption implies; therefore, the implied linear progression from shorter to longer text behind *lectio brevior potior* must be critically reevaluated, in my opinion.

---

141. Tov, *Collected Essays 3*, 166. See also Tov, *Collected Essays 3*, 154.
142. Tov, "Textual Harmonization in Exodus 1–24," 1.
143. Tov, "Textual Harmonizations in the Ancient Texts of Deuteronomy," 282.
144. Tov, "Textual Harmonizations in the Ancient Texts of Deuteronomy," 282. For Tov's excellent discussion of "coincidence" and "(in)consistency" in scribal transmission, see Tov, *Collected Essays 3*, 20–35, 36–44.
145. Tov, "Nature and Background of Harmonizations," 8; Tov, "Two Major Text Blocks," 7; Tov, "Textual Harmonization in Exodus 1–24," 7.
146. Tov, *Collected Essays 3*, 173.

Even though Tov does not use the term *scribal memory*, his discussion of harmonization certainly implies its validity.[147] This is implicit in Tov's definition, when he allowed that "some such changes were inserted unconsciously" and in his observations that "there is no overall guiding principle behind these harmonizing additions ... they could be inserted at any given moment by the changing instincts of the scribes."[148] The phrase "instincts of the scribes" seems to include when scribal memory recalls other passages, which then influences the copying of the text, whether the scribe does so intentionally or unintentionally.[149] However, since Tov asserted that "most [harmonizations] were inserted because of a theological concern for per-

---

147. I should also note that the influence of Carr's understanding of memory variants is present in this section of harmonization. Carr understood harmonizing variants as belonging (at least in some cases) to memory variants. See Carr, "Torah on the Heart," 31; Carr, *Formation of the Hebrew Bible*, 90–101, 132–37; Carr, "Scribal Processes of Coordination/Harmonization and the Formation of the First Hexateuch(s)," in Dozeman, Schmid, and Swartz, *Pentateuch*, 63–83.

148. Tov, "Textual Harmonization in Exodus 1–24," 2; Tov, "Textual Harmonizations in the Ancient Texts of Deuteronomy," 282.

149. Although he also does not use the term "scribal memory," Pardee's discussion of harmonization includes a much more explicit role for memory. The many harmonizing variants in the manuscripts are in most cases not the product of scribal intent; they are a testament to the pervasive quality of gospel material upon the memories of the scribes. They are the result of scribe's familiarity with multiple forms of a single story and their memory of different versions of the same saying (*Scribal Harmonization*, 429). Explicitly, avoiding the use of "unintentional" and "unconscious," Pardee concluded, "I have called the operation by which these changes occurred 'reflexive' or 'automatic' harmonization. As the scribe copied one Gospel, the text itself recalled parallel material latent in the scribe's horizon of expectation and in his general familiarity with alternative versions of sayings and stories" (430). In fact, these observations led Pardee to the following conclusion, which is really a refinement of his definition: "Therefore, one must take care when speaking about harmonizing variants. On the whole, scribes did not create harmonizations, if by harmonizations one means a reading *intended* to reduce discrepancies between the Gospels. It is more precise to say that a scribe created a *harmonizing* omission or *harmonizing* alteration under the influence of parallel material. The variant *functions* to align the passages quite apart from the scribe's intent in the creation of the alteration. Furthermore, scribes did not harmonize, if by harmonize one means espouse a deliberate agenda to assimilate the Gospels. Instead, scribes were *influenced* by external material to greater or lesser degrees and sometimes allowed parallel material to affect their copy of a Gospel. It is better to say, then, that parallel material is the *source* of the alteration or the *influence* at work upon the scribe" (430–31, emphasis original). Thus, although Pardee does not use the term scribal memory, his well-nuanced description of harmonization is certainly consistent

fection, especially in harmonizing pluses," I disagree with his estimation of frequency.[150] That is, based on my understanding of category-triggering, I have a larger role for unintentional harmonizations within scribal memory. When reading one passage that has a parallel passage or contains similar phrases as found in other passages, the scribe's memory of that other passage (in the same category) is triggered in ways that allow that other text to influence how the *Vorlage* is being copied into the new manuscript. That is, in Jefferson's terms the two passages can be understood as pairs, as comembers of their category describing the same saying or events.

Although Tov's focus has been primarily upon harmonizations between different books of the Torah, below I will provide examples of harmonization within the same book and then harmonization with a different book(s). I have selected all of the examples of harmonization within the same book from the Prophets and Writings, since the examples of harmonization with different book(s) are all from the Torah. Although I continue to use the presentation of the material based on the assumptions in the secondary literature with the presumed original text given in the first column, the same text with the harmonizing addition given next, and then the source text(s) given last, I do so simply because there must be some linear order to my presentation. *However*, since I assert that we need to reevaluate the presumed validity of what have been general principles in text criticism for a long time (e.g., *lectio brevior potior*), this arrangement of the texts should not be interpreted as my agreement with the scholarly consensus on what is and is not original or even earlier. Furthermore, in this section my reinterpretation of harmonization in these examples nevertheless remains fairly close to the secondary sources I am using; in the conclusion to this section I will explicate additional implications, when I discuss the phenomenon of harmonization itself rather than individual examples.

Below I break my discussion into two major subsections: harmonization within the same book and harmonizations between books. Since "What is a book?" is a reasonable question—for example, should 1 Kings and 2 Kings be understood as one book or two?—I do not put too much weight into this distinction.[151] Nevertheless, it provides a convenient orga-

---

with the notion of scribal memory and is in my opinion much better nuanced than Tov's discussion, even though there are important similarities.

150. Tov, "Textual Harmonization in Exodus 1–24," 2.

151. For my discussion of "book" in Deuteronomy, see Person, "Self-Referential Phrases in Deuteronomy," 217–42. See also pp. 15–19 above.

nizing principle to my discussion that is consistent with Tov's definition and with regular practice. Below in the section on harmonization within the same book, I will discuss the following examples: (1) harmonization between the passage describing Solomon building shrines to foreign gods (1 Kgs 11:7) and the passage describing the destruction of these shrines by Josiah (2 Kgs 23:13; example 2.39), (2) the harmonizing addition of a superscription from MT Jer 26:1 to MT Jer 27:1 (example 2.40), (3) the harmonizing influence of the passage concerning Shadrach, Meshach, and Abednego in the fiery furnace (Dan 3) on the passage concerning Daniel in the lion's den (Dan 6; examples 2.41–2.42), and (4) harmonization between restoration prophecies in Isa 51 and Isa 35 (example 2.43). In the section on harmonization between different books, I will discuss the following examples: (1) harmonization between the two versions of the Ten Commandments (Exod 20:10–12; Deut 5:14–16; example 2.44); (2) harmonization between two passages concerning the Nephilim and Anakites (Num 13:33–14:1; Deut 1:27–32; examples 2.45–2.46); (3) harmonization between Jethro's advice to Moses to ask for tribal leaders (Exod 18:21–27) and Moses's speech concerning tribal leaders (Deut 1:9–18; example 2.47); and (4) harmonization in 4Q365 of Exod 15:19 and Exod 14:28–29 (example 2.48). Although many more examples are discussed in the secondary literature, these examples are sufficient to illustrate my approach of applying category-triggering to harmonization within scribal memory.

Harmonization within the Same Book

Example 2.39: 1 Kgs 11:7 with 2 Kgs 23:13[152]

MT 1 Kgs 11:7	LXX 1 Kgs 11:5–6	MT 2 Kgs 23:13
At that time, Solomon built	At that time, Solomon built	The king defiled
a shrine [במה]	a shrine [ὑψηλόν = במה]	the high places [הבמות]
for Chemosh	for Chemosh	
the abomination [שקץ]	the idol [εἰδώλῳ]	

---

152. Sidnie White Crawford, Jan Joosten, and Eugene Ulrich, "Sample Editions of the Oxford Hebrew Bible: Deuteronomy 32:1-9, 1 Kings 11:1-8, and Jeremiah 27:1-10," *VT* 58 (2008): 352–66; my translation.

2. Category-Triggering and Text-Critical Variants

of Moab,	of Moab,	
on the mount near Jerusalem [בהר אשר על פני ירושלם]		near Jerusalem [אשר על פני ירושלם]
		to the south of the Mount of Destruction, [להר המשחית]
		which King Solomon of Israel had built
		for Astarte the abomination [שקץ; LXX = προσοχθίσματι] *of the Sidonians,*
		for Chemosh the abomination [שקץ] of Moab,
and one for Molech [ולמלך]	and to their king [τῷ βασιλεῖ αὐτῶν = ולמלכו]	and for Milcom [ולמלכם]
the abomination [שקץ]	the idol [εἰδώλῳ]	the abomination [תועבת]
of the Ammonites	of the Ammonites	of the Ammonites
	and to Astarte the abomination [βδελύγματι] *of the Sidonians*	

MT

    בהר אשר על פני ירושלם

    on the mount near Jerusalem

LXX: lacking

MT: lacking

LXX

    καὶ τῇ Ἀστάρτῃ βδελύγματι Σιδωνίων

    [= לעשתרת שקץ צידנים; see MT 2 Kgs 23:13][153]

    and to Astarte the abomination of the Sidonians

---

153. Because of the use of synonymous readings in both the Hebrew and the Greek for the "idol"/"abomination"/"offence" (שקץ, תועבת; εἰδώλῳ, βδελύγματι, προσοχθίσματι), any retroversion of this term must simply choose one arbitrarily. Therefore, I have simply followed the source for this harmonizing plus. Contra Crawford, Joosten, and Ulrich, "Sample Editions," 358.

Because of the significant differences between MT and LXX, some scholars have argued that they represent "two distinct Hebrew editions of 1 Kings."[154] For example, Jan Joosten's critical edition was to include two columns of his reconstructed Hebrew text, "Edition A" (≈ MT) and "Edition B" (≈ LXX *Vorlage*).[155] In his published preliminary discussion of 1 Kgs 11:1–8, he suggested that there are two possible cases of harmonizing pluses, one in MT and one in LXX, both of which were influenced by the passage in 2 Kgs 23:13 that specifically refers to the destruction of these same high places built by Solomon. His conclusion concerning the plus in MT, "on the mount near Jerusalem," clearly betrays the standard application of *lectio brevior potior* to the reconstruction of the original text: "The absence of these words from edition B [= LXX *Vorlage*] are hard to explain if they formed part of the original text. It is better, therefore, to suppose they were added in the M[T] tradition (including S[yriac], T[argum], and V[ulgate]) on the basis of 2 Kgs 23:13."[156] In his selective commentary on 1 Kgs 11:1–8, Joosten did not comment on the harmonizing plus in LXX, "and to Astarte the abomination of the Sidonians"; he simply provided a retroversion and noted "harm?" in his critical apparatus. However, other commentators have often concluded that it is an addition based on 2 Kgs 23:13.[157] Although I agree that harmonization occurred between these two passages, I do not think "it is better … to suppose" that the pluses are additions, since I reject the notion of an original text. Rather, I think we must accept that harmonization may also occur in the form of omissions, so that the influence of parallel texts could run in different directions at different times in the textual fluid-

---

154. Crawford, Joosten, and Ulrich, "Sample Editions," 359.

155. Because of Joosten's criminal conviction, he forfeited his assignment for the Kings volume in HBCE; therefore, late in the stage of writing this work I changed "will include" to "was to include" to indicate this. Otherwise, I have retained my references to his past work to reflect his influence on my thinking in this volume. My continuing to reference his work in this volume should in no way be construed as any kind of attempt to minimize the damage he did to the victims of child pornography and other sex crimes as well as his academic colleagues at Oxford and elsewhere.

156. Crawford, Joosten, and Ulrich, "Sample Editions," 362.

157. E.g., Mordechai Cogan, *1 Kings: A New Translation with Introduction and Commentary*, AB (New York: Doubleday, 2001), 325 n. b. Cogan also noted a harmonizing plus at the end of 11:5 in the Syriac: "Syr. adds (from v. 7): 'and after Chemosh, the abomination of the Moabites'" (325 n. a).

ity of their transmission. Of course, it is quite possible that, as Joosten suggested, both Hebrew editions underwent expansion independent of each other, but I would add that they also may have undergone contraction independent of each other in the earlier, wild time of their composition/transmission. However, either explanation nevertheless suggests that scribal memory of the source text influenced the copying of the *Vorlage*.

Example 2.40: Jer 27:1 with Jer 26:1[158]

MT Jer 27:1	LXX Jer 34:1	MT Jer 26:1
בראשית ממלכת יהויקם		בראשית ממלכת יהויקם
בן יאושיהו מלך יהודה	[lacking]	בן יאושיהו מלך יהודה
היה הדבר הזה אל ירמיה		היה הדבר הזה
מאת יהוה לאמר		מאת יהוה לאמר
In the beginning of the reign of Jehoiakim, son of Josiah, king of Judah, this word came to Jeremiah from the LORD.	[lacking]	In the beginning of the reign of Jehoiakim, son of Josiah, king of Judah, this word came from the LORD.

A common observation made about the relationship between MT Jeremiah and LXX Jeremiah is that MT contains many additions, including the addition of superscriptions to some passages where they are lacking in LXX (see also 7:1 and 16:1). In this case, this addition is widely seen as being taken from Jer 26:1 (both MT and LXX), especially since Jer 27 appears to be about Zedekiah, not Jehoiakim, since he is mentioned by name in MT Jer 27:3, 12 and LXX Jer 34:3, 12.[159] For example, in his preliminary published discussion of the critical text of Jer 27:1–10, Ulrich

---

158. Crawford, Joosten, and Ulrich, "Sample Editions," 365; my translation.

159. William L. Holladay, *Jeremiah 2: A Commentary on the Book of the Prophet Jeremiah Chapters 26–52*, Hermeneia (Minneapolis: Fortress, 1989), 112; Jack R. Lundbom, *Jeremiah 21–36: A New Translation with Introduction and Commentary*, AB 12B (New York: Doubleday, 2004), 302; Robert P. Carroll, *Jeremiah: A Commentary*, OTL (Philadelphia: Westminster, 1986), 526.

labeled this variant a harmonization based on Jer 26:1.[160] Many scholars correct the text in their translations to read "Zedekiah," not only due to the literary context but also based on a few manuscripts in the MT tradition and Syriac.[161] Although MT Jeremiah certainly suggests a tendency for additions in comparison with LXX Jeremiah, I am becoming more leery about applying such general observations to individual cases. It seems to me that even general tendencies have exceptions and as widely recognized there are additions in LXX Jeremiah as well (although fewer). Nevertheless, this seems to be a really good case for arguing for a harmonizing addition, especially because the majority of manuscripts in the MT tradition read "Jehoiakim." Then later, some scribes (evident in some manuscripts in MT and Syriac) harmonized the previous harmonizing addition taken from 26:1 with the immediate context (27:3, 12) by correcting the name of the king to "Zedekiah." Thus, even though I agree that this is a case in which I think we have a good basis for determining earlier and later readings—from lacking to harmonizing addition to correction of the name in that addition—I would not make this argument primarily based on the general principle of *lectio brevior potior* or even the general observation of MT Jeremiah as an expansive text, even though both of these generalities would apply here.

Daniel 6 with Daniel 3

The similar literary structures of the story of Shadrach, Meshach, and Abednego in the fiery furnace (Dan 3) and the story of Daniel in the lions' den (Dan 6) have often been noted. For example, Carol Newsom wrote the following:

> In both narratives jealous rivals imperil Jewish hero(es) by exploiting or manipulating their religious values and practices in a way that exposes their disobedience to a royal command or law. In both the king orders an execution.... In both stories, the form of execution involves a separated space where an element other than a human executioner is the agent (fire, lions). In both, either the executioners or the enemies of the hero(es) are killed by the same means that had been prepared for the

---

160. Crawford, Joosten, and Ulrich, "Sample Editions," 365.
161. With the NRSV: Lundbom, *Jeremiah 21–36*, 302; Carroll, *Jeremiah*, 526.

2. Category-Triggering and Text-Critical Variants   141

hero(es). Finally, in both accounts the climax of the narrative is a dramatic confession of the power of the God of the hero(es).[162]

Because of these similarities, Newsom suggested the possibility that Dan 6 was modeled on Dan 3. John Collins also noted similarities between Dan 6 and Bel and the Serpent and concluded that there must have been "an old layer of tradition which was developed in different ways" behind the extant versions of the motif of the lions' den.[163]

In some sense, these similarities can be understood at the level of the composition of these chapters, but, due to the complex text-critical issues, especially of chapters 4–6 of MT Daniel and LXX Daniel, they also must be understood at the level of transmission of these chapters or, even better, understood within the composition/transmission process of these chapters.[164] This is especially the case, if "the OG version of Dan 4–6 … once formed a distinctive booklet of Daniel stories and were perhaps the core of the developing collection."[165] Below I provide some good examples of how these similarities have influenced the harmonization of the texts. I have divided my discussion into two examples, one in which the material in MT Dan 6 is lacking in LXX Daniel and one in which the parallel material between MT Daniel and LXX Daniel has different readings.

---

162. Carol A. Newsom with Brennan W. Breed, *Daniel: A Commentary*, OTL (Louisville: Westminster John Knox, 2014), 190.
163. Collins, *Daniel: A Commentary on the Book of Daniel*, Hermeneia (Minneapolis: Fortress, 1993), 264.
164. For excellent overviews to the text-critical issues, see Collins, *Daniel*, 2–12; Newsom, *Daniel*, 3–6.
165. Newsom, *Daniel*, 10. Note that Collins provided an English translation with notes for his reconstructed MT and for the OG for Daniel 4–6 (*Daniel*, 208–73).

Example 2.41[166]

MT Dan 6:14	LXX Dan 6:14	MT Dan 3:12
Thereupon they answered and said to the king, "Daniel, one of the exiles of Judah,	[lacking]	There are certain Jews whom you appointed over the administration of the province of Babylon, Shadrach, Meshach, and Abednego. These men
has paid no attention to you, O king, [לא שם עלי מלכא טעם] or to the binding obligation that you issued. He makes his petition three times a day.		*have not paid attention to you, O king,* [לא שמו עליך מלכא טעם] they do not serve your god, and they do not worship the gold statue that you have set up.

MT Dan 6:24	LXX Dan 6:23	MT Dan 3:25
Then the king greatly rejoiced, and he commanded that Daniel be brought up out of the den. Daniel was brought up out of the den,	[lacking]	He answered and said, "Behold, I see four men, unbound, walking in the midst of the fire,
and no injury was found on him, [וכל חבל לא השתכה בה] because he trusted in his God.		*who have suffered no harm,* [וחבל לא איתי בהון] and the appearance of the fourth is like a divine being.

In his study of harmonization in Dan 6, Michael Segal concluded concerning these two examples that the pluses in MT are harmonizing

---

166. Michael Segal, "Harmonization and Rewriting of Daniel 6 from the Bible to Qumran," in *Hā-'îsh Mōshe: Studies in Scriptural Interpretation in the Dead Sea Scrolls and Related Literature in Honor of Moshe J. Bernstein*, ed. Binyamin Y. Goldstein, Michael Segal, and George J. Brooke, STDJ 122 (Leiden: Brill, 2018), 265–79. The translation is my adaptation of Collins's. See Collins, *Daniel*, 177–78, 256–59.

additions based on Dan 3 as the source text. Concerning 6:14, "the MT reading most probably reflects assimilation with the story in chapter 3."[167] Concerning 6:24, the "very similar language in MT is most probably the result of harmonization with chapter 3."[168]

Example 2.42[169]

MT Dan 6:23a	LXX Dan 6:19b	MT Dan 3:28a
My God *sent his angel* [אלהי שלח מלאכה] and shut the mouths of the lions, [וסגר פם אריותא] and they did not harm me.	The God of Daniel took providential care of him [τότε ὁ θεὸς τοῦ Δανιηλ πρόνοιαν ποιούμενος αὐτοῦ] and shut the mouths of the lions, [ἀπέκλεισε τὰ στόματα τῶν λεόντων] and they did not trouble Daniel.	Nebuchadnezzar proceeded to say: "Blessed be the God of Shadrach, Meshach, and Abednego, who *sent his angel* [אלההון ... די שלח מלאכה] and rescued his servants who trusted in him.

MT Dan 6:23a	LXX Dan 6:23a	MT Dan 3:28a
My God *sent his angel* [אלהי שלח מלאכה]	and God has saved me from the lions.	Nebuchadnezzar proceeded to say: "Blessed be the God of Shadrach, Meshach, and Abednego, who *sent his angel* [אלההון ... די שלח מלאכה]

---

167. Segal, "Harmonization and Rewriting of Daniel 6," 268. Similarly, Newsom, *Daniel*, 258.

168. Segal, "Harmonization and Rewriting of Daniel 6," 268.

169. Segal, "Harmonization and Rewriting of Daniel 6," 268. The translation is my adaptation of Collins's. See Collins, *Daniel*, 177–78, 256–59.

and shut the mouths of the lions [ואסגר פם אריותא] and they did not harm me.	[καὶ σέσωκέ με ὁ θεὸς ἀπὸ τῶν λεόντων]	and rescued his servants who trusted in him.

In his discussion of these two variants, Segal observed that MT and LXX have different versions of the story, specifically concerning who the divine agent related to Daniel's salvation is. "MT 3:28 and 6:23 both indicate that the protagonists were saved through the mediation of a divinely sent angel"; however, in LXX both the narrator (in 6:19b) and the character Daniel (in 6:23a) attribute Daniel's salvation as coming from "God's assistance, without any mention of angelic intercession."[170] Segal therefore concluded that "OG Dan 6 at times presents a more original version of the story, which has been altered in the MT edition due to harmonization or assimilation with the parallel story in chapter 3."[171] Although he is careful to state that "neither textual witness reflects the original version of the story" (in Dan 6), Segal still operated under the assumption of an original version so that he concludes that sometimes MT Daniel preserves the earlier/more original version and sometimes LXX Daniel does.[172] Using somewhat different language, Collins similarly concluded concerning Dan 6 that "neither text preserves the story in a pristine form."[173] Rather than assuming the existence of an original and pristine text, we should accept that there are multiple originals. For this reason, I prefer the conclusions of Young concerning the relationship of MT Daniel and LXX Daniel. Although his conclusion is based on his analysis of Dan 5, I think it applies equally well to Dan 6: "the earlier forms of the text which are developed in the OG and the MT were already parallel renditions of a common oral tradition, and thus there never was a common base *text* of Dan 5."[174]

If we take Young's approach to Daniel seriously, then we may also conclude that the different versions of MT Daniel and LXX Daniel can be understood as having synonymous readings in example 2.42 above. That is, rather than understanding that MT Dan 6:23a necessarily contains a different theological perspective from LXX Dan 6:19b, 23a (God's angel versus

---

170. Segal, "Harmonization and Rewriting of Daniel 6," 268–69.
171. Segal, "Harmonization and Rewriting of Daniel 6," 269.
172. Segal, "Harmonization and Rewriting of Daniel 6," 269.
173. Collins, *Daniel*, 263.
174. Young, "Original Problem," 272.

God acting directly), we can allow that oral traditions and traditional texts with roots in oral traditions have the characteristic of multiformity, so that what we may perceive as theological differences would not necessarily be seen as differences at all by the ancients. In this specific case, I do not think that the ancients would make a sharp distinction between the action of God and God's appointed agents, because in both cases God is responsible for the salvific action.[175] At the same time, the characteristic of multiformity would not rule out harmonization; however, when we take multiformity seriously, we must understand harmonization in ways that are more unintentional and unconscious than often assumed, because we should be far more cautious about assuming a theological rationale behind the purported change. Moreover, when we understand scribal performance and textual plurality as commonplace, we must not assume a particular unilinear direction of literary development (such as assumed in *lectio brevior potior*).

Example 2.43

Example 2.43 (see table on following page) is taken from Paulson Pulikottil's study of 1QIsa^a; however, my synopsis does not include MT Isa 51:11 and MT Isa 35:10, since they are so close to 1QIsa^a for these passages in relationship to this harmonizing variant. Pulikottil concluded "Isa. 51:11 and 35:10 are parallel and agree in their wording very closely. So this [the addition in 1QIsa^a 51:3] should be considered to be a harmonization under the influence of these passages."[176] Similarly, Joseph Blenkinsopp noted that "1QIsa^a mistakenly adds 'sorrow and mourning will flee' from 51:11b. cf. 35:10."[177] Once again we can see the assumption of an original text influencing the discussion of this variant, and I would refrain from concluding which reading was in the original text; rather, I assume more fluidity in the textual transmission of these texts.

---

175. For my fuller discussion of multiformity in oral traditions and traditional texts rooted in oral traditions, see Person, *Deuteronomic History and the Book of Chronicles*, especially ch. 3 and my discussion of what I also see as a somewhat false distinction between the Levites under David sacrificing versus David himself sacrificing in the extant versions of 2 Sam 6:12–19a // 1 Chr 15:25–16:3 (97–101)—that is, the king gets credit for what his servants do on his behalf.

176. Pulikottil, *1QIsa^a*, 60.

177. Blenkinsopp, *Isaiah 40-55: A New Translation with Introduction and Commentary*, AB 19A (New York: Doubleday, 2002), 324.

MT Isa 51:3	1QIsaᵃ 51:3	1QIsaᵃ 51:11	1QIsaᵃ 35:10
For the LORD will comfort Zion; he will comfort all her waste places, and will make her wilderness like Eden, her desert like the garden of the LORD; joy and gladness will be found in her, thanksgiving and the voice of song.	For the LORD will comfort Zion; he will comfort all her waste places, and will make her wilderness like Eden, her desert like the garden of the LORD; joy and gladness will be found in her, thanksgiving and the voice of song.	The scattered one of the LORD shall return, and come to Zion with singing; everlasting joy shall be upon their heads; they shall obtain joy and gladness,	And the ransomed of the LORD shall return, and come to Zion with singing; everlasting joy shall be upon their heads; they shall obtain joy and gladness,
	Sorrow and sighing shall flee away. [ינוסון יגון ואנחה]	*and sorrow and sighing shall flee away.* [וגם יגון ואנחה]	*and sorrow and sighing shall flee away.* [וגם יגון ואנחה]

* The synopsis is adapted from Pulikottil, *1QIsaᵃ*, 59–60, his translation.

Harmonization with a Different Book

Exodus 20:10–12 with Deuteronomy 5:14–16; Leviticus 16:29

In example 2.44, MT Exod 20:10–12 (and SP) agree against LXX Exod 20:10–12 (and for 20:10, 4Q149), which includes two harmonizing additions from MT Deut 5:14–16 and one harmonizing substitution from MT Lev 16:29.[178]

Example 2.44

In "Textual Harmonization in Exodus 1–24," Tov listed four harmonizations in the Exodus version of the Ten Commandments (Exod 20:10–17); for sake of brevity, example 2.44 (see table on following pages) includes only his first three. The first one concerns the harmonizing addition of "or your ox or your donkey, or any of [your livestock]" with Deut 5:14 as the source text. The second harmonization is a substitution of an obvious synonymous reading; that is, rather than "or the alien resident in your gates," the LXX has "or the alien resident who resides among you" with the source text being Lev 16:29. The third is the harmonizing addition of "so that it may go well with you" taken from Deut 5:16 as the source text. Tov implied that, in cases of harmonizations with a "remote context," scribal memory is influencing the scribe's copying of the manuscript and that he is consciously harmonizing the text to "reflect a certain conception, almost ideology, that intertextual links should be added in order to perfect the biblical stories."[179]

Although I too assume that such conscious or intentional harmonizations were possible, I think in most cases it is more probable that the

---

178. Tov, "Textual Harmonization in Exodus 1–24"; Eshel, "4QDeut^n," 143, 145–47. For the text of 4Q149 (4QMezA), see J. T. Milik, "Tefillin, Mezuzot et Targums (4Q128–4Q157)," in *Qumran Grotte 4.II*, ed. Roland de Vaux and J. T. Milik, DJD VI (Oxford: Clarendon, 1977), 80. Note that, although in the other examples I have followed the orthography of MT in my retroversion of the Greek into Hebrew, for v. 10 I follow the orthography of 4Q149. Neither of these decisions is intended to suggest that any retroversion can be precise enough to reconstruct the orthography of the Hebrew *Vorlage*; in fact, my decision to use a different orthography here is an attempt to highlight this difficulty. Every retroversion requires choosing a specific orthography, but the choice must be arbitrary.

179. Tov, "Textual Harmonization in Exodus 1–24," 5.

MT Exod 20:10–12 = SP	LXX Exod 20:10–12 (v. 10 = 4Q149)	MT Deut 5:14–16	MT Lev 16:29
¹⁰But the seventh day is a sabbath to the Lord your God; you shall not do any work—you, your son or your daughter you, your male or female slave,	¹⁰But the seventh day is a sabbath to the Lord your God; you shall not do any work—you, your son or your daughter you, your male or female slave, or your ox or your donkey, or any of [ὁ βοῦς σου καὶ τὸ ὑποζύγιόν σου καὶ πᾶν = ושו[רך] וחמרך וכל בהמתך	¹⁴But the seventh day is a sabbath to the LORD your God; you shall not do any work—you, your son or your daughter you, your male or female slave, or your ox or your donkey, or any of [ושורך וחמרך וכל בהמתך]	This shall be to you a statue forever: In the seventh month, on the tenth day of the month, you shall deny yourselves, and no work shall you do,
your livestock, or the alien resident in your gates.	your livestock, or the alien resident who resides among you. [καὶ ὁ προσήλυτος ὁ παροικῶν ἐν σοί = וגר הגר בתוככם]	your livestock, or the alien resident in your gates, [וגרך אשר בשעריך]	neither the citizen nor the alien resident who resides among you. [והגר הגר בתוככם]
[וגרך אשר בשעריך]		so that your male and female slave may	

2. Category-Triggering and Text-Critical Variants

¹¹For in six days the Lord made heaven and earth, the sea, and all that is in them, but rested the seventh day; therefore the Lord blessed the sabbath day and consecrated it.	rest as well as you. ¹⁵Remember that you were a slave in the land of Egypt, and the Lord your God brought you out from there with a mighty hand and an outstretched arm; therefore the Lord your God commanded you to keep the sabbath day.
¹²Honor your father and your mother,	¹⁶Honor your father and your mother, as the Lord your God commanded you,
so that it may go well with you [ἵνα εὖ σοι γένηται; = למען ייטב לך]	*so that your days may be long and that it may go well with you* [למען ייטב לך]
so that your days may be long in the land that the Lord your God is giving you.	in the land that the Lord your God is giving you.

scribe's memory of the broader tradition (including parallel passages but others as well) influenced his copying of his manuscript—a manuscript that the scribe assumed was an incomplete instantiation of the text within the broader tradition—as the scribe produced another manuscript that, even if he thought it was somehow a fuller representation of the tradition, was nevertheless also incomplete. What Tov presumed to be the influence of two different texts (Deut 5:14; Lev 16:29) upon the copying of one verse (Exod 20:10) suggests that scribal memory may be drawing from a larger pool of texts than often assumed and therefore scribal memory may be less conscious or intentional than Tov suggested, but, to use Tov's own words, more "inconsistent" and not systematic in any attempt to harmonize the texts.

Numbers 13:33–14:1 with Deuteronomy 1:27–32

I take this example from Reinhard Müller, Juha Pakkala, and Bas ter Haar Romeny's *Evidence of Editing*, an example of what they refer to as "late editorial changes," because "it lies beyond doubt that the plus in the SP of Num 13:33 is secondary."[180] Before discussing the example of harmonization (example 2.46), I want to note their discussion of the gloss found in MT Num 13:33 as compared to LXX Num 13:33, since it is important to their conclusion concerning this passage.

Example 2.45[181]

MT Num 13:33	LXX Num 13:33
[33]"And there we saw the Nephilim, the Anakites from the Nephilim, [בני ענק מן הנפלים] and we were in our own eyes as locusts, and so we were in their eyes."	[33]"And there we saw the giants; and we were in our own eyes as locusts, and so we were in their eyes."

---

180. Reinhard Müller, Juha Pakkala, and Bas ter Haar Romeny. *Evidence of Editing: Growth and Change of Texts in the Hebrew Bible*, RBS 75 (Atlanta: Society of Biblical Literature, 2014), 38–39; quotations from 35, 40.

181. Müller, Pakkala, and Ter Haar Romeny, *Evidence of Editing*, 36, their translation, adapted.

2. Category-Triggering and Text-Critical Variants

Based on standard redactional principles—presumably including *lectio brevior potior*—Müller, Pakkala, and Ter Haar Romeny argued that this addition occurred when a "marginal gloss" was incorporated into the text itself, causing a "disturbing repetition of הנפלים ('the Nephilim')."[182] They then stated that "the minus in LXX* empirically corroborates the assumption that the MT contains an addition in this verse."[183] They then turned their discussion to the following larger plus in SP.

Example 2.46[184]

MT Num 13:33–14:1	SP Num 13:33–14:1	MT Deut 1:27–32
³³"And there we saw the Nephilim, the Anakites from the Nephilim, and we were in our own eyes as locusts, and so we were in their eyes."	³³"And there we saw the Nephilim, the Anakites from the Nephilim, and we were in our own eyes as locusts, and so we were in their eyes."	
	And the Israelites grumbled in their tents and said, [ויהרגנו בני ישראל באהליהם ויאמרו]	And you grumbled in your tents and said, [ותרגנו באהליכם ותאמרו]
	"It is because YHWH hates us that he has brought us out of the land of Egypt, to hand us over to the Amorites to destroy us. Where are we headed? Our brothers have made our hearts melt by saying, 'The people are stronger and taller than we;	"It is because YHWH hates us that he has brought us out of the land of Egypt, to hand us over to the Amorites to destroy us. Where are we headed? Our brothers have made our hearts melt by saying, 'The people are stronger and taller than we;

---

182. Müller, Pakkala, and Ter Haar Romeny, *Evidence of Editing*, 36.
183. Müller, Pakkala, and Ter Haar Romeny, *Evidence of Editing*, 37.
184. Müller, Pakkala, and Ter Haar Romeny, *Evidence of Editing*, 38–39, their translation, adapted.

the cities are large and fortified up to heaven, and we also saw there the Anakites!'" And Moses said to the Israelites, [ויאמר משה לבני ישראל] "Have no dread or fear of them. YHWH your God, who goes before you, is the one who will fight for you, just as he did for you in Egypt before your very eyes, and in the wilderness, where you saw how YHWH your God, carried you, just as one carries a child, all the way that you traveled until you reached this place. But in spite of this, you have no trust in YHWH your God, who goes before you on the way to seek out a place for you to camp, in fire by night, and in the cloud by day, to show you the route you should take."	the cities are large and fortified up to heaven, and we also saw there the Anakites!'" And I said to you, [ואמר אלכם] "Have no dread or fear of them. YHWH your God, who goes before you, is the one who will fight for you, just as he did for you in Egypt before your very eyes, and in the wilderness, where you saw how YHWH your God, carried you just as one carries a child, all the way that you traveled until you reached this place. But in spite of this, you have no trust in YHWH your God, who goes before you on the way to seek out a place for you to camp, in fire by night, and in the cloud by day, to show you the route you should take."
[1]And all the congregation lifted up their voice, and cried; and the people wept that night.	[1]And all the congregation lifted up their voice, and cried; and the people wept that night.

Müller, Pakkala, and Ter Haar Romeny concluded as follows: "The additional text seems to have been inserted in an attempt to harmonize the passage with Deut 1:27–32."[185] After noting that the SP includes the gloss with MT Num 13:33, they then provided the following conclusion: "the MT would attest to a stage of textual development that lies between the LXX* and the SP."[186]

As they noted, their interpretation of this harmonizing addition in SP is consistent with most scholarship (including that of Tov) that suggests that SP has a harmonizing tendency. They clearly understand this harmonizing addition to be intentional, even stating that this occurred in the process of "copying … the donor text of Deut 1:27–32."[187] My understanding of scribal memory allows for such rare cases of copying from two *Vorlagen* (in this case, a scroll of Numbers and a scroll of Deuteronomy); however, I would not assume that even such "larger expansions" are necessarily the result of such a "mechanical technique of copying" that requires the scribe to consult another physical scroll. That is, when the scribe was copying one scroll, the similarity between the passage he was copying and some other passage triggered his memory of that other passage and he then copied the passage in the one scroll with the influence of the other passage in another scroll, whether the other passage was copied with or without a physical *Vorlage* before him. Although I can agree that the longer a harmonizing addition is the more likely it is copied from a physical manuscript, even these longer additions do not require such an interpretation when we take more seriously the important role of scribal memory in scribal performance. My disagreement with Müller, Pakkala, and Ter Haar Romeny (and many others in the scholarly consensus) is primarily based on what assumptions they share that I reject, especially their presumed ability based on the standard higher-critical methods to locate texts in a linear fashion between the original text and the extant texts (in this case, LXX >> MT >> SP). Although I allow that their reconstructions are possible, I am uncertain on what basis we can determine probability concerning such individual cases, especially when they occurred in the period prior to canonization.

---

185. Müller, Pakkala, and Ter Haar Romeny, *Evidence of Editing*, 40.
186. Müller, Pakkala, and Ter Haar Romeny, *Evidence of Editing*, 40.
187. Müller, Pakkala, and Ter Haar Romeny, *Evidence of Editing*, 40.

Exodus 18:21–27 with Deuteronomy 1:9–18

Sidnie White Crawford provided the following example to illustrate the type of intentional harmonization that she argued occurs often in the Pentateuch.

> To an ancient scribal exegete who takes a harmonizing approach to the text of Scripture, the events Moses rehearses in his speech [in Deut 1–9] should agree in detail with those events as narrated in Exodus and Numbers. If they do not, then the two accounts need to be brought into agreement, or harmonized.[188]

She understood such intentional harmonization as a characteristic of SP as well as the so-called proto-SP texts of Qumran (esp. 4Q27 [4QNum^b] and 4Q22).[189]

Example 2.47[190]

MT Exod 18:21–27	4Q22 18:21–27	MT Deut 1:9–18
[21]"You shall seek out for yourself from among all the people capable men who fear God, trustworthy men who spurn ill-gotten gain; and set these over	[21]"You shall seek out for yourself from among all the people capable men who fear God, trustworthy men who spurn ill-gotten gain; and set these over	

---

188. Crawford, *Rewriting Scripture in Second Temple Times*, SDSS (Grand Rapids: Eerdmans, 2008), 23.

189. In her more recent writings, Crawford expressed more skepticism in our ability to identify recensions or textual families and now prefers "pre-SamP" rather than "proto-SP." That is, due to her increasing understanding of textual plurality, she has possibly backed off from some of her earlier conclusions. Even though she continued to suggest that there is a "pre-SamP" textual family, she noted that there are so many nonaligned texts that we must understand that scribes had a much higher degree of freedom to change texts than we have generally considered. See esp., Crawford, "Interpreting the Pentateuch through Scribal Processes."

190. Crawford, *Rewriting Scripture*, 24–25; Jeffrey H. Tigay, "Conflation as a Redactional Technique," in *Empirical Models for Biblical Criticism*, ed. Jeffrey H. Tigay (Philadelphia: University of Pennsylvania Press, 1985), 63–68, his translation.

them as chiefs of thousands, chiefs of hundreds, chiefs of fifties, and chiefs of tens. ²²Let them exercise authority over the people at all times; let them bring every major matter to you, but decide every minor matter themselves. Make it easier for yourself, and let them share the burden with you. ²³If you do this—and God so commands you—you will be able to bear up; and all these people will go home content."
²⁴Moses heeded his father-in-law and did all that he had said.

them as chiefs of thousands, chiefs of hundreds, chiefs of fifties, and chiefs of tens. ²²Let them exercise authority over the people at all times; let them bring every major matter to you, but decide every minor matter themselves. Make it easier for yourself, and let them share the burden with you. ²³If you do this—and God so commands you—you will be able to bear up; and all these people will go home content."
²⁴Moses heeded his father-in-law and did all that he had said.

Moses said to *the people*, "I myself cannot bear the burden of you alone. The LORD your God has multiplied you until you are today as numerous as the stars in the sky. May the LORD, the God of your fathers, increase your numbers, a thousand-fold, and bless you as He promised you. How can I alone

⁹*I* said to *you* at that time "I cannot bear the burden of you alone. ¹⁰The LORD your God has multiplied you until you are today as numerous as the stars in the sky. ¹¹May the LORD, the God of your fathers, increase your numbers, a thousand-fold, and bless you as He promised you. ¹²How can I alone

²⁵Moses chose capable men out of all Israel and appointed them heads over the people: chiefs of thousands, chiefs of hundreds, chiefs of fifties, and chiefs of tens.	bear the trouble of you, the burden, and the bickering! Pick from each of your tribes men who are wise, discerning, and experienced, and I will appoint them as your heads." *They* answered and said, "What you propose to do is good." So *he* took *their* tribal leaders, wise and experienced men, and *he* appointed them heads over *them*: chiefs of thousands, chiefs of hundreds, chiefs of fifties, and chiefs of tens, and officials for *their* tribes. He charged *their* magistrates as follows: "Hear out your fellow men, and decide justly between any man and a fellow Israelite or a stranger. You shall not be partial in judgment; hear out high and low alike. Fear no man, for judgment is God's. And any matter that is too difficult for you, you shall bring near to me and I	bear the trouble of you, the burden, and the bickering! ¹³Pick from each of your tribes men who are wise, discerning, and experienced, and I will appoint them as your heads." ¹⁴*You* answered *me* and said, "What you propose to do is good." ¹⁵So *I* took *your* tribal leaders, wise and experienced men, and *I* appointed them heads over *you*: chiefs of thousands, chiefs of hundreds, chiefs of fifties, and chiefs of tens, and officials for *your* tribes. ¹⁶*I* charged *your* magistrates as follows: "Hear out your fellow men, and decide justly between any man and a fellow Israelite or a stranger. ¹⁷You shall not be partial in judgment; hear out high and low alike. Fear no man, for judgment is God's. And any matter that is too difficult for you, you shall bring near to me and I

	will hear it." Thus *he* commanded *them* about the various things that *they* should do.	will hear it." ¹⁸Thus *I* commanded *you at that time* about the various things that *you* should do.
²⁶And they exercised authority over the people at all times: the *difficult* matters they would bring to Moses, and all the minor matters they would decide themselves. ²⁷Then Moses bade his father-in-law farewell, and he went his way to his own land.	²⁶And they *would* exercise authority over the people at all times: the *major* matters they would bring to Moses, and all the minor matters they would decide themselves. ²⁷Then Moses bade his father-in-law farewell, and he went his way to his own land.	

Crawford gave an excellent description of this example of harmonization, which represents the consensus model's approach:

> The scribe accomplishes his harmonization in a straightforward manner; he begins with his Exodus text, in which Jethro gives Moses his advice; at the end of v. 24, which states that Moses heeded the advice, he interpolates the Deuteronomy passage, now presented as Moses' speech explaining to the people what he plans to do (on the basis of Jethro's advice above). He excises v. 25 in Exodus as redundant, since the Deuteronomy passage repeats the same information. At the end of the Deuteronomy interpolation, he resumes his Exodus text at v. 26. To ensure a smooth transition between the third person narrative of Exodus and the first person speech of Deuteronomy, he changes some of the first person verbs and pronouns of the Deuteronomy passage to third person. The resulting expanded narrative is very well made; the casual reader would not detect that the interpolation had taken place. This is a classic harmonization, and typical of the narrative portions of the pre-Samaritan text.[191]

---

191. Crawford, *Rewriting Scripture*, 26.

As I stated above concerning example 2.46, such longer harmonizing pluses are more likely additions and the kind of linear progression between copies of literary texts assumed in Crawford's analysis is certainly possible in my understanding of scribal memory. However, I think that the possibility that even such longer cases of harmonization occurred on the basis of how the oral text or mental text functions within scribal memory remains; I do not think that we must assume that this scribe had two manuscript *Vorlagen* physically before him to understand this as a case of a scribe producing a new manuscript with the harmonizing influence of a text other than the *Vorlage* of Exodus from which he was copying. Moreover, under either way of imagining what physical manuscripts were present, scribal memory continued to influence the copying of the new manuscript, a manuscript with a harmonization that, as Crawford noted, "is very well made" so that "the casual reader would not detect that the interpolation had taken place." That is, as is often the case, the new manuscript produced in the composition/transmission process under the influence of scribal memory is so traditional that our higher-critical methods (especially source- and redaction-criticism) would not inform us that such an interpolation had taken place; we can only identify this interpolation because we have text-critical evidence, especially since it is an example of classic harmonization.[192]

---

192. See similarly, Bénédicte Lemmelijn, "Text-Critically Studying the Biblical Manuscript Evidence: An 'Empirical' Entry to the Literary Composition of the Text," in Person, Rezetko, *Empirical Models*, 129–64. Although she pointed to harmonizing tendencies in the plague narrative (Exod 7:14–11:10), Lemmelijn noted that these harmonizing tendencies are only accessible to the modern scholar when we can carefully compare one text of Exodus with another (MT, SP, LXX). That is, if we only had Exod 7:14–11:10 in the LXX, we would not be able to identify these harmonizations at all (see esp. 154). Both Crawford's argument concerning the harmonization in Exod 18:21–27 and Lemmelijn's argument concerning harmonization in Exod 7:14–11:10 undercut Tigay's methodological argument, which is intended not only to support the higher-critical method in general, but also the JEDP source analysis of the Pentateuch. I.e, Crawford and Lemmemlijn recognize that without such empirical evidence, the higher-critical method would not be able to detect such harmonizing additions. For further discussion of Tigay's work and shortcomings of the source and redaction criticism, see Raymond F. Person Jr. and Robert Rezetko, "The Importance of Empirical Models to Assess the Efficacy of Source and Redaction Criticism," in Person and Rezetko, *Empirical Models*, 1–35.

2. Category-Triggering and Text-Critical Variants

4QPentateuch (4Q364–367) with Exodus 14:29; 15:19b

In his excellent application of media studies to the Dead Sea Scrolls, Miller discussed stichography as a means of graphically representing how the text should be performed/read aloud. He observed the following:

> Unlike the majority of scrolls written in continuous script, stichographic texts are divided into lines of verse (hemistich, colon, or line) through the strategic placement of *vacats* (spaces) and margins between poetic units. This scribal practice offers a paradigmatic example of oral-written textuality of the Scrolls because the spacing of stichographic texts represents both literary parallelism and oral performance.[193]

Although here I will not go into detail with Miller's analysis of the poetic structures of this passage from 4Q365, I first provide his table in which we can more easily see his poetic analysis based on the stichography before I provide a synopsis of the texts, which, due to my reformatting, does not represent his poetic analysis of the stichography very well (esp. since I have omitted the references to *vacats* and margins), but nevertheless helps readers see the example of harmonization in the passage with some consideration for space limitations.[194]

Example 2.48[195]

Song of the Sea, Strophe 17 (4Q365 6b:3–5 // Exod 15:19)		
1. For [Pharaoh's horse] went [*vacat*],	[כי בא [סוס פרעה	3
[with his chariot and riders amidst the sea *vacat*].	[ברכבו ובפרשיו בים]	3
2. [And the Lo]rd [brought] *margin* on them *vacat*,	[וישב יה[וֹה עליהמה	3–4
the waters of the sea *vacat*.	את מימי הים	4

---

193. Miller, *Dead Sea Media*, 28. I will discuss stichography, influenced significantly by Miller, further below in ch. 4 on visual-triggering.

194. For an excellent discussion of the history of scholarship on 4Q364–367 concerning what to call this literary document, see Emanuel Tov, "From 4QReworked Pentateuch to 4QPentateuch(?)," in Popović, *Authoritative Scriptures in Ancient Judaism*, 73–91.

195. Miller, *Dead Sea Media*, 135; Zahn, *Rethinking Rewritten Scripture*, 111; Miller's translation, adapted.

3. [For the sons of Israel walked *vacat*],	[ובני ישראל הלכו]	4
[on dry ground amidst the sea *margin*].	[ביבשה בתוך הים]	4
4. [And the wat]er was [a wall] for t[hem],	[והמי]ֹם לֹהֹ[ם] מה חומה]	5
[on] their right and on their left *vacat*.	[מ]ֹימינם ומשמאולם	5

4Q365	MT Exod 15:19	MT Exod 14:28–29
For Pharaoh's horse went with his chariot and riders	¹⁹For Pharaoh's horse went with his chariot and riders	²⁸The waters returned and covered the chariot and the riders, the entire army of Pharaoh that had followed
amidst the sea. And the Lord brought on them the waters of the sea.	amidst the sea. And the LORD brought on them the waters of the sea.	them amidst the sea; not one of them remained.
For the sons of Israel walked on dry ground amidst the sea.	For the sons of Israel walked on dry ground amidst the sea.	²⁹For the sons of Israel walked on dry ground amidst the sea.
And the water was a wall for them on their right and on their left.		And the water was a wall for them on their right and on their left.

Miller noted that most modern scholars understand the Song of the Sea to conclude with Exod 15:18; however, the stichography of 4Q365 demonstrates that "the poem continued [to the end of 15:19] for at least one ancient Jewish scribe."[196] He further observed that MT Exod 15:19 repeats the theme of horse and rider found at the beginning of the song in 15:1 and that it "consists of three nearly equally sized parallel clauses ending with 'sea.'"[197] In 4Q365, we find an additional clause that, according to Zahn, is a harmonizing addition taken from Exod 14:29.[198] Although he allowed

---

196. Miller, *Dead Sea Media*, 136.
197. Miller, *Dead Sea Media*, 136.
198. Zahn, *Rethinking Rewritten Scripture*, 111.

that this may be a harmonizing addition, Miller remained somewhat agnostic about what the original text may have been. In fact, he concluded as follows concerning this strophe as preserved in 4Q365, referring to the poetic lines as laid out in his table given above:

> This strophe offers a classic example of the definition of parallelism promoted by Kugel: A, and what's more, B. In Adele Berlin's equally insightful formulation, the relation between lines in this strophe is syntagmatic (i.e., the two lines contain a semantic continuation or progression of thought). Thus, "Pharaoh's chariot and his riders" in colon 1b (4Q365 6b 3) disambiguates by clarifying, or expanding, "Pharaoh's horse" in line 1a (4Q365 6b 3). Similarly, in line 2b (4Q365 6b 4), the "waters of the sea" is an explanation of line 2a (4Q365 6b 3–4), which describes God as "bringing." One can see this same parallelism in lines 3 and 4, too, where the second colon of each bicolon line is an expansion of the first: the sons of Israel did not just walk, but they walked on the dry ground amidst the sea (line 3; 4Q365 6b 4); the water was not just around them, but it formed a wall around them on both sides (line 4; 4Q365 6b:5).[199]

Although I am inferring more from his argument than he explicitly stated here, Miller seems to be suggesting that 15:19 provides an excellent poetic conclusion to the Song of the Sea and that both versions of this song with this conclusion (with or without the so-called harmonizing addition) can be understood as synonymous readings of the song. That is, even if we can conclude that "And the water was a wall for them, on their right and on their left" is a later harmonizing addition, this is an excellent example of how scribal memory works within the poetic register, so that even a later addition may be unrecognizable as an addition without text-critical evidence, because scribal memory can work so well within the poetic register of the literature.[200] In this hypothetical case, the poetic line 3 "For the sons of Israel walked on dry ground amidst the sea" in the *Vorlage* triggered the scribe's memory of this exact same line in Exod 14:28, so that the scribe continued with "And the water was a wall for them, on their

---

199. Miller, *Dead Sea Media*, 136–37.
200. For my discussion of scribal memory and text-critical variants in a tradition with more limiting poetics structures on word selection, see my discussion of Homeric hexameter in Person, "Formulas and Scribal Memory"; Person, "Poetics and List Formation."

right and on their left," an addition taken from 14:29 that nevertheless fits well within the poetic register of the passage. Miller's agnosticism concerning the original text here is more explicit in his introduction, where he rejected the notion of an original text.[201] I agree with Miller that in a real sense here we have multiple originals, none of which should be considered absolutely determinative for what ancient scribes must copy into their new manuscripts, even though what they perform in their manuscripts should nevertheless fit well within the poetic register of the literary text they are copying within the multiformity in which that text exists.

Harmonization: A Summary

Harmonization is a common feature of the textual fluidity found in the literature of the late Second Temple period and late antiquity, including not only the Hebrew Bible but also the New Testament and noncanonical literature.[202] Harmonization is most likely to occur in a passage that has a similar parallel located somewhere else, whether within the same book or in a different book.

Harmonization tends to be understood based on the standard MT-priority paradigm of an original text that can be reconstructed through the application of text-critical principles such as *lectio brevior potior*. Thus, in

---

201. Miller, *Dead Sea Media*, 1–38.

202. Although harmonization is a term (primarily?) restricted to biblical studies, the same phenomenon can be observed in other ancient literature, where "interpolation" and "assimilation" may be the term used. E.g., George Bolling identified cases of "interpolation" and Stephanie West identified some cases of "assimilation" between parallel passages in Homeric epic. See George Melville Bolling, *The External Evidence for Interpolation in Homer* (Oxford: Clarendon, 1925); Stephanie West, ed. *The Ptolemaic Papyri of Homer* (Cologne: Westdeutscher, 1967), 90, 112. On the basis of Bolling and West, Michaël van der Meer has recently used the Ptolemaic papyri of Homer as an analogue for pluses that he understands as duplications based on source texts throughout the Hebrew Bible, i.e., what we are understanding as harmonizations are found in the Hebrew Bible and Homer. See van der Meer, "Exclusion and Expansion: Harmonisations in the Samaritan Pentateuch, Pre-Samaritan Pentateuchal Manuscripts and Non-Pentateuchal Manuscripts," in *The Samaritan Pentateuch and the Dead Sea Scrolls*, ed. Michael Langlois, CBET 94 (Leuven: Peeters, 2019), 41–76. Therefore, I assume that this type of variant is more widespread in ancient and medieval literature than often noted in discussions of biblical texts, although this hypothesis is mostly based on the implications of what scribal performance and scribal memory suggest about the composition/transmission process in general.

2. Category-Triggering and Text-Critical Variants

the secondary literature, most cases of harmonization concern harmonizing additions (with some cases of harmonizing substitutions) with clear identifications of the influence of the source text upon the later text that contains the harmonization. Often the scribe is assumed to be consciously thinking of the source text and in some cases (esp. longer harmonizing additions) also had a second *Vorlage*—that of the source text—before him to consult while producing the new manuscript. Thus, even though he asserted that harmonization occurred inconsistently and haphazardly, Tov nevertheless could conclude as follows: "Some such changes were inserted unconsciously, but most were inserted because of a theological concern for perfection, especially in harmonizing pluses."[203] That is, despite there being no evidence for a systematic attempt at harmonization, this "theological concern for perfection" often manifested itself in fits and spurts when individual scribes made isolated harmonizing additions.

In contrast to the standard assumptions concerning harmonization, I think that textual plurality and textual fluidity requires a broader understanding of harmonization within the type of category-triggering that functions within scribal memory. During *Vorlage*-based copying by scribes, other texts are present in the room with the reading scribe due to scribal memory, including parallel passages and other passages that contain similar themes and phrases (i.e., passages that belong to some degree in the same category). Although it is certainly possible that a scribe had more than one scroll before him, I suspect that in most instances the other texts that are present are mental texts, including memories of oral texts. Furthermore, even though scribes are focused primarily on the physical manuscripts before them, they understood those manuscripts as incomplete in ways that allow them to draw from the other texts present in scribal memory, whenever they come to mind. Although he mostly operated under the assumption of an original text, Tov nevertheless seems to allow what I am referring to as scribal memory in his phrase "instincts of the scribes" when they unconsciously were influenced by another passage, especially when he identified two possible source texts as in example 2.44 (Exod 20:10 with Deut 5:14; Lev 16:29).[204] However, Tov seems to limit this to a few cases, whereas I think that this would have been much more common. Rather, I prefer how Cambry Pardee described the phenomenon

---

203. Tov, "Textual Harmonization in Exodus 1–24," 2.
204. Tov, "Textual Harmonizations in the Ancient Texts of Deuteronomy," 282.

of harmonization: "The many harmonizing variants in the manuscripts are in most cases not the product of scribal intent.... They are a consequence of a scribe's familiarity with multiple forms of a single story and their memory of different versions of the same saying."[205] There was no systematic attempt to harmonize, because the tradition embraced multiformity and textual plurality, and despite the dominant influence of the manuscript physically present in *Vorlage*-based copying, this was not the only text that determined what scribes wrote in the new manuscripts, because every manuscript was understood as necessarily an incomplete, imperfect representation of the broader tradition in its fullness. Therefore, sometimes when scribes were copying their *Vorlagen*, something in a passage—in the case of harmonization, phrases in common between the *Vorlage* and another passage(s)—triggered the scribes' memory of other relevant passages that then influenced the production of new manuscripts, which both were faithful copies of the *Vorlagen*, despite what we might understand as variants, and yet also necessarily incomplete representations of the fullness of the broader tradition. When we reimagine textual transmission in this way, the process should not be understood as unilinear as generally understood, for example, from shorter to longer. Each *Vorlage* has less influence on a scribe than generally assumed; moreover, the influence between similar texts can run in different directions in the context of textual plurality.

Since above I have closely followed the secondary literature from which I drew these examples, I have not explored how these examples of harmonization may also be examples of other types of text-critical variants, especially synonymous readings. For example, in example 2.44 (Exod 20:10 with Deut 5:14), the harmonizing addition of "or your ox or your donkey, or any of [your livestock]" may simply be another case of a synonymous reading within list construction. The list as given in MT Exod 20:10 ("you, your son or your daughter, you male or female slave, your livestock, or the alien resident in your towns") is simply one way to list all of the members of the agrarian household that necessarily implies "your ox or your donkey" in the use of "your livestock" as is illustrated in numerous other passages in which "ox"/"oxen" and/or "donkey"/"donkeys" are specified in other lists of "livestock" that are a part of the agrarian house-

---

205. Pardee, *Scribal Harmonization*, 429. Pardee is referring to harmonization in the gospels, but it applies equally well to harmonization in the Hebrew Bible and elsewhere.

hold (e.g., in MT, see Gen 12:16; 24:35; 30:43; 32:5, 15; 34:28; 47:17; Exod 2:17; 9:3; 22:2, 4, 9, 10; Num 31:28, 30, 33, 38, 44; Deut 5:21; 22:1, 4; 28:31; Josh 6:21; 7:24; 1 Sam 12:3; 22:19; 27:9; Job 1:3). That is, this example of harmonization may also be understood as a synonymous reading based on the widely understood lists of what livestock was included in the typical agrarian household. In fact, assuming that this variant is only the result of harmonization with the parallel passage in Deut 5:14, when scribal memory is involved, seems to be extremely problematic. Scribal memory is not confined to one specific manuscript of one specific literary text, but encompasses the entirety of the tradition (oral and written) that is held in the collective memory of scribes. Thus, parallel texts may be *one of many sources* of the *so-called* alteration or *one of many sources* of influence upon the scribe. In fact, I am not sure that the ancient scribes would necessarily agree that any harmonization is an alteration in the meaning of the text, because they seem to have a different understanding of word, and harmonizations may be better classified from their perspective as synonymous readings. In fact, I would maintain that the only reason we are able to identify them as harmonizations is because we have the extant parallel texts. If the parallel texts were not extant, we would most likely categorize them as synonymous readings. Moreover, even with the parallel texts, we tend to assume that we know what the original text was, so that we identify the harmonizing addition based on the anachronistic notion of original text.

Furthermore, we may need to reevaluate our understanding of text, especially when we are discussing harmonization. We continue to think about the text as the canonical books, but sometimes we probably should focus on shorter passages or pericopes as the most local text of scribal memory. That is, I am not sure that the ancient scribes would have understood that they were comparing, for example, the Exodus version of the Ten Commandments with the Deuteronomy version of the Ten Commandments. Rather, they probably thought of the Ten Commandments as the word of God that is preserved in the scribal memory, that is, preserved in the various written manuscripts of the scribes as well as in the oral/mental texts of the scribes and their audiences within the broader community. Thus, for example, it is possible that, according to Miller, various versions of the Song of the Sea (example 2.48) were considered faithful representations of the song, despite what we might see as an additional line being added in the form of a harmonization and, on an even broader scale, according to Young, both MT Daniel and LXX Daniel were considered faithful representations of the oral tradition of Daniel within the context of the textual plurality in the broader tradition.[206] Using the words of Jefferson on poetics, any version of the Song of the Sea or the Book of Daniel provides the scribes with access to their synonymous readings within scribal memory through the cognitive-linguistic mechanism of category-triggering for the events narrated in the literary text.

Before leaving the discussion of harmonization, I will close with some explicit reflections on methodology. Unlike in other sections, I identified what I think is a clear case of a set of variants that can be placed in chronological order as follows: (1) LXX Jer 34:1 that lacks a superscription, (2) MT Jer 27:1 that has an added superscription taken from MT Jer 26:1 but with the king improperly identified as Jehoiakim, and (3) a few manuscripts in the MT tradition of Jer 27:1 (with the Syriac) that have corrected the identification of the king to Zedekiah on the basis of harmonization with the references to him in that passage (27:3, 12; example 2.40). However, even in this case, I do not depend on the general principle of *lectio brevior potior* or even the observation that MT Jeremiah is expansive when compared to LXX Jeremiah, because it seems to me that these arguments are based on a linear progression from original text to the extant texts. That is, even though I generally avoid describing text-critical variants as errors or even as early/late, this is not because my idea of scribal memory eliminates the notion that scribes sometimes made errors or that there is never a linear progression of texts based on an ancestor text. Rather, I think that methodologically we do not have the tools to make those judgments in the vast majority of cases, due to textual plurality and the characteristic of multiformity I find present in these traditional texts. In fact, I agree with Crawford and Lemmelijn that the identification of most harmonizations is only possible on the basis of text-critical evidence, because most harmonizations (unlike MT Jer 27:1) fit so well into their literary contexts that they would remain unidentified without some empirical evidence.[207]

---

206. Young, "Original Problem."
207. Crawford, *Rewriting Scripture*, 26; Lemmelijn, "Text-Critically Studying the Biblical Manuscript Evidence," 154.

Variants and Person Reference

Person Reference in Conversation

The secondary literature in conversation analysis includes little reflection on what appears to be a close relationship between Jefferson's poetics and Schegloff's foundational work on person reference and this is partly because these are two areas of early work that have not seen as much attention since the 1970s as have other areas. Therefore, I think I must be more explicit about this relationship than is present in the secondary literature, even though I think that a careful reading of the secondary literature makes this relationship clear. I will proceed to establish this relationship below as follows: (1) a discussion of examples concerning person reference in Jefferson's 1996 article on poetics, (2) a summary of recent work in conversation analysis on person reference, (3) a discussion of those few places in the secondary literature that point in the direction of this synthesis, and (4) my own more explicit synthesis of category-triggering and person reference, which will serve as the theoretical basis for my discussion of the relevant text-critical variants. I will then make some general comments about the secondary literature in the study of the Hebrew Bible concerning text-critical variants of personal names and person reference before turning to my own discussion of selected text-critical examples.

Although person reference is not an explicit topic in her poetics article, Jefferson nevertheless provided numerous examples that include terms of person reference in her discussion of category-formed errors and in one of her subcollections she labeled "names in sound-rows."[208] Since "names in sound-rows" primarily concerns sound-triggering, I will not discuss those examples here, but do so in the next chapter on sound-triggering (example 3.2); however, here I provide some of her examples of category-formed errors, in which the trouble-source—that is, that which needs to be repaired—and the repair itself are comembers of the same category. Example 2.49 includes multiple examples from various conversations as given in Jefferson's article in which all of the talk is produced by the same speaker.

---

208. Jefferson, "On the Poetics of Ordinary Talk," 19.

Example 2.49[209]

> Larry: Hi. I'm Carol's sister-uh brother.
>
> Ellen: … a woman who eats like Hester's: (0.3) ↑ nee-e-neph ↓ ew ↑ nie:ce.
>
> Woman: … instead of you, studying us, 'n find out why white people cannot relate to- hh why white- why black people cannot relate tuh white people
>
> PMG: The Republicans are less efficient that the Democrats. I mean the Republicans are less efficient that the Democrats. ((laughs)) You know what I mean.
>
> Roger: The mother isn't holdin- the father isn't- ah Freudian Slip heh heh "Mother" hah hheh hhehh
> The mother, isn't the uh the one thet's holding you back.

In each of these examples, we can see how the speaker made a category-formed error. The first, second, and last examples concern opposite gendered terms for family members: sister/brother, nephew/niece, mother/father. The third and fourth examples come from socio-political discourse concerning race and political party: white people/black people and Republicans/Democrats. Such errors are so common in talk-in-interaction that they often occur without much commentary on them, although (as with the last two) sometimes they may lead to laughs and in one case even being identified as a Freudian slip in the talk itself. In fact, as the last two examples show, sometimes the error continues, even after it is explicitly referred to, yet the communication remains successful, because it is implicitly repaired; that is, all of the participants can successfully interpret the error and move on without an explicit repair being produced in the talk. These forms of category-formed errors occur so often that we understand what the trouble-source is, even when it is cut off in such a way that it is not complete, as illustrated in example 2.50, which includes two examples from different conversations.

---

209. Jefferson, "On the Poetics of Ordinary Talk," 10–13.

2. Category-Triggering and Text-Critical Variants

Example 2.50[210]

> Caller: ... my wi-uh my husband is ((up north)).
> Caller: ... that it would apply to any t- student.

Because categories are often word pairs that are comembers (e.g., sister/brother and nephew/niece above), we can readily interpret the implied word pairs here based on the initial sounds of the word and the category: wife/husband and teacher/student.

Each of the examples in examples 2.49–2.50 is an instance of self-initiated self-repair: the speaker both initiates the repair of the trouble-source and provides (or implies) the repair, sometimes within the same turn. The last of Jefferson's examples that I provide here (example 2.51) is a case of other-initiated other-repair: Beth makes the category-informed error (and is apparently unaware of it), so Jan simultaneously identifies the trouble-source and repairs it for Beth, who accepts that that is what she meant, even if she remains unsure about what she first said.

Example 2.51[211]

> Beth: ... the Black Muslims are certainly more provocative than the Black Muslims ever were.
> Jan: The Black Panthers.
> Beth: The Black Panthers. What'd I.
> Jan: You said the Black Muslims twice.
> Beth: Did I really?

Here Beth's error concerns simply repeating a comember term related to race relations in the 1970s in ways that Jan can repair it easily (Black Muslims/Black Panthers, both of whom were widely viewed by whites as provocative). With all of these examples, we can see how we can identify such category-formed errors related to person reference, whether we are the participants in the conversation (speaker or hearer) or even distant scholarly analysts, because this is a linguistic phenomenon with which we are familiar, even if we cannot identify it using the technical jargon of con-

---

210. Jefferson, "On the Poetics of Ordinary Talk," 11.
211. Jefferson, "On the Poetics of Ordinary Talk," 12.

versation analysis. Thus, although she does not explicitly discuss person reference in her poetics article, Jefferson nevertheless provided various examples of person reference related to category-triggering; that is, the category-formed errors are evidence of the existence of cognitive categories of comembers for person reference among other types of categories.

Conversation analysts have identified three preferences in their description of the practices for nonpresent, third-person, person reference in everyday conversation as follows: (1) the preference for achieving recognition, (2) the preference for minimalization, and (3) the preference for association. The preference for achieving recognition is the dominant preference in that it must always be considered. Tanya Stivers, N. J. Enfield, and Stephen Levinson described it as follows:

> referring expressions are designed to achieve recognition: They evidence the broader underlying principle of recipient design by which speakers make use of a referential form that should enable their recipients to link a referring expression with a real person.[212]

The preference for minimalization is a secondary preference to recognition. Sacks and Schegloff described it as follows: "*On occasions when reference is to be done, it should preferably be done with a single reference form.*"[213] The preference for association is also a secondary preference after recognition, which Stivers, Enfield, and Levison described as follows: "In certain situations speakers would work to explicitly associate the referent directly to the current conversation participants."[214] Based on cross-linguistic evidence, the preference for achieving recognition and minimalization appear to be universal. The preference for association has been identified only in some cultures and in some of those cultures it seems to take priority over minimalization; in others, minimalization seems to take priority.

---

212. Stivers, Enfield, and Levinson, "Person Reference in Interactions," in *Person Reference in Interaction: Linguistic, Cultural, and Social Perspectives*, ed. N. J. Enfield and Tanya Stivers, Language, Culture, and Cognition 7 (Cambridge: Cambridge University Press, 2007), 12–13.

213. Harvey Sacks and Emanuel Schegloff, "Two Preferences in the Organization of Reference to Persons in Conversation and Their Interaction," in *Everyday Language: Studies in Ethnomethodology*, ed. George Psathas (New York: Irvington, 1979), 16, emphasis original.

214. Stivers, Enfield, and Levinson, "Person Reference in Interaction," 14.

2. Category-Triggering and Text-Critical Variants

To illustrate these preferences, I will provide some examples with a brief discussion. The following examples come from different conversations in which the terms for person reference clearly provided ample recognition. Example 2.52 includes lines from four different conversations.

Example 2.52[215]

> Did *Varda* tell you what happened this weekend?
> Hey do you have a class with *Billy* this term?
> *Someone* said at the end of class "Could you pl-please bring in a microphone next time?"
> If *Percy* goes with *Nixon* I'd sure like that.

In each of these conversations the participants easily continued forward in the conversation without the need for any additional information to identify the persons sufficient for the conversational context (Varda, Billy, someone, Percy, and Nixon). However, in example 2.53 we have evidence of some difficulty in identifying the person at the beginning of this phone call.

Example 2.53[216]

> A: Hello?
> B: 'Lo,
> B: Is Shorty there,
> A: Ooo Jest—Who?
> B: Eddy?
> B: Wood[ward?
> A: [Oo jesta minnit.
>   (1.5)
> A: Its fer you dear.

Here the initial person reference ("Shorty") is insufficient for recognition; therefore, a repair is initiated by A ("Who?"), so that B now uses another way of referring to the same person ("Eddy? Woodward?"), which finally

---

215. Sacks and Schegloff, "Two Preferences in the Organization of Reference to Persons," 17; emphasis original.
216. Sacks and Schegloff, "Two Preferences in the Organization of Reference to Persons," 20.

achieves recognition. When we compare example 2.53 with example 2.52, we can see that the recognition probably would have been successful initially if the caller had used Eddy at first, which would have met the preference for recognition and minimalization, rather than the apparently more unfamiliar (at least to A) nickname Shorty. Example 2.54 illustrates this principle of minimalization.

Example 2.54[217]

>Mike: Paul de *Wa*:ld. Guy out of,=
>Curt: =De Wa:ld yeah I [°(know 'm.)
>Mike: [*Ti*ffen.
>Mike: =D'you know *h*im?
>Curt: °Uh*h*uh=
>Curt: =*I* know who 'e *i*:s.

Here Mike assumed that he needed to provide more information to achieve recognition than was actually necessary. Rather, Curt knew who "Paul de Wald" was without any additional information and interrupts Mike to communicate that recognition has been achieved and Mike should move on with the story-in-progress. That is, Curt is in some sense enforcing the principle of minimalization when Mike makes an erroneous assumption about whether or not the principle of recognition has been met. Examples 2.55–2.56 are English translations of examples in which the preference for association is important. Recognition is obviously achieved, but there would have been more minimal forms available for that recognition.

Example 2.55[218]

>Let's see if there's time for me to visit **my sister-in-law** with **your sister-in-law**.

---

217. Charles Goodwin, "Audience Diversity, Participation, and Interpretation," *Text* 6 (1986): 289.

218. William F. Hanks, "Person Reference in Yucatec Maya Conversation," in Enfield and Stivers, *Person Reference in Interaction*, 169, his translation.

Example 2.56[219]

> PK: Isn't there still your land there?
> AN: They have taken it then.
> PK: Who?
> AN: They just blocked it then the son of deceased my oldman uncle you know (.5) the husband of that madam, madam Xilom As.

Example 2.55 is telling in that "my sister-in-law" and "your sister-in-law" could have been substituted with the shorter forms "your wife" and "my wife" or even their names, but the formulation used here more clearly communicates the relationship between these two men; that is, the person references make explicit that this is a conversation between two brothers about their wives, emphasizing the association between the two speakers in relationship to the two third-party persons they are discussing. In example 2.56, note how long the person reference is ("the son of deceased my oldman uncle you know, the husband of that madam, madam Xilom As") in order to make explicit the various relationships between the speaker, his deceased cousin, his uncle, his aunt, and the addressee who apparently also knows, at least, the uncle. As these two examples demonstrate, person reference is one social action by which cultural norms about personal relationships can be communicated and reinforced.

When one is studying person references in talk-in-interaction, it is also important to distinguish between locally initial and locally subsequent *positions* and *forms*.[220] In English the locally initial position is generally filled by the locally initial form of a name and the locally subsequent positions are generally filled by the more minimal use of pronouns (a locally subsequent form). This is illustrated in example 2.57.

---

219. Penelope Brown, "Principles of Person Reference in Tzeltal Conversation," in Enfield and Stivers, *Person Reference in Interaction*, 197–98; her translation.

220. Emanuel Schegloff, "Some Practices of Referring to Person in Talk-In-Interaction: A Partial Sketch of a Systematics," in *Studies in Anaphora*, ed. Barbara Fox, Typological Studies in Language 33 (Amsterdam: Benjamins, 1996), 437–85.

Example 2.57[221]

> A: How is Missuz Hooper.
> B: uh oh, about the same.
> A: mm, mm mm mm. Have they uh th-uh
>   Then she's still continuing in the same way.
> B: Yes, mm hm.
> A: Well I hope uh **he** can con- uh can, carry on
>   that way, be[cause-
> B: [Well he wants to make a chay- a change.

The first time "Missuz Hooper" is referred to (the locally initial position) her name (a locally initial form) is used to ensure recognition. Once recognition has been achieved, then a more minimal form "she" (a locally subsequent form) can be used in the locally subsequent position. However, this example also has what might be seen as some person reference terms that are at first glance too minimal to achieve recognition: Who are "they," and who is "he"? In other words, these are typical locally subsequent forms used in what appears to be a locally initial position, since this *appears* to be the initial person reference to whoever "they" are and to whoever "he" is. However, as discussed by Celia Kitzinger, Rebecca Shaw, and Merran Toerien, the person reference "Missuz Hooper," at least for these two participants in this conversation, connotes a Mr. Hooper as "he" and together this married couple as "they."[222] Thus, when A refers to Mr. Hooper by himself for the first time with one of the most minimal forms—the pronoun "he"—it nevertheless achieves recognition, because the context provides all of the information necessary for such recognitional success. Example 2.57 comes from a study by Kitzinger, Shaw, and Toerien concerning what they called "locally initial indexicals"—that is, "instead of selecting a name or descriptor, speakers refer to third persons using an indexical reference form—i.e., *they, he, she*—without any explicit

---

221. Celia Kitzinger, Rebecca Shaw, and Merran Toerien, "Referring to Persons without Using a Full-Form Reference: Locally Initial Indexicals in Action," *Research on Language and Social Interaction* 45 (2012), 124–25.

222. Kitzinger, Shaw, and Toerien, "Referring to Persons without Using a Full-Form Reference," 124–25.

prior full-form reference."²²³ From their study of locally initial indexicals, they concluded as follows:

> Co-cultural knowledge is simply a resource upon which co-cultural members can draw for this purpose. The "common culture"—what Garfinkel describes as "the socially sanctioned grounds of inference and action that people use in their everyday affairs and which they assume that others use in the same way"—makes possible the use of (some) locally initial indexicals in the confident expectation that others will understand them, such that they can be successfully deployed for interactional ends—in this case, claiming continuity of focus between the prior talk (about Mrs. Hooper's health) and what might otherwise be hearable as a new departure dealing with a new referent (her husband).²²⁴

Although conversation analysis as a discipline has tended to shy away from systematic discussions about how presumed information between conversational participants influences the practices in talk-in-interaction, John Heritage has provided an excellent discussion of just this topic in his two 2012 articles, "Epistemics in Action" and "The Epistemic Engine."²²⁵ The above analysis of example 2.57 shows how useful such a discussion can be, but Heritage brought some helpful terminology to describing this phenomenon. Heritage asserted that "territories of knowledge," especially when there is "an imbalance of information between speaker and hearer," are often the engine that drives talk-in-interaction and, when that imbalance has been equalized, the topic for that particular sequence of conversation has run its course and comes to an end. Heritage made a distinction between "epistemic status" and "epistemic stance." Epistemic status refers to when "persons recognize one another to be more or less knowledgable concerning some domain of knowledge as a more or less settled matter of fact."²²⁶ "Epistemic stance concerns how speakers posi-

---

223. Kitzinger, Shaw, and Toerien, "Referring to Persons without Using a Full-Form Reference," 116.
224. Kitzinger, Shaw, and Toerien, "Referring to Persons without Using a Full-Form Reference," 125.
225. Heritage, "Epistemics in Action: Action Formation and Territories of Knowledge," *Research on Language and Social Interaction* 45 (2012): 1–29; Heritage, "The Epistemic Engine: Sequence Organization and Territories of Knowledge," *Research on Language and Social Interaction* 45 (2012): 30–52.
226. Heritage, "Epistemic Engine," 32.

tion themselves in terms of epistemic status in and through the design of turns at talk."[227] Thus, when applying Heritage's terminology to example 2.57, we can conclude that both speakers A and B have a similar epistemic status in relationship to the large domain of knowledge that includes Mrs. Hooper and Mr. Hooper as a married couple who are experiencing some real challenges due to her poor health. Otherwise, B's answer "about the same" to A's question "How is Missuz Hooper" would be nonsense, but A seems to know what "the same way" is concerning Mrs. Hooper's health and how it is affecting not only her, but also Mr. Hooper. Note that A uses the expression "in the same way" in the following line. However, the very fact that A asked the question "How is Missuz Hooper" suggests that she was temporarily assuming an epistemic stance of knowing less about the situation than B, even though it turns out that their epistemic statuses appear to be the same.

In the foundational 1979 publication devoted to person reference, Sacks and Schegloff identified the following problem facing person reference in conversation: "For reference to any person, there is a large set of reference forms that can do the work of referring to that one (e.g., he, Joe, a guy, my uncle, someone, Harry's cousin, the dentist, the man who came to dinner, et cetera)."[228] In a different chapter in the same volume, Schegloff wrote the following: "Humans, of course, make these sorts of identification, both categorical and 'recognitional,' (i.e., of particular, 'known' others), and differentiate their behavior toward them accordingly."[229] Since during this period Schegloff and Jefferson worked closely with each other (and their teacher, Sacks, before his untimely death in 1975), I think that Schegloff's distinction between categorical and recognitional is a reference to what Jefferson described as a category in her 1977 lecture on poetics, which was explicitly drawing from "stuff which we'd [presumably Sacks and Schegloff with Jefferson] pretty much kept to ourselves."[230] That is, person reference draws extensively from various relevant categories (such as family, race, gender, occupation) within the process of meeting the

---

227. Heritage, "Epistemic Engine," 33.
228. Sacks and Schegloff, "Two Preferences in the Organization of Reference to Persons," 16–17.
229. Emanuel A. Schegloff, "Identification and Recognition in Telephone Conversation Openings," in Psathas, *Everyday Language*, 25–26.
230. Jefferson, "On the Poetics of Ordinary Talk," 2. This 1996 article is explicitly based on the 1977 lecture.

2. Category-Triggering and Text-Critical Variants

preferences for recognition and minimalization, especially when a proper name may be insufficient for recognition. This idea is stated by Marianthi Makri-Tsilipakou in her study of the category of gendered person references in Greek for women: "it is often the case that categories do categorizing rather than simply referring to persons—to be worked out *in situ*, on the basis of 'interactional threads.'"[231] That is, "woman" and "girl" can be understood as coming from the same category (with somewhat different connotations?), but do not necessarily achieve recognition of specific individuals without the use of locally initial forms appearing earlier in the conversation. In their introduction to a special volume of *Discourse Studies* concerning person reference, Lerner and Kitzinger wrote the following:

> There is certainly much more to learn about when, how, and why speakers refer to themselves (or not)—as well as how they refer to their addressed recipient(s) and to third parties as well as to non-present persons. And beyond this, other domains of reference await the spotlight—for example, references to place, formulations of time and action, and, beyond reference, word selection (Jefferson, 1996) more generally.[232]

For my purpose, I want to highlight that they make an explicit connection between Jefferson's 1996 poetics article, word selection, and person reference, suggesting that such a more explicit synthesis is possible, maybe even needed.

On the basis of my reading of the secondary literature in conversation analysis and my analysis of text-critical variants related to person reference, the following is my limited contribution to such a synthesis that I will then illustrate with a selection of text-critical examples. When two people share cocultural traditional knowledge about persons—whether these persons are historical or fictional or are from the past, present, or

---

231. Makri-Tsilipakou, "The Category (Greek) 'Woman,' or 'Lady,' or 'Girl,' or 'Lass,' or …," *Gender and Language* 9 (2015): 36. Makri-Tsilipakou's contribution concerns not only how categories assist in word selection for person reference, but how word selection related to gendered categories ("woman" versus "girl" in Greek) can promote and preserve cultural values, specifically in her analysis patriarchal values.

232. Gene Lerner and Celia Kitzinger, "Introduction: Person-Reference in Conversation Analytic Research," *Discourse Studies* 9 (2007): 428. The significant contribution of this special volume of *Discourse Studies* concerns first-person references, since most work on person reference has emphasized third-person. However, for my present purpose, the literature on third-person references remains the most pertinent.

future—category and recognition may overlap substantially, even though they are distinct from an analytic perspective. In talk-in-interaction, person reference draws from a variety of categories to reach recognition within the preference for minimalization—for example, the category-formed errors I discussed above (examples 2.49–2.51) provide evidence of comembers in the same category as the triggering mechanism for the error or Freudian slip ("mother" versus "father"). I find that category-triggering (although I would not necessarily define these as errors) continues in the text-critical variants I have studied, for example when one comember term is substituted for another as a synonymous reading (see example 2.59: "pharaoh"/"king of Egypt" in Exod 3:10, 11, 18, 19). However, I also want to emphasize that in some sense every traditional character (historical and/or fictional) has his/her own category for person reference. For example, using the example from the above quotation from Schegloff, "he, Joe, a guy, my uncle, someone, Harry's cousin, the dentist, the man who came to dinner, et cetera" is Schegloff's list with a generalized list completer that defines a category of person reference terms, all of which can enable recognition of the same individual for those with the appropriate cocultural knowledge when used appropriately in conversation. Referring back to example 2.57 above, A's use of "Missuz Hooper" gave B access to the category that included "Missuz Hooper," Mister Hooper as "he," the two of them as a married couple as "they," because of the common cocultural knowledge that A and B shared. Similarly, the following example illustrates how a speaker may use the cocultural knowledge shared between participants in a word search related to person reference.

Example 2.58[233]

> B: Uh she asked me to stop by, she bought a chest of drawers from uhm
> (4.0)
> B: what's the gal's name? Just went back to Michigan
> (2.0)
> B: Helen uhm
> A: Oh I know who you mean,
> (1.0)

---

233. Schegloff, "Relevance of Repair to Syntax-For-Conversation," 266.

A: Brady- **Bra**dy.
B: Yeah! Helen Brady.
A: Mm hm
B: And she- she says she's uh never.

As noted above, there are various person reference terms, all of which can be understood as a category of comember terms for the same individual, in this case for "Helen Brady" who "just went back to Michigan" and apparently sold a chest of drawers to one of their common friends, which is the topic of the story B is telling. That is, the recognitional category for "Helen Brady" included various details about her, most relevantly her recent history, so that, even when the speaker was having trouble recalling her name, A and B together can draw from their cocultural knowledge to collaboratively remember the name to ensure adequate recognition for Helen as the character in the story who sold the chest of drawers, an event that A may not have been aware of, which is the reason for B's storytelling. In other words, even after B knew that recognition had been achieved with A ("Oh I know who you mean"), the word search for the name continued until the inserted sequence searching for the name was completed.

What I am asserting here on the basis of conversation analysis—that is, for each traditional character there is a category of person reference terms that produce recognition of that individual within the limits of minimalization for those with the relevant cocultural knowledge—has a strong analogy in the comparative study of oral traditions, especially related to noun-epithets for the purpose of person reference.

Person Reference in Literature, Especially the Hebrew Bible

Early critics of Parry and Lord focused on noun-epithet formulas in their criticism of oral-formulaic theory and the noun-epithet "swift-footed Achilles" became symbolic for these critics of what was wrong with the Parry/Lord approach.[234] The critics argued that Parry and Lord's perspective was so mechanical that it disallowed creativity and originality to these works and it meant that the one literary genius, Homer, whom Parry and Lord wanted to defend, composed problematic poetry, such as when "swift-footed Achilles" was used in contexts in which Achilles was

---

234. E.g., Roger Dunkle, "Swift-Footed Achilles," *CW* 90 (1997): 227–34.

being anything but swift-footed, for example, as he delivers a speech in the assembly (*Il.* 1.84) or sitting in his tent (*Il.* 9.307). Rather, they argued that such "mistakes" were created when later scribal interventions undermined the earlier literary quality of Homer's original text. According to Parry's and Lord's view, "swift-footed Achilles" simply referred to the character of Achilles, so that "swift-footed" was simply there as a metrical convenience in order to maintain the hexameter verse as required by the poetic tradition during performance. That is, the noun-epithet formula was a thrifty way to allow the poet to compose hexameter verse spontaneously and simply provided the essential idea carried by the noun—in this case, the character Achilles.

Foley refined Parry and Lord's explanation of "swift-footed Achilles" and similar problematic noun-epithets. Illustrating his idea of traditional referentiality and metonymy in oral traditional literature, Foley wrote: "'swift-footed Achilleus' is traditional epic code for the mythic entirety of the Achaean hero. It is an index for his character, a nominal part that stands by prior agreement for the whole of his personality."[235] Therefore, since Achilles is described as one of the "best of the Achaeans" and known for his superior speed and strength on the battlefield, this metonymic noun-epithet ("swift-footed") is quite appropriate as a description of the entirety of Achilles, even when he is sitting still.

There are significant differences between Homeric epic and the Hebrew Bible—most obviously, Homeric epic's strict adherence to hexameter poetic lines. Nevertheless, Foley's idea of traditional referentiality has been applied successfully to various ancient and medieval texts, including the Hebrew Bible.[236] If we translate the above quotation from Foley into the terminology of conversation analysis, we get something like the following: "swift-footed Achilles" is one of the comember terms from the category of person reference terms for the whole of Achilles's personality as preserved in the cocultural knowledge of the ancient Greeks. From the text-critical variants I have studied, this certainly applies analogously

---

235. John Miles Foley, *Homer's Traditional Art* (University Park: Pennsylvania State University Press, 1999), 210.

236. E.g., see Carole R. Fontaine, *Smooth Words: Women, Proverbs and Performance in Biblical Wisdom*, JSOTSup 356 (London: T&T Clark, 2002). Fontaine applied traditional referentiality to the characterization of the queen of Sheba from Kings and Chronicles through the New Testament and postbiblical Jewish literature into Islamic and Coptic sources.

2. Category-Triggering and Text-Critical Variants 181

to major characters of the Hebrew Bible (such as pharoah, Moses, David, Nebuchadnezzar, and God) as well as at least some minor characters (such as Ahab son of Kolaiah and Abner son of Ner), because the text-critical variants illustrate a degree of fluidity in the composition/transmission process in the substitution of pronouns and proper names/titles as well as the addition/omission of titles, patronyms, and other forms of person reference. That is, the text-critical variants can all be described as the result of category-triggering in the substitution/addition/omission of the person reference terms within scribal memory.

Although many text-critical variants include person reference terms, there have been few secondary studies of person reference in the Hebrew Bible and I am aware of none that use conversation analysis as the linguistic approach to the topic.[237] I will summarize below some selected studies that primarily concern person reference.

The close connection between proper nouns in the Bible and etymology is often noted. In his book *Biblical Names*, Moshe Garsiel studied what he labeled "Midrashic Name Derivations (MNDs)," which he defined as "interpretations of a midrashic (homiletic) nature applied to the name of people or of places on the basis of sound or semantic potential. Such an interpretation infuses a name with meaning in relation to past events, or looks forward to some future incidents."[238] His study begins with the assumption that the biblical author can be identified with a synchronic reading of MT. A more sophisticated study is *The Transformation of Biblical Proper Names* by Jože Krašovec, who analyzed the relationship between MT and the ancient translations, especially with regard to the different strategies of translation and transliteration of proper names and the relationship of these two strategies to the etymology of the names. He observed

---

237. Note that in her forthcoming review of conversation analysis as applied to the Hebrew Bible, Adina Moshavi does not discuss person reference. See Moshavi, "Conversation Analysis," in *Linguistics for Hebraists and Biblical Scholars*, ed. John A. Cook and Robert D. Holmstedt (University Park, PA: Eisenbrauns, forthcoming). In a recent essay, Frank Polak makes a passing reference to conversation analysis, but otherwise shows no influence in his study of person reference. See Polak, "Whodunit? Implicit Subject, Discourse Structure, and Pragmatics in the Hebrew and Greek Bibles," in *From Author to Copyist: Essays on the Composition, Redaction, and Transmission of the Hebrew Bible in Honor of Zipi Talshir*, ed. Cana Werman (Winona Lake, IN: Eisenbrauns, 2015), 227 n. 20.

238. Garsiel, *Biblical Names: A Literary Study of Midrashic Derivation and Puns* (Ramat Gan: Bar-Ilan University Press, 1991), 19.

that "well-known names are practically without variant"; however, "most rare names appear in numerous variant readings."[239]

In his study of "double and triple proper names," Frank Moore Cross applied observations from the Parry/Lord school to examples of "(1) multiple names of identical (or interchangeable) persons, tribes, or places in Greek epic; (2) multiple names of gods and places in Ugaritic epics; and finally, (3) multiple names, tribes, and places preserved in ... the Epic Source, the J and E strands of the Tetrateuch" in order to support his argument that the prose sources of the Tetrateuch have "their origin in old epic poetry, which stands as an ultimate source or sources behind the surviving prose documents."[240] Some of the examples he discussed from the Hebrew Bible (based exclusively on MT) include "Jacob"/"Israel," "Yahweh"/"Elohim," "El"/"Elyon"/"Shaddai," "Joshua"/"Hosea," and "Esau"/"Edom."[241] These examples provided him with evidence of "the survival of formulaic pairs in the prose documents that constitute the Tetrateuch."[242]

In his study of participant-reference shifts in Jeremiah, Oliver Glanz made the following initial observation based on a "first superficial reading": "On the one hand, the PNG (person, number, and gender) identity of a participant often shifts unexpectedly, on the other hand an identical PNG identity is used in order to refer to two different participants."[243] Based on both a synchronic analysis and diachronic analysis of the text,

---

239. Krašovec, *Transformation of Biblical Proper Names*, LHBOTS 418 (London: T&T Clark, 2010), 131.

240. Cross, "Telltale Remnants of Oral Epic in the Older Sources of the Tetrateuch: Double and Triple Proper Names in Early Hebrew Sources, and in Homeric and Ugaritic Epic Poetry," in *Exploring the Longue Durée: Essays in Honor of Lawrence E. Stager*, ed. J. David Schloen (Winona Lake, IN: Eisenbrauns, 2009), 83.

241. Cross, "Telltale Remnants of Oral Epic," 85–87. Note that according to Talmon's definition, all of these would be synonymous readings in cases of variants in the transmission history of the text.

242. Cross, "Telltale Remnants of Oral Epic," 87. I should point out that Cross is working with an early dichotomy that was often assumed in the Parry/Lord approach to oral traditions; that is, oral formulaic theory often assumed that epic poetry was necessary for the kind of oral composition imagined, so that this theory did not apply well to prose. This dichotomy (oral poetry versus written prose) is no longer accepted by scholars in the comparative study of oral tradition because of analogous formulaic structures in prose traditions (see examples 2.17 and 2.19 above), even though it continues to have some influence in biblical studies.

243. Glanz, *Understanding Participant-Reference Shifts in the Book of Jeremiah:*

he analyzed how participant-reference shifts have been interpreted in some of the standard commentaries on Jeremiah and he found two general approaches in the various translations in these commentaries with those that focused on diachronic methods generally assuming that these shifts denoted a change in author/redactor. He concluded that "participant-reference shifts do not disturb textual coherence and unity per se but even contribute to the readability of the text as the distribution of the diverse PNG shifts reflects the language competence and writing skills of the writer/redactor."[244] He therefore concluded that English translations should not smooth out the person, number, and gender shifts as is common practice, but rather should retain the shifts from the source text to the target language. Although he engaged in some text-critical analysis that was essential to his conclusions, his method is primarily a corpus linguistic approach using the Stuttgart Electronic Study Bible based on MT with his hermeneutical model coming explicitly from the influence of philosophical hermeneutics on Christian theology.

The study of person reference that most clearly anticipated some of my conclusions reached below is Rachelle Wenger's "Redundancy Is Information." She observed the following, which matches the notion of locally initial forms followed by locally subsequent forms, even though she makes no reference to works in conversation analysis:

> Biblical Hebrew is flexible in the ways it refers to participants who have already been introduced into a narrative. Person, gender, and number are shown by the form of the verb, and once a character is introduced, the thread of events in which that character is the subject can be carried forward by the verbs alone (e.g., Judg 15.4–5, 1 Kgs 18.31–34).... But sometimes when the referent of a verb is obvious, the author nevertheless goes to the trouble of referring to the participant with a full noun phrase—sometimes a complex one—repeating information the reader already knows.[245]

However, her approach to the text assumed that MT is the original text of the author, so that her results are really a statement about literary function

---

A Study of Exegetical Method and Its Consequences for the Interpretation of Referential Incoherence, SSN 60 (Leiden: Brill, 2013), 9.

244. Glanz, *Understanding Participant-Reference Shifts*, 345.

245. Wenger, "Redundancy Is Information: The Literary Function of Participant Reference in Biblical Hebrew Narrative," *BT* 63 (2012): 179.

in MT without noting that in some of her examples of the literary artistry of the author some of the details she focused on are lacking in other texts; for example, both MT Ruth 2:21 and MT Kgs 18:36 have a plus when compared to LXX—"Ruth **the Moabite**" and "Elijah **the prophet**"—both of which play an important role in her argument.[246] Thus, her following conclusion is problematic: "the redundant information is not random. It is deliberately reintroduced to shape the reader's attitudes and/or expectations concerning the character(s) involved."[247] Although I too would not describe the textual variants as random, I would also not assume all of them as "deliberately reintroduced." When we accept textual plurality and textual fluidity, such conclusions are clearly anachronistic. Unfortunately, all of the current secondary literature on person reference in the Hebrew Bible makes this methodological mistake, namely, assuming the priority of MT even when text-critical evidence is consulted.[248]

Below I will discuss selected examples of variants related to person reference. First, I will discuss a list of harmonizing additions from Tov's study of Exod 1–24. I will then analyze two passages that include more than one variant related to person reference: Jer 29:21 and 2 Sam 3:23–25. This selection of texts will allow me to discuss variants related to major characters (e.g., God, Moses, and David) as well as minor characters (e.g., Abner), demonstrating how variants related to person reference can occur for both major and minor characters within scribal memory in the context of textual fluidity.

Exodus 1–24

Example 2.59 includes various examples I have selected from Tov's article, "Textual Harmonization in Exodus 1–24." Because text-critical variants in Exod 1–24 occur so often, Tov was not exhaustive in his list of harmonizing variants, including those that pertain to person reference. For example, in his discussion of the example I have given below concerning the harmonizing addition of "Moses" as the explicit subject

---

246. On Ruth 2:21 and 1 Kgs 18:36, see Wenger, "Redunancy Is Information," 181.
247. Wenger, "Redunancy Is Information," 181.
248. Sometimes this methodological limitation is explicitly noted, e.g., Glanz is aware that most Jeremiah scholars argue that LXX Jeremiah represents an earlier version than MT Jeremiah (*Understanding Participant-Reference Shifts in the Book of Jeremiah*, 58).

2. Category-Triggering and Text-Critical Variants

of the verb from Exod 2:22, Tov wrote, "Similarly 4:13; 10:6; 11:8; 15:25; 16:23; 24:4" to alert his readers that in each of these cases LXX agrees against MT and SP in the harmonizing addition of "Moses" based on the near context.[249] As has been my practice above, the order of the variants given should not be interpreted as implying anything about my judgment concerning early and late variants. I also have given these selected examples in canonical order, rather than in the different subsets used by Tov.

Example 2.59[250]

Exod 2:3
MT: ותקח לו: and she took for him
SP: ותקח לו אמו: and **his mother** took for him

Exod 2:6
MT: ותחמל עליו: and she took pity on him
4QExod[b]: [ותחמו]ל עליו בת פרעה: and **the daughter of pharaoh** took pity on him

Exod 2:22
MT, SP: ויקרא: and he called
LXX: καὶ ἐπωνόμασεν Μωυςῆς = ויקרא משה: and **Moses** called

Exod 3:10, 11
MT: פרעה: Pharaoh
LXX: Φαραω βασιλέα Αἰγύπτου = פרעה מלך מצרים: Pharaoh, **king of Egypt**

Exod 3:18, 19
MT: מלך מצרים: king of Egypt
LXX: Φαραω βασιλέα Αἰγύπτου = פרעה מלך מצרים: **Pharaoh**, king of Egypt

---

249. Tov, "Textual Harmonization in Exodus 1–24," 11.
250. Tov, "Textual Harmonization in Exodus 1–24," 11–12, my translation, his retroversions.

Exod 3:18
MT: יהוה אלהינו: **the Lord**, our God
LXX: τῷ θεῷ ἡμῶν = אלהינו: our God

Exod 4:31b
MT: ויקדו: and they bowed
LXX: ὁ λαὸς προσεκύνησεν = ויקדו העם: and **the people** bowed

Exod 12.31
MT: יהוה: the Lord
LXX: κυρίῳ τῷ θεῷ ὑμῶν = יהוה אלהיכם: the Lord, **your God**

In each of these cases, what Tov identified as a harmonizing addition can be understood as either a comember term from the category of person reference terms for the character implied in the subject of the verb ("**his mother**," "**the daughter of pharaoh**," "**Moses**," "**the people**") or as an additional reference term for the character ("pharaoh, **king of Egypt**," "**pharaoh**, king of Egypt," "**the Lord**, our God," "the Lord, **our God**"). As discussed more thoroughly above, I do not share Tov's assumption that harmonization primarily occurs through additions. Furthermore, it seems to me that, even though some extant texts may suggest certain tendencies, individual scribes were most likely inconsistent in their practice of using person reference terms on the basis of scribal memory from the copying of one manuscript to another and different scribes may have had different general tendencies in ways that would at least complicate (if not eliminate) our ability to make such generalizations as assumed in principles like *lectio brevior potior*. Thus, each of these readings should be understood as synonymous readings related to person reference rather than harmonizing additions.

Jeremiah 29:21

Most Jeremiah scholars have concluded that the majority of variants between LXX Jeremiah and MT Jeremiah consist of additions of titles, proper names, adjectives, adverbs, divine names and epithets, and standard prophetic formula in the expansive MT.[251] Note that many of these

---

251. E.g., see Emanuel Tov, "Some Aspects of the Textual and Literary History of

types of variants concern person reference, including the identification of prophet, God, and addressee often found in prophetic superscripts. Thus, I could provide a similar list to what I have given above for Exod 1–24 for Jeremiah; however, I have chosen to focus on one verse that illustrates this well-known phenomenon, which contains five different variants related to person reference when MT and LXX are compared.

Example 2.60: Jer 29:21

MT

כה אמר יהוה צבאות אלהי ישראל אל אחאב בן קוליה ואל צדקיהו בן מעשיה הנבאים לכם בשמי שקר הנני נתן אתם ביד נבוכדראצר מלך בבל והכם לעיניכם

Thus says the LORD **of hosts, the God of Israel** concerning Ahab **son of Kolaiah** and Zedekiah **son of Maaseiah, who are prophesying to you in my name a lie**: Behold, I am giving them into the hand of **Nebuchadrezzar**, king of Babylon, and he shall kill them before your eyes.

LXX

οὕτως εἶπεν κύριος ἐπὶ Αχιαβ καὶ ἐπὶ Σεδεκιαν Ἰδοὺ ἐγὼ δίδωμι αὐτοὺς εἰς χεῖρας βασιλέως Βαβυλῶνος, καὶ πατάξει αὐτοὺς κατ' ὀφθαλμοὺς ὑμῶν.

Thus says the LORD concerning Ahab and Zedekiah: Behold, I am giving them into the hand of the king of Babylon, and he shall kill them before your eyes.

MT: יהוה צבאות אלהי ישראל: the LORD **of hosts, the God of Israel**
LXX: κύριος = יהוה: the LORD

---

the Book of Jeremiah," in *Le livre de Jérémie: Le prophéte et son milieu, les oracles et leur transmission* ed. Pierre-Maurice Bogaert, BETL 54 (Leuven: Leuven University Press, 1981), 145–67; Tov, "The Literary History of the Book of Jeremiah in the Light of Its Textual History," in Tigay, *Empirical Models for Biblical Criticism*, 211–39; William A. McKane, *A Critical and Exegetical Commentary on Jeremiah 1: Introduction and Commentary of Jeremiah I–XXV*, ICC (Edinburgh: T&T Clark, 1986), l–lxxxiii; Louis Stulman, *The Prose Sermons of the Book of Jeremiah*, SBLDS 83 (Atlanta: Scholars Press, 1986), 141. For my early discussion of these types of variants, see Person, "Ancient Israelite Scribe as Performer," 605–6.

MT: אחאב בן קוליה: Ahab **son of Kolaiah**
LXX: Αχιαβ = אחאב: Ahab

MT: צדקיהו בן מעשיה: Zedekiah **son of Maaseiah**
LXX: Σεδεκιαν = צדקיהו…‏ : Zedekiah

MT: הנבאים לכם בשמי שקר: **who are prophesying to you in my name a lie**
LXX: [lacking]

MT: נבוכדראצר מלך בבל: **Nebuchadrezzar**, king of Babylon
LXX: βασιλέως Βαβυλῶνος = מלך בבל: the king of Babylon

Before discussing each of these five variants, I should note the person reference terms that both MT and LXX have in common, all of which are pronouns. I have given the antecedents in brackets, all of which are possible substitutions for the (implied) pronouns as imagined variants: "*I* [the LORD] am giving," "am giving *them* [the people]," "*he* [Nebuchadrezzar] shall kill," "shall kill *them* [the people]," and "before *your eyes* [the people]." Of course, none of the extant texts has completely eliminated (implied) pronouns from the text and that should not be expected; however, even in my comparison of only two of the extant textual traditions (MT and LXX), at least half of the terms for person reference in this one verse have a variant in the other text.

If we assume with the scholarly consensus that each of these variants is the result of an addition in MT, maybe even a harmonizing addition to the near context as in Tov's analysis of similar variants in Exodus 1–24, *then* I can list them as follows with the closest possible source text (i.e., in both MT and LXX of Jeremiah) given in parentheses: "the LORD **of hosts, the God of Israel**" (MT Jer 33:12 // LXX Jer 40:12), "Ahab **son of Kolaiah**" (no possible source text in common), "Zedekiah **son of Maaseiah**" (possibly MT Jer 37:3 // LXX Jer 44:3, *if* we assume a confusion between "Zedekiah" the king and "Zephaniah son of Maaseiah" the prophet), "**who are prophesying to you in my name a lie**" (MT Jer 27:10 // LXX Jer 34:10), and "**Nebuchadrezzar**, king of Babylon" (MT Jer 27:6 // LXX Jer 34:6). However, it seems to me that harmonization is not a necessary explanation for these variants, especially if it implies the necessary influence of a particular source text. Rather, we can simply explain these variants as the result of category-triggering within scribal memory; that is, these variants (whether additions or omissions) reflect different tendencies related to the preferences of recognition and minimization in relationship to person reference, both of which could have occurred in the textual plurality allowed within scribal memory.

In some sense we may have two groups of variants in this list. Two of the variants, "the Lord **of hosts, the God of Israel**" and "**Nebuchadrezzar**, king of Babylon," can easily be explained as synonymous readings within scribal memory, because there is no doubt that the additional terms of person reference refer to the same individual. However, the other three may be grouped together with a *possible* interpretation that the earlier form of the prose oracle as given in the LXX concerns the kings Ahab (son of Omri) and Zedekiah (son of Josiah), both of whom are associated with the end of the kingdoms of Israel and Judah, respectively. *If* this is the case, *then* the additions in MT change the oracle to apply possibly to otherwise unknown (i.e., not in the extant texts) false prophets, "Ahab **son of Kolaiah** and Zedekiah **son of Maaseiah, who are prophesying to you in my name a lie**." However, even *if* we accept this interpretation identifying early and late forms of the oracle, it seems to me that scribal memory remains a likely explanation—in fact, an even more likely explanation, since there are no clear source texts for these variants, suggesting in some sense a faulty memory, especially *if* MT Jer 37:3 // LXX Jer 44:3 is the mental source text for the harmonizing addition of the patronymic for Zedekiah. Nevertheless, even in this case, I prefer to avoid the language of error, because the characteristic of multiformity that is found in traditional literature and underlies textual plurality and fluidity allows us to conclude that, in some sense, these prose oracles can be understood as synonymous. Because of multiformity, the ancients may not have regarded the identification of the specific leaders, whether kings or false prophets, as necessarily referring to the same individuals, because the category of leaders who did evil clearly included kings and their servants, including the false prophets.[252]

2 Samuel 3:23–25

In these three verses we have three primary characters—Joab, Abner, and David—and there are variants related to both David and Abner, variants that are nevertheless found within the broader passage (2 Sam 3:6–39).

---

252. See further my discussion of this same example in the next chapter concerning the sound-triggering that may be functioning in the patronym for Ahab (example 3.10).

Example 2.61: 2 Sam 3:23–25
MT

ויואב וכל הצבא אשר אתו באו ויגדו ליואב לאמר בא אבנר בן נר אל
המלך וישלחהו וילך בשלום ויבא יואב אל המלך ויאמר מה עשיתה הנה
בא אבנר אליך למה זה שלחתו וילך הלוך ידעת את אבנר בן נר כי לפתתך
בא ולדעת את מוצאך ואת מבואך ולדעת את כל אשר אתה עשה

[23]When Joab and all the army that was with him came, it was reported to Joab, "Abner son of Ner came to **the king**, and he has dismissed him, and he has gone away in peace." [24]Then Joab went to the king and said, "What have you done? Behold, **Abner** came to you; why did you dismiss him, so that he surely got away? [25]You know that **Abner son of Ner** came to deceive you, and to learn your comings and goings and to learn all that you do."

4Q51

בן נר אל דויד וישלחהו וילך [בשלום ויבוא יואב אל המלך ויאמר מה]
עשיתה הן בא אבנר אליך למה זה [שלחתו וילך הלוא ידעת את] אבנר כי
הלפתותך [בא ולדעת את מוצאך ואת מבואך דלעת את] כול אשר אתה
עושה [vacat]

[23]"son of Ner came to **David**, and he has dismissed him, and he has gone away [in peace." [24]Then Joab went to the king and said, "What] have you done? Behold, **Abner** came to you; why did you [dismiss him, so that he surely got away? [25]You know that] **Abner** [came] to deceive you, [and to learn your comings and goings and to learn] all that you do."

LXX[B]

καὶ Ιωαβ καὶ πᾶσα ἡ στρατιὰ αὐτοῦ ἤχθησαν, καὶ ἀπηγγέλη τῷ Ιωαβ λέγοντες "Ηκει Αβεννηρ υἱὸς Νηρ πρὸς Δαυιδ, καὶ ἀπέσταλκεν αὐτὸν καὶ ἀπῆλθεν ἐν εἰρήνῃ. καὶ εἰσῆλθεν Ιωαβ πρὸς τὸν βασιλέα καὶ εἶπεν Τί τοῦτο ἐποίησας; ἰδοὺ ἦλθεν Αβεννηρ πρὸς σέ, καὶ ἵνα τί ἐξαπέσταλκας αὐτὸν καὶ ἀπελήλυθεν ἐν εἰρήνῃ; ἢ οὐκ οἶδας τὴν κακίαν Αβεννηρ υἱοῦ Νηρ, ὅτι ἀπατῆσαί σε παρεγένετο καὶ γνῶναι τὴν ἔξοδόν σου καὶ τὴν εἴσοδόν σου καὶ γνῶναι ἅπαντα, ὅσα σὺ ποιεῖς;

[23]When Joab and all the army that was with him came, it was reported to Joab, "Abner son of Ner came to **David**, and he has dismissed him, and he has gone away in peace." [24]Then Joab went to the king and said, "What have you done? Behold, **Abner** came to

2. Category-Triggering and Text-Critical Variants 191

you; why did you dismiss him, so that he got away in peace? ²⁵Do you not know about the evil of **Abner son of Ner**, that he came to deceive you and to learn your goings and comings, all that you do?"

MT: המלך: "the king"
4Q51: דויד: "David"
LXX: Δαυιδ = דויד: "David"

MT: אבנר: "Abner"
4Q51: אבנר: "Abner"
LXX^B: Αβεννηρ = אבנר: "Abner"
LXX^L: Αβεννηρ υἱοῦ Νηρ = אבנר בן נר: "Abner son of Ner"

MT: אבנר בן נר: "Abner son of Ner"
4Q51: אבנר: "Abner"
LXX^B: Αβεννηρ υἱοῦ Νηρ = אבנר בן נר: "Abner son of Ner"

In contrast to example 2.60, all of these variants are most obviously cases of synonymous readings, in that in every case the variants related to the same character can be found in the nearby context of the passage. For the first variant in 3:23, both the MT reading of "the king" and the 4Q51 and LXX reading of "David" are found in MT and LXX (*vacats* in 4Q51), for example, "the king" in 3:24 and "David" in 3:22. For the second variant and third variants ("Abner" and "Abner son of Ner"), both MT and LXX have both readings within these same three verses, much less the larger passage. (4Q51 is so fragmentary that it is difficult to determine—for example, should we restore the beginning of the fragment as "Abner son of Ner"? The published critical edition justifiably does not, because "son of Ner" within the context of the broader passage could be a good reading.)[253] Here I have provided a variant within the Greek tradition itself: the LXX^L reading of "Abner son of Ner" (against MT, 4Q51, and LXX^B: "Abner"). With others, I suspect that this variant occurred in the transmission of the Greek text and does not reflect a different Hebrew *Vorlage*; however, even if that is the case, it demonstrates how category-triggering of terms

---

253. For an excellent discussion of problems related to reconstructions of manuscript *vacats*, see Martone, "Textual Plurality and Textual Reconstructions." Martone demonstrated that reconstructions generally assume the priority of MT in an uncritical way.

of person reference can occur throughout the composition/transmission process under the influence of scribal memory, including into the transmission process of the ancient translations. That is, category-triggering functions not only within the transmission process of the Hebrew, but during the translation process and within the transmission process of the ancient translations themselves; therefore, determining the Hebrew *Vorlage* of any apparent text-critical variant in the ancient translations is methodologically problematic.[254]

Variants and Person Reference: A Summary

As with other sections in this chapter, I argue that category-triggering helps us to explain text-critical variants, in this case those related to person reference. I think it is important to make an analytic distinction between categories of groups of people (based on gender, ethnicity, etc.) and recognitional categories that are related to historical/fictional characters; however, recognitional categories draw significantly from the other types of categories related to person reference. For example, "king" comes from a category for the royal house that would include comembers (king's servants, daughter of the king, queen, etc.) and can be used for different kings, such as "pharaoh" (Exod 3:10, 11, 18, 19) and "David" (2 Sam 3:23–25). Obviously, in such instances, "king" alone does not supply the necessary details for adequate recognition; therefore, the names of the kings are generally provided elsewhere in the nearby literary context with a notable exception of "pharaoh."

Conversation occurs in a much more sequential fashion than the reading of traditional literature requires. That is, in any talk-in-progress, the sequence of turns is not yet decided and each speaker is producing their turns at talk within the ongoing context of the conversation. In contrast, the transmission of traditional literature like the Hebrew Bible occurs in communities in which not only the scribes copying a manuscript knew the literary text as preserved in scribal memory (and to some degree in the *Vorlage* before them), but the scribes' audience (readers and/or hearers of the new manuscripts) also may have known the literary text as preserved in scribal memory. Therefore, the sequential character of conversation is

---

254. See similarly, John Screnock, "A New Approach to Using the Old Greek in Hebrew Bible Textual Criticism," *Textus* 27 (2018): 229–57.

not as strong in traditional literature. Furthermore, it is highly unlikely that every reading of a book would begin at the beginning of the manuscript, thereby creating different locally initial readings based on where the scribe began to read. In the terminology of conversation analysis, the distinctions between locally initial and subsequent locations and between locally initial and subsequent forms become less important. Familiarity with the literary text makes recognition of the biblical characters easier to achieve. Nevertheless, a certain degree of what in conversation are locally initial forms (most importantly, personal names) is necessary for the social function of the traditional literature in defining the community and its identity in relationship to its traditional literature, especially in the education of children into the community. Therefore, even though recognition may be achieved more easily for those most familiar with the literature (competent adults), the educational purpose of traditional literature for the purpose of socialization suggests that a minimal approach to all person references may prove problematic. At least based on the observation that person reference in the Hebrew Bible is often a location for variation between the extant manuscript traditions, it seems that textual plurality and textual fluidity in scribal performance allows for significant variation in the copying of manuscripts with regard to person reference. Although recognition may be easier to achieve and there is in some sense no locally initial location, the exclusive use of the most minimal forms (typically locally subsequent forms, such as pronouns) would undercut recognition, especially for those in the community who are the most unfamiliar with the texts, that is, those whose epistemic status with regard to the literature is among the lowest. Therefore, the locally initial forms can appear in various locations within the literature, so that what we perceive as additions/omissions can occur in relationship to a certain percentage of person reference terms within a given passage. Individual scribes may have differing tendencies related to the selection of person reference terms based on their assumptions concerning their audiences' epistemic status and therefore their epistemic stance in relationship to the perceived epistemic status of their audience. Some scribes may assume a high epistemic status for their audience and therefore be more prone to minimize/omit the more explicit terms of person reference. Some scribes may assume a low epistemic status for their audience and therefore be more prone to add terms of person reference to facilitate better recognition. Of course, the same scribe may make one assumption for one audience when copying one text and another assumption for the same or another audience when copying another text.

Because of what seem to be competing/conflicting tendencies based on the preferences for recognition and minimalization in the text-critical evidence, I think that it is probably best to assume that variants related to person reference are understood as synonymous readings. For example, "pharaoh," "king of Egypt," and "pharaoh, king of Egypt" (Exod 3:10, 11, 18, 19) are synonymous readings and as such should all be treated as original and authentic, at least on methodological grounds. That is, although I do not discount that scribes sometimes made changes to the text on ideological bases, I think that too often biblical scholars assume that that is the case, based on a presumed original text with later ideological changes. Once we accept textual plurality and textual fluidity in the context of scribal performance under the influence of scribal memory, we have little (if any) methodological basis to distinguish early from late readings, especially when all of the extant variants can be understood as comembers of a recognitional category for a specific individual.

If this is the case, then future studies of person reference of the Hebrew Bible for the purpose of understanding the composition/transmission process of the literary texts can no longer be based exclusively on MT, but must take into account at least some limited text-critical evidence so that the conclusions reached reflect somewhat the textual plurality found in the extant manuscript traditions studied. My analysis confirms with Glanz that shifts in person reference do not necessarily inhibit literary unity and therefore do not coincide with the identification of sources and/or redactional layers. My analysis also cautions us from making the sharp distinction between random and deliberate that Wenger made in her study. At first glance, the text-critical evidence may suggest randomness to some or to others a trend toward expansion with a linear movement from short to longer texts. Upon closer reflection, such generalizations themselves are problematic. Moreover, although I do not rule out deliberate and intentional changes during the transmission process, I think that too often we assign such motivations to scribes who are simply operating within the boundaries allowed in connection with multiformity and textual plurality. Furthermore, the practices of person reference as identified by conversation analysis are not described well by limiting ourselves to random or deliberate. These practices are actually systematic, even though few of us are conscious of these principles and therefore we cannot use them deliberately, if that term implies some form of conscious intentionality. Thus, although I am confident that the change from everyday conversation to the copying of manuscripts of traditional literature led to significant adaptations of the principles of recognition and minimalization, I nevertheless suspect that they remain present in the transmission process in ways that affect the influence of scribal memory in *Vorlage*-based copying. At least it seems to me that the text-critical evidence strongly suggests that this is the case.

Category-Triggering and Variants: A Summary

In my application of Jefferson's poetics to text-critical variants, I began with category-triggering, because it most easily corresponds with a well-accepted category in text-critical studies, what Talmon labeled as "synonymous readings." Talmon observed that some text-critical variants reflect the same cognitive-linguistic phenomenon that is a characteristic of Hebrew poetry—synonymous parallelism—so he coined the term "synonymous reading" to describe this type of variant. That is, both Hebrew poets when composing a text and scribes when copying a text draw, in the words of conversation analysis, from a category of comembers, thereby respectively producing synonymous parallelism and synonymous readings. Thus, Talmon concluded, "the diverse practitioners involved in the process, viz., authors, redactors, and scribes, employed the same or similar literary tenets and techniques."[255]

When we take Talmon's conclusions seriously and combine them with Jefferson's category-triggering, we can broaden Talmon's observations to other types of text-critical variants that also involve the selection of comembers from the same category. That is, the one thing that ties together "authors, redactors, and scribes" is that they were using linguistic practices across the various acts within the composition/transmission process (both oral and written) that are the same linguistic practices that they used in their everyday conversations, practices that appear to be linguistically universal. This initial observation of combining Talmon's and Jefferson's insights demanded a broader reassessment of text-critical variants, which was the topic of the rest of the chapter by analyzing variants in lists, harmonizations, and variants concerning person reference.

As observed in conversation analysis, list-construction requires adequate representativity in its selection of items to establish the category that the list itself represents; that is, lists are a series of comembers of the same

---

255. Talmon, *Text and Canon*, 83.

category that represent the category as a whole, even when only two or three of the many comembers are actually listed. When we apply this insight to variants that occur within lists in the Hebrew Bible, we find that those variants related to the items in the list itself are often comembers of the same category, at least from the perspective of the tradents that preserved that specific version of the list. If the list establishes the relevant category, then variation of the specific items in the list, all of which are comembers of the category, does not distract at all from the cognitive-linguistic function of the list; that is, the same list can have different comember items, because both versions of the list nevertheless represent the same category of comembers in that the given items have adequate representativity for that category. Therefore, different versions of the same list can be understood as synonymous readings or synonymous lists.

When we understand that larger units of meaning, such as lists, can be synonymous readings, then we need to reevaluate what we mean by the category of text-critical variants understood as harmonization. The definition of harmonization assumes that a scribe consciously or unconsciously changed the wording in one passage to reflect the wording in another passage, often a closely related or parallel passage in the same book or a different book. The definition assumes that the scribes understood that the two passages are different and somehow have their own literary integrity and furthermore that the change in wording improves the harmonized passage by moving the two passages into closer verbal agreement. That is, the standard seems to be that the same wording is an improvement in harmonizing the two different texts. However, Tov insists that, even though some textual traditions appear to have more harmonizing tendencies (in his opinion, especially SP and LXX), there nevertheless seems to be no systematic effort to harmonize the texts. For example, although there are some harmonizing variants present between the two forms of the Ten Commandments, none of the manuscripts systematically try to harmonize the two versions; rather, the harmonizing variants occur more haphazardly. Thus, even though Tov does not use the term "scribal memory," his description seems to support its use when discussing harmonization, since this haphazard character of harmonization suggests that scribes did not typically have more than one *Vorlage* physically before them, but must have depended on their memory of the parallel passages.

Despite the careful definition of harmonization that is widely accepted, it seems to me that harmonizing variants are only labeled as such because we have the similar or parallel passage in the extant texts. Without that similar or parallel passage I strongly suspect that harmonizing variants (with the possible exception of especially long additions) would be classified simply as synonymous readings. To continue with the example of the Ten Commandments: although there is an Exodus version and a Deuteronomy version, it is quite possible that the ancients mostly understood these two versions as synonymous readings. Since scribes may have been fairly conservative when copying one of the books so that they copied the version found in that specific book in the *Vorlage* before them, they did not attempt to systematize the two versions into one. Occasionally, the memory of the other version may have asserted itself in the process of copying, so that some of the wording of that other version influenced the copying of a *Vorlage* before the scribe, but that is because in some sense the scribe did not change anything, even though the new manuscript may now differ somewhat from the *Vorlage* from our modern perspective. Nevertheless, both versions are synonymous readings of the Ten Commandments, so that substituting the wording from one to another does not create a different text, but simply provides a variant of the same text within textual plurality.

Also according to conversation analysis, an initial person reference requires sufficient information so that the speaker's audience can recognize to whom the speaker is referring. The speaker chooses from a category of terms that are associated with that specific person, including proper name, title, gender, familial relationship, and the rest, in a way that is both economical (that is, preferring minimalization) but sufficient for recognition. When this insight is applied to text-critical variants concerning person reference in the Hebrew Bible, we can see that (at least in many cases) the variants simply draw from the same category of person reference terms for that specific biblical character. For example, in 2 Sam 3:23–25 (example 2.61) the same character can be referred to as "David," "the king," and "he," all of which in the literary context clearly refer to the category of person reference terms (among others) for David, the king of Judah and Israel. Thus, in this particular literary context any variant readings related to person references for David can be understood as synonymous readings, because they all are comembers of this same recognitional category.

In sum, this chapter has analyzed four types of text-critical variants—synonymous readings, variants within lists, harmonizations, and variants related to person reference—all of which can be understood from the perspective of conversation analysis as comembers of the same category. As such, all of these variants can be understood as synonymous readings.

Although this greatly expands upon Talmon's initial definition of synonymous readings, it seems to me that the cognitive-linguistic practices behind these four types is the same: the category-triggering of comembers. This cognitive-linguistic practice influences scribal memory, so that, when scribes copy manuscripts physically before them, the new manuscripts that they produce may contain synonymous readings of any of these four types. This is due to the fact that scribal memory includes not only the physical representation of the literary text at hand but also a scribe's memory of every manuscript of that same literary text that the scribe has read, has heard read aloud, or has heard otherwise recited or quoted, including what we might regard as a different literary text but that the ancients considered to be the same literary text. Therefore, methodologically we must accept that much of what we perceive to be a variant may not have been understood as a variant in the world of the ancient scribes who composed and transmitted the traditional literature of the Hebrew Bible.

3
Sound-Triggering and Text-Critical Variants

The observation that writing represents sound has a very long history and the history of biblical scholarship includes various works in which sound-patterning is the focus. For example, in his 1893 article entitled "Paronomasia in the Old Testament," Immanuel Casanowicz cataloged 502 cases of paronomasia, which he understood as "the union of similarity of sound with dissimilarity of sense."[1] Even though many have criticized how broad his definition is, Casanowicz's study remains an important resource for discussions of sound-patterning.[2]

---

1. Casanowizc, "Paronomasia in the Old Testament," *JBL* 12 (1893): 106.

2. For an example of an excellent critique of Casanowicz, see Valérie Kabergs and Hans Ausloos, "Paronomasia or Wordplay? A Babel-Like Confusion: Towards a Definition of Hebrew Wordplay," *Bib* 93 (2012): 1–20. In addition to secondary works cited throughout the rest of the chapter, see the following: On alliteration: Scott B. Noegel and Gary A. Rendsburg, *Solomon's Vineyard: Literary and Linguistic Studies in the Song of Songs*, AIL 1 (Atlanta: Society of Biblical Literature, 2009); Urmas Nõmmik, "The Idea of Ancient Hebrew Verse," *ZAW* 124 (2012): 400–408; Jonathan Yogev and Shamir Yona, "Opening Alliteration in Biblical and Ugaritic Poetry," *ZAW* 127 (2015): 108–13. On wordplay: Noegel, ed., *Puns and Pundits: Word Play in the Hebrew Bible and Ancient Near Eastern Literature* (Bethesda, MD: CDL, 2000); Noegel, *Janus Parallelism in the Book of Job*, JSOTSup 223 (Sheffield: Sheffield Academic, 1996); Al Wolters, "ṢÔPIYYÂ (Prov 31:27) as Hymnic Participle and Play on Sophia," *JBL* 104 (1985): 577–87; William L. Holladay, "Form and Word-Play in David's Lament over Saul and Jonathan," *VT* 20 (1970): 153–89; Anthony R. Ceresko, "The Function of *Antanaclasis* (*mṣʾ* 'to find' // *mṣʾ* 'to reach, overtake, grasp') in Hebrew Poetry, Especially in the Book of Qoheleth," *CBQ* 44 (1982): 551–69; David R. Blumenthal, "A Play on Words in the Nineteenth Chapter of Job," *VT* 16 (1966): 497–501; Karolien Vermeulen, "To See or Not To See: The Polysemy of the Word עין in the Isaac Narratives (Gen 17–35)," *JHS* 9 (2009), https://doi.org/10.5508/jhs.2009.v9.a22; Jack M. Sasson, "Word-Play in Gen 6:8–9," *CBQ* 37 (1975): 165–66; Aaron D. Rubin, "Genesis 49:4 in Light of Arabic and Modern South Arabian," *VT* 59 (2009): 499–502; Emanuel Tov, "Loan-Words,

Unfortunately, the history of interpretation concerning sound-patterning shows that this literary phenomenon has been mostly divorced from text-critical studies. On the one hand, most literary studies of sound in the Hebrew Bible operate on the basis of the MT-priority paradigm and assume that the authors/redactors/poets intentionally produced the sound-patterns during the compositional process of the original text. In these literary studies MT is often assumed to be the best text produced by authors with the variants found in the other textual traditions representing the later transmission of the corrupted text by copyists. For example, Gary Rendsburg wrote, "For almost always this proto-Masoretic text … reflects an older linguistic layer of Hebrew, a more conservative orthography (that is, spelling), and a more complex and sophisticated literary style."[3] On the other hand, many text-critical studies pay too little attention to the sound-patterns in the text. In short, the traditional division between lower and higher criticism continues to distort our understanding of sound-patterning in the composition/transmission process. The examples of sound-patterns I discuss below sometimes come from studies that are exceptions to these general observations, but most of the time they illustrate this methodological problem based on the MT-priority paradigm.

As noted in chapter 1, Jefferson's sound-triggering included what literary scholars would understand as alliteration and wordplay. Here I

Homophony and Transliterations in the Septuagint," *Bib* 60 (1979): 216–36; Aron Dotan, "Homonymous Hapax Doublets in the Masora," *Textus* 14 (1988): 131–45; Shalom Paul, "Polysensuous Polyvalency in Poetic Parallelism," in Fishbane and Tov, *Sha'arei Talmon*, 147–63; Paul, "Polysemous Pivotal Punctuation: More Janus Double Entendres," in *Texts, Temples, and Traditions: A Tribute to Menahem Haran*, ed. Michael V. Fox et al. (Winona Lake, IN: Eisenbrauns, 1996), 369–74. On soundscape and sound-patterning: Rhiannon Graybill, "'Hear and Give Ear': The Soundscape of Jeremiah," *JSOT* 40 (2016): 467–90; Aloysius Fitzgerald, "The Interchange of L, N, and R in Biblical Hebrew," *JBL* 97 (1978): 481–88; Aaron Schart, "Totenstille und Endknall: Ein Beitrag zur Analyse der Soundscape des Zwölfprophetenbuches," in *Sprachen—Bilder—Klänge: Dimensionen der Theologies im Alten Testament und in seinem Umfeld: Festschrift für Rüdiger Bartelmus zum seinem 65. Geburtstag*, ed. Christiane Karrer-Grube et al., AOAT 359 (Münster: Ugarit-Verlag, 2009), 257–74. New Testament studies has had much less interest in sound than Hebrew Bible studies (probably because of the relative lack of poetry); however, see the most recent contribution of "sound-mapping" in Margaret E. Lee, ed. *Sound Matters: New Testament Studies in Sound Mapping*, Biblical Performance Criticism 16 (Eugene, OR: Cascade, 2018).

3. Gary A. Rendsburg, *How the Bible Is Written* (Peabody, MA: Hendrickson, 2019), 5.

provide a few more examples as a way of reminding my readers of this phenomenon that occurs in everyday conversation. The first example concerns alliteration in what Jefferson understands as a "gist-preserving error." Jefferson described this case from election coverage on TV as follows: "someone is attempting to quote a bon mot, a catch-phrase, and gets it wrong.... What's said is wrong, but catches a great deal of the correct item. In this case, the wrong item captures not only the sense of the correct item but its alliteration."[4]

Example 3.1[5]

> McGee: What was it he [s]aid? [S]omething about [s]ubstituting [s]ideburns for [s]ense?
> Delegate: Beards for brains.
> McGee: Beards for brains. Right.

Jefferson noted that the incorrect quotation—"sideburns for sense"—follows an s-alliterative pattern in "said? Something about substituting." That is, McGee is obviously searching for the correct words and the incorrect quotation has certain elements closely connected to the correct quotation—"beards for brains"—including an alliterative pattern (with different consonants) as well as category-triggering between "sideburns"/"beards" and "sense"/"brains." Thus, this is a gist-preserving error that betrays how word selection works cognitively and linguistically, including sound-triggering (and category-triggering) as a gross-selection mechanism. The next set of examples illustrates what Jefferson called "co-class puns," what in this chapter we are referring to as wordplay. This is a set of eleven examples from American football broadcasts that specifically refer to the proper names of the players:

Example 3.2[6]

> (a) Bill [Knox] [knocked] the ball loose ...
> (b) Kenny [Stabler] has really [stabilized] the club.
> (c) [Chester] Markol [checks] in ...

---

4. Jefferson, "On the Poetics of Ordinary Talk," 14.
5. Jefferson, "On the Poetics of Ordinary Talk," 17.
6. Jefferson, "On the Poetics of Ordinary Talk," 19.

(d) And [Eischeid] has really been [shining] here in the second half.
(e) A nineteen yard touchdown run by Gregg [Pruitt]. So the Browns are really [proving] tough today.
(f) Willie [Lanier] [nearly] took his head off!
(g) And we have Lawrence [McCutcheon], a [clutch] runner.
(h) Jim Le[Clair] had a good [clear] shot at Franco.
(i) Plunkett may make a [last] ditch attempt throwing to Jim [Lash].
(j) [Norm Stead] throwing to his favorite receiver who has [enormous speed] potential.
(k) [Fore]man is stopped at the [for]ty, thirty yard line.

I agree with Jefferson that this list is pretty self-explanatory concerning the sound-selection of words.

Above I have selected these specific examples of sound-triggering from Jefferson, because below I will discuss examples of alliteration and then wordplay, with the first examples of wordplay related to person reference. As in Jefferson's article and in literary studies in general, alliteration refers to the repetition of the same or similar consonantal sounds. For wordplay I will borrow the definition of Valérie Kabergs and Hans Ausloos: "wordplay is defined as a specific play and a reciprocal interaction between sound patterns brought up by the variation in morphological structures, on the one hand, and meaning—defined by the use of a word in a specific literary context—on the other."[7] In most of our examples of wordplay, alliteration will also be present as the sound-triggering connection between the two (or more) words, something quite similar to Jefferson's examples from football broadcasts. Thus, I hope to show the obvious connection between Jefferson's identification of sound-triggering in ordinary talk and the sound-patterns of alliteration and wordplay in the composition/transmission process of the Hebrew Bible.

This chapter emphasizes alliteration and wordplay (mostly with alliterating sound-patterns) and contains little discussion of other forms of sound-patterns (e.g., assonance, rhyme, rhythm) in the Hebrew texts. This decision on my part is simply practical and should not in any way be considered as a statement that other forms of sound-patterning did not exist in the composition/transmission of the Hebrew texts and/or are no longer evident in the texts. I had to make some decisions on how

---

7. Kabergs and Ausloos, "Paronomasia or Wordplay?," 11–12.

to limit my discussion and these decisions were driven primarily by the available secondary literature. Of course, the dominance of studies in alliteration with few concerning assonance and other sound-patterns should not come as a surprise, since we are dealing with a consonant-only alphabet. However, I strongly suspect that, in the spoken forms of Biblical Hebrew, these other forms of sound-patterning would have been more prominent than the written record can easily suggest. This should be another reminder of how little we really can know about the spoken Hebrew in antiquity and even the sounds that the Hebrew Bible itself represents. Nevertheless, I think we have enough evidence to make some safe generalizations about the composition/transmission process, including how both authors and copyists, or better simply all scribes, could have been influenced in their composition/transmission of the Hebrew texts by sound-triggering as a gross-selection mechanism for word selection.

Alliteration

Although most studies of alliteration in the Hebrew Bible ignore the text-critical evidence, I have found the following examples in which the alliterative patterns are present in both the MT and at least one other textual witness. Thus, the assumptions generally made concerning the author of the original text as the source for the alliteration (most often assumed to be the MT) are demonstrated to be inaccurate, at least methodologically. Both authors and copyists can be influenced by the sound-pattern(s) in the text, so that these variants can arise at various times in the composition/transmission process. Below I will briefly discuss five examples in which the alliteration is in the Hebrew text itself (Prov 15:32; Amos 6:4–7; Isa 48:7; 48:9–11; 47:1) and two additional examples in which the Greek translators used alliteration in their translations to preserve something of the alliterative pattern in the Hebrew *Vorlage* (Isa 33:20; Prov 26:17). We will see that both the presumed original reading and the implied later reading (no matter which one we choose as which) can both be influenced by the same sound-triggering.

Example 3.3: Prov 15:32[8]

MT

פורע מוסר מואס נפשו ושומע תוכחת קונה לב
He who ignores instruction despises himself,
But he who **hears** admonition gains understanding.

LXX

ὃς ἀπωθεῖται παιδείαν, μισεῖ ἑαυτόν·
ὁ δὲ τηρῶν ἐλέγχους ἀγαπᾷ ψυχὴν αὐτοῦ.
פורע מוסר מואס נפשו ושומר תוכחת קונה לב
He who ignores instruction despises himself,
But he who **heeds** admonition gains understanding.

Although most commentators prefer the MT reading, Fox concluded as follows: "In this context, שומר and שומע are pragmatic synonyms and there is no basis for preferring one to the other."[9] He also noted that ר and ע are "similar in some varieties of the archaic script" and noted other examples of ר-ע substitutions (Prov 3:10; 6:16; 15:4; 19:27 and possibly 8:3).[10] Overall, Fox concluded, "Often both the M[T] and G[reek] forms differ considerably but make equal good sense. We can accept both as variant proverbs, without determination of priority" and this appears to be one such example.[11]

In *Biblical Sound and Sense*, Thomas McCreesh provided excellent discussions of examples of sound patterning in Prov 10–29, including a discussion of this proverb. However, since his analysis was based exclusively on MT, he apparently was unaware that his sound analysis of 15:32 is equally valid for both the MT and LXX versions of this proverb. Noting the fourfold repetition of the participles, McCreesh noted five sound-patterns: (1) the assonance of *ô* and *e* in both colons, (2) the alliteration of פ, מ, and ס/שׁ in the first colon, (3) the connection of the שׁ-syllable at the end of the first colon and the beginning of the second colon, (4) the alliteration/assonance of the syllables קׁ and כֹ in the second colon, and (5) the alliteration/assonance between פּוֹרֵעַ and שׁוֹמֵעַ, the first words in

---

8. Fox, *Proverbs*, 244.
9. Fox, *Proverbs*, 244.
10. Fox, *Proverbs*, 134.
11. Fox, *Proverbs*, 59.

both cola (the vowels in all three syllables and the final ע).[12] Fox's conclusion is at most only slightly affected by McCreesh's analysis—that is, the ע-alliteration between פּוֹרֵעַ and שׁוֹמֵעַ disappears in the possible LXX-*Vorlage*; however, it is replaced by a ר-alliteration between פּוֹרֵעַ and שׁוֹמֵר. In other words, in my opinion, these are not only equal proverbs (following Fox) but equal proverbs that share to a high degree their poetic structure of sound-patterning (adapting McCreesh). Thus, if we were to insist on one being the original and the other being later, we would also have to recognize that the later scribe produced a variant that had virtually no affect on the poetic sound-patterning—that is, both the original and the variant were possibly produced under the influence of the same sound-triggering mechanisms. However, a better interpretation would be to insist that they are equal proverbs, both of which are influenced by the same sound-triggering combination of alliteration and assonance.

Example 3.4: Amos 6:4–7[13]

MT

השכבים על מטות שן וסרחים על ערשותם
ואכלים כרים מצאן ועגלים מתוך מרבק
הפרטים על פי הנבל
כדויד חשבו להם כלי שיר
השתים במזרקי יין וראשית שמנים ימשחו
ולא נחלו על שבר יוסף
לכן עתה יגלו בראש גלים
וסר מרזח סרוחים

Alas for those who lie on beds of ivory, and lounge on their couches,
and eat lambs from the flock, and calves from the stall;
who sing idle songs to the sound of the harp,
and like David improvise on instruments of music;
who drink wine from bowls and anoint themselves with the finest oils.
But are not grieved over the ruin of Joseph!

---

12. Thomas P. McCreesh, *Biblical Sound and Sense: Poetic Patterns in Proverbs 10–29*, JSOTSup 128 (Sheffield: Sheffield Academic, 1991), 95–96.

13. Retroversion of LXX taken from Casanowicz, "Paronomasia in the Old Testament," 146 (no. 279).

Therefore they shall now be the first to go into exile,
And the revelry of the loungers shall pass away.

MT

וסר מרזח סרוחים

the revelry of the loungers shall pass away

LXX

καὶ ἐξαρθήσεται χρεμετισμὸς ἵππων
וסר מסחר סוסים =
the neighing of the horses shall pass away

Although I have given the full passage in the MT, I am interested here only in the last poetic line, so I have not provided the full passage in the LXX; however, the analysis of this last line requires reference to previous verses. The MT phrase וסר מרזח סרוחים is widely recognized as a case of alliteration. Shalom Paul noted the "alliterative hissing effect of the sibilants" and "the twofold repetition of the two letters סר."[14] Göran Eidevall described it as "an elegant combination of alliteration (*sār, sĕrûḥîm*) and assonance (*mirzaḥ, sĕrûḥîm*)."[15] Hans Walter Wolff translated the phrase as "und fertig ist das Fest der Fläzenden" [in the English translation of Wolff: "and suppressed is the spree of the sprawlers"] "to reflect the alliteration of the three Hebrew words."[16] When we look at this phrase in the context of Amos 6:4–7, we should note the repetition of ס, ר, ח, and מ throughout the passage, which reaches its fullest expression in the last poetic line of the Hebrew. What is often not noted, despite Casanowicz's observation, is that וסר מסחר סוסים of the possible LXX-*Vorlage* also includes the alliteration of the same consonants.[17] In fact, the Greek of the LXX is often understood as a misreading of the Hebrew text, whether

---

14. Paul, *Amos: A Commentary on the Book of Amos*, Hermeneia (Minneapolis: Fortress, 1991), 210.

15. Eidevall, *Amos: A New Translation with Introduction and Commentary*, AB (New Haven: Yale University Press, 2017), 181.

16. Wolff, *Dodekapropheten: Joel–Amos*, BKAT 14.2 (Neukirchen-Vluyn: Neukirchener Verlag, 1963), 314; Wolff, *Joel and Amos: A Commentary on the Books of the Prophets Joel and Amos*, Hermeneia (Philadelphia: Fortress, 1977), 273.

17. Casanowicz, "Paronomasia in the Old Testament," 146 (#279).

due to a damaged *Vorlage* or to the translator's difficulty with the Hebrew.[18] Although the two variants clearly have different meanings at the lexical level, I maintain that they both fit within their literary context, not only in terms of the alliteration but also in terms of how they relate to the passage. Even *if* the Greek can be demonstrated as a misreading (which I doubt), the source of the misreading was not only the Hebrew word that was misread, because the larger literary context contributed through scribal memory to the misreading. However, I prefer to avoid the language of "misreading" here, because of its presumption of an original text. Rather, the broader literary context within scribal memory allows for textual plurality. The MT reading repeats סרוחים ("those that lounge") from 6:4 (translated in LXX as κατασπαταλῶντες ἐπὶ ταῖς στρωμναῖς αὐτῶν; "and live lewdly on their couches" NETS; with s- and r-sounds reoccurring in the Greek [σ, ρ] possibly triggered by the repetition of סר in the Hebrew) as those who will experience the punishment of exile. The reading of LXX here continues the categorical references to livestock found in 6:4 ("lambs" and "calves"), all of which imply wealth. Moreover, the reference to "horses" probably also connects with the reference to the destruction of the Northern Kingdom of Israel in 6:6 ("the ruin of Joseph"), since horses are associated with military campaigns rather than livestock for food. That is, while the Northern Kingdom was being destroyed by the Assyrians, the wealthy Judahites simply enjoyed their luxurious lifestyle (including lounging around and eating a lot of meat) and did not mount their horses to help the north; however, they will soon find themselves in the same fate, being "the first to go into exile" (6:7a) after a serious military defeat that is symbolized by their (dead or stolen?) horses no longer neighing. Thus, it seems to me that both of these readings fit into their literary context, including the alliterative pattern of Amos 6:4–7, so that both should be understood as authentic or original.

---

18. E.g., see Anthony Gelston, "Some Hebrew Misreadings in the Septuagint of Amos," *VT* 52 (2002): 494–96; Gelston, *Twelve Minor Prophets*, BHQ 13 (Stuttgart: Deutsche Bibelgesellschaft, 2010), 85; W. Edward Glenny, "Hebrew Misreadings or Free Translation in the Septuagint of Amos?," *VT* 57 (2007): 540–41; Glenny, *Finding Meaning in the Text: Translation Technique and Theology in the Septuagint of Amos*, VTSup 126 (Leiden: Brill, 2009), 90–91.

Example 3.5: Isa 48:7[19]

MT

עתה נבראו ולא מאז ולפני יום ולא שמעתם פן תאמר הנה ידעתין
Now they are created, not long ago;
before today you have never heard of them,
so that you could not say, "I already knew **them (fem. pl.)**"

1QIsa[a]

עתה נבראו ולוא מאז ולפני יום ולוא שמעתים פן תואמר הנה ידעתים
Now they are created, not long ago;
before today you have never heard of them,
so that you could not say, "I already knew **them (masc. pl.)**"

The change in the MT of the third-person masculine plural suffix in 7b (שמעתם) to the third-person feminine plural suffix in 7c (ידעתין) often receives comment. One explanation for this grammatical abnormality is based on alliteration.[20] Lawrence Boadt wrote:

> The poet changes the object of *šěma'tām* from the masculine plural to the feminine plural with the following verbs *yěda'tîn*, even though both have the same referent. The reason is alliterative. The second colon has a triple *mem* pattern while the third emphasizes the strong *nun* pattern in *pen* and *hinnēh* by the change of suffix on *yāda'* to *în*.[21]

This quotation comes from Boadt's article "Intentional Alliteration in Second Isaiah," in which he gave "sixteen examples of alliterative lines which attempt to show that the technique is indeed purposely chosen, for all the

---

19. The reading for 1QIsa[a] is taken from Ulrich, *Biblical Qumran Scrolls*, 425.
20. Another possible explanation for what appears to be grammatical incongruence in the MT related to number or gender is that they are colloquial forms. See Gary A. Rendsburg, *Diglossia in Ancient Hebrew*, AOS 72 (New Haven: American Oriental Society, 1990), 69–83. Yet another possible explanation is the possibility that final-*mem* and final-*nun* were pronounced very similarly in the Second Temple period. For a discussion of this possibility, see Ian Young, Robert Rezetko, and Martin Ehrensvärd, *Linguistic Dating of Biblical Texts*, 2 vols. (London: Equinox, 2008), 1:226–27.
21. Lawrence Boadt, "Intentional Alliteration in Second Isaiah," *CBQ* 45 (1983): 361. Note that in this example I followed Boadt's analysis of the poetic structure/line rather than that of BHS.

cases involve something unusual done with words—in grammar, morphology, or arrangement—in order to achieve an alliterative effect."[22] Here we see that Boadt's argument for this change refers to the poet, presumably the author of the original text. That is, he is assuming the priority of the MT (he does not even mention the variant in 1QIsa[a]) and then explains this oddity. However, an argument based on alliteration can be made for a change in either direction. If we assume the priority of MT as Boadt does, then the author's grammatical change can be explained in terms of "the strong *nun* pattern" with the later reading in 1QIsa[a] being explained in terms of the "triple *mem* pattern." If we assume the priority of 1QIsa[a], then the author built upon the "triple *mem* pattern" with the later reading of the MT being explained in terms of the "strong *nun* pattern." However, the best approach may be not to assume the priority of either and regard both readings as synonymous, since both fit within their alliterative literary context. Furthermore, authorial intention is not necessary to understand either variant in terms of alliteration on the basis of sound-triggering.

Example 3.6: Isa 48:9–11[23]

MT

למען שמי אאריך אפי ותהלתי אחטם לך לבלתי הכריתך
הנה צרפתיך ולא בכסף
בחרתיך בכור עני
למעני למעני אעשה כי איך יחל
וכבודי לאחר לא אתן

For the sake of my name I defer my anger,
of my praise I restrain it for you,
so that I may not cut you off.
Behold, I have refined you, but not like silver,
I have tested you in the furnace of adversity.
For my own sake, for my own sake, I do it,
For why should [my name] be profaned?
And my glory to another I will not give.

---

22. Boadt, "Intentional Alliteration in Second Isaiah," 356.
23. The 1QIsa[a] reading is taken from Ulrich, *Biblical Qumran Scrolls*, 425.

MT

בחרתיך בכור עני

I have tested you in the furnace of adversity

1QIsa^a

בחנתיכה בכור עני

I have chosen you in the furnace of adversity

Modern commentators are divided concerning which of the readings in 48:10 they follow as the original. Some prefer the reading in 1QIsa^a, because בחן ("test") is often paired with צרף ("refine") in poetry in connection to the metallurgical metaphor being used for punishment and restoration (e.g., Zech 13:9).[24] After noting connections between בחן ("test") and צרף ("refine") in the psalms, Chris Franke also noted the connection between בחר ("choose") and כסף ("silver") in the phrase בכסף נבחר ("choice silver"; i.e., "refined silver") in Prov 8:19; 10:20 in a similar metallurgical metaphor; therefore, he noted, "These connections could possibly explain why the scribe wrote *bḥr* instead of *bḥn*."[25] Nevertheless, Franke concluded, "The parallelism between *ṣrp* and *bḥn* makes better sense than adopting the reading of the MT."[26] That is, Franke concluded that the author used בחן ("test"; reading with 1QIsa^a) and a later scribe changed it to בחר ("choose"; leading to MT), despite his awareness of how both readings have parallels elsewhere in Hebrew poetry.

In "The Interchange of *L*, *N*, and *R* in Biblical Hebrew," Aloysius Fitzgerald noted that the interchange of these three consonants (ל, נ, and ר) is common in Semitic languages; however, he understood his study as follows: "this review will make clear that what the poet is doing is using a dialectal form that fits better the sound-patterning of his line."[27] That is, the various dialectal forms available to the poet provided him with a

---

24. E.g., Claus Westermann, *Isaiah 40–66: A Commentary*, OTL (Philadelphia: Westminster, 1969), 195; Klaus Baltzer, *Deutero-Isaiah: A Commentary on Isaiah 40–55*, Hermeneia (Minneapolis: Fortress, 2001), 286; Blenkinsopp, *Isaiah 40–55*, 286.

25. Chris Franke, *Isaiah 46, 47, and 48: A New Literary-Critical Reading*, BJSUCSD 3 (Winona Lake, IN: Eisenbrauns, 1994), 203.

26. Franke, *Isaiah 46, 47, and 48*, 204.

27. Fitzgerald, "Interchange of L, N, and R," 481. For 48:10, I have divided the verse into two poetic lines following Fitzgerald. For 48:9, 11, I simply followed BHS, since Fitzgerald did not discuss these verses.

3. Sound-Triggering and Text-Critical Variants 211

rich reservoir for creating sound-patterns. When he discussed Isa 48:10, he wrote the following:

> The concern here is with MT *bḥr* in the sense of normal Hebrew *bḥn*. Aramaic combines both "to test" and "to choose" in the one root *bḥr*; and *bḥr* of Isa 48:10 is frequently regarded as an Aramaism. Probably the roots are ultimately identical, with Hebrew specializing the variant forms in different ways. Whether the form here is Aramaic or simply dialectal Hebrew is impossible to decide, but clearly it ought not to be changed to *bḥrntyk*. The *r* fits the alliterative pattern of the colon and the line and presents the verb in a form that better echoes the parallel *ṣrptyk*.[28]

Fitzgerald specifically refers to the "alliterative pattern" of ר in his defense of the MT reading as original, an argument that is lacking in the other discussions cited above. However, Fitzgerald ignored that fact that there is also an alliterative pattern for ב in this passage. In 48:10a, both ב and ר occur once and also in 48:10b both ב and ר occur once without counting the variant under discussion. In fact, there is an alliterative pattern for ב, ר, and ב throughout 48:9–11, so that no matter which variant one chooses as the original an analogous supporting argument on the basis of alliteration can be made. Therefore, maybe it is best to accept both readings as synonymous. Of course, Fitzgerald himself suggested that these two "roots are ultimately identical," even though he then preferred one over the other.

Example 3.7: Isa 47:1

MT

רדי ושבי על עפר בתולת בת בבל
שבי לארץ אין כסא בת כשדים

Come down and sit in the dust, virgin daughter Babylon!
Sit on the ground without a throne, daughter Chaldea!

MT/1QIsa[b]

שבי לארץ: Sit on [to] the ground

1QIsa[a]

שבי על הארץ: Sit on [against] the ground

---

28. Fitzgerald, "Interchange of L, N, and R," 487.

MT/1QIsa^a
אין כסא: without a throne

LXX[29]
εἴσελθε εἰς τὸ σκότος = ובאי בחשך: go into the darkness

Both of these variants include the possibility of sound-triggering by alliteration. Few commentators comment on such slight variations concerning prepositions, because, as in this case, their semantic ranges overlap so much that they often have synonymous meanings. However, Boadt wrote the following:

> The poet does not use parallel prepositions in constructing his parallel cola. The ʿal-ʿāpār in the first line balances lāʾāreṣ in the next line. The verb yāšab can take either ʿal or lĕ.... Because he had the option, the prophet chose to employ ʿal in the first line to emphasize the ʿayin alliteration in the two word combination, ʿal-ʿāpār. He may possibly have also seen an advantage in balancing the syllable count, although..., it would only be of concern to him in the initial colon of the bicolon.[30]

Consistent with his overall understanding of "intentional alliteration," Boadt understood the preposition על in the phrase על עפר as something the poet/"prophet chose ... [in order] to emphasize the ʿayin alliteration," despite what he seems to assume would have been more common, that is, the use of parallel prepositions between the two cola: לעפר and לארץ. However, because of his exclusive use of MT, Boadt apparently did not realize that just such a parallel use of prepositions is found in 1QIsa^a (על עפר and על הארץ) that fits even better with the alliterative pattern of ע. At the same time, it may be best to not focus so much on variants concerning prepositions, because we seem to have two sets of synonymous readings (על הארץ/לארץ/לעפר and על הארץ), but sound-triggering certainly can be an explanation for why על is selected in the passage, whether it is original or a later variant.

---

29. Although he reads with MT, Blenkinsopp notes this LXX variant and that it was possibly taken from 47:5. See Blenkinsopp, *Isaiah 40–55*, 276.

30. Boadt, "Intentional Alliteration in Second Isaiah," 359. Note that in this example I followed Boadt's analysis of the poetic structure/line rather than that of BHS.

The MT reads שבי לארץ אין כסא ("sit in the dust without a throne"); the possible LXX-*Vorlage* reads ובאי בחשך (or על הארץ) שבי לארץ ("sit in [to/against] the dust and go into the darkness"). Both readings have connections to the broader literary context. The MT reading draws from the royal imagery associated with the virgin daughter of Babylon, whose privilege will end so that she will do domestic work and will experience the horror of war like most women (47:1–4). The LXX reading draws from the similar oracle in 47:5–7, which begins "Sit in silence [שבי דומם] and go into darkness [ובאי בחשך], daughter Chaldea [בת כשדים]!" The LXX reading in 47:1c also parallels the poetic line in 47:1a in that both have two imperative verbs in a chiastic structure—"come down" (רדי) and "sit" (שבי); "sit" (שבי) and "go" (באי)—pairing "sit" with a verb of motion. Furthermore, both readings have alliterative connections to their immediate literary context. The MT reading (אין כסא) connects with the א in the preceding word (ארץ; "dust"), the כ in כשדים, and probably the ס with the ש in שבי (twice) and כשדים. The LXX reading (ובאי בחשך) connects with the ב in שבי (twice), בתולת, בת בבל, and בת כשדים; the א in the preceding word (ארץ; "dust"); and the ש with the ש in שבי (twice) and כשדים. Thus, even if one insists that one of these readings must be original, both the original and the later variant provide evidence of sound-triggering through the use of alliteration within the immediate poetic context. I prefer to think of them both as authentic readings within the composition/transmission processes of the Hebrew poetic tradition.

Example 3.8: Isa 33:20

MT

חזה ציון קרית מועדנו
עיניך תראינה ירושלם נוה שאנן אהל בל יצען
בל יסע יתדתיו לנצח וכל חבליו בל ינתקו

Behold, Zion, the city of our appointed festivals!
Your eyes will see Jerusalem, a quiet habitation, an immovable tent, whose stakes will never be pulled up, and none of whose ropes will be broken. (NRSV)

LXX

ἰδοὺ Σιων ἡ πόλις τὸ σωτήριον ἡμῶν·
οἱ ὀφθαλμοί σου ὄψονται Ιερουσαλημ, πόλις πλουσία, σκηναὶ αἳ οὐ μὴ σεισθῶσιν,

οὐδὲ μὴ κινηθῶσιν οἱ πάσσαλοι τῆς σκηνῆς αὐτῆς εἰς τὸν αἰῶνα χρόνον, οὐδὲ τὰ σχοινία αὐτῆς οὐ μὴ διαρραγῶσιν.
Look, the city of Sion is our salvation!
Your eyes will see Ierousalem, a wealthy city: tents that will not be shaken,
nor will the stakes of its tent be moved forever, nor will its ropes be broken. (NETS)

This is the first example in this section on alliteration that does not involve a text-critical variant in the Hebrew tradition, but concerns the influence of alliteration on the Greek translation of the LXX-*Vorlage* that appears to be the same as the MT. Throughout the verse in the Hebrew, we find alliteration of three sibilants (צ, שׁ, and ס) and נ. This alliteration is most focused in three words that begin with a sibilant and end with ן: ציון ("Zion"), שאנן ("quiet"/"untroubled"), and יצען ("immovable"). Jan de Waard concluded that "the translator wanted to save some phonological features of his source text" and therefore created a "good example of phonological translation."[31] De Waard noted that the Hebrew אהל בל יצען, including the *hapax legomenon* of יצען, is translated into σκηναὶ αἵ οὐ μὴ σεισθῶσιν, so that the alliteration of the Hebrew sibilants in the passage is represented in this Greek phrase by alliteration of the Greek sibilant σ. He also observed that the translator likely substituted the Greek alliterative phrase πόλις πλουσία ("a rich city") for the phrase נוה שאנן ("a quiet habitation") that includes one of the three most important words. Of course, the alliteration of the Greek π does not correspond exactly to the Hebrew that has no פ in the verse, but de Waard concluded that this Greek phrase replaces one alliteration (an initial sibilant) with another consonant, so that the translator produced a good phonological translation (that still has the sibilant σ). Thus, sound-triggering is not limited to the composition/transmission process of the Hebrew text, but can also be observed in the translation process of the LXX or the early transmission of the Greek text.

---

31. De Waard, "'Homophony' in the Septuagint," *Bib* 62 (1981): 553.

Example 3.9: Prov 26:17

MT

מחזיק באזני כלב עבר מתעבר על ריב לא לו
Like one who takes a passing dog by the ears
is one who meddles in the quarrel of another

LXX
ὥσπερ ὁ κρατῶν κέρκου κυνός, οὕτως ὁ προεστὼς ἀλλοτρίας κρίσεως.
Like one who takes a dog by the tail
Is one who meddles in the quarrel of another.

Michael Fox noted the "strong paranomasia" in the phrase עבר מתעבר, but we should note that the proverb includes alliteration of ע, ב, and ר throughout.[32] Fox also concluded that the LXX reading does not suggest a different Hebrew text, but rather is the translator's creation of κ-alliteration in the Greek as a substitute for the ע-alliteration in the Hebrew.[33] Of course, both the Hebrew and Greek versions of the proverb, despite minor differences, suggest that it is just as foolish to involve oneself in someone else's quarrel as it is to grab a stray dog, whether it is by the ears or tail.

These last two examples (Isa 33:20; Prov 26:17) demonstrate that sound-triggering occurred not only in the composition/transmission process of Hebrew texts, but could also occur in their translation into Greek or in the early transmission of the Greek text. Although I might accept an argument that the translators were more consciously aware of such sound-triggering than authors and copyists, I would nevertheless insist that this was not always the case and that methodologically it would be difficult (if not impossible) to distinguish between intentional/conscious alliteration and unintentional/unconscious alliteration, even in the translation process. Furthermore, even a scribe copying the Greek translation who is familiar with the Hebrew *Vorlage* may have made some changes in the Greek text under the influence of alliterative patterns. Thus, sound-triggering in the form of alliteration could occur in various places along

---

32. Fox, *Proverbs 10–31: A New Translation with Introduction and Commentary*, AB (New Haven: Yale University Press, 2009), 799. See also Casanowicz, "Paronomasia in the Old Testament," 147 (#291).

33. Fox, *Proverbs*, 347.

the composition/transmission process, including the transmission of texts in translation.

Wordplay

Wordplay in Hebrew obviously builds upon alliteration, in that the wordplay occurs among different lexemes that have an alliterative (and/or assonant) pattern in common. Although commentators generally regard wordplay as likely being intentional on the part of the authors (or at least more intentional than alliteration), Jefferson's examples of wordplay in oral discourse undercuts such an assumption (see above examples 2.1, 2.2, 3.2). Even if we concur that authorial intention is more likely in wordplay than other forms of alliteration, it remains methodologically problematic in determining what is or is not intentional.[34] In fact, even if an author becomes conscious of the wordplay and decides to build upon it further, this does not necessarily require us to conclude that the initial wordplay was intentional; it may have been unintentional and, once recognized, then intentionally expanded. Therefore, although I am certainly not ruling out the possibility of intentional sound-patterning, I will refrain from deciding what is or is not intentional, due to the methodological problems of any such determination based on how sound-triggering can work cognitively and linguistically without such conscious intentionality.

Below I provide seven examples, beginning with two examples of wordplay connected to person reference (Jer 29:21–22; Gen 5:29) and then four examples in which the ambiguity of the Hebrew consonantal text led to purported variants when vocalization was added (in the form of MT pointing) or when the Hebrew was translated (thereby losing the ambiguity; Prov 31:21–22; Ps 91:8; Prov 3:8; Song 1:2). I close my discussion of wordplay with an example concerning how the Greek translator of Numbers had a consistent pattern of translating toponyms connected to etiologies, so that the wordplay carried over into the translation (Num 11:3). In all of these examples, I conclude that we may not have true variants—that is, even though there appear to be variants in

---

34. For a similar argument concerning intentionality when applying Jefferson's poetics to the novel *Martin Chuzzlewit* by Charles Dickens, see Hugo Bowles, "The Poetics of Mrs Gamp's Conversation—Are They Dickens's 'Slips of the Pen'?," in Person, Wooffitt, and Rae, *Bridging the Gap*, 119–39.

the text, these variants either do not detract from the wordplay or in some cases simply choose to transmit only one of the meanings found in the ambiguity of the Hebrew consonantal text, which is not necessarily a rejection of the other meaning(s). In fact, it is interesting to note that the broader textual tradition tends to preserve the ambiguity as a collective, even when the transmission of the text represented a particular vocalization (either pointing in MT or the translation of the text) required the scribe to prefer one meaning over another in its transmission. In other words, it remains possible that at least at an early stage of transmission both readings were present in the tradition as preserved in scribal memory.

Example 3.10: Jer 29:21–22

MT

כה אמר יהוה צבאות אלהי ישראל אל אחאב בן קוליה ואל צדקיהו בן מעשיה ... ולקח מהם קללה לכל גלות יהודה אשר בבבל לאמר ישמך יהוה כצדקיהו וכאחב אשר קלם מלך בבל באש

Thus says the LORD **of hosts, the God of Israel**, concerning Ahab **son of Kolaiah** and Zedekiah **son of Maaseiah**.... And on account of them this curse shall be used by all the exiles from Judah in Babylon: "The LORD make you like Zedekiah and Ahab, whom the king of Babylon roasted in the fire." (NRSV)

LXX

οὕτως εἶπεν κύριος ἐπὶ Αχιαβ καὶ ἐπὶ Σεδεκιαν ... καὶ λήμψονται ἀπ' αὐτῶν κατάραν ἐν πάσῃ τῇ ἀποικίᾳ Ιουδα ἐν Βαβυλῶνι λέγοντες Ποιήσαι σε κύριος, ὡς Σεδεκιαν ἐποίησεν καὶ ὡς Αχιαβ, οὓς ἀπετηγάνισεν βασιλεὺς Βαβυλῶνος ἐν πυρὶ

Thus says the Lord, concerning Ahab and Zedekiah.... And on account of them this curse shall be used by all the exiles from Judah in Babylon: "The Lord make you like Zedekiah and Ahab, whom the king of Babylon roasted in the fire."

MT: יהוה צבאות אלהי ישראל: the LORD **of hosts, the God of Israel**
LXX: κύριος = יהוה: the LORD

MT: אחאב בן קוליה: Ahab **son of Kolaiah**
LXX: Αχιαβ = אחאב: Ahab

MT: צדקיהו בן מעשיה: Zedekiah **son of Maaseiah**
LXX: Σεδεκιαν = צדקיהו... : Zedekiah

The potential for wordplay concerning Ahab's father's name, Kolaiah (קוליה), with "curse" (קללה) and "roast" (קלם) is often observed.[35] The sound-repetition of the initial two consonants קל in these three words suggests to Garsiel that this is an example of what he called "Midrashic name derivations" ("MNDs"), which he defined as "interpretations of a midrashic (homiletic) nature applied to the name of people or of places on the basis of sound or semantic potential. Such an interpretation infuses a name with meaning in relation to past events, or looks forward to some future incidents."[36] Garsiel has devoted an entire book to his study of Midrashic name derivations, all of which are excellent illustrations of the kind of sound-triggering related to names that Jefferson identified in spoken discourse (see above example 3.2).

Garsiel's study is based exclusively on MT, ignoring in this example the fact that many Jeremiah scholars have argued that the shorter LXX-*Vorlage* represents an earlier recension than MT. Because of the significant difference between MT and LXX, some Jeremiah commentators have questioned whether wordplay is present in this passage. For example, William Holladay based his translation on the LXX reading (lacking the patronyms) and, even though he noted that others think that there is a possible wordplay here, he asked them, "but if the names are genuine, why would G[reek translator] have omitted them?"[37] That is, he assumed that the patronym, "son of Kolaiah" (בן קוליה), was necessarily included in the written text for the wordplay to be present and, if it was present in the earlier text, he could not imagine a reason why it would have been omitted in the LXX-*Vorlage* or in the translation process. Others (e.g., Robert Carroll) use the wordplay as a justification for reading with MT here, *even if* they generally prefer the LXX-*Vorlage* as earlier.[38]

What all of these interpretations have in common is an emphasis on the linear transmission from the biblical author of the original text to a later text. This is explicit in Garsiel's study: "The greatness of the biblical

---

35. Garsiel, *Biblical Names*, 51; Carroll, *Jeremiah*, 554; Lundbom, *Jeremiah 21–36*, 357; Holladay, *Jeremiah 2*, 134.
36. Garsiel, *Biblical Names*, 19.
37. Holladay, *Jeremiah 2*, 134.
38. Carroll, *Jeremiah*, 554.

author consists in his ability so to combine them as to create a correspondence between a name (and one of its latent implications) and some other elements in the literary unit."[39] This is also implicit in Holladay's interpretation that the wordplay was not present in the earlier text of the LXX-*Vorlage* (and presumably the original text), due to his understanding that "son of Kolaiah" was a later addition. However, Garsiel himself provided various examples that illustrate that such details were not necessary for the presence of such wordplay to occur, even though he worked exclusively with MT. In his chapter 3, he provided numerous examples of "tacit MNDs as to which the ear cannot register any sound effects, because the direct derivation from the name is replaced by another word or phrase which merely alludes to it."[40] In his chapter 4, he provided numerous examples of "MNDs where it is the name which is concealed, or at any rate placed far away on the textual continuum."[41] This insight by Garsiel is strengthened significantly by the discussion in the previous chapter on person reference and category-triggering as understood in conversation analysis and the use of proper names and titles in the Hebrew Bible.[42] That is, a competent early reader of Jeremiah might have known that Ahab is the "son of Kolaiah" on the basis of their traditional knowledge of Ahab the prophet, even when the patronym is not explicit in the written text. In other words, rather than necessarily determining which reading is original, the sound-triggering found in this wordplay can be understood in *both* the MT and LXX-*Vorlage* readings, even if the wordplay is only tacit. At least, this is implied in Garsiel's own work of such "tacit MNDs" and "MNDs related to names not mentioned in the text."[43] The scribal memory of the writers may have included the phrase "Ahab, son of Kolaiah" even when the written text read only "Ahab," under the influence of category-triggering, that is, the category identifying Ahab. Therefore, even if we decide that in this type of wordplay later scribes are more likely to add the

---

39. Garsiel, *Biblical Names*, 266. Garsiel's examples of wordplay were not limited to "the name of a particular person" but also included "the names of his father, grandfather or clan progenitor, his wife or his mother" (255). Thus, this example based on a patronym is consistent with his understanding of wordplay and puns related to biblical names.

40. Garsiel, *Biblical Names*, 98.

41. Garsiel, *Biblical Names*, 127.

42. See specifically my discussion of this same example (pp. 187–89).

43. The title of his chapter 4; Garsiel, *Biblical Names*, 127.

patronym rather than omit it (as in Holladay's interpretation), we should not rule out the possibility that the wordplay is nevertheless present in both readings (contra Holladay), because the tacit wordplay was active in scribal memory.

Example 3.11: Gen 5:29

> MT
>
> ויקרא את שמו נח לאמר זה ינחמנו ממעשנו ...
> He called his name Noah, saying, "This one **shall bring us relief** from our work ..."
>
> LXX
> καὶ ἐπωνόμασεν τὸ ὄνομα αὐτοῦ Νωε λέγων Οὗτος διαναπαύσει ἡμᾶς ἀπὸ τῶν ἔργων ἡμῶν ...
> = ויקרא את שמו נח לאמר זה יניחנו ממעשנו
> He called his name Noah, saying, "This one **shall cause us to cease** from our work ..."

In his work on paronomasia, Casanowicz used this example to illustrate his general observation that "in many cases it is quite apparent that it is not an etymology which is intended, but a paronomasia."[44] He quoted the rabbinic tradition on the unsuitability of this etymology: "the explanation does not suit the name, nor the name the explanation; it should either read, Noah will give us rest, or Naḥman will comfort us" (Gen. Rab. 25:2). He further noted that the LXX reads καταπαύσει ("will give us rest").[45] He concluded that "in most of the explanations of proper names in the Old Testament we have examples of popular etymology, which is satisfied with a partial agreement in sound," but "in the plays upon proper names, still less regard is had to the real meaning."[46] That is, the

---

44. Casanowicz, "Paronomasia in the Old Testament," 117, 144 (#255). This is only one of the fifty-two instances of paronomasia found in "explanations of proper names" in his list. See also, Garsiel, *Biblical Names*, 32, 203.

45. Casanowicz, "Paronomasia in the Old Testament," 117. Note that Casanowicz refers to a LXX reading of καταπαύσει here; however, this reading is not given in the text-critical apparatus of John William Wevers, *Genesis*, SVTG 1 (Göttingen: Vandenhoeck & Ruprecht, 1974), 107.

46. Casanowicz, "Paronomasia in the Old Testament," 117.

wordplay is more important than the accuracy of the implied etymology. Casanowicz also noted that "the same name is sometimes variously played upon, either with reference to different meanings of the same word, or to a different word."[47]

Umberto Cassuto also noted this wordplay:

> Apparently two traditions were current among the Israelites with regard to the name of the righteous man who was saved from the waters of the Flood: according to the one his name was *Noah*, according to the other his name was *Menahem* or *Nahman*, and the Torah ... accepted the first view but did not wish to disregard the second.[48]

That is, the MT has the name "Noah" but the etymology for "Nahman" (ינחמנו). He then concluded that the LXX reading is the "result of the harmonizing tendency ... in that version."[49] Cassuto noted that "both traditions are recorded in the late Haggada."[50] Since these two traditions are evident in rabbinic literature, it seems to me that we should explore the probability that the two traditions are also ancient in ways that affected the early transmission of this text. That is, rather than choosing one wordplay on the name "Noah" as original, it is probably best to assume that both wordplays were sometimes understood in the texts and their earliest transmission and that both names were considered (near-)synonyms, that is, referring to the category for the same individual.

Example 3.12: Prov 31:21–22[51]

MT

לא תירא לביתה משלג כי כל ביתה לבש שָׁנִים
מרבדים עשתה לה שש וארגמן לבושה

She is not afraid for her household when it snows,
    for all her household are clothed in crimson.
She makes herself coverings; her clothing is fine linen and purple.

---

47. Casanowicz, "Paronomasia in the Old Testament," 118.
48. Umberto Cassuto, *From Adam to Noah, Genesis I–VI:8*, part 1 of *A Commentary on the Book of Genesis* (Jerusalem: Magnes, 1961), 288.
49. Cassuto, *From Adam to Noah*, 288.
50. Cassuto, *From Adam to Noah*, 288.
51. The translation of MT is NRSV; the translation of LXX is from Fox, *Proverbs*, 395.

LXX
οὐ φροντίζει τῶν ἐν οἴκῳ ὁ ἀνὴρ αὐτῆς, ὅταν που χρονίζῃ·
πάντες γὰρ οἱ παρ' αὐτῆς ἐνδιδύσκονται.
δισσάς χλαίνας ἐποίησεν τῷ ἀνδρὶ αὐτῆς,
ἐκ δὲ βύσσου καὶ πορφύρας ἑαυτῇ ἐνδύματα.

Her husband does not worry about those who are in his house,
whenever he tarries (away from home),
because those who are with her are well clothed.
She made for her husband a two-ply mantle,
And from linen and purple (she made) clothing for herself.

MT: שָׁנִים [at the end of v. 21] = scarlet
LXX: δισσάς [at the beginning of v. 22] = שְׁנַיִם = two

This example comes from the acrostic poem of the worthy woman in Prov 31:10–31, but concerns only two lines, for ל and מ. The NRSV translation of MT and Fox's translation of LXX given above contrast with the translation of MT given by Rendsburg: "She does not fear for her house on account of snow, for all her house is clothed šānîm, Garments she has made for herself, linen and purple are her clothing."[52] (Although there are other differences between the MT and the LXX, I will only comment on the šānîm wordplay and how it relates to possible variants.[53]) Rendsburg did not translate šānîm, because he understood this to be a case of Janus parallelism—that is, the same word carries two different meanings, one connected to what precedes it and one connected to what follows it. The varied interpretations of šānîm between the MT (as pointed) and the LXX (assuming a different vocalization) are both understood in the consonantal text in Rendsburg's interpretation—that is, "the consonantal string s-n-y-m at the end of v. 21 bears two meanings: with the meaning 'double' it looks back to the first part of the verse, and with the meaning 'scarlet' it looks ahead to the next verse."[54] This wordplay, however, can only be maintained in a consonantal

---

52. Gary A. Rendsburg, "Q Word Play in Biblical Hebrew: An Eclectic Collection," in Noegel, *Puns and Pundits*, 146. Later Rendsburg revised this translation as follows: "She does not fear for her house on account of snow, Because her entire house is clothed in scarlet/doubly (šanim). Coverings she has made for herself, Linen and purple are her clothing" (*How the Bible Is Written*, 378).

53. For other variants, see Fox, *Proverbs*, 395.

54. Rendsburg, "Word Play in Biblical Hebrew," 147.

text. As soon as the vocalization is specified as in the MT or as soon as the consonantal text is translated as in LXX (or a modern translation) the wordplay is undermined. Thus, what may appear to be textual variants are not necessarily variants based on a different Hebrew text, but are based on different vocalizations of the same Hebrew consonants. We should not assume that the ancient scribes necessarily missed the wordplay, even when their later specific standards of transmission (with pointing or in translation) required them to choose one specific meaning of the Hebrew consonants. We, therefore, should allow both meanings to be considered part of the earliest readings of the text within scribal memory, even when the specific manuscript may *appear* to be suppressing one in favor of the other. Note that this requires the ambiguity to be communicated both visually (in the consonantal text) and aurally (in terms of the two possible vocalizations), because, once the vocalization is made explicit (including in pointing or translation), the visual undercuts (at least to some degree) the aural. Therefore, the ambiguity of the consonant-only text would need to be supplied (when it remained available) in scribal memory.

Example 3.13: Ps 91:8[55]

MT

רק בעיניך תביט וְשִׁלֻּמַת רשעים תראה
You will look with your eyes and the punishment of the wicked you will see.

11Q11

רק] תביט[בעיניך] ותרא[ה שלום רשע]ים
You will look with your eyes and the punishment of the wicked you will see. [reading שִׁלּוּם, "punishment"]

This example is taken from Jonathan Kline, *Allusive Soundplay in the Hebrew Bible*, in which he focused upon nonhomonymic allusive paronomasia—that is, the use of wordplay in one text that appears to be alluding to another text that has similar wording according to sound. Kline noted that Ps 91:8 has the following pattern in common with both Ps 37:34

---

55. This example is taken from Jonathan G. Kline, *Allusive Soundplay in the Hebrew Bible*, AIL 28 (Atlanta: SBL Press, 2016), 59–62. The text for 11Q11 (11QapocrPs) is taken from Ulrich, *Biblical Qumran Scrolls*, 654.

and Ps 73:3: "the unique phrase 'to look upon the X of the wicked.'"⁵⁶ He understood Ps 91:8 as alluding back to both of these earlier psalms in a wordplay that builds on the following phrases in the other two:

Ps 37:34: בהכרת רשעים תראה = on the destruction of the wicked you will see
Ps 73:3: שְׁלוֹם רשעים אראה = on the prosperity of the wicked I will see

Kline noted that Ps 37 and Ps 73 are more nuanced than Ps 91 concerning the fate of both the righteous and the wicked—that is, "Ps 91 focuses almost entirely on the idea that God protects the righteous."⁵⁷ The allusive wordplay of Ps 91:8 that draws from both "the destruction [הכרת] of the wicked" in 37:34 (based on its synonymous meaning with שלום) and "the prosperity [שְׁלוֹם] of the wicked" in 73:3 (based on the same consonants) suggests that the psalmist is using the wordplay as a form of commenting on these earlier psalms. "Here, in Ps 91:8, the psalmist concurs with the thought expressed in Ps 37:34 by employing a turn of phrase similar to the last phrase of that verse and to the last phrase of Ps 73:3, but that states the opposite of what the latter phrase states."⁵⁸ That is, the psalmist is agreeing with "the destruction of the wicked" in 37:34 by the use of a synonym that nevertheless sounds somewhat like "the prosperity of the wicked" in 73:3 as a way of commenting negatively upon the more nuanced message of Ps 73.

Kline noted the variant reading in 11Q11. Although the context of שלום in Ps 73:3 requires the meaning "peace"/"prosperity" (with the MT pointing of שְׁלוֹם), he noted that the MT pointing would make no sense in the context of Ps 91, so that שלום in 11Q11 must be read as "punishment" (שִׁלּוּם), which is also found in Isa 34:8 and Hos 9:7. He also observed that the LXX reading in Ps 91:8 (ἀνταπόδοσιν) could reflect either the MT or the 11Q11 reading, since they are synonymous. However, he concluded as follows:

If שִׁלּוּם is the original reading in Ps 91:8—which would, in fact, make the wordplay with שְׁלוֹם in Ps 73:3 even more remarkable, since the words would differ only on the level of vocalization—a later scribe may have

---

56. Kline, *Allusive Soundplay*, 59.
57. Kline, *Allusive Soundplay*, 59.
58. Kline, *Allusive Soundplay*, 59.

changed the consonantal form שלום (to be read שָׁלוֹם) in Ps 91:8 to שלמת (i.e., שְׁלֻמַּת) in order to make the meaning of the word absolutely clear.

Nevertheless, Kline's conclusion is justifiably tenuous, because, as we have argued throughout the volume, the creation of the specifics of wordplay based on sound-triggering is not confined to the act of composition by authors, but could occur throughout the composition/transmission process. Therefore, no matter which of these synonymous readings may be original or even earlier, they both participate within the allusive sound-play influenced by sound-triggering within scribal memory. Competent scribes of Ps 91:8 recalled the phrases alluded to in Ps 37:34 and Ps 73:3 (whether the allusion was conscious or not) and this led to the two extant variant readings, both of which participate in the wordplay.

Example 3.14: Prov 3:8

> MT
>
> רפאות תהי לשרך ושקוי לעצמותיך
> It will be healing for your navel and a refreshment for your bones.
>
> LXX
> τότε ἴασις ἔσται τῷ σώματί σου καὶ ἐπιμέλεια τοῖς ὀστέοις σου
> = רפאות תהי לשארך ושקוי לעצמותיך
> It will be healing for your flesh and a refreshment for your bones.

Many commentators find the MT reading problematic. For example, Fox wrote, "M[T]'s 'healing … for your navel' does not make good sense."[59] Therefore, many commentators follow the LXX reading in their translation to create a better parallelism with "to your bones" in the following colon (לעצמותיך). However, in his study of synonyms and near-synonyms, Yair Zakovitch explained the MT reading as a wordplay in a way that makes sense of both the readings based on the same consonantal text. He referred to Song 7:3, in which the navel is described as a goblet from which the lover drinks wine; therefore, he understood the poet of this proverb using a similar imagery for the healing tonic and suggested that the navel here also functions as a *pars pro toto* in that it metonymically represents

---

59. Fox, *Proverbs*, 99. See also Fox, *Proverbs 10–31*, 151.

the whole body, thereby paralleling "bones" in the second colon. However, he also asserted that the consonantal text allows for a reference to "flesh" as well, since לשארך ("to your flesh") can also be written לשרך with an elided א.[60] "Keeping the present vocalization while hearing also the implied שארך-שרך extends to the verse greater meaning. שר i.e. the 'navel' and 'goblet' to the tonic; שר i.e., שאר, man's flesh, body, and health that is protected from all harm by the tonic pouring into it: the fear of God."[61] If we follow Zakovitch, we once again seem to have a case where the modern efforts of most commentators to determine the original text with one fixed meaning for each word has hampered our understanding of the poetry of the Hebrew consonantal text under the influence of the MT pointing and the LXX translation, both of which necessarily had to choose one vocalization over another. Therefore, we may not have variants here at all, but the larger tradition preserves the ambiguity of the consonantal Hebrew when the two readings are read not in opposition to each other, but as mutually supporting the wordplay of the text.

Example 3.15: Song 1:2

MT

ישקני מנשיקות פיהו כי טובים דדיך מיין

Let him kiss me with the kisses of his mouth!
For your breasts/your love are/is better than wine.

In *Multiple Originals*, Gary Martin provided an excellent survey of how differently דדיך is understood and translated before the Protestant Reformation consistently as (1) "your breasts" in Western Christian circles and (2) "your love" in both Jewish circles and among Syriac-speaking Christians.[62] In fact, he concluded,

> The individual manuscript traditions are remarkably firm within their own domains: I have found no "mixed" traditions. All extant Greek and

---

60. Yair Zakovitch, "Implied Synonyms and Antonyms: Textual Criticism vs. The Literary Approach," in Paul et al., *Emanuel*, 836; Fox, *Proverbs*, 99. See discussion of text-critical variants based on "orthography: quiescent *'Aleph*" in Tov, *Textual Criticism* (3rd ed.), 237.

61. Zakovitch, "Implied Synonyms and Antonyms," 837.

62. Martin, *Multiple Originals*, 99.

Latin (classical languages of the Mediterranean world) witnesses read "breasts." All extant Hebrew, Syriac, and Aramaic (Semitic languages of the Near and Middle East) witnesses read "love."[63]

He explained this variance on the basis of his discussion of Semitic cognates and parallel erotic literature in the ancient Near East, arguing that דדיך is best understood as a double entendre of "love" and "genitalia" (either male or female).[64] Therefore, the purported variant readings of דדיך point not to a different vocalization (as some have proposed) but to what Martin suggested as a new category for the identification of variants, "ambiguous vocalization."[65]

Example 3.16: Prov 23:10

MT

אל תסג גבול עולם ובשדי יתומים אל תבא

Do not remove the ancient boundary stones or encroach on the fields of orphans.

Vulgate
ne adtingas terminus parvulorum et agrum pupillorum ne introeas
אל תסג גבול עוללים ובשדי יתומים אל תבא =
Do not remove the boundary stones of children or encroach on the fields of orphans.

Most commentators and translators read with the MT for the meaning of "ancient," so that the first colon of the proverb reads something like "Do not remove ancient boundary stones."[66] In fact, few commentators even note the two variants given above. Many commentators, however, have noted the close connections to Amenemope, as illustrated in the following excerpts from Fox's translation of the Egyptian wisdom text (with **bold** denoting close connections to Prov 23:10):

---

63. Martin, *Multiple Originals*, 108.
64. Martin, *Multiple Originals*, 112–25.
65. Martin, *Multiple Originals*, 191.
66. Zakovitch, "Implied Synonyms and Antonyms," 841; his translation.

7.12: **Do not displace the stone on the boundary of fields** …
7.15: nor **encroach on the boundary** of the widow …
7.19: **he will be caught by the powers** of the Moon …
8.9: **Beware of encroaching on the boundaries of fields** …
8.15: **Do not traverse the furrow of another** …

Fox also noted the connection to Deut 19:14: לא תסיג גבול רעך אשר גבלו ראשנים ("Do not remove boundary stones of your neighbor, which the first [generations] set up"); however, he concluded that "Deuteronomy is not the source of Prov 22.28, for the editor of Part IIIa [22:17–23:11] is using Amenemope extensively."[67] (Why the editor cannot be influenced by two [or more] sources is unclear, even if one source is primary.) Thus, the prohibition against stealing another's property (whether "widow," "orphan," and/or "neighbor") by moving the boundary stones marking property lines is clearly present in ancient Near Eastern culture.

In contrast to most commentators who understand עולם as "ancient," Zakovitch discussed this proverb as another example of wordplay using near-synonyms:

> In our verse, reading עולם as עולים (a difference of the vowels only), carries then also the reading עוללים, "infants" (see also Isa 49:15; 69:20). In this way we see that the author of Prov 23:10 in fact divided the term עולים יתומים—babies who are orphans, babies who have no one to protect them—between the two hemistichs of the verse.[68]

Thus, according to Zakovitch, the consonantal Hebrew text (some variation of עלם) carries the connotations of "ancient boundary stones" (as in MT), "the boundary stones of infants" (as in OL), and "the boundary stones of the poor" (עולים as in m. Pe'ah 5:6; 7:3). I would add that all three readings are consistent with the larger cultural phenomenon as represented by Amenemope and Deut 19:14 (following Fox). Furthermore, all three readings have parallel connections based on category-triggering to the following colon: the MT reading ("ancient boundary stones") clearly relates to "the *field* of the orphans" and the other readings ("infants" and "poor") relate well to "the field of the *orphans*."

---

67. Fox, *Proverbs 10–31*, 733.
68. Zakovitch, "Implied Synonyms and Antonyms," 843.

Example 3.17: Num 11:3

MT

ויקרא שם המקום ההוא תבערה כי בערה בם אש יהוה
So that place was called Taberah, because the fire of the LORD burned against them. (NRSV)

LXX

καὶ ἐκλήθη τὸ ὄνομα τοῦ τόπου ἐκείνου ʼΕμπυρισμός, ὅτι ἐξεκαύθη ἐν αὐτοῖς πῦρ παρὰ κυρίου.
The name of that place was called Burning, because fire was kindled among them from the Lord. (NETS)

This example does not include any purported variant in the Hebrew text, but demonstrates that the Greek translator understood the wordplay in the Hebrew and adjusted his standard translation style accordingly. This example comes from a study of the LXX-Numbers by Ausloos. He noted that typically this translator transliterated toponyms as illustrated by his treatment of many of the toponyms in Num 33:5–37, a passage that summarizes Israel's wandering in the wilderness (e.g., רעמסס = Ραμεσση and סכת = Σοκχωθ in 33:5).[69] Despite this general tendency, some toponyms are translated, but Ausloos identified a pattern: "the translator of Numbers specifically and deliberately chooses to consistently translate (and thus not to transliterate) every toponym that occurs within an etiology, in order to emphasize the connection between the place name and the incident related."[70] Furthermore, toponyms in etiologies are consistently translated throughout the entire book, not only in the etiology. Hence, in Num 11:3, the translator translated תבערה (in transliteration as found in most English translations, "Taberah") as ʼΕμπυρισμός ("Burning"). This translation emphasizes the etiology found in the Hebrew text of Num 11:1–3. "Now when the people complained in the hearing of the LORD about their misfortunes, the LORD heard it and his anger was kindled [ויחר אפו]. Then the fire of the LORD burned against them [ותבער בם אש יהוה], and consumed some outlying parts of the camp.... So that place was called Taberah

---

69. Hans Ausloos, "The Septuagint's Rendering of Hebrew Toponyms as an Indication of the Translation Technique of the Book of Numbers," in Otero and Morales, *Textual Criticism and Dead Sea Scrolls Studies*, 49.

70. Ausloos, "Septuagint's Rendering of Hebrew Toponyms," 49.

[Burning; תבערה], because the fire of the Lord burned against them [ותבער בם אש יהוה]" (11:1, 3; NRSV). The translation insured that the Greek readers understood the etiology: "The name of that place was called Burning ['Ἐμπυρισμός], because fire was kindled among them from the Lord [ὅτι ἐξεκαύθη ἐν αὐτοῖς πῦρ παρὰ κυρίου]" (NETS). Because he identified this consistent pattern (illustrated by his discussion of Num 11:3, 34; 13:23; 20:13; 21:3; 27:14), Ausloos concluded as follows: "the phenomenon of the wordplay, tested against the way in which the LXX-translator of Numbers deals with etiologies, gives clear indications as to the characterisation of the translation technique."[71] Thus, as in the previous section, we have observed that sound-patterning, both alliteration and wordplay, can occur throughout the composition/transmission process, including when transmission includes the translated text.

Sound-Triggering and Variants: A Summary

The current predilection to use only MT for studies in biblical poetics is problematic. As these examples demonstrate, the typical distinction between authors and composition, on the one hand, and copyists and transmission, on the other, distorts the evidence according to the text-critical and literary-critical history of the texts. The interpretive preference for identifying one meaning and thereby overlooking potential ambiguities often leads to a narrow view of the texts' history, suppressing the ambiguity found in the consonant-only Hebrew texts. Furthermore, the assumption that alliteration and wordplay is intentional is problematic. Rather, we have seen that sound-triggering can influence both authors and copyists—or even better all scribes in the composition/transmission process—so that the distinctions often made must be abandoned.

In the above examples of alliteration, we have seen that the alliterative patterns are found in the text-critical variants, so that no matter which variant we may choose as original, both the author of the text and later scribes are influenced by the same (or equally alternative) alliterative patterns. The influence of the alliterative patterns may extend beyond the transmission of the Hebrew text as well in that we have seen two examples of alliteration in the Hebrew *Vorlage* influencing either the translation of the text into Greek or the transmission of the Greek

---

71. Ausloos, "Septuagint's Rendering of Hebrew Toponyms," 49.

translation, but again we may want to avoid setting up too strong a distinction here as well.

In the above examples of wordplay, we have observed both how etiologies can hint at more than one interpretation of personal names and how the consonant-only text of the Hebrew may be ambiguous, thereby allowing more than one meaning being understood for what appears to be one lexeme. Therefore, even though the later tradition specified the vocalization of the Hebrew—for example, in the pointing of MT or the translation of the Hebrew into another language—the later tradition nevertheless could preserve the ambiguity in that different textual traditions often chose one vocalization over another but, when taken collectively, the ambiguity could remain. Of course, even in MT, such ambiguity can be preserved in the paratextual material as an aid to scribal memory, for example, in the *ketiv-qere* system.[72]

These examples strongly suggest that sound-triggering influenced the composition/transmission process through scribal memory. Much like participants in ordinary conversation may be completely unaware of the sound-patterns of alliteration and wordplay that they are producing in their talk, the ancient scribes may have unknowingly been influenced by sound-patterns in the texts as they copied their *Vorlagen*. In other words, scribal memory and its effect on the composition/transmission process could have included instances of sound-triggering. This influence could have been unintentional and unrecognized in some instances; in other cases, the sound-triggering may have begun in unintentional ways but was then recognized so that the scribes played off of the sound-patterns even more. Consistent with Jefferson's observations, poets are in the business of word selection on the basis of aesthetic sensibilities based on the exaggeration of the poetics in ordinary talk, so some cases most certainly could have been intentional. However, since sound-triggering can work all along a continuum of unintentional/unrecognized to intentional throughout the composition/transmission process, we lack any clear methodology for distinguishing intentional from unintentional cases. Although it is probably accurate to assume that the more elaborate and complex any particular case of sound-patterning is the more likely it is intentional, this does not, however, rule out the possibility that

---

72. For an excellent discussion of homonyms in the *ketiv-qere* of MT, see Dotan, "Homonymous Hapax Doublets."

even a complex case was unintentional or was initially generated in its earliest stages unintentionally, as Jefferson's discussion of sound-flurries illustrates (see above, example 1.11). Furthermore, even in those cases in which we might be able to determine earlier and later variants, the later variants could be understood as intentional or unintentional. Therefore, we should generally refrain from questions of authorial intention in cases of sound-patterning for methodological reasons.

Those who remain skeptical of my arguments above may correctly note that I have not found a large quantity of supportive examples—that is, such quantitative limitations are often used as sources of critique. In their application of a qualitative method of research, conversation analysts often face this very type of criticism within the social sciences and the response can be summarized in a quote from Schegloff: "one is also a number."[73] In fact, some sophisticated studies in conversation analysis are based on a close analysis of only one example.[74] The assumption is that, if an example of a successful interaction can be found in a conversation, then both participants in that conversation must have understood whatever social practice is being illustrated in that example in order for the communication to have been successful. In other words, conversation has complex mechanisms by which participants can repair misunderstandings whenever they occur and, when such repair mechanisms are lacking, the participants appear to have understood each other well enough, based on their knowledge of social action, for the conversation to continue successfully. Thus, from this perspective of qualitative research, even my small collection of examples is highly suggestive. That is, if these scribes had the cognitive-linguistic abilities to participate in the composition/transmission of texts in this way, those same abilities would have been available to other scribes as well, especially since these processes seem to be universally valid in modern linguistic studies. Furthermore, even Jefferson understood sound-triggering and category-triggering as a second-level mechanism (beyond the necessity of the pragmatic context), so that it is not always operative in word selection. Nevertheless, Jefferson's poetics remains highly suggestive for word selection in talk-in-interaction.

---

73. Emanuel A. Schegloff, "Reflections on Quantification in the Study of Conversation," *Research on Language and Social Interaction* 26 (1993): 101.

74. For an excellent discussion, see Jeffrey D. Robinson, "The Role of Numbers and Statistics within Conversation Analysis," *Communication Methods and Measures* 1 (2007): 65–75.

Another response by conversation analysts to such criticisms is that statistically based research requires some understanding of representative data for the purpose of comparison. Since every study is based on a small set of data recorded and transcribed by conversation analysts, it is unclear what a representative data set of conversation would look like. For example, how much of the data set should be conversation in the family home, how much at work, how much in retail establishments, and so on? In my case, I can also respond that, due to the lack of sufficient text-critical evidence from the early period of textual transmission, I strongly suspect that we have a distorted perception of the transmission history of the Hebrew text, *even though* the discovery of the Dead Sea Scrolls moved our time line of evidence back centuries and revolutionized the field. Furthermore, as I have noted above, few literary studies have made good use of the text-critical evidence and too few text-critical studies have explored the literary issues of the text-critical variants. Thus, in my opinion, the secondary literature on this topic is most likely far from a good representation of the limited ancient evidence. Therefore, I can acknowledge the quantitative limitations of my study, but nevertheless assert that my conclusions are highly suggestive that sound-triggering within scribal performance influenced all ancient scribes in their composition/transmission of the text, both when they reproduced their *Vorlagen* verbatim (even though I do not think that this was necessarily their goal) and when they produced what we perceive as text-critical variants (even though they may not have understood them as different). Thus, I will close quoting Tov's observation concerning translation homophony in LXX and reapply it to my own discussion above: "the phenomenon described here occurs only sporadically."[75] However, even though it is sporadic, the phenomenon remains valid as a description of at least some tradents of the text. Or, in the words of Jefferson, sound-triggering may be a "gross-selection mechanism" not only in ordinary talk, but in forms of institutional talk, including *Vorlage*-based copying in the composition/transmission process of the Hebrew Bible.

Although this chapter has emphasized sound-triggering, I should remind my readers of the artificiality of my dividing category-triggering, sound-triggering, and visual-triggering into separate chapters. For example, note that in my discussion above of the wordplay in Prov 23:10 concerning some variation of עלם, I also described how the three vari-

---

75. Tov, "Loan-Words," 227.

ants ("ancient boundary stone," "boundary stones of the infants," and "boundary stone of the poor") relate to the parallel phrase in the second colon "the field of the orphans" in terms of category-triggering, that is, a category for the "field" as defined by "boundary stones" and a category of "infants"/"poor"/"orphans." Furthermore, as we transition to the next chapter concerning visual-triggering, I will quote from Scott Noegel's article "'Wordplay' in Qoheleth": "though both alliteration and assonance fit generally under the category of paronomasia or 'similarities of sound,' it is important to keep in mind that all examples of paronomasia are also effective on a visual register."[76] Certainly, some of the examples of wordplay discussed above may be best represented with the unpointed and therefore unvocalized consonantal text as a form of visually triggering the ambiguity of sound represented (Prov 31:21–22; Prov 3:8; Prov 23:10).[77] Nevertheless, as argued in the discussion of Ps 91:8 and Song 1:2, even when the consonantal text is necessarily vocalized in one particular way, the sound (in addition to the visual cues) can still communicate the wordplay.

---

76. Scott B. Noegel, "Word Play in Qoheleth," *JHS* 7 (2007), https://doi.org/10.5508/jhs.2007.v7.a4. See similarly, Karolien Vermeulen, "Two of a Kind: Twin Language in the Hebrew Bible," *JSOT* 37 (2012): 140.

77. These examples can also be understood as wordplay based on homographs. See below for my discussion of homographs in visual-triggering.

4
Visual-Triggering and Text-Critical Variants

In the previous two chapters I explicitly drew upon Jefferson's observations concerning category-triggering and sound-triggering as practices used in word selection in everyday conversation. Moreover, I contended that these same cognitive-linguistic practices underlie word selection in the process of *Vorlage*-based copying within scribal memory and I provided examples to illustrate this contention. In this chapter I discuss a category of text-critical variants that I have not yet discussed: those that appear to have occurred due to visual errors. Since Jefferson's poetics concern face-to-face social interactions that do not involve written texts, and since her poetics were developed during the earlier period of conversation analysis when visual cues in face-to-face social interactions had not yet been studied as rigorously as audible practices, it is not surprising that she did not discuss something like what I will call visual-triggering in my discussion of visual text-critical variants in this chapter. That is, below I will extrapolate from the practices of category-triggering and sound-triggering and identify a third practice that I will analogously call visual-triggering to suggest how the visual medium of writing affected scribal memory in *Vorlage*-based copying and apply it to variants that are widely understood to have occurred in the transmission process as visual errors. Before discussing visual-triggering, however, I will review how conversation analysis now includes the analysis of multimodalities in face-to-face interactions and how conversation analysis is now applied to written data as one possible medium of social interaction. I will then turn to a discussion of various examples that illustrate how visual-triggering helps us understand some text-critical variants and scribal memory.

Multimodality in Everyday Conversation

The early studies in conversation analysis primarily focused on audible data, especially since the data for many of the earliest studies were from telephone conversations in which even the participants did not have access to visual cues. However, the emphasis from the beginning was on social interaction, not talk itself, so now a preferred way of describing the object of study in conversation analysis is "talk-in-interaction" to denote that more than talk is involved (e.g., gaze, nods, and gestures). These early studies were also influenced to some degree by technological limitations—that is, video-recording in the 1970s required bulky, expensive equipment that could have been intrusive to recording natural conversations. However, Sacks and his students, including Jefferson, asserted from the beginning that visible behavior should be incorporated into the study of talk-in-interaction. One of the earliest studies that demonstrated the promise of including visual data was Charles Goodwin's 1981 study of restarts and gaze. Previous studies in linguistics had assumed that pauses indicated that the speaker was cognitively planning what to say, but Goodwin provided a detailed analysis of how a pause can be used by a speaker to request the hearer's gaze as a way of drawing the hearer's attention to the talk. Then, after the pause, the speaker would often restart the utterance so as to produce the complete utterance after the pause. This is illustrated in the following:

Example 4.1[1]

    Marsha: ..... X_____
                    'N he ca- *he* calls me a Vassar sno:b
    Dianne: .... X_____

Marsha begins her utterance as she is turning to look at Dianne (denoted by the dots above). When she sees that Dianne is not looking at her (denoted by the first X), she stops with a glottal stop ("ca-"), requesting Diane's attention. When she sees Dianne turning toward her (denoted by the dots below), she restarts her turn and, as she says "Vassar," they make

---

1. Charles Goodwin, *Conversational Organization: Interaction between Speakers and Hearers, Language, Thought and Culture* (New York: Academic Press, 1981), 72.

eye contact (denoted by the line above and the second X). Thus, Goodwin demonstrated how turn construction is also influenced by nonvocal aspects of talk-in-interaction—that is, participants orient to both vocal and nonvocal contributions to the interaction as they construct their turns at talk.

In their chapter "Embodied Actions and Organizational Activity," Christian Heath and Paul Luff reviewed the secondary literature in conversation analysis, including Goodwin's work, that has led to the consensus that "the production and intelligibility of social action in face-to-face or co-present gatherings is accomplished by virtue of a complex range of resources—the spoken, the bodily and the material."[2] They noted that all of these resources, both audible and visual, significantly influence the interaction between speaker and hearer within specific physical settings, even at the level of a single turn-at-talk. They illustrated this observation with a detailed discussion of an example from a doctor-patient interaction, in which the patient's response to the doctor's questions concerning what was the medical problem included not only speech but also gaze, visual orientation, and gesture, all of which helped the patient describe the reason for the medical visit and encouraged the doctor to respond in a particular way, including directing the doctor's gaze.[3] Thus, this example helps to illustrate two important basic observations concerning talk-in-interaction: (1) how copresent speech combines with body movement in everyday interactions, thereby describing how the most basic of social interactions is multimodal, involving various audible and visual elements, within whatever physical setting the participants are present, and (2) how this basic form of social interaction is also carried over into more institutional forms of interactions, such as doctor-patient interaction.[4]

---

2. Heath and Luff, "Embodied Actions and Organizational Activity," in *The Handbook of Conversation Analysis*, ed. Jack Sidnell and Tanya Stivers, BHL (Oxford: Wiley-Blackwell, 2013), 283.

3. Heath and Luff, "Embodied Actions and Organizational Activity," 295–99.

4. This example also illustrates how institutional talk (in this case, doctor-patient interactions) is adapted from practices in everyday conversation. For my discussion of how literary discourse itself is a type of institutional talk, see Person, *Structure and Meaning in Conversation and Literature*; Person, *From Conversation to Oral Tradition*. For my application of multimodality/embodied actions to literature connected to rituals (specifically Deut 26:1–11), see Raymond F. Person Jr., "Multimodality and Metonymy: Deuteronomy as a Test Case," in *Orality and Narrative: Performance and*

In his recent study, "Poetics and Performativity in the Management of Delicacy and Affiliation," Ian Hutchby expanded the understanding of poetics in ordinary talk beyond Jefferson's emphasis on word selection to include "vocal, facial, and bodily modulations."[5] That is, Hutchby's analysis includes not only Jefferson's insights on category-triggering and sound-triggering, but also a fuller account of poetics informed by more recent understandings of face-to-face talk-in-interaction that include multimodality. Although he does not use the term visual-triggering that I have coined as an analogous triggering mechanism, his analysis nevertheless confirms my intuition that such a thing must also occur in ordinary talk as he extended Jefferson's early analysis of poetics. However, his analysis still does not include written data.

Studies in Conversation Analysis That Include Written Data

With its emphasis on naturally occurring data, conversation analysts have generally avoided discussions of written texts, especially since the early studies were most interested in everyday conversation or face-to-face talk-in-interaction. Nevertheless, the theoretical basis for studies in conversation analysis including written texts as a form of naturally occurring data was expressed in 1983 by J. Maxwell Atkinson: "an adequate understanding of how texts are produced and responded to may remain elusive so long as the issue is pursued without making close comparative reference to how talk works."[6] That is, following a basic assumption in conversation analysis, institutional talk (such as doctor-patient interactions or producing and responding to written texts) can only be understood when compared to the most basic form of social interaction, everyday conversation. Atkinson's study concerned political speeches and the newspaper accounts of these same speeches. Other early work using written texts was that of Michael Mulkay, who analyzed the exchange of letters

---

Mythic-Ritual Poetics, vol. 12 of *Orality and Literacy in the Ancient World*, ed. Anton Bierl, David Bouvier, and Ombretta Cesca, MNSup (Leiden: Brill, forthcoming).

5. Hutchby, "Poetics and Performativity in the Management of Delicacy and Affiliation," in Person, Wooffitt, and Rae, *Bridging the Gap*, 31–51.

6. J. Maxwell Atkinson, "Two Devices for Generating Audience Approval: A Comparative Study of Public Discourse and Texts," in *Connectedness in Sentence, Discourse and Text*, ed. K. Ehlich and Henk van Riemsdijk, Tilburg Studies in Language and Literature 4 (Tilburg: Tilburg University, 1983), 230.

between scholars.[7] Due to the increasing influence of electronic media on communication, more recent studies have included an analysis of written texts in various social interactions, for example, studies concerning texting and Facebook chat.[8] Therefore, even though the earliest studies in conversation analysis did not include written texts and therefore Jefferson did not acknowledge something like visual-triggering in her poetics, it seems to me that the theoretical underpinning for such an analogous gross selection-mechanism for visual aspects of talk-in-interaction and within the institutional setting of reading in the ancient world, which includes scribal memory, was implied even in the early studies. Moreover, more recent studies now include the analysis of written texts even within what is becoming increasingly understood as everyday forms of social interaction. I assert that reading written texts has been an everyday practice for some of us, including the scribal elites in the ancient world, not unlike texting and Facebook chat for many contemporary readers. Therefore, something like visual-triggering should be considered as an analogous practice to category-triggering and sound-triggering.

Visual-Triggering: An Analogous Practice

As noted in Jefferson's article and in the previous two chapters, sometimes category-triggering and sound-triggering occur together. Although I think that that would also be the case for what I am labeling visual-triggering—that is, that all three forms of triggering can be related since talk-in-interaction is embodied and multimodal—in this chapter I am focusing primarily on visual-triggering alone based on types of variants often identified in text criticism. In the next chapter I will provide some examples of the interactions between these three different forms of triggering mechanisms. However, here I will simply note that written alphabetic letters represent sound, so that a sharp distinction between sound-triggering and visual-triggering should not be maintained. Furthermore, I assert that when a scribe is copying a manuscript the scribe

---

7. Mulkay, "Agreement and Disagreement in Conversation and Letters," *Text* 5 (1985): 201–27; Mulkay, "Conversations and Texts," *Human Studies* 9 (1986): 303–21.
8. Johanna Rendle-Short, "Dispreferred Responses When Texting: Delaying That 'No' Response," *Discourse & Communication* 9 (2015), 643–61; Joanne Meredith and Elisabeth Stokoe, "Repair: Comparing Facebook 'Chat' with Spoken Interaction," *Discourse & Communication* 8 (2014): 181–207.

is drawing from what Heath and Luff described as "a complex range of resources—the spoken, the bodily and the material."[9] That is, during *Vorlage*-based copying, the scribes necessarily *both* (1) read a manuscript that in some sense represented the spoken in the written script (and may even be vocalized), which was the result of a previous scribe's bodily movement of his hand involving writing materials, *and* (2) the scribes wrote new manuscripts that represented the spoken as a result of their own bodily movement interacting with writing materials (especially in those cases in which dictation was the means of producing the new manuscript). Moreover, scribes imagined future readers interacting with their manuscripts as well, either as readers (silent or aloud; alone or in public) or as copyists. Therefore, my extraction of the visual in this chapter should be understood strictly as an analytic solution in my attempt to discuss a complex social interaction that underlies scribal performance and scribal memory, that is, the communication that occurs between at least two scribes within the context of their collective memory of the traditional text that they are transmitting. Therefore, below I will focus on text-critical variants that are generally understood as being caused by errors based on similar visual shapes and orders of alphabetic letters representing voiced words. In the following sections I will discuss different words that can be represented by the exact same consonants (homographs), the confusion of similar letters, the division of letters into words, the change in order of the same letters (metathesis), and skipping over of words due to their similar beginning or ending letters (haplography). I will end with a discussion of stichography, which is the arrangement of poetic texts by spaces and/or lines in a manuscript as a visual representation of things such as poetic lines and half-lines as sound units.

Homographs

Homographs are words that look the same, but have different meanings.[10] Homophonic homographs are words that look the same in writing *and* are pronounced the same (also referred to as "homonyms")—for example, in English, "spring" can be a noun referring to a water source or a verb referring to quick movement. Heterophonic homographs are words that

---

9. Heath and Luff, "Embodied Actions and Organizational Activity," 283.
10. Note that some of the examples of wordplay in the previous chapter are examples of homographs within my discussion of sound-triggering.

look the same, but are pronounced differently—for example, in English, "lead" can be a noun referring to a metal or a verb referring to leadership.[11] In writing systems that use consonant-vowel alphabets, homographs are rare—for example, "there are fewer than 20 common [heterophonic] homographs in English."[12] Other writing systems have more homographs—for example, modern Hebrew and Arabic have a much higher percentage of homographs, especially when they use the unvoweled/unpointed systems.[13] Cognitive studies of reading have consistently demonstrated that the processing time for heterophonic homographs is higher than that for homophonic homographs *and* that the processing time for homophonic homographs is higher than that of words that are not homographs. That is, there is a hierarchy in relationship to word-processing during reading that strongly suggests that homographs complicate word recognition, especially heterophonic homographs. For example, in English the processing time increases from control words that are not homographs (e.g., "clock") to homophonic homographs/homonyms (e.g., "spring") to heterophonic homographs (e.g., "lead").[14]

The cognitive study of reading suggests that "phonology generally contributes to visual word perception."[15] That is, "the retrieval of meaning requires the activation of the phonological structure to which the printed word refers."[16] The study of heterophonic homographs has been critical to these general observations, because they present a higher degree

---

11. The secondary literature on the cognitive processing of homographs during reading contains some variety in the use of terms, e.g., some scholars simply use "homograph" to refer to "heterophonic homographs." See Alan H. Kawamoto and John H. Zemblidge, "Pronunciation of Homographs," *Journal of Memory and Language* 31 (1992): 349; Lawrence R. Gottlob et al., "Reading Homographs: Orthographic, Phonologic, and Semantic Dynamics," *Journal of Experimental Psychology: Human Perception and Performance* 25 (1999): 562. I have chosen to follow the terminology as used in Ram Frost and Shlomo Bentin, "Processing Phonological and Semantic Ambiguity: Evidence from Semantic Priming at Different SOAs," *Journal of Experimental Psychology: Learning, Memory, and Cognition* 18 (1992): 58–68; Frost and Michal Kampf, "Phonetic Recoding of Phonologically Ambiguous Printed Words," *Journal of Experimental Psychology: Learning, Memory, and Cognition* 19 (1993): 23–33.

12. Gottlob et al., "Reading Homographs," 562.

13. Frost and Bentin, "Processing Phonological and Semantic Ambiguity," 59; Gottlob et al. "Reading Homographs," 562.

14. Gottlob et al., "Reading Homographs."

15. Gottlob et al., "Reading Homographs," 561.

16. Frost and Bentin, "Processing Phonological and Semantic Ambiguity," 67.

of difficulty in recognizing which word the grapheme represents phonologically, due to its ambiguity. This explains why the processing time is higher for homographs. When a reader sees a heterophonic homograph, the ambiguity presents both phonological possibilities that continue until the reader has gained enough information from the context to select one of the phonological possibilities, in order to select the word's meaning in that context.[17] Once this selection has occurred, the reader then inhibits the alternative meanings of the homograph (with their pronunciation), while continuing to read with the selected meaning of the homograph (with its pronunciation).[18] The necessity of selecting among the phonological alternatives represented by the homograph before selecting the word's meaning is so strong that this principle applies to the word processing of interlingual homographs by readers who are bilingual. For example, when presented with experimental texts designed to test English-French and French-English bilinguals concerning their reading of both English and French texts with two homographs—"or" (in English, a high frequency conjunction and in French a low frequency noun meaning "gold" as well as a high frequency conjunction meaning "whereas" with all uses of "or" in the experimental readings in French as the low frequency noun) and "pour" (in English, a low frequency verb related to liquid and in French a high frequency preposition meaning "for")—the bilinguals required more processing time than the control group of monolinguals, presumably because the interlingual participants perceived additional phonologically possible pronunciations.[19] "The language context in which a word appears is insufficient to maximize selection in the bilingual; it is, rather, structure or meaning that contributes to the selection process."[20] That is, bilingualism can increase the frequency of homographs during reading, especially when the bilingual reader encounters a homograph in one language in which the homograph represents a low frequency word in contrast to the

---

17. Frost and Bentin, "Processing Phonological and Semantic Ambiguity"; Kawamoto and Zemblidge, "Pronunciation of Homographs"; Gottlob et al., "Reading Homographs."

18. David S. Gorfein, Stephanie Berger, and Andrea Bubka, "The Selection of Homograph Meaning: Word Association When Context Changes," *Memory & Cognition* 28 (2000): 766–73.

19. Seth N. Greenberg and Jan Saint-Aubin, "Letter Detection for Homographs with Different Meanings in Different Language Texts," *Bilingualism: Language and Cognition* 7 (2004): 241–53.

20. Greenberg and Saint-Aubin, "Letter Detection for Homographs," 252.

same homograph representing a high frequency word in the bilingual's other fluent language.[21]

Below I will discuss two heterophonic homographs that I have taken from Stefan Schorch's essay, "Dissimilatory Reading and the Making of Biblical Texts."[22] The first example concerns the different vocalization of the same verbal root and the second example concerns vocalizations that represent different noun forms. These two examples do a good job of representing the dissimilar readings of homographs that can occur more easily in the writing system of ancient Hebrew before any pointing system was developed.

Example 4.2: Gen 45:2[23]

MT

ויתן את קלו בבכי וַיִּשְׁמְעוּ מצרים וַיִּשְׁמַע בית פרעה

And he wept so loudly that the Egyptians heard it, and the house of Pharaoh **heard** it.

SP

ויתן את קולו בבכי וַיִּשְׁמְעוּ מצרים וַיַּשְׁמִעוּ בית פרעה[24]

And he wept so loudly that the Egyptians heard it and **let it hear** the house of Pharaoh.

---

21. This discussion concerns homographs in the reading process, but an analogous problem is presented in the written recording of homophones, e.g., in English there are three different graphemes for the homophones "to"/"too"/"two." That is, in oral discourse an analogous word-processing must occur when hearing homophones that may be differentiated in their written graphemes. Such differentiation of homophones (whether in oral discourse or in their recording in graphemes) likewise depends on context.

22. Schorch, "Dissimilatory Reading and the Making of Biblical Texts: The Jewish Pentateuch and the Samaritan Pentateuch," in Person and Rezetko, *Empirical Models*, 109–27.

23. Schorch, "Dissimilatory Reading," 117. The SP translation is Schorch's. Since he adapted the NRSV, I have provided the NRSV for the MT translation. The LXX translation is my own adaptation of the NRSV.

24. Schorch provided the Tiberian pointing system of vocalization in the SP for the purpose of comparison to MT as justified in Stefan Schorch, *Das Buch Genesis*, vol. 1 of *Die Vokale des Gesetzes: Die samaritanische Lesetradition als Textzeugin der Tora*, BZAW 339 (Berlin: de Gruyter, 2004), 79–80.

LXX
καὶ ἀφῆκεν φωνὴν μετὰ κλαυθμοῦ· ἤκουσαν δὲ πάντες οἱ Αἰγύπτιοι, καὶ ἀκουστὸν ἐγένετο εἰς τὸν οἶκον Φαραω.
[= SP] ויתן את קלו בבכי וַיִּשְׁמְעוּ מצרים וַיַּשְׁמִעוּ בית פרעה =
And he wept so loudly that the Egyptians heard it and **let it hear** the house of Pharaoh.

The MT reading repeats the *qal* form for both occurrences of the verb root of שמע ("heard it"). In contrast, both the SP reading and the LXX reading assume the *piel* form for the second occurrence of שמע ("let it hear" in Schorch's translation of SP and "it came to be heard" in NETS). Since SP and LXX preserve the *lectio difficilior*, Schorch concluded that "LXX … attests an example for successful transmission" of the original text as "intended by the scribe" of the "originally encoded text."[25] From the perspective of scribal memory, however, these two readings can be understood as synonymous readings, even though the heterophonic homograph would require different vocalizations. That is, within the multiformity allowed within the tradition, the difference between the pharaoh hearing Joseph's crying directly (the *qal* reading in MT) or indirectly by way of a report (the *piel* reading in SP and LXX) is really insignificant, since both are clearly exaggerations. In either case, Joseph's crying was so unusually loud that all of the Egyptians heard it, including the pharaoh (directly and/or indirectly). Therefore, I would resist the tendency to determine which reading is original within the broader tradition that preserved both readings in scribal memory.

When he introduced the problem of reading unpointed texts, Schorch provided two clear examples of heterophonic homographs: (1) the nine different ways that the verb וישב can be pointed and pronounced and (2) the four different ways that מטה can be pointed and pronounced, the latter of which are as follows: "מטה: (1) מִטָּה ('bed,' Gen 37:1); (2) מַטֶּה ('staff,' Gen 38:25); (3) מַטָּה ('below,' Deut 28:43); (4) מֻטֶּה ('corruption,' Ezek 9:9)."[26] Example 4.3 illustrates the homograph מטה.

---

25. Schorch, "Dissimilatory Reading," 118.
26. Schorch, "Dissimilatory Reading," 111.

4. Visual-Triggering and Text-Critical Variants

Example 4.3: Gen 47:31[27]

MT

וַיֹּאמֶר הִשָּׁבְעָה לִי וַיִּשָּׁבַע לוֹ וַיִּשְׁתַּחוּ יִשְׂרָאֵל עַל רֹאשׁ הַמִּטָּה

And he said, "Swear to me." And he swore to him. Then Israel bowed himself **at the head of his bed**.

LXX

εἶπεν δὲ Ὀμοσόν μοι. καὶ ὤμοσεν αὐτῷ. καὶ προσεκύνησεν Ισραηλ ἐπὶ τὸ ἄκρον τῆς ῥάβδου αὐτοῦ.

= וַיֹּאמֶר הִשָּׁבְעָה לִי וַיִּשָּׁבַע לוֹ וַיִּשְׁתַּחוּ יִשְׂרָאֵל עַל רֹאשׁ הַמַּטֶּה

And he said, "Swear to me." And he swore to him. Then Israel bowed himself **at the top of his staff**.

In example 4.3, MT-Gen 47:31 identified the homograph מטה with (1) "at the head of the bed" and LXX-Gen 47:31 identified it with (2) "at the top of his staff." Schorch concluded as follows:

> the context makes it [the LXX reading] highly unlikely that this is a correct rendering of the text [T^a] originally encoded in the consonantal framework. The general narrative is concerned with Jacob's illness and impending death, and the act of prostration can hardly be carried out on the top of a staff. Thus, although the Greek rendering was ultimately understood as a meaningful text [T^b] as proven by its quotation in Heb 11:21, the underlying Hebrew reading is clearly erroneous in terms of transmission, since it did not retrieve the original message in the right way.[28]

Once again we can see how the assumption of an original text is influencing Scorch's interpretation of variants. When we are not pressed into finding one original reading, I suggest that both Hebrew readings are not only "meaningful texts," but can be understood as (near-)synonymous readings and as multiple originals. Both versions of the narrative presume that Jacob is so ill that he is confined to bed and near death, especially since "bed" is

---

27. Schorch, "Dissimilatory Reading," 116, his translations.
28. Schorch, "Dissimilatory Reading," 116. Similarly, James Barr, "Vocalization and the Analysis of Hebrew," in *Hebräische Wortforschung: Festschrift zum 80. Geburtstag von Walter Baumgartner*, ed. Benedikt Hartmann et al., VTSup 16 (Leiden: Brill, 1967), 3.

understood in both versions in 48:2 (κλίνην = הַמִּטָּה). I agree with Scorch that "prostration can hardly be carried out on the top of a staff"; however, I do not think that that is the only possible interpretation of the LXX reading. It seems to me that "Israel bowed himself at the top of his staff" (Scorch's translation of the LXX reading) can imply that Jacob is using his staff as he (partially?) rises by the side of his bed to support himself in his frailty—that is, maybe the staff is on the floor and Jacob must use the staff to sit up to whatever degree he can manage. It seems to me that this is not far from what a possible interpretation of the MT reading may imply—that is, rather than assuming that the MT reading implies that he could get out of bed to prostrate himself on the floor "at the head of his bed" (presumably "in front of his bed"), we can interpret the MT reading as he cannot prostrate himself on the floor as generally expected and, therefore, he somehow does so while staying in bed. In other words, in both versions Jacob is so frail that his prostration does not follow generally accepted practice, so he improvises in his frailty by somehow staying in his bed with the possible assistance of his staff. That is, the LXX reading may be pointing us to a different interpretation of the MT reading than is sometimes made.[29]

As Schorch's essay clearly demonstrates, the consonantal Hebrew text allows for some ambiguity in the interpretation of homographs and the textual plurality evident in the written transmission of the text was paralleled by a textual plurality of how the consonantal text was voiced in different reading traditions. That is, I began my discussion of visual-triggering with homographs to illustrate the arguments made in recent studies of the cognitive processing of reading homographs that insist that word recognition depends significantly on phonological recognition. Although this is true for English, French, and other modern writing systems that use consonantal-vowel alphabets, it is even more relevant for ancient Hebrew and other languages with consonantal alphabets. Thus, the textual plurality that relates to which Hebrew letters were actually written in the

---

29. Similarly, S. R. Driver, *The Book of Genesis: With Introduction and Notes*, 3rd. ed. (New York: Gorham, 1904), 375; E. A. Speiser, *Genesis: Introduction, Translation, and Notes*, AB (Garden City, NY: Doubleday, 1964), 356–57; Robert Davidson, *Genesis 12–50*, CBC (Cambridge: Cambridge University Press, 1979), 292–93; Nahum N. Sarna, *Genesis: The Traditional Hebrew Text with the New JPS Translation*, JPS Torah Commentary (Philadelphia: Jewish Publication Society, 1989), 324. These commentators note the difficulty in interpreting the text, but agree that whatever Jacob's actions were, he was confined to his bed.

ancient manuscript tradition does not fully describe the textual plurality that was preserved in scribal memory, because even the exact same consonantal text may have more than one interpretation, all of which may nevertheless be understood as authentic, based significantly on different pronunciations of homographs. The consonantal Hebrew text required the application of scribal memory, especially when a reader was confronted with homographs, because the visual-triggering of the Hebrew letters did not in every case produce unambiguous readings. The following discussion now turns to variants within the consonantal text itself.

Confusion of Similar Letters or Interchanges

Some text-critical variants are understood as reading errors on the part of the scribe, including especially the confusion of letters that are visually similar. Hendel labeled this type "graphic confusion" and Tov referred to them as "interchange of similar letters."[30] "When referring to interchanges I [Tov] mean that one letter is replaced with another one, or even two, presumably because of their external similarity."[31] The interchange of ד and ר is one of the more common interchanges and, as Tov noted, "the interchange ד/ר is possible in both the square Aramaic script and the earlier paleo-Hebrew script."[32] The three examples I discuss below all include the interchange ד/ר with the last one having additional common interchanges.

Example 4.4: Prov 14:34[33]

MT

צדקה תרומם גוי וחסד לאמים חטאת

Righteousness exalts a nation, but sin is **a reproach** to any people.

---

30. Hendel, *Steps to a New Edition*, 152; Tov, *Textual Criticism* (3rd ed.), 227–33.

31. Emanuel Tov, "Interchanges of Consonants between the Masoretic Text and the *Vorlage* of the Septuagint," in Fisbane and Tov, *Sha'arei Talmon*, 257.

32. Tov, "Interchanges of Consonants," 266. For an excellent discussion of how paleography relates to text criticism, see Hila Dayfani, "The Relationship between Paleography and Textual Criticism: Textual Variants Due to Graphic Similarity between the Masoretic Text and the Samaritan Pentateuch," *Textus* 27 (2018): 3–21. She provides examples comparing MT and SP with close comparisons of letters in the paleoscript of the Dead Sea Scrolls as an empirical reference to how the variants could have arisen.

33. Fox, *Proverbs*, 229.

LXX
δικαιοσύνη ὑψοῖ ἔθνος, ἐλασσονοῦσι δὲ φυλὰς ἁμαρτίαι.
= צדקה תרומם גוי וחסר לאמים חטאת
Righteousness exalts a nation, but sin **diminishes** any people.

Here the interchange ד/ר is between the two words וחסד and וחסר. Fox noted that, although the MT reading is a "rare Aramaism," an argument of *lectio difficilior* does not apply in this case because the LXX "recognized the rare Aramaism חסד 'disgrace' in 25:10 and could have done so here."[34] Furthermore, the LXX reading has the support from the Syriac. Whether the reading is the noun חסד ("reproach") or the verb חסר ("diminishes"), both readings present a proverb that contrasts "righteousness" and "sin" and their opposite effects on "a nation"/"people." Thus, it seems as if here we have another case of equally good proverbs.[35] That is, within scribal memory, this variant is a synonymous reading producing synonymous proverbs; therefore, the presumed confusion of similar letters did not result in a significant variant.

Example 4.5: Isa 47:10[36]

MT

ותבטחי ברעתך

You felt secure **in your wickedness**.

1QIsa^a

ותבטחי בדעתך

You felt secure **in your knowledge**.

This example is taken from Pulikottil's study of harmonization in 1QIsa^a; however, he seems to have overlooked that this variant may also be the result of the interchange ד/ר in this literary context that could be understood as (near-)synonyms. Pulikottil wrote,

> The substitution of בדעתך ("in your knowledge") for ברעתך ("in your wickedness") in 47.10 is influenced by ודעתך in 47.10a. The scroll reading is very much in line with the rest of the verse, which goes on talking

---

34. Fox, *Proverbs*, 229.
35. Fox, *Proverbs*, 29.
36. Pulikottil, *1QIsa^a*, 51, his translation.

about the wisdom and knowledge of Babylon.... This example shows that the scribe, when faced with incongruities, prefers to go with the dominant idea of the passage and also for the substitution that would bring forth better parallelism. רעה is hardly parallel to חכמה nor has it a place in the context of חכמה and דעת.[37]

Pulikottil's assumption of an original text seems to push him to choose one reading over the other, thereby missing how these two readings can be understood as synonymous with an interchange of ר/ד. I disagree that "רעה is hardly parallel to חכמה nor has it a place in the context of חכמה and דעת," because the חכמה and דעת that is referred to here is clearly the knowledge and wisdom of the people separated from God, the knowledge and wisdom that leads them astray from God. This is not the knowledge and wisdom of God, but its opposite, and it leads to evil and their disaster as divine punishment (Isa 47:11). Therefore, it seems to me that these readings can be understood as synonymous readings within the context of scribal memory, which explains further how the interchange of ר/ד in this context could easily occur. Obviously, a *Vorlage* would have one reading or the other, but, if both readings were preserved in scribal memory, then the so-called confusion of similar letters would be much more likely to occur.

In example 4.6 below, according to Fox's interpretation, we not only have a case of the interchange ר/ד, but the interchanges ח/ה and ד/כ (denoted by the abbreviation "graph") as well as a case of haplography. Fox concluded that, when multiple interchanges occur, there are two possible explanations for the process that led to the variant. "The change from one word-form to another can take place by a series of steps or all at once."[38] This example is one that Fox used to illustrate how multiple interchanges can occur at once. After quoting the two proverbs, I provide the three variants as understood by Fox for further clarification.

Example 4.6: Prov 25.27[39]

    MT

אכל דבש הרבות לא טוב וחקר כבדם כבוד

Eating honey too much is not good, or to seek honor on top of honor.

---

37. Pulikottil, *1QIsa*ᵃ, 52.
38. Fox, *Proverbs*, 79.
39. Fox, *Proverbs*, 339, his translation.

LXX
ἐσθίειν μέλι πολὺ οὐ καλόν, τιμᾶν δὲ χρὴ λόγους ἐνδόξους.
= אכל דבש הרבות לא טוב והקר דברים מכבד
Eating honey too much is not good, and being sparing of words is honorable.

MT: וחקר
LXX: τιμᾶν δὲ χρή = והקר
   graph ה → ח

MT: כבדם
LXX: λόγους = דברים
   graph ר → ד
   graph ד → כ

MT: כבוד
LXX: ἐνδόξους = מכבד
   haplog ממ → מ

Noting the graphic similarities in the Hebrew, Fox rejected the possibility that these changes occurred as a series of individual interchanges:

> I do not think that the change occurred in a series of unrelated accidents but rather that a scribe looked at a group of consonants and grasped them wrongly. Taken as a whole, the change is not unlikely, especially if we picture the text as written continuously and without final letters: והקרדברממכבד.[40]

In this case, the description that Fox used suggests an original reading (the LXX reading included in his critical text) and a later reading (the MT reading). Note that Fox imagined the text "written continuously" as וחקר כבדם (= וחקרכברמכבד), not as והקרדברממכבד (= והקר דברים מכבד) כבוד). That is, his comments might suggest that the confusion ran only in one direction. However, since he often makes the case that the proverbs in MT and LXX are equally good proverbs, I wonder why Fox rejected this possibility here.[41] It seems to me that these can be understood as synony-

---

40. Fox, *Proverbs*, 339.
41. Fox, *Proverbs*, 59.

mous proverbs, even though the parallelism between the first strophe and the second strophe differs—that is, in the MT reading the second strophe has a synonymous vice to eating too much honey (seeking too much honor) and in the LXX reading the second strophe uses antonomy, in that "being sparing of words" implies moderation of a good thing. Fox summarized the reconstructed proverb based on the LXX reading as "don't overdo good things, not even speech."[42] However, it seems to me that "don't overdo good things, even seeking honor" would be synonymous, in that the general principle applies equally to speech and seeking honor. Furthermore, as Fox noted, both versions of this proverb use the same honey analogy as Prov 25:16.[43]

The standard interpretation of these type of variants tends to be that the scribe misread the word by confusing similarly shaped letters; what is implied but often not explicitly acknowledged is that the variant that results from this error made enough sense in the mind of the scribe within the literary context that the scribe could make that kind of a mistake and apparently later scribes continued to copy this mistake, because it likewise made some sense in the literary context. However, once we take into account the role of scribal memory within the context of textual plurality, we need to broaden the definition of synonymous readings, so that some of these scribal errors may not be errors at all, but may simply reflect the multiformity of the broader tradition. That is, although the similarly shaped letters may have played a visual role, the different words do not significantly change the meaning of the text, so that we have multiple originals with words that may have been influenced by visual-triggering, due not only to the contribution to the synonymous reading but also their similarly shaped letters.

Division of Words

Since ancient manuscripts were sometimes written without spaces between the words (*scriptio continua*; or at least without sufficient spacing), variants may have resulted from different interpretations of how to divide a string of letters into separate words. Below I discuss two examples.

---

42. Fox, *Proverbs*, 339.
43. Fox, *Proverbs*, 339.

Example 4.7: Isa 40:12[44]

MT

מי מדד בשעלו מים

Who measured **the water** with the hollow of His hand.

1QIsa^a

מיא מדד בשועלו מי ים

Who measured **the water of the sea** with the hollow of His hand.

In example 4.7, the string of letters מים (or מיים) are divided in two different ways: מים ("the water") and מי ים ("the water of the sea") with the possible duplication or omission of a *yod*. Tov concluded, "The reading of 1QIsa^a is preferable because of the parallel hemistich+ ('and gauged the sky with a span')."[45] It is unclear to me why one reading should be preferred over the other on the basis of the parallelism here, because the two readings are often found in synonymous parallelism (e.g., Ps 74:13; 78:13; Isa 43:16; 51:10). Therefore, it seems to me that this variant based on the erroneous division of letters is also a synonymous reading and that we should therefore consider both readings as authentic within the multiformity of the tradition as preserved in scribal memory.

Example 4.8: Prov 13:14[46]

MT

תורת חכם מקור חיים לסור ממקשי מות

The law of the wise is a spring of life,
  so that one may avoid the snares of death.

LXX

νόμος σοφοῦ πηγὴ ζωῆς, ὁ δὲ ἄνους ὑπὸ παγίδος θανεῖται.
= תורת חכם מקור חיים וכסיל ממקש ימות

The law of the wise is a spring of life,
  but the fool will die by a trap.

---

44. Tov, *Textual Criticism* (3rd ed.), 235, his translation.
45. Tov, *Textual Criticism* (3rd ed.), 235.
46. Fox, *Proverbs*, 211, his translation.

4. Visual-Triggering and Text-Critical Variants 253

In his interpretation, Fox clearly preferred the MT reading over the LXX reading. "The change from לסור to וכסיל was provoked by different word division, ממקש ימות. This left the resulting verb, 'he will die,' without a subject. The change of לסור to וכסיל provided the subject, but it is unclear whether this was a scribe's or the translator's doing."[47] Since he sometimes concludes that the different proverbs in MT and LXX are equally good, it is not clear to me why he rejects the possibility of the change in word division being ממקשי מות ("snares of death") with a resulting change from וכסיל to לסור. In his work on paranomasia, Casanowicz argued that the alliteration in the Hebrew is preserved in both readings, but he provided a different retroversion of the Greek: ופתי ממקש ימות.[48] Fox's retroversion of ὁ δὲ ἄνους as וכסיל rather than ופתי recognizes the similar letters between לסור and וכסיל, so that it is preferred. Nevertheless, Casanowicz's observation that the alliteration is preserved in the LXX reading remains, since it is based on the repetition of מק in both stichs. Thus, it seems to me that sound-triggering is also in play in this example in terms of both the alliteration of מק between both stichs and in the alliteration between the two words וכסיל and לסור (as well as their graphic similarities). Therefore, we may have another case of synonymous proverbs, since the moral of the two versions of the proverb is the same.

As these two examples illustrate, sometimes the explanation of variants based on the division of words can be understood as two equally valid interpretations of the same sequence of consonants within the multiformity of the tradition as preserved in scribal memory. That is, these variants may not truly be variants at all, especially when we look at the different lexemes within their larger literary context in which they appear to be the same.

Metathesis

Variants containing metathesis are variants in which two readings differ simply in the transposition of two letters, usually consecutive letters. Although variants due to metathesis are widely understood as scribal errors, David Tsumura has suggested that these scribal errors are sometimes best understood as "phonetic spellings":

---

47. Fox, *Proverbs*, 211.
48. Casanowicz, "Paronomasia in the Old Testament," 142 (#229).

While "scribal errors" are concerned with orthographic mistakes, "phonetic spellings" are concerned with the relationship between scripts and sounds. They are the graphic representations of the "phonic" features of a word or a phrase as it is pronounced. They intend to reproduce the actual pronunciation. Hence they often deviate from the normal and "correct" spelling.[49]

Tsumura also noted that the *ketiv-qere* tradition supports his conclusion: "the K. *tends* to represent 'phonic' reality by a phonetic spelling. By contrast, the Q. points to the 'correct' historical spelling."[50] Tsumura provided various examples from the book of Samuel, including the following three:

Example 4.9[51]

1 Sam 27:8
(K) והגזרי – (Q) והגרזי

2 Sam 15:28
(K) בערבות – (Q) בעברות

2 Sam 20:14
(K) ויקהלו – (Q) ויקלהו

Concerning these three variant readings, Tsumura concluded, "Both forms are the phonetic variants of the same word."[52] In an analogous way to how many text critics disregard orthographic differences, Tsumura was advocating for treating such phonetic spellings in a similar way—that is, these different spellings simply reflect different pronunciations of the same word and should not be considered scribal errors that resulted in different words. In fact, he noted that the *ketiv* reading in 2 Sam 20:14 "is sometimes vocalized as /wayyiqlēhû/ based on a different root *qlh"; however, he rejected this interpretation, preferring to understand it as a different phonetic spelling from the root קהל.[53]

---

49. David Tsumura, "Scribal Errors or Phonetic Spellings? Samuel as an Aural Text," *VT* 49 (1999): 390.
50. Tsumura, "Scribal Errors or Phonetic Spellings?," 391.
51. Tsumura, "Scribal Errors or Phonetic Spellings?," 392.
52. Tsumura, "Scribal Errors or Phonetic Spellings?," 392.
53. Tsumura, "Scribal Errors or Phonetic Spellings?," 392.

4. Visual-Triggering and Text-Critical Variants

Although Tsumura's arguments may caution us from too quickly concluding that the transposition of consecutive letters (metathesis) may be due to a visual error, his last example concerning 2 Sam 20:14 illustrates a problem for his own argument—that is, 2 Sam 20:14 can reasonably be translated as "and they [all the Bichrites] assembled" (following Tsumura's argument that Q and K represent the same word from the root קהל) and "and they assembled" (using the root קלה, the option Tsumura discussed but rejected). It seems to me that both of these translations are possible, especially if we understand that they are (near-) synonymous readings. Below I provide three examples of metathesis from Fox's HBCE volume, *Proverbs*. In all three examples, Fox identified each of the proverbs in both the MT and LXX versions as meaningfully good proverbs.

Example 4.10: Prov 12:21[54]

MT

לא יאנה לצדיק כל און ורשעים מלאו רע

No misfortune will happen to the righteous man,
    but the wicked are filled with trouble.

LXX

οὐκ ἀρέσει τῷ δικαίῳ οὐδὲν ἄδικον, οἱ δὲ ἀσεβεῖς πλησθήσονται κακῶν.

= לא ינאה לצדיק כל און ורשעים מלאו רע

No injustice will please the righteous person,
    but the wicked are filled with trouble.

Fox noted the metathesis אנ → נא in לא יאנה ("no misfortune") and לא ינאה ("no injustice"). Although יאנה and ינאה are not synonyms, he concluded that "both G[reek] and M[T] offer meaningful proverbs. G describes the good man's attitude, M the consequence of his righteousness."[55] Therefore, if we think of this variant as occurring at the level of the proverbs rather than the lexeme, we have synonymous proverbs, so that this can be understood as a synonymous reading.

---

54. Fox, *Proverbs*, 203, his translation.
55. Fox, *Proverbs*, 203.

Example 4.11: Prov 15:30[56]

MT

מאור עינים ישמח לב שמועה טובה תדשן עצם
The light of the eyes makes the heart glad,
    and a good saying fattens the bones.

LXX

θεωρῶν ὀφθαλμὸς καλὰ εὐφραίνει καρδίαν, φήμη δὲ ἀγαθὴ πιαίνει ὀστᾶ.
The eye, beholding good things, makes the heart glad,
    and a good saying fattens the bones.
= מראה עינים ישמח לב שמועה טובה תדשן עצם
The sight of the eyes makes the heart glad,
    and a good saying fattens the bones.

Fox identified the metathesis אר → רא in מראה עינים ("The sight of the eyes") and מאור עינים ("The light of the eyes"); however, he noted other possible influences: "The change was partly graphic, due to the similarity of מראה and מאור, but it was facilitated by the association of both words with 'eyes.' Two directions of change are possible."[57] After discussing the possibilities of change in both directions, Fox concluded: "Although מראה is preferable,... both variants can be accepted as forming meaningful proverbs."[58] His preference for מראה is primarily based on a literary argument of wordplay and his evaluation of the MT reading as "awkward and tautologous"; therefore, he provided מראה in his eclectic text as the preferred reading.[59] However, in his introduction Fox cautioned his readers that text criticism must proceed "in spite of contradictions and insoluble dilemmas" and in this case he is aware that some other text critics may apply a different standard (e.g., *lectio difficilior potior*) and reach a different conclusion.[60] Thus, even though he prefers one over the other, Fox's argument suggests that these are not only meaningful proverbs, but (near-)synonymous proverbs. Furthermore, I want to note here that Fox's

---

56. Fox, *Proverbs*, 243, his translation.
57. Fox, *Proverbs*, 243.
58. Fox, *Proverbs*, 243.
59. Fox, *Proverbs*, 243.
60. Fox, *Proverbs*, 15.

4. Visual-Triggering and Text-Critical Variants

argument concerning how both readings are closely connected to "eyes" suggests that category-triggering is involved in this example. That is, the two variants based on metathesis nevertheless belong to the same category of lexemes related to the human sense of sight.

Example 4.12: Prov 12:23[61]

> MT
> אדם ערום כֹּסֶה דעת ולב כסילים יקרא אולת
> The intelligent man conceals knowledge,
>   but the heart of the foolish broadcasts folly.

> LXX
> ἀνὴρ συνετὸς θρόνος αἰσθήσεως, καρδία δὲ ἀφρόνων συναντήσεται ἀραῖς.
> = אדם ערום כִּסֵּא דעת ולב כסילים יקרא אלות
> The intelligent man is a throne of knowledge,
>   but the heart of the foolish will meet with curses.

According to Fox, the differences between these two versions involved three changes, all of which can easily be understood as part of the reading process within scribal memory:

> G[reek] differs from M[T] by (1) construing כסא as כִּסֵּא ("throne"), (2) equating יקרא ("calls") with יקרה ("meets," "happens"), and (3) reading אלות ("curses") in its source text.... Difference 1 gets rid of an apparent logical difficulty: that the wise man should conceal wisdom, whereas he presumably should be revealing it to all. Differences 2 and 3 are trivial errors.[62]

That is, כסא/כסה can be read in two ways (as the noun "throne" and as the verb "conceals"), יקרה can be read two ways when וקרה is considered ("calls" and "meets"), and the last word consists of the metathesis ול → לו in אולת ("folly") and אלות ("curses"). Therefore, according to Fox, "The result was a meaningful, new proverb."[63] Although Fox prefers the MT

---

61. Fox, *Proverbs*, 203, his translation.
62. Fox, *Proverbs*, 203.
63. Fox, *Proverbs*, 203.

version, it seems to me that these are (near-)synonymous proverbs contrasting the wise and the foolish.

Tsumura's arguments concerning phonetic spellings rather than scribal errors may caution us from too quickly concluding that variants based on metathesis are scribal errors. Fox provided numerous examples of metathesis that resulted in equally good proverbs, of which the three discussed above are representative. When I combine their arguments, it seems to me that at least in these cases we really have synonymous readings that can easily be explained from the perspective of scribal memory in that what is visually presented on the manuscript can be read in slightly different ways that nevertheless preserve the general meaning of the proverb within the context of textual fluidity and textual plurality. That is, the visual error of metathesis may be, at least in some cases, not an error, but the alternative readings may simply represent the textual plurality of the tradition.

Haplography

Haplography is widely understood as one means by which the text was shortened due to a scribal error of visually skipping over some text. "Haplography, 'writing once' (ἅπλος, 'once,' and γραφή, 'writing'), is the erroneous omission of one or more adjacent letters, clusters of letters, or words that are identical or similar."[64] Haplography is sometimes referred to as parablepsis (that is, "overseeing") and can be due to both homoioarchton ("same beginning") and homoioteleuton ("same ending")—that is, the repetition of letters or word(s) at the beginning or ending of a word or phrase caused the scribe's eye to jump over the text that occurs between the identical or similar beginning/ending word or phrase. Because of the dominance of *lectio brevior potior* in typical assumptions of textual transmission, haplography is often understood as one of the few ways in which a text is shortened. "According to the traditional conception in biblical studies, the older text was only expanded during its transmission. Omissions would have been almost exclusively scribal lapses (such as homoioteleuton) or caused by other unintentional corruptions."[65] In *God's Omitted Word*, Juha Pakkala has challenged the dominant assumption of

---

64. Tov, *Textual Criticism* (3rd ed.), 222.

65. Juha Pakkala, *God's Omitted Word: Omissions in the Transmission of the Hebrew Bible* (Göttingen: Vandenhoeck & Ruprecht, 2013), 16.

lectio brevior potior by suggesting that omission was more common than generally assumed, including omissions other than haplography. Similarly, Freedman and Overton have concluded that the majority of text critics have overlooked that "haplography is the most common error in the copying of manuscripts," so that in their opinion haplography is "widespread and ruthless."[66] Because of their conclusion of the prevalence of haplography, they explicitly criticized the widely accepted assumptions of textual transmission: "The shorter, more difficult reading is *not* always better; haplography always produces a shorter text, and almost always a more difficult one."[67]

In past publications and again throughout this work, I share similar criticisms of the standard assumptions of textual transmission; however, I also go further than Pakkala, Freedman, Overton, and others are willing to go, in that I am rejecting the very idea of an original text.[68] Furthermore, I am also arguing that methodologically we need to be more closely engaged with how word selection works within language in general as well as how the material mechanics of textual transmission should temper our conclusions, drawing significantly from the notion of scribal memory in the composition/transmission process. Concerning haplography, I find Vroom's arguments in "A Cognitive Approach to Copying Errors: Haplography and Textual Transmission of the Hebrew Bible" very convincing. In the introduction I discussed my adaptation of Vroom's insights on textual transmission in general as it related to word selection, which included the possibility of scribes returning to the wrong location in the *Vorlage*; here I will focus only on his observations about haplography.

Like others before him, Vroom noted that subjectivity is often involved in identifying haplography.[69] "In many cases, when a variant can be explained as either a secondary insertion or an accidental omission, text-critical judgments become arbitrary; conclusions can be determined according to each scholar's assumptions about the nature of scriptural transmission."[70] As one corrective to this subjectivity, Vroom drew substantially from cognitive psychology as it applies to the copying process. He identified the two most important insights from discussions of short-term

---

66. Freedman and Overton, "Omitting the Omissions," 99.
67. Freedman and Overton, "Omitting the Omissions," 100.
68. See esp., Person and Rezetko, "Importance of Empirical Models."
69. E.g., Tov, *Textual Criticism* (3rd ed.), 222–23.
70. Vroom, "Cognitive Approach to Copying Errors," 263.

memory or what he prefers to refer to as "working memory" as the "phonological loop" and the "visuospatial sketchpad." He quoted the following definition of "phonological loop" from *A Dictionary of Psychology*:

> A subsystem of working memory that functions as a buffer store, holding information with the help of inner speech, as when a person mentally rehearses a telephone number over and over while searching for a pen and paper to write it down. It contains two components, a short-term phonological buffer store, holding phonologically coded information for very short periods only, and a subvocal rehearsal loop that maintains information by repeating it mentally from time to time.[71]

As noted above in my discussion of homographs, the study of reading within cognitive psychology has demonstrated that visual word perception is closely connected to sound—that is, the recognition of the visual representation of sounds in writing requires what is described here as "inner speech" and "phonologically coded information." Thus, the phonological loop is an important element of working memory in the reading process. Vroom described the visuospatial sketchpad and its implications on *Vorlage*-based copying as follows:

> In contrast to the phonological loop, the visuospatial sketchpad has to do with the processing of *non-verbal* information; this includes both visual and spatial information.... When it comes to physical handwritten manuscripts, such visual information might include the shape of a word (such as small, crammed, or messy handwriting), as well as any distinct marking on the scroll (such as lacuna, tears, scuffs, smears etc.).[72]

He noted that during *Vorlage*-based copying the visuospatial sketchpad is important so that the scribe can accurately return to the *Vorlage* where he left off, in order to select the next transfer unit to store in his working memory as he moves back to the same space where he left off in the new manuscript.

When he combined these insights, Vroom reached two sound conclusions that greatly eliminate what have been widely understood as related to haplography: "(1) haplography does not occur with the repetition of

---

71. Vroom, "Cognitive Approach to Copying Errors," 271. Quoting "Phonological Loop," in *Dictionary of Psychology*, ed. Andrew M. Colman (Oxford: Oxford University Press, 2008), 573.

72. Vroom, "Cognitive Approach to Copying Errors," 271.

individual letters; (2) haplography does not typically result in the loss of large chunks of text."[73] He illustrated his conclusions with Exod 22:4, which has a minus widely understood as an example of haplography in the secondary literature. Note that I have varied my general practice of simply giving the MT reading first here, because the possible case of haplography is demonstrated best by starting with the presumed visuospatial layout of the earlier reading within Vroom's discussion, which seems to assume an original text.

Example 4.13: Exod 22:4[74]

> SP
> וכי יבעיר איש שדה או כרם ושלח את בעירו ובער בשדה אחר שלם ישלם
> משדהו כתבואתה ואם כל השדה יבעי מיטב שדהו ומיטב כרמו ישלם
> And if a man causes a field or a vineyard to be grazed and he sends out his animal and it grazes the field of another **he shall surely make restitution from his field according to its yield. But if it grazes the whole field**, from the best of his field and from the best of his vineyard he shall make restitution.

> MT
> וכי יבער איש שדה או כרם ושלח את בעירו ובער בשדה אחר מיטב שדהו ומיטב כרמו ישלם
> And if a man causes a field or a vineyard to be grazed and he sends out his animal and it grazes the field of another, from the best of his field and from the best of his vineyard he shall make restitution.

Vroom noted: "Numerous scholars have argued that the MT's text was shortened due to haplography, in which case SP preserves the preferable reading."[75] In order for this interpretation to work, scholars typically emend the יבעי in SP to יבער to align with the verbs as found in MT and then explain the omission as follows: "after the scribe finished copying the ר on the word אחר, he mistakenly thought he had finished copying the ר on יבער, which resulted in an accidental omission of the

---

73. Vroom, "Cognitive Approach to Copying Errors," 273.
74. Vroom, "Cognitive Approach to Copying Errors," 264, his translation.
75. Vroom, "Cognitive Approach to Copying Errors," 264.

intervening material."[76] Because of the necessity of the phonological loop, Vroom countered that "it is simply not possible for a scribe to finish copying the ר on יבער, and then turn back to the ר on אחר in his *Vorlage*; the eye would not return to a single letter."[77] That is, the transfer unit that the scribe selected is at least a whole word (probably a phrase) in the phonological loop; therefore, this minus should not be explained as a case of haplography, because it does not make sense from the perspective of the cognitive process of reading and copying texts. Furthermore, Vroom insisted that the observation of how the visuospatial sketchpad works would also eliminate this minus (and other similar lengthy minuses) as likely examples of haplography:

> Supposing that the scribe's eye did return to the wrong ר—which, cognitively speaking, is virtually impossible—then such an explanation would also imply that the scribe's eye returned to a substantially different location on his *Vorlage* than where he left off. Such a scenario does not seem plausible given what is known about spatial working memory.[78]

Vroom does not completely rule out the possibility of haplography, even of longer minuses. For example, he provided an excellent discussion of how haplography might have occurred in a large minus in MT-Lev 15:3 compared to SP, 11Q1 (11QpaleoLev[a]), and LXX when the repetition that possibly triggered the haplography is longer (או החתים בשרו מזובו; "or his body is blocked up by his discharge"), thereby meeting the requirements of the phonological loop in the transfer unit. He also provided two options for how this repeated phrase may have occurred on the *Vorlage*, one in which the visuospatial sketchpad would make sense—that is, the repeated phrase occurred in the same location at the end of two different lines of text, so that the eye simply skipped from one line to the next—and one option in which the visuospatial sketchpad would make no sense—that is, where the repeated phrase occurs in quite different locations on the *Vorlage*. Here I simply provide this example with the visuospatial layout that makes haplography a possibility (his option 1).

---

76. Vroom, "Cognitive Approach to Copying Errors," 265. Here Vroom is describing what is widely accepted by others.

77. Vroom, "Cognitive Approach to Copying Errors," 274.

78. Vroom, "Cognitive Approach to Copying Errors," 276.

Example 4.14: Lev 15:3[79]

SP

> ... וזאת תהיה טמאתו
> בזובו רר בשרו את זובו או חתום בשרו מזובו
> טמא הוא כל ימי זוב בשרו או החתים בשרו מזובו
> טמאתו היא ...

And this is the law of his uncleanness for a discharge:
whether his body runs with his discharge, **or his body is blocked up by his discharge,**
he is unclean. All the days his body flows **or his body is blocked up by his discharge,**
it is his uncleanness.

MT

> ... וזאת תהיה טמאתו
> בזובו רר בשרו את זובו או החתים בשרו מזובו
> טמאתו הוא ...

And this is the law of his uncleanness for a discharge:
whether his body runs with his discharge, **or his body is blocked up by his discharge,**
it is his uncleanness.

Since every manuscript was hand-copied and the physical characteristics of each manuscript (e.g., length and breadth of the writing surface, size of the margins, size of the handwritten letters) differed somewhat, such a specific layout that would allow the case of haplography in this passage would occur accidentally and therefore somewhat rarely. The repeated words would appear in different locations on the visuospatial sketchpad of each manuscript, most of which would make haplography improbable.

Although he acknowledged that haplography remains as a possible explanation of text-critical variants, Vroom nevertheless cautioned scholars from using haplography as a common explanation for minuses, because the combined circumstances in which the phonological loop and the visuospatial sketchpad line up well to support such an explanation

---

79. Vroom, "Cognitive Approach to Copying Errors," 276–77, his translation.

occur far less often than the traditional application of haplography suggests. Thus he concluded:

> First, haplography does *not* occur with the repetition of individual letters; it is *only* possible with the repetition of words. Second, haplography should *only* be considered a viable text-critical explanation for small variants; it should *not* be used to account for large differences among a text's witnesses.[80]

Vroom's observations concerning haplography are an important contribution to my effort to analogously apply visual-triggering to the composition/transmission process, in that both the phonological loop and the visuospatial sketchpad provide excellent limitations on how visual-triggering may have been operative within scribal memory, when a scribe is producing a new manuscript. First, all of the examples I have discussed in this chapter as cases of visual-triggering are "for small variants" that can be easily understood as fitting within a phonological loop *and* filling the same space in the visuospatial sketchpad, no matter where they are located in the specific visuospatial sketchpad of the *Vorlage*. They all consist of a different word recognition within the same grapheme (homographs, confusion of similar letters, and metathesis) or the division of letters into different words that nevertheless occupy the same location—that is, the division creates two different lexemes from the same string of letters. In other words, the limitations that Vroom insisted must be met for haplography based on what we know of the copying process from cognitive psychology are met in the other types of text-critical variants I discussed throughout this chapter on visual-triggering. Therefore, despite drawing from different resources concerning the cognitive-linguistic processes behind the composition/transmission process, Vroom and I have nevertheless reached complementary conclusions concerning visual-triggering.

However, I should also note another difference between my approach and his—that is, he is focusing solely upon working memory/short-term memory, whereas my notion of scribal memory also includes long-term memory. Scribes' knowledge of the broader tradition in its multiformity and textual plurality influenced their copying of a text, in that their memory of variant readings in other manuscripts may have influenced their copying of the *Vorlage* before them. Nevertheless, scribes' working memory must

---

80. Vroom, "Cognitive Approach to Copying Errors," 279.

also have been involved, as demonstrated in Vroom's discussion. Scribal memory included the interaction between working memory and long-term memory of the literary text represented by the specific *Vorlage*, so that variation from the *Vorlage* may have been intentional or unintentional, conscious or unconscious, but was always organic to the traditional literature—that is, within scribal memory whatever was copied was to some degree authentic in that it drew from the traditional register or special grammar of the broader tradition.

Stichography

Some ancient manuscripts of the Hebrew Bible may have been written in *scriptio continua*, that is, without spaces between words, punctuation, or other graphical ways of representing word division and sentence grammar; therefore, some text-critical variants may be due to the difficulty of reading such a text (see above on the division of words). Moreover, as just observed in my discussion of haplography, even when manuscripts are written in a running script with spaces between words, the visuospatial sketchpad often differs from manuscript to manuscript, because of the variation in the writing material (e.g., the width and length of the folios) or the handwriting (e.g., size of letters). In this section, I examine an exception to these general practices, that is, stichography. Stichography refers to the visual layout of poetic texts in manuscripts so that poetic units (stichs or hemistichs) are represented graphically.[81] In *Dead Sea Media*, Miller has made a convincing argument that this visual representation of poetry is also connected to how the poetic texts were performed:

> Stichography reflects an interface between the written tradition and the performative tradition of poetic songs. Stichography demonstrates that the scribes who produced the Dead Sea Scrolls were both (1) copyists who reproduced the (written) text of compositions and (2) performers who incorporated the oral register of language into their written copies.… Stichography graphically displays a scribal understanding of the manner in which compositions were read.[82]

---

81. Tov, *Textual Criticism* (3rd ed.), 201–2; Tov, *Scribal Practices and Approaches Reflected in the Texts Found in the Judean Desert*, STDJ 54 (Leiden: Brill, 2004), 166–78.
82. Miller, *Dead Sea Media*, 118.

That is, the poetic structure may be represented on the manuscript visually in ways that nevertheless represent (imperfectly) how the poetic text is sounded out when read aloud from the manuscript or recited within that community.

Miller discussed various examples of stichography of biblical and nonbiblical manuscripts among the Dead Sea Scrolls and illustrated the diverse stichographic systems that are represented among the scrolls. He demonstrated "the intrinsic link between parallelism and stichography."[83] His examples include illustrations of how "the multiformity of stichographic systems can be traced to scribal episodic memory of the different ways in which stichographic poetry was read by ancient Jews."[84] Below I will summarize his arguments with a discussion of one of his examples, his discussion of the Song of the Sea (Exod 15) as visually presented in two manuscripts: 4Q14 (4QExod^c) and 4Q365 (4QPentateuch^c).[85] In his transcription and translation of 4Q14, Miller has represented "minor intervals" (similar to *vacats*), respectively, as an underscore (e.g., יהוה_עד) and with "*interval*" ("Lord; *interval* until"). That is, even though 4Q14 is written in a running script (not *scriptio continua*, but also not with stichographic layout), Miller's analysis takes into account these minor intervals, which are spaces between words in the running script that are somewhat larger spaces than the space found between some of the words. Miller noted that these four intervals correspond with *vacats* in 4Q365 (see below).

Example 4.15: Exod 15:16–20[86]

4Q14 33 II, 40–42

40   כֹּאבן עד יעבר עמךֹ יהוה עד יעבֹ[ר] עַםֹ [זו] קֹנית תֹּבִיאם ותטֹעם
בהר נחלֹתֹ[ךֹ] מכון לשבתך פעלת]

41   יהוה מקדש יהוהֹ כוננוֹ ידך יהוה יֹמֹלֹךֹ עֹולם ועד כי בא סוס פֹּ[רעה
ב]רֹֹכבו ובֹפֹּ[רשיו בים וישב יהוה]

---

83. Miller, *Dead Sea Media*, 132.

84. Miller, *Dead Sea Media*, 237.

85. Miller, *Dead Sea Media*, 158–61. Miller also provided an excellent discussion of how the visual layouts of 4Q14 and 4Q365 relate well to the Leningrad Codex (MT^L) as one of his many illustrations of the complex relationships between the stichographic layout of the Dead Sea Scrolls and the visual layout and accent systems of the Masoretes. For the sake of brevity, I will not provide his transcription and translation of the Leningrad Codex; rather, I refer readers to his excellent discussion.

86. Miller, *Dead Sea Media*, 126, his translation.

4. Visual-Triggering and Text-Critical Variants

42 עליהם אֵת מִי הים ובני ישׂראל הלכו בִּיבָּ[שׁ]ה בתוך הים ותקֹ[ח]
מרים [הנביאה אחות אהרן את התוף]

40. as a stone. Until they pass over, your people, O Lord; *interval* until they pas[s] over, [this] people whom you have bought. You will bring them and plant them in the mountain of [your] inheritance. [A place for your dwelling, you have made],

41. O Lord. A sanctuary of the Lord, your hands have established. The Lord will rule forever and ever. *interval* For Ph[araoh's] horse went [with] his chariot and [his] ri[ders into the sea. And the Lord brought]

42. on them, the waters of the sea. *interval* For the sons of Israel walked on d[r]y ground amidst the sea. *interval* And Miriam [the prophetess, the sister of Aaron, too[k] the tambourine

Since 4Q14 is in a running script, the poetic units are not laid out stichographically as in 4Q365 (see below); nevertheless, the corresponding use of intervals in 4Q14 and *vacats* in 4Q365 suggests that both scribes are aware of a similar division of the text into poetic units.[87] Below is Miller's transcription and translation of the Song of the Sea in 4Q365.

Example 4.16: Exod 15:16–21[88]

4Q365 6b 1–6

1 עַ֭ד יֹ[עֲבוּר vacat עמכה יהוה עד יעבור vacat עם זו קניתה vacat תביאמו ותטעמו]

2 בהר נחלתכה vacat מכון לשבתּֽ[ה vacat פעלתה יהוה vacat מקדש יהוה vacat כוננו ידיכה]

3 יהוה ימלוך עולם ועד vacat כי בא [סוס פרעוה vacat ברכבו ובפרשיו בים vacat וישב]

4 [יה]וֹה עליהמה את מימי הים vacat [ובני ישראל הלכו vacat ביבשה בתוך הים]

5 [והמי]ֹ֫ם לֹ֫ה[מה חומה מ]יֹמינם ומשמאולם vacat ותקֹח [מרים הנביאה אחות אהרון]

6 [את התוף בידה ו]תֹצינה [כו]ל הנשֹׁיֹם אחֹריֹהֹ ב[תופים ובמחולות ותען]

---

87. Miller, *Dead Sea Media*, 128.
88. Miller, *Dead Sea Media*, 125.

1. Until t[hey pass over, *vacat* your people, O Lord; *vacat* until they pass over, *vacat* this people whom you have bought. *vacat* You will bring them and plant them]
2. in the mountain of your inheritance. *vacat* A place for yo[ur] dwelling, [*vacat* you have made, O Lord. *vacat* A sanctuary of the Lord, *vacat* your hands have established.]
3. The Lord will rule forever and ever. *vacat* For [Pharaoh's horse] went [*vacat* with his chariot and riders into the sea. *vacat* And brought]
4. [the Lo]rd on them, *vacat* the waters of the sea. *vacat* [For the sons of Israel walked *vacat* on dry ground amidst the sea.]
5. [And the wat]er was [a wall] for t[hem, on] their right and on their left. *vacat* And [Miriam the prophetess, the sister of Aaron,] took
6. [the tambourine in her hand;] and [al]l the women went out after her with [tambourines and with dancing. And she answered]

Among the various stichographic systems that Miller discussed, 4Q365 illustrates what he called "running stichography," that is, a type in which "poetic units can 'run' across the margin from one column line to the next."[89] Miller's detailed description of the stichographic layout of 4Q365 includes the following:

> Overall, 4Q365's stichography illustrates three characteristics of stichography exhibited in a number of other stichographic texts. First, *vacats* delineate varying numbers of cola and each column line contains varying numbers of poetic units (hemistiches). For example, lines 1-2 have five hemistiches, and lines 3-5 have four hemistiches. Second, the *vacats* rather than margins consistently demarcate cola. For example, the colon "and brought *margin* the Lord on them" (וישב יהוה עליהמה) is broken up between lines 3 and 4 after "and (he) brought" (וישב). Third, the lineation of the column does not correspond to lines of verse—that is, each column line does not begin with a new poetic line. For example, "[You will bring them and plant them], in the mountain of your inheritance" (תביאמו ותטעמו [בהר נחלתכה)]) is split between lines 1 and 2.[90]

---

89. Miller, *Dead Sea Media*, 123.
90. Miller, *Dead Sea Media*, 127–28.

4. Visual-Triggering and Text-Critical Variants

According to Miller, this stichographic layout represents not only the scribe's understanding of the poetic structure of the passage, but also the scribe's understanding of the public performance of this passage. That is, the visuospatial sketchpad has been designed by a scribe to represent more accurately the traditional oral performance of the passage by breaking it up into poetic units to facilitate scribes reading the text aloud in the context of liturgy.

Miller's analysis explicitly includes a discussion of scribal memory.[91] As noted above, he argued that the scribes are both copyists and performers.[92] That is, during the copying process, scribes drew from both their working memory of the *Vorlage* before them and their long-term memory of the text in performance. "By incorporating their memory of both the written text and the spoken text into their copies, scribes interacted with compositions as traditional performers."[93] This dynamic interplay between the written and the oral helps Miller explain how there is a diversity of interpretations of the poetic structure of some of the texts that he examines as visually represented in the stichographic layout of the texts:

> Stichographic texts are arranged in a bewildering array of manners, usually with inconsistencies in stichographic systems. What gives rise to this multiformity? Similar to other spacing techniques, the multiformity of stichographic systems can be traced to scribal episodic memory of the different ways in which stichographic poetry was read by ancient Jews.... This diversity is typical of texts copied and transmitted in oral-written contexts in which ancient Jews read and used biblical poetry. In other words, variations and inconsistencies between stichographic systems represent the wide variety of manners in which biblical poetry was performed by ancient Jews and remembered by ancient scribes.[94]

Although Miller sometimes pointed out text-critical variants among the stichographic passages he discussed, his discussion is mostly focused on the stichographic layouts, which in most cases (probably because of the paucity of stichographic texts) contain few, if any, text-critical variants. However, his argument for the multiformity found among the stichographic texts is analogous to the argument I am making concerning

---

91. Miller, *Dead Sea Media*, esp. 226–66.
92. Miller, *Dead Sea Media*, 28.
93. Miller, *Dead Sea Media*, 275.
94. Miller, *Dead Sea Media*, 237.

text-critical variants. That is, both text-critical variants and stichographic layouts represent the interplay between the scribe's copying of a *Vorlage* and that scribe's memory of the text represented by the *Vorlage* as it has been and will be performed in the scribe's community.

Implicit in Miller's analysis is the possibility of a scribe copying a manuscript without a stichographic layout (similar to 4Q14), but performing the text in the new manuscript by adding a stichographic layout (similar to 4Q365). Presumably, stichographic layouts (or at least their standardization in terms of which passages required stichography and the preference for a particular stichographic system) were a later development of the composition/transmission process. However, even if this was not the case, the fact that some poetic passages are found without stichographic layouts and others with them suggests that it was certainly possible that a scribe added the stichographic layout when copying a text without one *or* that a scribe may copy a manuscript with a stichographic layout into a manuscript without stichography. In either possibility, it seems to me that scribal memory must be present. The addition of stichographic divisions assumes a traditional interpretation of the text informed by how it is performed in the scribe's community by the scribe visually representing what is held in his scribal memory. The omission of stichographic divisions assumes a traditional interpretation of the text contained in scribal memory could nevertheless inform the reading of the text without the stichographic layout. No matter which possibility was more common, Miller has pointed out that stichography remains a visual means of triggering scribal memory of how the text is sounded out in performance. In that sense, stichography is a form of both visual-triggering and sound-triggering.

Although I suspect that stichographic texts sometimes may have asserted themselves more on scribes as copyists so that they were less likely to introduce memory variants during the copying process, I would not rule out that stichography may also more easily trigger the sound that the written text represents to the scribes as performers, since the relationship between the written and the spoken is more obvious. Moreover, no matter which of these tendencies may be most prominent in the composition/transmission process, Miller's argument concerning stichography and my argument concerning text-critical variants both suggest that the written text represented imperfectly what was preserved more fully in scribal memory, so that any manuscript facilitated access to the literary text as preserved in the collective memory of the community for the purpose of traditional performances.

Visual-Triggering and Variants: A Summary

Above I have argued for visual-triggering as an analogous gross-selection mechanism to both category-triggering and sound-triggering and have provided examples of text-critical variants that are commonly understood to have been caused by visual scribal errors. A common misunderstanding of studies concerning the interaction of the oral and the written in relationship to memory is that the visual influence of the *Vorlage* is assumed to be unimportant, a misunderstanding that tends to be based on various dichotomies that I am rejecting, such as oral-versus-written, author-versus-copyist, and composition-versus-transmission. Therefore, although in the previous two chapters I might be accused of minimalizing the influence of *Vorlagen* (unfairly, in my opinion), in this chapter I am being explicit about how the physical writing on a *Vorlage* plays an important role within scribal memory by taking seriously how those types of variants generally understood as visual errors can be understood differently from the perspective of the cognitive-linguistic processes of word selection within scribal memory. Homographs by their very nature require something more than the physical written consonants, because they represent more than one possible pronunciation and therefore potentially different lexemes. The ambiguity of homographs was necessarily overcome when scribal memory informed the scribe's selection of the transfer unit in the phonological loop of working memory, so that what we identify as variants may represent different reading traditions of the same consonantal text. Variants that are due to similarly shaped letters likewise suggest that visual-triggering was active; however, rather than emphasizing how some of these variants were misreadings, I have argued that within the context of scribal memory some of these variants may be understood as synonymous readings, especially when we look at these variants within their larger literary context. Similarly, variants that are based on differing divisions of letters into words are based on differing visual recognitions of lexemes, but, when we look at some of the variants within their larger literary context, they appear to be candidates for synonymous readings in that they nevertheless appear to be the same. Tsumura has cautioned us that some variants based on metathesis (i.e., the interchange of letters) may be phonetic spellings rather than scribal errors. Nevertheless, some variants based on metathesis remain, but some of these can be understood as synonymous readings that preserve the general meaning of the text within the context of textual fluidity and textual plurality. That is, rather than seeing one lexeme in the text, a scribe may perceive another lexeme based on his memory of alternative readings of the literary text preserved in his *Vorlage* that is nevertheless closely related visually in terms of having the same consonants only in a somewhat different order.

After reassessing these types of variants often understood as visually inspired scribal errors, I then turned to a discussion of two important recent studies that are closely related to my arguments of visual-triggering, Vroom's study of haplography and Miller's study of stichography. Vroom's study of haplography is an excellent example of the application of cognitive psychology to the copying process, which leads to conclusions that minimizes the use of the category of haplography as applied to scribal omissions. That is, the assumptions that scribes would sometimes easily skip over words and even parts of words due to similar beginnings or endings does not adequately take into account the idea of transfer units in working memory and, when applied to longer blocks of text, does not adequately take into account the visuospatial sketchpad that assists scribes in returning to the same location in the *Vorlage* during the copying process. When I apply Vroom's observations that limit the identification of haplography more generally to visual-triggering as discussed earlier in this chapter, we can see that all of the examples I have discussed are consistent with the two most important observations that Vroom adapted from cognitive psychology: the phonological loop and the visuospatial sketchpad. All of the examples of visual-triggering I have discussed assert that the scribes necessarily would need to identify the phonological loop for what they see visually in the written letters (especially obvious in the case of homographs) and that the visual-triggering would be based on the scribes' identification of a lexeme or phrase located in the same space on the visuospatial sketchpad. However, where I differ from Vroom is that his discussion is really limited to the influence of working memory on the copying process, whereas my notion of scribal memory includes not only the scribes' working memory related to the transfer units taken from the *Vorlagen* physically present before them, but also the scribes' long-term memory of how the literary text has been performed in previous manuscripts, recitations, and/or public readings.

Miller's study of stichography is an excellent example of how studying the visual layout—what Vroom would refer to as the visuospatial sketchpad—of specific manuscripts (rather than critical editions) can provide important results in our understanding of textual transmission and its close connection to oral performance. The fact that some manuscripts include

4. Visual-Triggering and Text-Critical Variants

stichography, the visual layout of poetry according to its poetic structure, may at first seem to undercut my argument that places visual-triggering within the context of both category-triggering and sound-triggering rather than insisting that visual-triggering is so primary that variations from the *Vorlage* must be rejected as either scribal errors or ideologically motivated scribal revisions. However, Miller argued convincingly that stichography is a visual representation of how the poetry was orally performed, so much so that we can see in some cases how the different stichographic layouts of the same poetic passage may reflect different interpretations of the poetry. In his analysis, Miller found the concept of scribal memory as indispensible to his discussion of stichography, in that stichography is a memory aid for scribes in the oral performance of the poetry; nevertheless, stichography does not represent the fullness of oral performance, so that scribal memory is aided but not displaced by the stichographic layout. In other words, Miller's application of scribal memory to stichography is analogous to my application of scribal memory to text-critical variants in ways that our arguments are mutually supportive.

In the previous chapters on category-triggering and sound-triggering, my arguments emphasized long-term memory within scribal memory. That is, these variants represented what we would refer to as different versions of the literary text represented imperfectly by *Vorlagen* before the scribes. In this chapter, my argument more seriously takes into account how working memory/short-term operates within scribal memory in addition to long-term memory. The visually written consonantal texts on the *Vorlagen* asserted themselves within the working memory of the scribes as they selected transfer units from the *Vorlagen* to copy into the new manuscripts and this visual selection may include misreading what the consonants were in the *Vorlage*. However, some of these misreadings may also represent what we would refer to as different versions of the same literary text as operative in the long-term storage in scribal memory.

I want to close this chapter with a disclaimer. I am not suggesting that scribes never made visual errors, never misread the text. However, what I reject is the assumption that the transmission process insisted on scribes copying their *Vorlagen* verbatim in ways that would preserve so many of these errors once they entered a text. It seems to me that, given textual plurality and textual fluidity, such errors would likely have been corrected and not preserved in the numbers that they are often assumed to exist. Rather, it seems to me that these errors are less likely errors, but simply represent the multiformity preserved within scribal memory based on the ambiguity of the consonantal text in a time when what we identify as scribal errors could be phonetic spellings or simply alternative readings. That is, many of these errors seem to me to be synonymous readings, when we step back and look at the larger literary context rather than focusing on the individual lexemes and when we adjust our understanding of what different-but-the-same word may have been to the ancient scribes as performers.

5
Text-Critical Variants and Category-Triggering, Sound-Triggering, and Visual-Triggering: Conclusions and Implications

In chapter 1, I drew insights from both conversation analysis and the comparative study of oral traditions to argue that a word—that is, the smallest unit of meaning—can be less than a lexeme or more than a lexeme. Word selection then works within the particular linguistic registers and pragmatic contexts in which words occur based on a variety of factors, including the meaning(s) that each word may carry, the sounds of the spoken word, and the relationship of the word to other words that occur within the larger pragmatic context. This argument was based significantly on Jefferson's poetics, including category-triggering and sound-triggering. In chapter 4 I extended Jefferson's poetics by an analogous gross-selection mechanism for writing, what I labeled "visual-triggering." That is, I extended the understanding of word selection so that the relationship of the word to other words that occurs within the larger pragmatic context not only includes meaning and sound but also graphic (dis)similarities.

In chapters 2–4 I explored respectively category-triggering, sound-triggering, and visual-triggering, emphasizing each of them separately. Concerning category-triggering, I analyzed four types of text-critical variants—synonymous readings, variants within lists, harmonizations, and variants related to person reference—all of which can be understood from the perspective of conversation analysis as comembers of the same category and, by my extension of Talmon's definition, as synonymous readings. In each of the examples explored in chapter 2, the cognitive-linguistic practice of category-triggering influenced scribal memory, so that even when scribes may have copied *Vorlagen* that were physically present, the new manuscripts that they were producing contained some synonymous readings of any of the four types of text-critical variants, because scribal memory includes not only the physically present representation of the text in the *Vorlage* lying before them, but their memory of every manuscript of that same literary text that the scribes have read, have heard read aloud, or have heard otherwise recited or quoted. These texts include what we might assume to be a different literary text, but that from the perspective of the ancients was nevertheless the same literary text. Therefore, methodologically we must accept that much of what we perceive to be a variant may not be understood as a variant in the world of the ancient scribes who composed and transmitted traditional literature, some of which later became the Hebrew Bible. That is, what we perceive as different word(s) may be understood by the ancients as the same word, so that what we perceive as different texts may be understood by the ancients as the same text.

In chapter 3, I applied sound-triggering to text-critical variants connected to alliteration and wordplay and reached the conclusion that these types of variants can also be understood as synonymous readings. Much like participants in ordinary conversation may be completely unaware of the sound-patterns of alliteration and wordplay that they are producing in their talk, the ancient scribes may have unknowingly been influenced by sound-patterns in the texts as they copied their *Vorlagen*. In other words, scribal memory and its effect on the composition/transmission process could have included instances of sound-triggering. Although some of these instances may have been unintentional and unrecognized, in other cases sound-triggering may have begun unintentionally but was then recognized so that the scribes played off of the sound patterns, thereby expanding them within a single manuscript and therefore within the broader tradition preserved in scribal memory. Of course, some cases may have been intentional from the beginning. However, our ability to discern intentional versus unintentional cases is severely lacking (if not, impossible), given the spontaneous character of sound-triggering as a gross-selection mechanism in everyday conversation, oral traditions, and literature.

In chapter 4, I expanded on Jefferson's poetics, identifying what I labeled "visual-triggering," to account for those types of text-critical variants often associated with what others call visual scribal errors, including confusion of similar letters, division of words, metathesis, and haplography. Once again, my analysis suggested that many of these so-called scribal errors should be understood as synonymous readings. I also agreed with Vroom that cases of haplography should be considered rare, only possible when certain conditions are met that make sense of the cognitive-linguistic processes of copying as understood from the perspective of cognitive psychology. Before I looked at these types of text-critical variants, I provided examples of homographs to demonstrate that the consonantal text can trigger more than one possible interpretation, *even when* the consonants are exactly the same. That is, homographs are technically not variants, even though variant readings may be associated with them and these variants readings may lead to variants in the transmission of the text. Then, building on the work of Miller, I ended the chapter with a discussion of stichography to demonstrate that visual-triggering in the form of how poetic structures are graphically represented can also be present, again *even with* the same consonantal text. Thus, the graphic text remains somewhat ambiguous in its representation of meaning and sounds (especially in homographs), which opens up the possibility that the graphic text represents the textual plurality and textual fluidity in which the literature exists within scribal memory. Even though there are graphic means for representing to some degree reading practices and other forms of performance (e.g., stichography), the diversity of these very practices further emphasizes the textual plurality and textual fluidity of the literature that can only be understood from the perspective of scribal memory, in which the interplay of written texts and mental texts are a necessary reality, even in *Vorlage*-based copying.

Multimodality and Text-Critical Variants

In chapters 2–4 I emphasized each of the respective gross-selection mechanisms; however, I nevertheless pointed out here and there how these three mechanisms are interrelated. Moreover, I reached the same conclusion in each chapter: Many of the instances of these types of variants should be understood as synonymous readings within the multiformity of the traditional literature, some of which later became the Hebrew Bible, rather than understanding them as scribal errors. Below I will discuss four examples that will help me illustrate that category-triggering, sound-triggering, and visual-triggering can work in combination within scribal memory: Song 4:5; 7:4; Exod 26:24; 36:29; 1 Sam 11; and 2:8–10. That is, as discussed above in chapter 4 from the perspective of conversation analysis, embodied actions in everyday conversation consist of both audible and visual forms of communication in face-to-face talk-in-interaction, so that we should now consider that this multimodality may carry over into the act of *Vorlage*-based copying, such that category-triggering, sound-triggering, and visual-triggering may interact with each other in ways that affect how scribal memory works in the composition/transmission process. The following examples will help me illustrate how this interaction may occur in text-critical variants.

Example 5.1[1]

MT Song 4:3a, 5–6

כחוט השני שפתתיך ומדבריך נאוה ...
שני שדיך כשני עפרים תאומי צביה
הרועים בשושנים
עד שיפוח היום ונסו הצללים
אלך לי אל הר המור ואל גבעת הלבונה

Your lips are like a scarlet thread, and your mouth is lovely....
Your two breasts are like two young deer, twins of a gazelle
that graze among the lilies.
Until the day breathes and the shadows flee,
I will hasten to the mountain of myrrh and the hill of frankincense.

4Q107 (4QCant[b]) lacking 4:4–7[2]

MT Song 7:3–5a

שררך אגן הסהר אל יחסר המזג
בטנך ערמת חטים סוגה בשושנים
שני שדיך כשני עפרים תאמי צביה
צוארך כמגדל השן

Your navel is a rounded bowl that never lacks mixed wine.
Your belly is a heap of wheat, encircled with lilies.
Your two breasts are like two young deer, twins of a gazelle.
Your neck is like an ivory tower.
Syriac: 7:5 includes 4:5b: = הרועים בשושנים = that graze among the lilies

My analysis of the poetics in these two passages in Song of Songs (as well as the next example of Exod 26:24; 36:29) is based significantly on Karo-

---

1. The translation is taken from the NRSV with adaptations from Vermeulen, "Two of a Kind," 147.
2. See Ulrich, *Biblical Qumran Scrolls*, 743.

5. Conclusions and Implications

lien Vermeulen's excellent article, "Two of a Kind: Twin Language in the Hebrew Bible," in which she carefully analyzed every occurrence of the noun תואמים ("twins") in MT. She observed the following:

> The six attestations of תואמים in the Hebrew Bible appear in pairs: two in Genesis (Gen. 25.24; 38.26), two in Exodus (Exod. 26.24; 36.29) and two in the Song of Songs (Song 4.5; 7.4). Each of the pairs deals with a different kind of twins. In Genesis the twins are human; in Exodus, they are inanimate (one usage of the word is talking about double beams of the Tabernacle); and in the Song of Songs, the twins are animals as a metaphor for human body parts. Furthermore, there is a considerable amount of material between the occurrences of תואמים in the respective books, meaning that the occurrences belong to different stories or parts of the story.[3]

Furthermore, "the passages use three devices that add to the emphasis on the twins: geminates, alliterations, and (numerical) paronomasia."[4] I will summarize her arguments below, noting how they represent category-triggering, sound-triggering, and visual-triggering, and then look at the text-critical evidence, which she did not analyze. That is, Vermeulen's study fits the pattern I noted in chapter 3, in which few studies of biblical poetics are informed by text-criticism. In my summary of her discussion of these two passages in Song of Songs, I will discuss numerical paronomasia, alliteration, and then geminate roots.

Vermeulen concluded that "all occurrences of the word תואמים come along with play on the number 'two'" as a form of numerical paronomasia (what Jefferson identified as a form of numerical category-triggering) and this is certainly the case in these two passages:[5] "Your **two** [שְׁנֵי] breasts are like **two** [שְׁנֵי] young deer, **twins** [תּוֹאֲמֵי] of a gazelle" (Song 4:5; 7:4). In 4:3a, "your lips are like a scarlet [שָׁנִי] thread" also participates in this numerical paronomasia, in that we have a pair of lips, each of which can be described by the homophonous word "scarlet" (שָׁנִי); therefore, "your two lips" are certainly implied here. In 7:3b–4, the word "scarlet" (שָׁנִי) does not explicitly occur; however, as Vermeulen noted, the use of שֵׁן ("ivory") in the poetic wordplay of "ivory tower" (מִגְדַּל הַשֵּׁן) recalls the homophones of שְׁנֵי ("two"), שָׁנִי ("scarlet"), and שִׁנֵּי ("teeth"), which in 4:2 are not only white

---

3. Vermeulen, "Two of a Kind," 136.
4. Vermeulen, "Two of a Kind," 140.
5. Vermeulen, "Two of a Kind," 149.

like the "tower" but also "all of which bear twins" (מתאימות).⁶ Therefore, Vermeulen could conclude that "though absent, the word שָׁנִי, 'scarlet,' is here understood as well."⁷

Vermeulen's arguments concerning numerical paronomasia (or numerical category-triggering) is based heavily on homophones; however, she also discussed alliteration that extends beyond the homophones in these passages. In addition to שֵׁן ("ivory" in 7:5a), שְׁנֵי ("two" twice in 4:5; 7:4), שָׁנִי ("scarlet" in 4:3a), and שִׁנֵּי ("teeth" in 4:2), the following occur in these passages, repeating the sibilant שׁ: שפתתיך ("your lips" in 4:3a), שדיך ("your breasts" in 4:5; 7:4), בשושנים ("among the lilies" in 4:5; 7:3), שיפוח ("breathes" in 4:6), and שררך ("your navel" in 7:3). Furthermore, as Vermeulen noted, the closely related sibilant צ also makes some appearances in צביה ("gazelle" in 4:5; 7:4), הצללים ("the shadows" in 4:6), and צוארך ("your neck" in 7:5a). Thus, Vermeulen connects these additional words to the homophones by way of alliteration of the sibilants שׁ and צ, a type of sound-triggering.⁸ As noted in chapters 3 and 4 above, homophones and alliteration are not only forms of sound-triggering, but can also be understood as forms of visual-triggering. Similarly, Vermeulen stated that here "the alliteration works visually as well."⁹

Vermeulen also connected the use of geminate roots to the phenomenon associated with the noun תואמים ("twins"). She noted the following geminate roots: שושנים ("lilies" in 4:5; 7:3b), הצללים ("the shadows" in 4:6), שררך ("your navel" in 7:3), all of which participate in the alliterative pattern. That is, in addition to the שׁ/צ alliteration, these roots have "twin" letters, so they participate in the numerical paronomasia in that way as well.

Vermeulen's analysis was limited to MT, so that her conclusions concern the poetry of the author of the original text: "the author deliberately chose words and combinations in which two identical consonants occurred."¹⁰ That is, Vermeulen is operating under the MT-priority paradigm. Admittedly, the text-critical evidence for this passage may not be that substantial: (1) Song 4:4–7 is lacking in 4Q107 and (2) the Syriac includes what is widely seen as a harmonization, when it includes 4:5b

---

6. Vermeulen, "Two of a Kind," 148 n. 51.
7. Vermeulen, "Two of a Kind," 148.
8. See also, J. Cheryl Exum, *Song of Songs: A Commentary*, OTL (Louisville: Westminster John Knox), 166.
9. Vermeulen, "Two of a Kind," 140.
10. Vermeulen, "Two of a Kind," 142.

5. Conclusions and Implications

at the end of 7:4 ("that graze among the lilies"). However, the difference between these two passages has often led to speculation about their differences with what seems to be an assumption that the original text would have been consistent in both passages. For example, Roland Murphy's uncertainty is evident when, on the one hand, he concluded that "browsing among the lilies" (his translation of 4:5b) might have been omitted in 7:4, because of the reference to lilies in 7:3, but, on the other hand, he saw no apparent reason for why it should be omitted, "unless it is a gloss in 4:5?," since the phrase occurs in 2:16–17, where the man is compared to a gazelle, so its presence in 4:5 may be due to harmonization with 2:16–17.[11] Thus, when we combine the differences between these two passages with the scant text-critical evidence, it is not difficult to conclude, when we operate under the text-critical paradigm, that the text of Song of Songs may have also been more fluid than the extant text-critical evidence suggests. This would especially be the case if, as Vermeulen argued for the implicit understanding of שני ("scarlet") in Songs 7:3b–4, the very existence of the phenomenon of category-triggering, sound-triggering, and visual-triggering associated with the noun תואמים ("twins") implies textual plurality, so that even though some word may be physically absent in the consonantal text, it is nevertheless understood as implied within scribal memory in ways that would explain any variants between these two passages and between MT and the other textual traditions. Furthermore, the category-triggering, sound-triggering, and visual-triggering associated with the noun תואמים ("twins") illustrates how these gross-selection mechanisms can nevertheless work together in the triggering process of poetics throughout the composition/transmission process.

In the next example, I continue to draw significantly from Vermeulen's analysis of the noun תואמים ("twins") in MT; however, the "twins" in these passages are beams in the tabernacle.

Example 5.2[12]

MT Exod 26:24
ויהיו תאמים מלמטה ויחדו יהיו תמים על ראשו אל הטבעת האחת
כן יהיה לשניהם לשני המקצעת יהיו

---

11. Murphy, *Song of Songs: A Commentary on the Book of Canticles or The Song of Songs*, Hermeneia (Minneapolis: Fortress, 1990), 182, 186.
12. Vermeulen, "Two of a Kind," 145; her translation.

And they shall be twins from downwards
and together they will be complete above the head of it into one ring;
thus shall it be for them both, for the two corners they will be.

MT Exod 36:29

והיו תואמם מלמטה ויחדו יהיו תמים אל ראשו אל הטבעת האחת
כן עשה לשניהם לשני המקצעת

And they shall be twins from downwards
and together they will be complete to the head of it into one ring;
thus he did to them both, for the two corners.

Concerning Gen 25:24; 38:26; Exod 26:24; 36:29; and Song 4:5; 7:4, Vermeulen concluded that "the language of biblical passages including the 'twin' word exteriorizes and emphasizes the twin concept by means of devices that mimic the twinning formally."[13] She noted that these devices included geminates, alliterations, and numerical paranomasia; however, she also noted that Exod 26:24; 36:29 does not include geminate roots like the other passages. Nevertheless, Exod 26:24; 36:29 are a pair of parallel passages in the same book that use the noun תואמים ("twins") with alliteration and paronomasia in ways consistent with her overall argument. The numerical paronomasia (or numerical category-triggering) is evident in that the noun תואמים occurs in combination with שְׁנֵי ("two") not only twice in each of these two verses, but also in the larger literary context of Exod 26:19, 21, 26; 36:24, 26, 30. Furthermore, שְׁנֵי ("two") occurs in the literary context in which the homophone שָׁנִי ("scarlet") is used to describe the curtain in the tabernacle (Exod 26:1, 31, 36; 36:8, 35, 37), continuing the wordplay of these homophones. In addition to the alliteration between these two homophones, Vermeulen identified the alliteration of ו, י, ש, ת, and מ in both of these verses, noting that תואמים ("twins") participates in this alliteration with the exception of the ש-alliteration that is closely connected to ever present שְׁנֵי ("two") that appears in all of three pairs of passages. Furthermore, she noted that the ו-alliteration "only works on the visual level, since some of them are *matres lectionis*," and I would add that this is also the case for the י-alliteration.[14] Vermeulen also discussed the paronomasia of the words תאמים and תמים: "they are more than mere

---

13. Vermeulen, "Two of a Kind," 135.
14. Vermeulen, "Two of a Kind," 145.

5. Conclusions and Implications

alliteration. They create an impression of an etymological relationship connecting twins with completeness."[15]

Vermeulen's argument would have been enhanced by a discussion of the text-critical variants. For both Exod 26:24; 36:29, SP reads תאמם rather than תמים in MT, thereby explicitly repeating the "twin"-word with a defective spelling compared to the תאמים of MT Exod 26:24 or the תואמים of MT Exod 36:29; the SP reading is also reflected in LXX and targum.[16] However, a discussion of the variants from the perspective of the MT-priority paradigm would not be helpful. For example, even though he noted some of these variants and that the root *tmm* ("to be whole, complete") is common in Semitic languages but the root *t'm* ("to be a twin") is "unique in Biblical Hebrew" (thereby implying a case of *lectio difficilior potior*), William Propp nevertheless preferred the MT reading, rejecting the versions for their "redundancy," which diminishes "the author's punning diction."[17] Rather than insisting on only *one* correct reading of the original text, I think that we should consider another possibility of what Martin called "ambiguous vocalization" that carries with it a double entendre.[18] Especially when we note the dissimilar spelling of "twins" in MT Exod 26:24 (תאמים), MT Exod 36:29 (תואמם), and SP-Exod 26:24; 36:29 (תאמם), we should consider the possibility that even תמים in the MT may be a phonetic spelling of "twins" and, even if it is not, the similarity of the roots suggests the possibility of a double entendre of "twins"/"complete." This interpretation is certainly consistent with Vermeulen's identification of these two words in MT having "an impression of an etymological relationship."[19]

---

15. Vermeulen, "Two of a Kind," 145–46. This wordplay is often identified by others, e.g., Umberto Cassuto, *A Commentary on the Book of Exodus* (Jerusalem: Magnes, 1967), 356.

16. LXX Exodus has a significantly different text in Exod 36–37, especially in terms of arrangement; however, for my purpose I will simply note that here and refer readers interested in pursuing this further to John William Wevers, *Exodus*, SVTG 2 (Göttingen: Vandenhoeck & Ruprecht, 1991), 596.

17. Propp, *Exodus 19–40: A New Translation with Introduction and Commentary*, AB (New York: Doubleday, 2006), 647, 414.

18. Martin, *Multiple Originals*, 191.

19. Vermeulen ("Two of a Kind," 145–46) described the difference between the two MT passages as "dissimilar spelling," but did not refer to SP at all, and insisted on a "close resemblance" between תאמים and תמים. Here I am not only drawing from Martin's "ambiguous vocalization" (*Multiple Originals*, 191), but also Tsumura's discussion

Even if we stay closely to Vermeulen's discussion of only MT, we can see how category-triggering (numerical paronomasia), sound-triggering (alliteration, wordplay), and visual-triggering (alliteration, wordplay) combine in interesting ways within the composition/transmission process. This is more evident in that the so-called variants can be seen as alternative readings in the literary context that nevertheless reflect the same sort of poetics as found in MT; therefore, we can suggest that all of these various connections could have resided in the scribal memory of this literary text in its characteristic textual fluidity and plurality throughout the composition/transmission process.

Example 5.3[20]

MT 1 Sam 10:27–11:2

זה ויבזהו ולא הביאו לו מנחה ויהי כמחריש
ויעל נחש העמוני ויחן על יבש גלעד ויאמרו כל אנשי יביש אל נחש כרת
לנו ברית ונעבדך ויאמר אליהם נחש העמוני בזאת אכרת לכם בנקור לכם
כל עין ימין ושמתיה חרפה על כל ישראל

They despised him [Saul] and brought him no present. But he held his peace.

Nahash the Ammonite went up and besieged Jabesh-gilead; and all the men of Jabesh said to Nahash, "Make a treaty with us, and we will serve you." But Nahash the Ammonite said to them, "On this condition I will make a treaty with you, namely, that I gouge out everyone's right eye, and thus put disgrace upon all Israel."

---

of how some scribal errors should be understood as alternative phonetic spellings. See Tsumura, "Scribal Errors or Phonetic Spellings?"

20. The translation for MT 1 Sam 11:1–2 is NRSV; for 4Q51 10:27–11:2, my adaptation of NRSV. Note that the NRSV translation of 4Q51 10:27–11:2 follows MT, where available, so that I have corrected it to follow the Hebrew of 4Q51 10:27–11:2. Also, with NRSV, I have chosen not to indicate the lacuna in the manuscript and to translate the *editio princeps* as found in Frank Moore Cross et al., eds., *Qumran Cave 4.XII. 1–2 Samuel*, DJD XVII (Oxford: Clarendon, 2005), 65–66, which is reprinted in Ulrich, *Biblical Qumran Scrolls*, 271. Note that this differs from Cross's earlier reconstruction as given in Frank Moore Cross, "The Ammonite Oppression of the Tribes of Gad and Reuben: Missing Verses from 1 Samuel 11 Found in 4QSam[a]," in *The Hebrew and Greek Texts of Samuel, 1980 Proceedings IOSCS, Vienna*, ed. Emanuel Tov (Jerusalem: Academon, 1980), 107.

5. Conclusions and Implications

4Q51 (4QSam^a) 10:27^{sup}–11:2

[זה וי]בזוהו ולוא הביאו לו מנחה <i>vacat</i>
[ונ]חש מלך בני עמון הוא לחץ את בני גד ואת בני ראובן בחזקה ונקר להם
כ[ול] [ע]ין ימין ונתן אין [מושי]ע ל[י]שראל ולוא נשאר איש בבני ישראל
אשר בע[בר הירדן] [אש]ר ל[וא נ]קר לו נח[ש מלך בני ע]מון כול עין ימין
ו[ה]ן שבעת אלפים איש [נצלו מיד] בני עמון ויבאו אל [י]בש גלעד {ויהי
כמו חדש ויעל נחש העמוני ויחן על יביש} ויאמרו כול אנשי יביש אל נחש
מ[לך] [בני עמון כרת] ל[נו ברית ונעבדך ויאמר א]ל[יה]ם נחש [העמוני
בזאת אכרת לכם]

end of fragment

… They despised him [Saul] and brought him no present.

Now Nahash, king of the Ammonites, had been grievously oppressing the Gadites and the Reubenites. He would gouge out the right eye of each of them and would not grant Israel a deliverer. No one was left of the Israelites across the Jordan whose right eye Nahash, king of the Ammonites, had not gouged out. But there were seven thousand men who had escaped from the Ammonites and had entered Jabesh-gilead. {About a month later, Nahash the Ammonite went up and besieged **Jabesh**}; and all the men of Jabesh said to Nahash, **king of the Ammonites**, "Make a treaty with us, and we will serve you." But Nahash the Ammonite said to them, "On this condition I will make a treaty with you [end of fragment]

To further organize the following discussion of this passage, I provide first a list of variants between MT 1 Sam 11:1–2 and 4Q51 11:1–2 (and, in some cases, LXX), that is, where the two texts overlap:

MT 1 Sam 11:1: ויהי כמחריש, But he (Saul) held his peace.
4Q51 1 Sam 11:1: ויהי כמו חדש, About a month later
LXX 1 Sam 11:1: Καὶ ἐγενήθη ὡς μετὰ μῆνα = ויהי כמו חדש, About a month later

MT 1 Sam 11:1: יבש גלעד, Jabesh-Gilead
4Q51 11:1: יביש, Jabesh

MT 1 Sam 11:1: נחש, Nahash
4Q51 11:1: נחש מ[לך] [בני עמון], Nahash, king of the Ammonites

LXX 1 Sam 11:1: Ναας ὁ Αμμανίτης = נחש העמוני נחש, Nahash the Ammonite[21]

I should also note that Cross identified {ויהי כמו חדש ... יביש} as a scribal correction in 4Q51 written above line 9 to be inserted after גלעד בש[י]: "The scribe himself corrected the error by copying it above the point of omission."[22] Cross identified this scribal error as a case of haplography based on homoioteleuton (יבש to יביש). In my judgment, Cross's identification of haplography as a scribal error here meets the limiting criteria Vroom argued for, since we can easily imagine (1) how the *Vorlage* may have had the repetition of יביש (in whatever orthography) in approximately the same visuospatial sketchpad—that is, the repeated words may have been in the same location in two adjacent lines—and (2) the first phrase (אל [י]בש גלעד) is so similar to the second phrase (על יביש) that they can be understood as synonymous readings in various contexts, in ways that could meet the requirements of a phonological loop.[23] Note that within the larger passage both versions have both "Jabesh" and "Jabesh-Gilead" as synonymous toponyms (see further below). Furthermore, since the same scribe corrected his own text, this suggests that the cognitive processes that would allow haplography to occur were not fully met and the same scribe recognized his error. In that sense, this scribal error does not really constitute a variant that can be understood as a synonymous reading, even though an omission of this phrase would not necessarily create significant difficulties in the reading of this text under the influence of scribal memory in my judgment (see further below). This case illustrates how I do not rule out scribal errors, but I think that methodologically they are really difficult to identify, with this case being an exception. Nevertheless, even though I agree with him in this one case, I reject Cross's underlying general assumption of the original text.

Within this case of a scribal error based on haplography, we have a variant between MT and 4Q51 (with LXX) that is based on what is widely

---

21. This is Cross's reconstruction of the OG and its *Vorlage* with the support of the Latin (*Naas Ammonites*).

22. Frank Moore Cross et al., *Qumran Cave 4.XII*, 66. See also Cross, "Missing Verses," 108; P. Kyle McCarter Jr., *1 Samuel: A New Translation with Introduction, Notes, and Commentary*, AB 8 (Garden City, NY: Doubleday, 1980), 199.

23. See Vroom, "Cognitive Approach to Copying Errors." For my discussion of Vroom on haplography, see above.

understood as a visual error of a division of words. Both readings begin with ויהי ("and it came to pass") followed by the letters כמוחד(י)ש, which can be read together as כמוחדיש ("as [his] keeping silent"; generally connected to the preceding text concerning Saul as translated in the NRSV: "They despised him and brought him no present. *But he held his peace*") or divided as כמו חדש ("about a month"; generally connected to the following text about Nahash as translated in the NRSV: "*About a month later*, Nahash the Ammonite went up." Note that the NRSV translates this phrase twice). The graphic string of letters כמוחד(י)ש is ambiguous, so that the visual-triggering of these letters allows for both readings; however, once pointing is added as in MT or it is translated into Greek, this ambiguity is lost. In my judgment, both readings can be understood as original within the ambiguity of the consonantal text, especially since neither reading really changes the meaning of the text. That is, in both readings, Saul remained silent or did nothing in face of a challenge, in MT with regard to an internal challenge by "worthless fellows" among his own people and in 4Q51 with regard to an external challenge by Nahash for a period of a month. Both readings can be interpreted as shedding light on a time when Saul may not have immediately defended himself or his subjects as a good king presumably would have.

The long plus in 4Q51 has been understood by Cross and others as part of the original text, with its omission being understood as a case of haplography related to a reconstruction in which the consonantal string of כמוחד(י)ש was repeated (as reflected in the NRSV translation, the first translation to include the plus); however, this assertion has been challenged by some recent scholars.[24] Here I will not repeat the detailed arguments for or against its originality, because I do not share the assumption of an original text. I will simply note that both sides of this debate make close reference to Josephus, who seems to know of a *Vorlage* closer to 4Q51 than MT, even though differences remain between Josephus's account and 4Q51, so that Josephus is used to support the plus's originality (based on its similarities) or reject it as a late addition (based on its differ-

---

24. For its originality, see Cross, "Missing Verses"; McCarter, *1 Samuel*, 199; Tov, *Textual Criticism* (3rd ed.), 311. Contra A. Graeme Auld, *I and II Samuel: A Commentary*, OTL (Louisville: Westminster John Knox, 2011), 118; Reinhard G. Kratz, "Nahash, King of the Ammonites, in the Deuteronomistic History," in Müller and Pakkala, *Insights into Editing*, 163–88; Müller, Pakkala, and Ter Haar Romeny, *Evidence of Editing*, 79–99.

ences). Rather than choosing one version as the original or reconstructing the original, I will simply note that all of these versions make sufficient sense of the text when we consider that no single manuscript alone can fully represent the literary text as housed in scribal memory. Again, this does not require that no scribal errors were ever made—in fact, I acknowledge one such error in this example; however, much of what we assume is based on a scribal error should not be understood as such. For example, based on my extension of Vroom's limitations on identifying haplography, it seems to me that those who argue for the original text being lost in MT *due to haplography* need to assert a different explanation for its supposed omission. That is, the omission is so long as to be effectively eliminated as a possible case of haplography based on Vroom's arguments. *However*, it also seems to me that omissions may have been more common than generally accepted, especially since an omission in one manuscript would not necessarily imply that the scribe was attempting to omit the material from the tradition as a whole, as preserved in scribal memory. That is, there was probably little or no ideological motivation implied in most omissions or additions. Therefore, whether this plus is an addition or an omission in any particular manuscript, the plus seems to fit organically within the broader tradition, but is also unnecessary.

Above my comments have mostly concerned visual-triggering, especially in terms of the word division of כמוחד(י)ש and the possibility of haplography, a form of a visual scribal error. Now I want to turn my attention to the two remaining variants I identified above: (1) "Jabesh-Gilead" in MT 1 Sam 11:1; "Jabesh" in 4Q51 and (2) "Nahash" in MT 1 Sam 11:1; "Nahash, the king of the Ammonites" in 4Q51 11:1; and "Nahash the Ammonite" in LXX 1 Sam 11:1. Both of these variants represent how category-triggering can occur in relationship to geographical reference and person reference. Concerning (1): both texts include both forms—in MT, "Jabesh-Gilead" followed by "Jabesh" in 11:1; in 4Q51, "Jabesh-Gilead" in the long plus (10:27^{sup}) followed by "Jabesh" twice in 11:1. Clearly, these are synonymous readings. Concerning (2): both texts include two different forms—in MT, "Nahash the Ammonite," "Nahash," and "Nahash the Ammonite" in 11:1; in 4Q51, "Nahash, king of the Ammonites," "Nahash, king of the Ammonites," and "Nahash the Ammonite" in the long plus (10:27^{sup}) as well as "Nahash, king of the Ammonites," and "Nahash the Ammonite" in 11:1. When we expand our analysis, we find that "Nahash, king of the Ammonites" also occurs in MT in 1 Sam 12:12. Clearly, these are synonymous readings. Furthermore, Garsiel identified a form of sound-triggering related to Nahash in 11:1–2 as noted in his translation: "Then Nahash (***nhs***) the Ammonite [*h-ʿmwny*] ... and encamped (***wyhn***) ... Nahash [***nhs***] the Ammonite (*h-ʿmwny*) ... may thrust out all your right eyes (*ʿyn ymyn*)."[25] That is, "Nahash the Ammonite" (נחש העמוני) triggered the selection of both the verb "encamped" (ויחן) with the alliteration of the נ and ח and "right eyes" (עין ימין) with the alliteration of the ע, מ, נ, and י. Whether or not the plus in 4Q51 is an addition or an omission (or really neither), we can see that the sound-triggering Garsiel identified is also present in the plus with the repetition of "Nahash, the king of the Ammonites" and "right eye." Furthermore, the plus (with the published reconstruction) continues the alliteration of the נ, מ, ע, ח, and י throughout. Therefore, within these few verses we find examples of category-triggering, sound-triggering, and visual-triggering regardless of which version of the text we read, but even more so when we consider both texts are original.

Although I will focus my next discussion on 1 Sam 2:8–10, I am providing the fuller passage (2:3–10), since my arguments concerning the variants in 2:8–10 depend significantly on the broader literary context. Although there are variants in 1 Sam 2:1–7, I will not comment on them.

Example 5.4: 1 Samuel 2:3–10[26]

MT

ותתפלל חנה ותאמר עלץ לבי ביהוה רמה קרני ביהוה רחב פי על אויבי כי שמחתי בישועתך אין קדוש כיהוה כי אין בלתך ואין צור כאלהינו אל תרבו

---

25. Garsiel, *Biblical Names*, 54 (emphasis added).

26. See Reinhard G. Kratz, "Textual Supplementation in Poetry: The Song of Hannah as a Test Case," in *Supplementation and the Study of the Hebrew Bible*, ed. Saul M. Olyan and Jacob L. Wright, BJS 361 (Providence, RI: Brown University, 2018), 25–29. The English translations are Kratz's adaptation of NRSV, except he provided the NETS for LXX and I have repeated his translation of 4Q51 when he argued that LXX represents the same (or very similar) Hebrew text as 4Q51. Note that I have also strictly followed the main text in BHS, rather than including the suggested emendations given in the notes of BHS as Kratz did. In a few cases, I have given my own retroversion of the Greek into Hebrew, but in most cases I have simply noted with Kratz (and others) that LXX and 4Q51 agree. Kratz discussed some of the other proposed reconstructions of 4Q51 in this passage; however, I have chosen not to enter that discussion and, like Kratz, continue with the published reconstruction. In fact, none of the alternatives would significantly alter my arguments or conclusions.

תדברו גבהה גבהה יצא עתק מפיכם כי אל דעות יהוה ולא נתכנו עללות
קשת גברים חתים ונכשלים אזרו חיל שבעים בלחם נשכרו ורעבים חדלו
עד עקרה ילדה שבעה ורבת בנים אמללה יהוה ממית ומחיה מוריד שאול
ויעל יהוה מוריש ומעשיר משפיל אף מרומם מקים מעפר דל מאשפת ירים
אביון להושיב עם נדיבים וכסא כבוד ינחלם כי ליהוה מצקי ארץ וישת
עליהם תבל רגלי חסידו ישמר ורשעים בחשך ידמו כי לא בכח יגבר איש
יהוה יחתו מריבו עלו בשמים ירעם יהוה ידין אפסי ארץ ויתן עז למלכו וירם
קרן משיחו

Hannah prayed and said, "My heart exults the LORD; my strength is exalted in my LORD. My mouth derides my enemies, because I rejoice in your victory. There is no Holy One like the LORD, no one besides you; there is no Rock like our God. Talk no more so very proudly, let not arrogance come from your mouth; for the LORD is a God of knowledge [pl.], and by him actions are weighed. The bow(s) of the mighty are broken, but the feeble gird on strength. Those who were full have hired themselves out for bread, but those who were hungry are fat with spoil. The barren has borne seven, but she who has many children is forlorn. The LORD kills and brings to life; he brings down to Sheol and raises up. The LORD makes poor and makes rich; he brings low, he also exalts. He raises up the poor from the dust; he lifts the needy from the ash heap, to make them sit with princes and inherit a seat of honor. For pillars of the earth are the LORD's, and on them he has set the world. He will guard the feet of his faithful ones, but the wicked shall be cut off in darkness; for not by might does one prevail. The LORD! His adversaries shall be shattered. The Most High will thunder in heaven. The LORD will judge the ends of the earth; he will give strength to his king, and exalt the power (horn) of his anointed."

4Q51 (fragmentary)[27]

vacat עלץ לבי ביהוה] רמה קרני בי[הו]ה [רחב]
[פי על אובי שמחתי בישועתך כ]יא ואין קדוש כיה[וה]
[ואין צדיק כאלהינו ואין בלת]ך ואין צור כאלוהינו
[אל תרבו תדברו גבהה אל יצא ע]תק מפיכם כי אל דעת
[יהוה ואל תוכן עללותיו קשת גבורי]ם חתה ונ[כ]שלים אז[רו]

---

27. Ulrich, *Biblical Qumran Scrolls*, 260–61.

5. Conclusions and Implications

[חיל שבעים בלחם נשכרו ורעבים חד]ל[ו עד ע]קרה ילדה
[שבעה ורבת בנים אמללה יהוה ממית ומח]יה מוריד
[שאול ויעל יהוה מוריש ומעשיר משפיל]אף [מרומם]
[מקים מעפר דל ומאשפות ירים אביון להושיב עם]
נדיב[ים וכסא כבוד ינחלם כי ליהוה מצוקי ארץ וישת]
עליהם תב[ל] ודרך ח[סידיו ישמור ורשעים בחשך ידמו]
נתן נד[ר]ל[נוד]ר ויברך ש[נות צדיק כי לוא בכח יגבר איש]
יהוה יהת מר[י]בו מי ק[דוש כיהוה
[   ]◦[   ]ותם בשלמ◦[אל יתהלל חכם]
[בחכמתו]ואל ית[ה]ל[ל הגבור בגבורתו ואל יתהלל עשיר]
[בעשרו כי בזאת יתהלל המתהלל השכל וידע את יהוה]
[ולעשו]ת מש[פט וצדקה בתוך הארץ יהוה עלו בשמים]
וירעם [יהוה ידין אפסי ארץ ויתן עז למלכנו וירם קרן]
משיחו

My heart exults the LORD; my strength is exalted in my LORD. My mouth derides my enemies, I rejoice in your victory, for there is no Holy One like the LORD, no one righteous like our God, no one besides you; there is no Rock like our God. Talk no more so proudly, let not arrogance come from your mouth; for the Lord is a God of knowledge, and a God who balances his own actions. The bow of the mighty is broken, but the feeble gird on strength. Those who were full have hired themselves out for bread, but those who were hungry are fat with spoil. The barren has borne seven, but she who has many children is forlorn. The LORD kills and brings to life; he brings down to Sheol and raises up. The LORD makes poor and makes rich; he brings low, he also exalts. He raises up the poor from the dust; he lifts the needy from the ash heap, to make them sit with princes and inherit a seat of honor. For pillars of the earth are the LORD's, and on them he has set the world.

He will guard the **way** of his faithful ones, but the wicked shall be cut off in darkness; **he grants the vow to the one who takes vows, he blesses the years of the righteous,** for not by might does one prevail. **The LORD shatters his adversary (adversaries). Who is holy like the LORD ... when he repays (?) ... Let not the wise boast of his wisdom, and let not the strong boast of his strength, and let not the rich boast of his riches, but let the one who boasts boast about this: that he has the understanding and knows the LORD and to exercise justice and righteousness in the midst of the land. The Most High will thunder in heaven.**

The Lord will judge the ends of the earth; he will give strength to his king, and exalt the power (horn) of his anointed.

To further organize the following discussion, I provide first a list of variants between MT and 4Q51 1 Sam 2:8–10, including LXX, since the reconstruction of the *lacuna* of 4Q51 depends significantly on the purported LXX *Vorlage*.[28]

MT 2:8b   כי ליהוה מצקי ארץ וישת עליהם תבל, For the pillars of the earth are the Lord's, and on them he has set the world

4Q51 2:8b   [כי ליהוה מצוקי ארץ וישת] עליהם תב[ל], For the pillars of the earth are the Lord's, and on them he has set the world

LXX 2:8b   [lacking]

MT 2:9   רגלי חסידו ישמר ורשעים בחשך ידמו, He will guard the **feet** of his faithful ones, but the wicked shall be cut off in darkness;

4Q51 2:9   [ודרך ח]סידיו ישמור ורשעים בחשך ידמו] [ ], He will guard the **way** of his faithful ones, but the wicked shall be cut off in darkness;

LXX 2:9   [lacking]

MT 2:9   [lacking]

4Q51 2:9   נתן נד[ר] ל[נוד]ר ויברך ש]נות, **he grants the vow to the one who takes vows, he blesses the years of the righteous,**

LXX 2:9   διδοὺς εὐχὴν τῷ εὐχομένῳ καὶ εὐλόγησεν ἔτη δικαίου· ὅτι οὐκ ἐν ἰσχύι δυνατὸς ἀνήρ = 4Q51

MT 2:10   יהוה יחתו מריבו, The Lord! His adversaries shall be shattered.

4Q51 2:10   יהוה יחת מר[י]בו, **The Lord shatters his adversary (adversaries).**

---

28. Since it often corresponds closely to 4Q51, I have not provided the Hebrew *Vorlage* of LXX here and simply refer my readers to Tov's reconstruction: Emanuel Tov, "Different Editions of the Song of Hannah and of Its Narrative Framework," in *Tehillah le-Moshe: Biblical and Judaic Studies in Honor of Moshe Greenberg*, ed. Mordechai Cogan, Barry L. Eichler, and Jeffrey H. Tigay (Winona Lake, IN: Eisenbrauns, 1997), 149–70.

5. Conclusions and Implications 293

LXX 2:10   κύριος ἀσθενῆ ποιήσει ἀντίδικον αὐτοῦ = 4Q51

MT 2:10   עלו בשמים ירעם, The Most High will thunder in heaven.
4Q51 2:10 ירעם [עלו בשמים], The Most High will thunder in heaven. [Note different location.]
LXX 2:10   κύριος ἀνέβη εἰς οὐρανοὺς καὶ ἐβρόντησεν = 4Q51

MT 2:10   [lacking]
4Q51 2:10 מי ק]דוש כיהוה, Who is holy like the Lord?
LXX 2:10   κύριος ἅγιος = קדוש כיהוה, The Lord is holy.

MT 2:10   [lacking]
4Q51 2:10 [   ]ºתם בשלמº, when he repays (?)
LXX 2:10   [lacking]

MT 2:10   [lacking]
4Q51 2:10 אל יתהלל חכם [בחכמתו   ]], Let not the wise boast of his wisdom,
LXX 2:10   μὴ καυχάσθω ὁ φρόνιμος ἐν τῇ φρονήσει αὐτοῦ = 4Q51

MT 2:10   [lacking]
4Q51 2:10 [ואל ית]ה[ל]ל הגבור בגבורתו], and let not the strong boast of his strength,
LXX 2:10   καὶ μὴ καυχάσθω ὁ δυνατὸς ἐν τῇ δυνάμει αὐτοῦ = 4Q51

MT 2:10   [lacking]
4Q51 2:10 [ואל יתהלל עשיר] [בעשרו], and let not the rich boast of his riches,
LXX 2:10   καὶ μὴ καυχάσθω ὁ πλούσιος ἐν τῷ πλούτῳ αὐτοῦ = 4Q51

MT 2:10   [lacking]
4Q51 2:10 [כי בזאת יתהלל המתהלל השכל וידע את יהוה] [ולעשו]ת [מש]פט וצדקה בתוך הארץ], but let the one who boasts boast about this: that he has the understanding and knows the Lord and to exercise justice and righteousness in the midst of the land.
LXX 2:10   ἀλλ' ἢ ἐν τούτῳ καυχάσθω ὁ καυχώμενος, συνίειν καὶ γινώσκειν τὸν κύριον καὶ ποιεῖν κρίμα καὶ δικαιοσύνην ἐν μέσῳ τῆς γῆς. = 4Q51

Text-critical assessments of the Song of Hannah tend to assume an original text from which the variants are explained in a linear fashion. For some commentators, this linear progression is from the shorter version (MT) to the longer version (LXX; 4Q51), assuming *lectio brevior potior*; for others, it is from the longer version to a shorter version due to some form of textual corruption.[29] In my discussion here I will mostly dialogue with Reinhard Kratz's discussion as representative.

In his discussion, Kratz is obviously aware of the discussion of textual fluidity. For example, he concluded that his analysis of the text-critical variants in 1 Sam 2 demonstrates that "the text remained in this processing flow for a long time and was being continually reworked."[30] Nevertheless, he remained confident that, despite such textual fluidity, he could discern the textual and redactional layers behind the extant texts. For example, the following is my summary of his argument for the development of 1 Sam 2:8–9 based on his text-critical and redactional study, in which I have bolded what he understood to be additional material.[31]

Original
He raises up the poor from the dust; he lifts the needy from the ash heap, to make them sit with princes and inherit a seat of honor, for not by might does one prevail. (8a, 9b)

Additions made independently in LXX and MT:

LXX
He raises up the poor from the dust; he lifts the needy from the ash heap, to make them sit with princes and inherit a seat of honor. **He**

---

29. For the short original, see Kratz, "Hannah"; Tov, "Different Editions." For the long original, see Anneli Aejmelaeus, "Hannah's Psalm: Text, Composition, and Redaction," in *Houses Full of All Good Things: Essays in Memory of Timo Veijola*, ed. Juha Pakkala and Martti Nissinen, PFES 95 (Helsinki: Finnish Exegetical Society; Göttingen: Vandehoeck und Ruprecht, 2008), 354–76; Aejmelaus, "Hannah's Psalm in 4QSam[a]," in *Archaeology of the Books of Samuel: The Entangling of the Textual and Literary History*, ed. Phillippe Hugo and Adrian Schenker, VTSup 132 (Leiden: Brill, 2010), 23–37.
30. Kratz, "Hannah," 33. See similarly Tov, "Different Editions," 151.
31. Kratz, "Hannah," 39. Here I provide the English translation; he provided this same summary in Hebrew. I should note that Tov's analysis produced much the same result. See Tov, "Different Editions," 164. The two differences are that Tov included 8b in his original and did not include 9b in his discussion.

grants the vow to the one who takes vows, he blesses the years of the righteous, for not by might does one prevail. (8a, **9a**, 9b)

MT
He raises up the poor from the dust; he lifts the needy from the ash heap, to make them sit with princes and inherit a seat of honor. **For pillars of the earth are the LORD's, and on them he has set the world. He will guard the feet of his faithful ones, but the wicked shall be cut off in darkness,** for not by might does one prevail. (8a, **8b, 9a,** 9b).

LXX and MT conflated in 4Q51:[32]

4Q51
He raises up the poor from the dust; he lifts the needy from the ash heap, to make them sit with princes and inherit a seat of honor. **For pillars of the earth are the LORD's, and on them he has set the world. He will guard the way of his faithful ones, but the wicked shall be cut off in darkness, he grants the vow to the one who takes vows, he blesses the years of the righteous,** for not by might does one prevail. (8a, **8b, 9a,** 9b).

Since I do not share his assumption of an original text from which the extant versions can be traced in a linear fashion back to this original, I will not summarize his arguments here. However, in my discussion below of these diverse variants I will draw upon his discussion (and others) as I present my own analysis of how category-triggering (in the forms of synonymous readings, parallel poetic lines, and harmonization), sound-triggering (in the form of alliteration), and visual-triggering (also in the form of alliteration) underly these variants within scribal memory.

In Kratz's analysis, the phrase "For the pillars of the earth are the LORD's, and on them he has set the world" (8b, MT and 4Q51) and the phrase "He will guard the feet/way of his faithful ones, but the wicked shall be cut off in darkness" (9a, MT and 4Q51) are regarded as late additions

---

32. Despite different overall conclusions, 4Q51 is considered a conflated text here. See also Aejmelaeus, "Hannah's Psalm," 372; Aejmelaeus, "Hannah's Psalm in 4QSam^a," 31; Tov, "Different Editions," 164.

in MT that were then copied into 4Q51, since they are lacking in LXX.³³ The variant reading in 4Q51 (דרך "way") is widely considered to be a harmonization with Prov 2:8: ודרך חסידו ישמר ("He will guard the way of his faithful ones"), presumably based on scribal memory of this passage.³⁴

In Kratz's analysis, the following phrases—all of which are lacking in MT but are extant in LXX and 4Q51—are additions:

9b he grants the vow to the one who takes vows, he blesses the years of the righteous
10 Who is holy like the LORD? (4Q51); The Lord is holy (LXX)
10 Let not the wise boast of his wisdom and let not the strong boast of his strength and let not the rich boast of his riches, but let the one who boasts boast about this: that he has the understanding and knows the LORD and to exercise justice and righteousness in the midst of the land.

All these additions are understood as harmonizations:

9b "He grants the vow…" is a harmonization with the preceding narrative of Hannah, "insert[ing] the idea of fulfillment of vows and blessing of the righteous with old age."³⁵
10 "Who is holy like the LORD?" in 4Q51 and "The Lord is holy" in LXX is a harmonization with 2:2 ("For there is no one holy like the LORD").³⁶
10 "Let not the wise … in the midst of the land" is an addition taken from Jer 9:22–23 based on the following connections between the two passages: "keyword associations ('god of knowledge,' 'heroes,' 'rich,' in 1 Sam 2:3, 4, 7), the idea of pride in v. 3, the universalistic plus in v. 8b (cf. Jer 10:10–13), and, finally, the statement about the powerlessness of people in v. 9b."³⁷

---

33. Kratz, "Hannah," 39. See also Tov, "Different Editions," 159, 161.
34. Kratz, "Hannah," 32. See also McCarter, *1 Samuel*, 70; Aejmelaeus, "Hannah's Psalm," 370; Aejmelaeus, "Hannah's Psalm in 4QSamᵃ," 32; Tov, "Different Editions," 161 n. 43.
35. Kratz, "Hannah," 39; Tov, "Different Editions," 162.
36. Kratz, "Hannah," 41; Tov, "Different Editions," 168.
37. Kratz, "Hannah," 41, 43. Similarly Tov, "Different Editions," 165; Aejmelaeus, "Hannah's Psalm," 373; Aejmelaeus, "Hannah's Psalm in 4QSamᵃ," 33–34.

Although he does not use the term scribal memory, Kratz's analysis implies it, especially in his discussion of how keywords in 1 Sam 2 "suggested to the scribe that he cite Jer 9:22–23 in 1 Sam 2."[38] These clearly are examples of harmonization as a form of category-triggering. Of course, the parallel structure of the poetry in Jer 9:22–23 // 1 Sam 2:10 itself is a form of category-triggering—that is, "wise"/"wisdom," "strong"/"strength," and "rich"/"riches" describe the same category of persons (as coclass members) within the wisdom tradition; "let not … boast" versus "let … boast" uses contrast as a category; and "understanding," "knows the Lord," and "exercise justice and righteousness" are qualities of the wise, who know that they are not holy like the Lord.

What Kratz and others have not noticed is the role of sound-triggering in these variants in the form of alliteration of ר (twenty-eight times in MT; thirty-one in 4Q51) and ב (sixteen in MT; twenty-two in 4Q51) throughout 1 Sam 2:1–10 and that some of the variants participate in these alliterative patterns as follows:

- For the pillars of the earth [ארץ] are the Lord's, and on them he has set the world (8b, MT and 4Q51)
- [Both of the variants in] He will guard [ישמר] the feet [רגלי]/way [ודרך] of his faithful ones, but the wicked [רשעים] shall be cut off in darkness (9a, MT and 4Q51, respectively)
- he grants [נתן] the vow [נדר] to the one who takes vows [לנודר], he blesses [ויברך] the years [שנות] of the righteous (9a, 4Q51 and LXX)
- and let not the strong boast of his strength [הגבור בגבורתו] (10, 4Q51 and LXX)
- and let not the rich boast in his riches [עשיר בעשרו] (10, 4Q51 and LXX)
- but let the one who boasts boast about this: that he has the understanding and knows the Lord and to exercise justice and righteousness in the midst of the land [הארץ] (10, 4Q51 and LXX)

That is, *if* these are (harmonizing) additions, the scribes who added these phrases were influenced by the sound-triggering of the ר and ב alliteration in the *Vorlage* that they were copying; however, it is better to understand

---

38. Kratz, "Hannah," 43.

that such sound-triggering can be at work in scribal memory throughout the composition/transmission process in ways that complicate our discerning earlier versus later readings in the context of textual fluidity and textual plurality, *even if* we continue to insist on an original text. Thus, it seems to me that we have multiple originals once again.

The four above examples have allowed me to demonstrate how category-triggering, sound-triggering, and visual-triggering can work in combination with each other within scribal memory as scribes engaged in *Vorlage*-based copying. The following summarizes what forms of triggering we observed in the four examples:

Example	Category-Triggering	Sound-Triggering	Visual-Triggering
5.1. Song 4; 7	Numerical Paronomasia	Alliteration Wordplay Homophones	Alliteration Homographs
5.2. Exod 26:24; 36:29	Numerical Paraonomasia	Alliteration Wordplay Homophones	Alliteration Homographs
5.3. 1 Sam 10:27–11:2	Synonymous Readings	Alliteration Wordplay	Haplography Division of Words
5.4. 1 Sam 2:8–10	Synonymous Readings Parallelism Harmonization	Alliteration	Alliteration

These and other forms of category-triggering and sound-triggering are found in everyday conversation combined with body movements (for which there may be something comparable to what I have labeled visual-triggering that has yet to be described in conversation analysis).[39] Above I have argued that these and other forms of category-triggering and sound-triggering as well as the analogous visual-triggering can be found in text-critical variants, *even if* we assume a linear progression from an origi-

---

39. For recent movement in this direction, see Wooffitt et at., "Poetics in Jefferson's Poetics Lecture"; Hutchby, "Poetics and Performativity."

nal text to the extant versions. It seems best, however, to assume that these gross-selection mechanisms occur in the cognitive-linguistic practices of language, whether in ordinary talk, composition of new literary works, or in what would have been one of the most literate tasks in the ancient world: *Vorlage*-based copying. Even in *Vorlage*-based copying, scribes drew from scribal memory as they performed these traditional texts for their imagined future readers of the manuscripts that they were producing based not only on the *Vorlagen* physically present before them, but all of the *Vorlagen* that they held in scribal memory and applied within the process of copying. Within scribal memory, category-triggering, sound-triggering, and visual-triggering were operative in ways that contributed to the textual fluidity and textual plurality that was not accidental but characteristic of their understanding of traditional literary texts, none of which can be fully contained in any one manuscript. Therefore, even though every manuscript was a memory aid through which readers and hearers had access to the literary text as preserved in scribal memory, every manuscript was also an imperfect instantiation of that literary text. This cultural reality allowed scribes to both copy their *Vorlagen* verbatim *and* to vary from their *Vorlagen*, all the while that they were producing faithful copies in their scribal performance enabled by scribal memory within a tradition that valued textual plurality. Here I want to quote an important insight from Hans Debel to emphasize that textual fluidity and textual plurality do not create an environment with no limitations, because the new manuscripts must nevertheless be faithful copies of the literary text within the tradition:

> The room for change was not infinite: some form of collective memory seems to have created certain expectations and, in practice, put limits to the variance that could be tolerated in a text that represented an authoritative tradition. Although there seems to have been plenty of opportunity to introduce new elements within texts and to change their details, certain elements within the tradition could not be omitted.[40]

Debel's insight from text criticism compares well with what we know about the performance of oral traditions, once again demonstrating the value in scribal performance and scribal memory, even though he does not use these terms.[41]

---

40. Debel, "Anchoring Revelations," 474.
41. See esp. Foley's distinction of how a poet's own repertoire (idiolect) is lim-

Throughout this volume I have drawn from secondary literature that assumes, based on the assumptions held in the MT-priority paradigm, that these poetic characteristics are generally connected to authors who intentionally use these poetic features in the composition of their literary texts. This assumption, in my opinion, is significantly influenced by uncritical assertions that everyday conversation lacks such poetics, which is too often extended even to orally composed literature. However, Jefferson's "poetics of ordinary talk" demonstrates how conversation has poetic features that often go unnoticed in conversation, but are the basis for more intentional forms of poetic literature. When we apply Jefferson's insights to text-critical variants that are widely understood as late additions or scribal errors, we nevertheless see that some variants share in the poetic characteristics of the literary texts in which they are found. That is, rather than assuming that poetics is something limited to literary authors during composition, we should reimagine poetics as a basic feature of language in general, so that category-triggering and sound-triggering occur in the most basic form of language—face-to-face talk-in-interaction—and in the most "advanced" form of language—literary texts in which poetics has been exaggerated for aesthetic effect.[42] Because category-triggering and sound-triggering can occur throughout language, we should not limit its influence to composition, but consider its influence spanning the composition/transmission process, including in *Vorlage*-based copying of manuscripts. Because these gross-selection mechanisms occur throughout the composition/transmission process, we also must accept that the determination of when a particular example is intentional versus unintentional is at best extremely difficult (if not impossible), especially in ancient

---

ited to some degree by his local tradition (dialect) as well as by the larger oral tradition (language). I.e., the larger tradition sets limits on what is essential and therefore cannot be omitted with additional limitations possibly set within a local tradition. See Foley, *Traditional Oral Epic*, 390.

42. Here I want to point out how often the distinction between oral and literate have promoted Western values that are demeaning of much of the world's population and their "primitive" oral traditions. I hope that I have not participated in such colonizing tendencies in this and previous works (thus the scare quotes for "advanced" and "primitive" here), but I also know that I need to constantly pay close attention to the Western biases I carry with me. I highly recommend the work of Althea Spencer-Miller, who has helped me see these biases better. See Althea Spencer-Miller, "Rethinking Orality for Biblical Studies," in *Postcolonialism and the Hebrew Bible: The Next Step*, ed. Roland Boer, SemeiaSt 70 (Atlanta: Society of Biblical Literature, 2013), 35–68.

5. Conclusions and Implications

literary traditions that are characterized by scribal performance, scribal memory, and textual fluidity.[43]

Now I want to return to questions I asked in the introduction: What is a word? How are words selected? What is a text? What were scribes doing? and What is the role of textual plurality in the work of scribes copying manuscripts?

What is a word? A word is the smallest unit of meaning, which can be less than a lexeme (e.g., "hm") or more than a lexeme (e.g., "y'know" in conversation, "Vino pije licki Mustajbeze" in South Slavic epic, and "until the day of his death" // "all the days of his life" in a biblical variant in Jer 52:34).

How are words selected? Words are selected within the particular linguistic registers and pragmatic contexts in which they occur based on a variety of factors, including the meanings that each word may carry (sometimes with category-triggering), the sounds of the spoken word (sometimes with sound-triggering), and the relationship of the word to other words that occur within the larger pragmatic context. Thus, for example, in the following list taken from a naturally occurring conversation, the generalized list completer ("and crap") was "selected from among such candidates as 'as stuff,' 'and junk,' 'and things,' etc.," because of the preceding k-sounds, including the first two items in the list: "cakes and candy and crap" (ex. 2.22).[44] In literature, either "the revelry of the loungers" (מרזח סרוחים; MT Amos 6:7) or "the neighing of the horses" (מסחר סוסים; LXX Amos 6:7) can be selected, since both participate in the repetition of ס, ר, ח, and מ throughout the passage and connect with other keywords in the passage, a repetition that functions as both sound-triggering and visual-triggering (ex. 3.4).

What is a text? Any text is a collection of selected words, whether the text is oral or written; however, our focus has been on What is a literary text in the context of ancient Hebrew literature? First, a literary text does not reside in any one text, that is, in any one oral performance (whether composed orally, recited by memory, or read aloud from a manuscript)

---

43. However, note that Bowles made this same argument even for the modern author Charles Dickens, i.e., he argued that the category-triggering and sound-triggering found in the speech of one of Dickens's most colorful characters is probably a combination of intentional design and unintentional poetics. See Bowles, "Poetics of Mrs Gamp's Conversation."

44. Jefferson, "List-Construction," 69.

or in any one manuscript. A literary text is bigger than any single text, because it resides in scribal memory, that is, the knowledge of the traditional literary texts (oral and/or written) held in the collective memory of scribes. This is even the case for some texts that exist only in conversation—for example, a list of three items can be understood as a text that nevertheless can represent a longer list of coclass items, despite its incompleteness. Thus, even in the act of *Vorlage*-based copying, scribes drew from their knowledge of the literary text represented by the manuscript physically present before them, but also from their knowledge of the literary text that nevertheless transcended that one manuscript to include every encounter of the literary text that they had had in their reading of other manuscripts of the same literary text and their hearing of the literary text as recited by memory or read aloud from a manuscript. Scribal memory gave them access to the literary text in its characteristic textual plurality and textual fluidity.

What were scribes doing? Even in *Vorlage*-based copying, scribes were transmitting the literary text, not only the manuscript physically present before them. Although the physically present manuscript may play the most significant role in *Vorlage*-based copying, thereby encouraging a high degree of verbatim copying, the scribes' performance of the literary text was not limited to this one manuscript, because scribal memory provided the scribes with access to the literary text beyond this one manuscript.

What is the role of textual plurality in the work of scribes copying manuscripts? In the MT-priority paradigm, textual plurality is primarily the result of scribal errors with a limited number of ideologically motivated revisions; it is, therefore, understood as a by-product of transmission that occurs after composition. What I am advocating for is taking textual plurality as central to the composition/transmission process, not simply a by-product of things gone awry. Textual plurality is not the result of copyists who have failed at their task of copying; rather, textual plurality is the reality in which scribal performance always occurs, because the literary text cannot be identified with some anachronistic original text contained in a first pristine manuscript, but the literary text must be identified within scribal memory, which includes the entire collection of all of the manuscripts of the same literary text and all of the scribes' interactions (oral/aural and/or written) with these manuscripts as well as oral texts and mental texts. As long as scribal performance produces a new manuscript that fits well within this textual plurality within scribal memory, the new manuscript is a faithful performance of the same literary text, despite what we moderns might insist are additions, omissions, transpositions, and substitutions. In other words, as long as these scribal changes, that is, those places in the new manuscript that vary from the physically present *Vorlage*, reside elsewhere within the textual plurality of the literary text in scribal memory, the same-but-different manuscript is not really new. Thus, we can have multiple originals within a tradition that characteristically values textual plurality.

Since I suspect that I have introduced scribal memory to many of my readers, and since I have extended previous discussions of scribal memory with the addition of insights concerning word selection for all of my readers, I want to end this summary with a quotation from the monograph *Memory in Oral Traditions* by the cognitive psychologist David Rubin:

> A theory was proposed for recall in oral tradition. Recall starts with the first word of the song and proceeds in a linear fashion. Words sung are cues for words yet to be sung. If words are to be recalled, they must be discriminated from other words in memory. The general constraints of the genre and piece, especially rhythm, acts as cues from the start, with the singing filling in other cues as it progresses. A piece fitting the constraints of the genre results, not necessarily a verbatim reproduction of a piece produced earlier. Where the constraints are strong, they will limit variation without the help of particular cue-item associations formed when a piece was heard. Where only one variant has been heard, especially when it has been heard repeatedly using spaced practice, individual cue-item associations will be more important and will further decrease variation. This process, after the initial, often conscious decision to sing a song has been made, can go on without conscious intervention, using what has been called implicit or indirect memory. The serial-recall method, however, means that knowledge in oral traditions is not routinely accessed without the cues provided by a running start and often cannot be accessed without them. Thus questions about the contents of a piece can often be answered only after the piece is sung. [45]

Although I have some difficulties with his description—for example, his description of oral composition may overemphasize the "linear fashion" of

---

45. David C. Rubin, *Memory in Oral Traditions: The Cognitive Psychology of Epic, Ballads, and Counting-Out Rhymes* (Oxford: Oxford University Press, 1995), 192.

memory—Rubin nevertheless makes some insights that may prove helpful to my project. If I translate his insights into my own as they relate to the role of scribal memory in *Vorlage*-based copying, it seems to me that scribal performance parallels oral composition to some extent as described by Rubin. That is, the *Vorlage* is the "cue-item." To paraphrase Rubin: This process, after the scribe's initial, often conscious decision to copy the *Vorlage* has been made, can go on without conscious intervention, using what has been called implicit or indirect memory, including scribal memory, resulting in a copy of the manuscript, fitting the constraints of the literary text within its characteristic textual plurality, but not necessarily a verbatim reproduction of the *Vorlage* physically present before the scribe. To return to the quotation I used in the introduction from Goshen-Gottstein's law of scribes: "the better [a scribe] knows his Bible, the better he knows its grammar—the more numerous may his inventions become;" however, I would avoid "inventions."[46] Rather, I would state that the deeper and broader a scribe's scribal memory was the more numerous the variants within the tradition's textual plurality he had to draw from as he produced a new manuscript that nevertheless was a faithful performance of the traditional text at home in textual plurality.

Methodological Reflections on Historical Criticism

In previous publications, I have called for a "new model of the development of literary texts in the ancient world."[47] In the introduction, I placed this monograph in a larger context in which such a new model is being advocated in the study of ancient and medieval literature and beyond, including what Young referred to as the "text-critical paradigm" and what Kelber referred to as the "oral-scribal-memorial-performative paradigm." These various efforts at establishing a new paradigm are based on the inefficacy of the historical-critical model as currently practiced, because, as Kelber noted, "the historical-critical paradigm is not historical enough."[48] In his critique of text criticism of the Hebrew Bible, Troxel lamented that text critics too often fail to take into account "textual materiality and its sociological entailments"—that is, they are not grounded enough in the

---

46. Goshen-Gottstein, "Biblical Philology and the Concordance," 10.
47. Person, *Deuteronomic History and the Book of Chronicles*, 171.
48. Kelber, *Collected Essays*, 2.

5. Conclusions and Implications

historical, social reality of the ancient world.[49] Foley observed that the failure of historical-criticism is that it is based on an "inadequate theory of verbal art"—that is, it fails to comprehend the historical and cultural influences upon oral traditions and literature because it remains too bound to a modern post-Gutenberg notion of word and text.[50] In this volume, I have attempted to provide a more adequate theory of verbal art that is deeply rooted in the historical and cultural realities of the ancient world, drawing especially from the notions of scribal performance and scribal memory as a means to providing the "new conceptual tools" and "new framework and vocabulary" for which Zahn seeks.[51] In this final section of the conclusion, I will review methodological critiques I have made in previous publications and then explicate the methodological implications of this study. That is, even though this volume focuses on *Vorlage*-based copying, the implications of the conclusions reached in this volume have far-reaching methodological consequences, especially in terms of how we understand source and redaction criticism.

In previous publications, I have drawn from conversation analysis, the comparative study of oral traditions, and text criticism as ways of critiquing methodological assumptions commonly held in biblical scholarship. In my use of conversation analysis, I argued for how ineffective *Wiederaufnahme* is as a scribal practice that enables us to locate redactional additions, because analogous structures can be found in everyday conversation and in literature that is clearly authored by a single individual.[52] In various publications, I have also advocated for the use of text-critical controls on redactional arguments.[53] The publication that most directly addresses the methodological crisis related to source criticism and redaction criticism is the collection of essays I coedited with Robert Rezetko, *Empirical Models Challenging Biblical Criticism*.

My own chapter concerns the anachronistic assumptions concerning literary unity behind source and redaction criticism. Biblical scholars

---

49. Troxel, "What Is the 'Text'?," 611.
50. Foley, *Immanent* Art, 5.
51. Zahn, *Rethinking Rewritten Scripture*, 241.
52. Raymond F. Person Jr., "A Reassessment of *Wiederaufnahme* from the Perspective of Conversation Analysis." *BZ* 43 (1999): 241–48. See also ch. 6 in Person, *From Conversation to Oral Tradition*.
53. E.g., Person, *Deuteronomic History and the Book of Chronicles*; Person, "Text Criticism as a Lens."

regularly assume that literary unity requires both linguistic consistency and consistency of story based on modern Western notions; therefore, inconsistencies in terms of language and content presumably provide discernible traces that enable scholars to identify sources and redactional layers. I challenged these assumptions by showing how what is regularly understood as inconsistencies can occur within a performance of oral traditions as a model of how some cultural expressions, including traditional literature, include what we anachronistically assume must be the result of multiple authors/redactors, each of whom consistently uses a linguistic system based on their historical and/or geographical setting.[54] Here I will add that such assumptions are a post-Gutenberg development based on the logic of Lachmann's notion of an original text as the literary text, which allows differences to be understood as variants, even though the ancient scribes may have understood them as the same. Therefore, without a stable literary text that can be traced back to the original text, it seems to me that the use of historical linguistics for the purpose of dating biblical texts is seriously undermined.[55] Moreover, what we often assume is required for consistency of story ignores the reality of textual plurality, which is more akin to multiformity in oral traditions.

In the introduction to *Empirical Models Challenging Biblical Criticism*, Rezetko and I put forth arguments concerning source and redaction criticism based on our collective reading of all of the essays in the volume.[56] We noted that all of the contributors accept the notion of composite texts in the context of textual fluidity and textual plurality, which provides some agreement with how source and redaction critics understand basic elements of literary development in the ancient world. That is, authors sometimes compose literary texts using sources and those texts are sometimes revised by later redactors. Furthermore, empirical evidence provides some evidence of discernible traces of such literary

---

54. Person, "Problem of 'Literary Unity.'"
55. For my earlier discussion of historical linguistics, see Person, *Deuteronomic History and the Book of Chronicles*, 23–40. I find the collective work of Rezetko, Young, and Ehrensvärd on historical linguistics convincing. See Young, Rezetko, and Ehrensvärd, *Linguistic Dating of Biblical Texts*; Young, "Starting at the Beginning"; Robert Rezetko and Ian Young, *Historical Linguistics and Biblical Hebrew: Steps Toward an Integrated Approach*, ANEM 9 (Atlanta: SBL Press, 2014). In my opinion, their approach to historical linguistics takes seriously the problem of textual plurality that is too often ignored in such discussions.
56. Person and Rezetko, "Importance of Empirical Models."

development. *However*, these traces cannot be used effectively without other empirical controls (such as text-critical evidence) with any degree of certainty, especially since the literary history of any one text may be so complex as to defy description. In fact, this complex literary history included documented evidence of opposing tendencies, so that the kind of general observations necessary to how historical criticism functions (for example, *lectio difficilior potior*) can no longer be considered accurate generalizations. Thus, we concluded:

> The most that source and redaction criticism may be able to do *even with empirical evidence* is help us understand in general ways the composite nature of the text with only sketchy notions of what sources and redactional layers may have contributed to the literary character of the text. Once we devote much time to analyzing these reconstructed sources and redactional layers themselves as literary objects worthy of close literary and theological study, we probably have crossed a line of plausibility that becomes much too speculative, at least in most cases.[57]

In our estimation, empirical models cut both ways, both affirming that in some *limited* cases there may be what are often understood as discernible traces *and* demonstrating that such characteristics that may be labeled as discernible traces may, on the one hand, occur in single-authored texts or the performance of traditional literature and, on the other hand, may be eliminated in the later stages of the composition/transmission process in the literary history of the text, especially in omissions.

Conversations with colleagues since the publication of *Empirical Models Challenging Biblical Criticism* have sometimes demonstrated fundamental misunderstandings of the argument that we put forward there, so here I want to be even more explicit about our conclusions. For example, we have been accused of not understanding that no one criterion should be applied in isolation, but all of the available criteria should be utilized collectively in source and redaction criticism. We agree and nowhere do we suggest otherwise. The question we are asking is not how to apply a list of criteria, but what criteria should even be on the list in the first place. In other words, why was a particular criterion added to the list of criteria as a generally effective method to identify discernible traces and does that reason for its inclusion on the list remain valid?

---

57. Person and Rezetko, "Importance of Empirical Models," 35.

Based on empirical evidence identified by the contributors of *Empirical Models Challenging Biblical Criticism*, we think that the criteria we have been using are problematic and must be completely reevaluated. The list of criteria we have been using for more than one hundred years needs to be seriously reassessed and the results of that reassessment will likely be a much shorter list of criteria, meaning that some future list of criteria *even when applied collectively* will lose much of its efficacy. Therefore, we may have to accept much more modest results in our source-critical and redaction-critical work before we begin to use the Hebrew Bible in our historical reconstructions of ancient Israel and Judah. Otherwise, our historical reconstructions are built upon seriously flawed arguments of the literary history of the Hebrew Bible. We have also been accused of assuming that we need complete objectivity, but again we have not suggested that anywhere. However, the historical-critical method purports to deliver a certain degree of objectivity through its rigorous methodology and we are convinced that the methodology has some significant flaws, so that whatever level of objectivity it purports to deliver is unfounded. Although complete objectivity will never be reached and therefore is not our goal, we nevertheless think that rigorous debate about methodology is important in order to improve whatever degree of objectivity any methodology may reach. In short, we are not interested in abandoning historical-criticism, but in improving it, so that it can provide better methodological guidance in our work and that of others. Nevertheless, we are confident that this improvement is not a simple revision, but will likely require a paradigm shift in which even basic terms need to be reinterpreted.[58]

Although I have often drawn significantly from text-critical evidence, many of my previous publications can justifiably be seen as my attempt at source and redaction criticism with some text-critical controls. In fact, that was often my explicitly stated purpose. This is even the case with all of the essays in *Empirical Models Challenging Biblical Criticism*, which as the volume's title clearly implies is designed to challenge the rhetorical force of the volume edited by Jeffrey Tigay entitled *Empirical Models for Biblical*

---

58. For an interesting discussion of the incommensurability between paradigms, specifically in recent discussions of historical linguistics of ancient Hebrew, see Martin Ehrensvärd, Robert Rezetko, and Ian Young, "Counting and Weighing: On the Role of Intuition in Philology and Linguistics," *JSem* 29 (2020), https://doi.org/10.25159/2663-6573/8180.

Criticism and to dialogue with other works that were clearly influenced by Tigay's volume in their exploration of methodological issues related to biblical criticism, especially source and redaction criticism.[59] For example, in her chapter, text critic Bénédicte Lemmelijn advocates for a model for researching the literary history of texts that requires that text criticism take priority over source and redaction criticism, explicitly challenging the distinction between composition and transmission; nevertheless, her target audience is consistent with the volume as a whole as intended by Rezetko and me as its editors, that is, those scholars who generally engage in source and redaction criticism.[60]

Although throughout this volume I have rejected the strong distinction between composition and transmission, preferring instead the composition/transmission process, I nevertheless understand the composition/transmission process as a continuum, even if there are no places on that continuum where we can easily distinguish one from the other. I acknowledge that my previous publications have tended toward the composition end of the continuum, so that in this volume I am emphasizing *Vorlage*-based copying, which is clearly on the transmission end. In other words, even though in previous publications I have combined text criticism with source and redaction criticism, this is my first monograph that is emphasizing text criticism in this larger project to evaluate how the historical-critical paradigm currently functions and why biblical scholarship requires a new paradigm. Another way of stating this is that this volume focuses on the most literate end of the oral/literate continuum, but nevertheless does so in a way that emphasizes the connection of this most literate activity of *Vorlage*-based copying with practices on the most oral end of that continuum: everyday conversation. I now want to explicate how this study emphasizing transmission has profound implications on composition too or, even better stated, has significant implications throughout the

---

59. Jeffrey H. Tigay, ed., *Empirical Models for Biblical Criticism* (Philadelphia: University of Pennsylvania Press, 1985). In *Empirical Models Challenging Biblical Criticism* we referred to the following publications influenced by Tigay: Carr, *Formation of the Hebrew Bible*; Müller and Pakkala, *Insights into Editing*; Müller, Pakkala, and Ter Harr Romeny, *Evidence of Editing*; and Pakkala, *God's Omitted Word*. Since the publication of *Empirical Models Challenging Biblical Criticism,* the conversation has continued, both in conference sessions and in print. See esp. Juha Pakkala and Reinhard Müller, *Editorial Techniques in the Hebrew Bible: Toward a Refined Literary Criticism*, RBS 97 (SBL Press, 2022).

60. Lemmelijn, "Text-Critically Studying the Biblical Manuscript Evidence."

composition/transmission process in the interplay of the oral and written within scribal memory.

In previous publications and especially in this work, I have challenged our much too narrow understanding of "word" and how words are selected. I have also challenged our much too narrow understanding of "text," especially arguing against the simplistic equation of original text with the literary text. These two challenges fatally undercut current assumptions behind source and redaction criticism. Without an original text composed by an author our understanding of sources and redactional layers is deeply compromised. Although throughout this work I have generally avoided the use of authors and copyists and preferred the term scribes, here I will revert to their use for purposes of illustration for why the current paradigm is so inadequate. Without an original text, we cannot assume that one author used a source to compose his literary text in a way that future copyists would be uninfluenced by the author's first source. Furthermore, the author's source would not be contained in a single manuscript, but would reside in scribal memory, even if we can conclude that the author had a physical copy of the *Vorlage* of the source before him. Therefore, any future addition to the literary text by a redactor could be informed by the same source in ways that may leave no discernible traces and even what we may identify as a different source would not necessarily be understood as different by the author and redactor in how they accessed that source in its textual plurality in scribal memory. Too often under the current paradigm, synonymous readings are identified as having significant literary and/or theological value in such a way as to distinguish between sources and literary texts; between authors, redactors, and copyists; or between different redactors. However, I have given numerous examples of synonymous readings (admittedly significantly expanding Talmon's definition) that inhibit these typical anachronistic distinctions between authors, redactors, and copyists. The problematic nature of these distinctions requires us to find new vocabulary or greatly reinterpret existing vocabulary to better represent the historical reality of scribes in the ancient world as they perform their texts even in the most literate activity at the transmission end of the composition/transmission continuum: *Vorlage*-based copying. As they copy their *Vorlagen*, scribes use their scribal memory to access the literary text that resides in more than the one physically present *Vorlage* before them.

Bibliography

Aejmelaeus, Anneli. "Hannah's Psalm: Text, Composition, and Redaction." Pages 354–76 in *Houses Full of All Good Things: Essays in Memory of Timo Veijola*. Edited by Juha Pakkala and Martti Nissinen. PFES 95. Helsinki: Finnish Exegetical Society; Göttingen: Vandenhoeck & Ruprecht, 2008.

———. "Hannah's Psalm in 4QSam^a." Pages 23–37 in *Archaeology of the Books of Samuel: The Entangling of the Textual and Literary History*. Edited by Philippe Hugo and Adrian Schenker. VTSup 132. Leiden: Brill, 2010.

Albright, William Foxwell. "The List of Levitic Cities." Pages 49–73 in *Louis Ginzberg: Jubilee Volume on the Occasion of His Seventieth Birthday*. New York: American Academy for Jewish Research, 1945.

Arnold, Patrick M. "Geba." *ABD* 2:921–22.

Askin, Lindsey A. *Scribal Culture in Ben Sira*. JSJSup 184. Leiden: Brill, 2018.

———. "Scribal Production and Literacy at Qumran: Considerations of Page Layout and Style." Pages 23–36 in *Material Aspects of Reading in Ancient and Medieval Cultures: Materiality, Presence, and Performance*. Edited by Jonas Leipziger, Anna Krauß, and Friederike Schücking-Jungblut. Materiale Textkulturen 26. Berlin: de Gruyter, 2020.

Atkinson, J. Maxwell. "Two Devices for Generating Audience Approval: A Comparative Study of Public Discourse and Texts." Pages 199–236 in *Connectedness in Sentence, Discourse and Text*. Edited by K. Ehlich and Henk van Riemsdijk. Tilburg Studies in Language and Literature 4. Tilburg: Tilburg University, 1983.

Auld, A. Graeme. "The 'Levitical Cities': Texts and History." *ZAW* 91 (1979): 194–206.

———. *I and II Samuel: A Commentary*. OTL. Louisville: Westminster John Knox, 2011.

Ausloos, Hans. "The Septuagint's Rendering of Hebrew Toponyms as an Indication of the Translation Technique of the Book of Numbers." Pages 35–50 in *Textual Criticism and Dead Sea Scrolls Studies in Honour of Julio Trebolle Barrera: Florilegium Complutense*. Edited by Andrés Piquer Otero and Pablo A. Torijano Morales. JSJSup 157. Leiden: Brill, 2012.

Baltzer, Klaus. *Deutero-Isaiah: A Commentary on Isaiah 40–55*. Hermeneia. Minneapolis: Fortress, 2001.

Barr, James. "Vocalization and the Analysis of Hebrew." Pages 1–11 in *Hebräische Wortforschung: Festschrift zum 80. Geburtstag von Walter Baumgartner*. Edited by Benedikt Hartmann, Ernst Jenni, E. Y. Kutscher, Victor Maag, Isaac Leo Seeligmann, and Rudolf Smend. VTSup 16. Leiden: Brill, 1967.

Ben Zvi, Ehud. "The List of the Levitical Cities." *JSOT* 17.54 (1992): 77–106.

Bird, Graeme D. *Multitextuality in the Homeric Iliad: The Witness of the Ptolemaic Papyri*. Hellenic Studies 43. Washington, DC: Center for Hellenic Studies, 2010.

Blenkinsopp, Joseph. *Isaiah 40–55: A New Translation with Introduction and Commentary*. AB 19A. New York: Doubleday, 2002.

Blumenthal, David R. "A Play on Words in the Nineteenth Chapter of Job." *VT* 16 (1966): 497–501.

Boadt, Lawrence. "Intentional Alliteration in Second Isaiah." *CBQ* 45 (1983): 353–63.

Bolling, George Melville. *The External Evidence for Interpolation in Homer*. Oxford: Clarendon, 1925.

Bowles, Hugo. "The Poetics of Mrs Gamp's Conversation—Are They Dickens's 'Slips of the Pen'?" Pages 119–39 in *Bridging the Gap between Conversation Analysis and Poetics: Studies in Talk-in-Interaction and Literature Twenty-Five Years after Jefferson*. Edited by Raymond F. Person Jr., Robin Wooffitt, and John P. Rae. Research in Language and Communication. London: Routledge, 2021.

Breed, Brennan W. *Nomadic Text: A Theory of Biblical Reception History*. ISBL. Bloomington: Indiana University Press, 2014.

Brettler, Marc Z. "Alemeth." *ABD* 1:145–46.

Brooke, Alan England, Norman McLean, and Henry St. John Thackeray, eds. *The Later Historical Books: I and II Samuel*. Vol. 2 .1 of *The Old Testament in Greek according to the Text of Codex Vaticanus, Supplement from Other Uncial Manuscripts, with a Critical Apparatus Containing the Variants of the Chief Ancient Authorities for the Text of the Septuagint. Cambridge: Cambridge University Press, 1927.

Brooke, George J. "4QGen^d Reconsidered." Pages 51–70 in *Textual Criticism and Dead Sea Scrolls Studies in Honour of Julio Trebolle Barrera: Florilegium Complutense*. Edited by Andrés Piquer Otero and Pablo A. Torijano Morales. JSJSup 157. Leiden: Brill, 2012.

———. "Deuteronomy 5–6 in the Phylacteries from Qumran Cave 4." Pages 57–70 in *Emanuel: Studies in Hebrew Bible, Septuagint, and the Dead Sea Scrolls in Honor of Emanuel Tov*. Edited by Shalom M. Paul, Robert A. Kraft, Lawrence H. Schiffman, and Weston W. Fields. VTSup 94. Leiden: Brill, 2003.

———. "Hot at Qumran, Cold in Jerusalem: A Reconsideration of Some Late Second Temple Period Attitudes to the Scriptures and Their Interpretation." Pages 64–77 in *Hā-'îsh Mōshe: Studies in Scriptural Interpretation in the Dead Sea Scrolls and Related Literature in Honor of Moshe J. Bernstein*. Edited by Binyamin Y. Goldstein, Michael Segal, and George J. Brooke. STDJ 122. Leiden: Brill, 2018.

———. "The Qumran Scrolls and the Demise of the Distinction between Higher and Lower Criticism." Pages 26–42 in *New Directions in Qumran Studies: Proceedings of the Bristol Colloquium on the Dead Sea Scrolls, 8–10 September 2003*. Edited by Jonathan G. Campbell, William John Lyons, and Lloyd K. Pietersen. LSTS. London: T&T Clark, 2005.

———. *Reading the Dead Sea Scrolls: Essays in Method*. EJL 39. Atlanta: Society of Biblical Literature, 2013.

———. "What Is Editing? What Is an Edition? Towards a Taxonomy for Late Second Temple Jewish Literature." Pages 23–39 in *Insights into Editing in the Hebrew Bible and the Ancient Near East: What Does Documented Evidence Tell Us about the Transmission of Authoritative Texts?* Edited by Reinhard Müller and Juha Pakkala. CBET 84. Leuven: Peeters, 2017.

Brouwer, Catherine E. "Word Searches in NNS-NS Interaction: Opportunities for Language Learning?" *Modern Language Journal* 87 (2003): 534–45.

Brown, Penelope. "Principles of Person Reference in Tzeltal Conversation." Pages 172–202 in *Person Reference in Interaction: Linguistic, Cultural, and Social Perspectives*. Edited by N. J. Enfield and Tanya Stivers. Language Culture and Cognition 7. Cambridge: Cambridge University Press, 2007.

Carr, David M. *The Formation of the Hebrew Bible: A New Reconstruction.* Oxford: Oxford University Press, 2011.

———. "Scribal Processes of Coordination/Harmonization and the Formation of the First Hexateuch(s)." Pages 63–83 in *The Pentateuch: International Perspectives on Current Research.* Edited by Thomas B. Dozeman, Konrad Schmid, and Baruch J. Swartz. FAT 78. Tübingen: Mohr Siebeck, 2011.

———. "Torah on the Heart: Literary Jewish Textuality within Its Ancient Near Eastern Context." *Oral Tradition* 25 (2010):17–39.

———. *Writing on the Tablet of the Heart: Origins of Scripture and Literature.* Oxford: Oxford University Press, 2005.

Carroll, Robert P. *Jeremiah: A Commentary.* OTL. Philadelphia: Westminster, 1986.

Casanowicz, Immanuel M. "Paronomasia in the Old Testament." *JBL* 12 (1893): 105–67.

Cassuto, Umberto. *A Commentary on the Book of Exodus.* Jerusalem: Magnes, 1967.

———. *From Adam to Noah, Genesis I–VI:8.* Part 1 of *A Commentary on the Book of Genesis.* Jerusalem: Magnes, 1961.

Ceresko, Anthony R. "The Function of *Antanaclasis* (*mṣʾ* 'to find'//*mṣʾ* 'to reach, overtake, grasp') in Hebrew Poetry, Especially in the Book of Qoheleth." *CBQ* 44 (1982): 551–69.

Cerquiglini, Bernard. *In Praise of the Variant: A Critical History of Philology.* Translated by Betsy Wing. Parallax. Baltimore: Johns Hopkins University Press, 1999.

Cogan, Mordechai. *1 Kings: A New Translation with Introduction and Commentary.* AB. New York: Doubleday, 2001.

Collins, John J. *Daniel: A Commentary on the Book of Daniel.* Hermeneia. Minneapolis: Fortress, 1993.

Cook, Johann. "The Relationship between Textual Criticism, Literary Criticism and Exegesis—An Interactive One?" *Textus* 24 (2009): 119–32.

Crawford, Sidnie White. "Interpreting the Pentateuch through Scribal Processes: The Evidence from the Qumran Manuscripts." Pages 59–80 in *Insights into Editing in the Hebrew Bible and the Ancient Near East: What Does Documented Evidence Tell Us about the Transmission of Authoritative Texts?* Edited by Reinhard Müller and Juha Pakkala. CBET 84. Leuven: Peeters, 2017.

———. *Rewriting Scripture in Second Temple Times.* SDSS. Grand Rapids: Eerdmans, 2008.

---. *The Text of the Pentateuch: Textual Criticism and the Dead Sea Scrolls*. Berlin: de Gruyter, 2022.

Crawford, Sidnie White, Jan Joosten, and Eugene Ulrich. "Sample Editions of the Oxford Hebrew Bible: Deuteronomy 32:1–9, 1 Kings 11:1–8, and Jeremiah 27:1–10." *VT* 58 (2008): 352–66.

Cross, Frank Moore. "The Ammonite Oppression of the Tribes of Gad and Reuben: Missing Verses from 1 Samuel 11 Found in 4QSam[a]." Pages 105–19 in *The Hebrew and Greek Texts of Samuel, 1980 Proceedings IOSCS, Vienna*. Edited by Emanuel Tov. Jerusalem: Academon, 1980.

---. "Telltale Remnants of Oral Epic in the Older Sources of the Tetrateuch: Double and Triple Proper Names in Early Hebrew Sources, and in Homeric and Ugaritic Epic Poetry." Pages 83–88 in *Exploring the Longue Durée: Essays in Honor of Lawrence E. Stager*. Edited by J. David Schloen. Winona Lake, IN: Eisenbrauns, 2009.

Cross, Frank Moore, Donald W. Parry, Richard J. Saley, and Eugene Ulrich, eds. *Qumran Cave 4.XII. 1–2 Samuel*. DJD XVII. Oxford: Clarendon, 2005.

Czachesz, István, and Risto Uro, eds. *Mind, Morality and Magic: Cognitive Science Approaches in Biblical Studies*. Bible World. Durham: Acumen, 2013.

Davidson, Robert. *Genesis 12–50*. CBC. Cambridge: Cambridge University Press, 1979.

Dayfani, Hila. "The Relationship between Paleography and Textual Criticism: Textual Variants Due to Graphic Similarity between the Masoretic Text and the Samaritan Pentateuch." *Textus* 27 (2018): 3–21.

Debel, Hans. "Anchoring Revelations in the Authority of Sinai: A Comparison of the Rewritings of 'Scripture' in *Jubilees* and in the P Stratum of Exodus." *JSJ* 45 (2014): 471–92.

---. "Rewritten Bible, Variant Literary Editions and Original Text(s): Exploring the Implications of a Pluriform Outlook on the Scriptural Tradition." Pages 65–91 in *Changes in Scripture: Rewriting and Interpreting Authoritative Traditions in the Second Temple Period*. Edited by Hanne von Weissenberg, Juha Pakkala, and Marko Marttila. BZAW 419. Berlin: de Gruyter, 2011.

DeConick, April D. *The Original Gospel of Thomas in Translation with a Commentary and New English Translation of the Complete Gospel*. LNTS. London: T&T Clark, 2006.

Delnero, Paul. "Memorization and the Transmission of Sumerian Literary Compositions." *JNES* 71 (2012): 189–208.

Doane, Alger N. "'Beowulf' and Scribal Performance." Pages 62–75 in *Unlocking the Wordhord: Anglo-Saxon Studies in Memory of Edward B. Irving*. Edited by Mark Amodio and Kathleen O'Brien O'Keeffe. Toronto: University of Toronto Press, 2003.

———. "The Ethnography of Scribal Writing and Anglo-Saxon Poetry: Scribe as Performer." *Oral Tradition* 9 (1994): 420–39.

———. "Oral Texts, Intertexts, and Intratexts: Editing Old English." Pages 75–113 in *Influence and Intertextuality in Literary History*. Edited by Jay Clayton and Eric Rubinstein. Madison: University of Wisconsin Press, 1991.

———. "Spacing, Placing and Effacing: Scribal Textuality and Exeter Riddle 30 a/b." Page 45–64 in *New Approaches to Editing Old English Verse*. Edited by Sarah Larratt Keefer and Katherine O'Brien O'Keeffe. Rochester, NY: Brewer, 1998.

Dotan, Aron. "Homonymous Hapax Doublets in the Masora." *Textus* 14 (1988): 131–45.

Driver, S. R. *The Book of Genesis: With Introduction and Notes*. 3rd. ed. New York: Gorham, 1904.

Dunkle, Roger. "Swift-Footed Achilles." *CW* 90 (1997): 227–34.

Ehrensvärd, Martin, Robert Rezetko, and Ian Young. "Counting and Weighing: On the Role of Intuition in Philology and Linguistics." *JSem* 29 (2020): 1–10. https://doi.org/10.25159/2663-6573/8180.

Eidevall, Göran. *Amos: A New Translation with Introduction and Commentary*. AB. New Haven: Yale University Press, 2017.

Epp, Eldon Jay. "The Multivalence of the Term 'Original Text' in New Testament Textual Criticism." Pages 551–93 in *Perspective on New Testament Criticism: Collected Essays, 1962–2004*. NovTSup 116. Leiden: Brill, 2005.

Eshel, Esther. "4QDeut[n]—A Text That Has Undergone Harmonistic Editing." *HUCA* 62 (1991): 117–54.

Exum, J. Cheryl. *Song of Songs: A Commentary*. OTL. Louisville: Westminster John Knox, 2005.

Fitzgerald, Aloysius. "The Interchange of L, N, and R in Biblical Hebrew." *JBL* 97 (1978): 481–88.

Foley, John Miles. "Comparative Oral Traditions." Pages 65–81 in *Voicing the Moment: Improvised Oral Poetry and Basque Tradition*. Edited by Samuel G. Armistead and Joseba Zulaika. Reno: University of Nevada at Reno, 2005.

———. "Editing Oral Epic Texts: Theory and Practice." *Text: Transactions of the Society of Textual Scholarship* 1 (1981): 75–94.

———. *How to Read an Oral Poem*. Urbana: University of Illinois Press, 2002.

———. *Homer's Traditional Art*. University Park: Pennsylvania State University Press, 1999.

———. *Immanent Art: From Structure to Meaning in Traditional Oral Epic*. Bloomington: Indiana University Press, 1991.

———. *Traditional Oral Epic: The Odyssey, Beowulf, and the Serbo-Croatian Return Song*. Berkeley: University of California Press, 1990.

Foley, John Miles, and Ramey, Peter. "Oral Theory and Medieval Studies." Pages 71–102 in *Medieval Oral Literature*. Edited by Karl Reichl. Berlin: de Gruyter, 2012.

Fontaine. Carole R. *Smooth Words: Women, Proverbs and Performance in Biblical Wisdom*. JSOTSup 356. London: T&T Clark, 2002.

Fox, Michael V. *Proverbs: An Eclectic Edition with Introduction and Textual Commentary*. HBCE. Atlanta: SBL Press, 2015.

———. *Proverbs 10–31: A New Translation with Introduction and Commentary*. AB. New Haven: Yale University Press, 2009.

———. "Text Criticism and Literary Criticism." Pages 341–56 in *Built by Wisdom, Established by Understanding: Essays on Biblical and Near Eastern Literature in Honor of Adele Berlin*. Edited by Maxine Grossman. Bethesda: University Press of Maryland, 2013.

Franke, Chris. *Isaiah 46, 47, and 48: A New Literary-Critical Reading*. BJSUCSD 3. Winona Lake, IN: Eisenbrauns, 1994.

Freedman, David Noel, and Shawna Dolansky Overton. "Omitting the Omissions: The Case for Haplography in the Transmission of the Biblical Text." Pages 99–116 in *"Imagining" Biblical Worlds: Studies in Spatial, Social and Historical Constructs in Honor of James W. Flanagan*. Edited by David M. Gunn and Paula M. McNutt. JOTSup 359. Sheffield: Sheffield Academic, 2002.

Frog. "Repetition, Parallelism, and Non-Repetition: From Ordinary Talk to Ritual Poetry and Back Again." Pages 180–217 in *Bridging the Gap between Conversation Analysis and Poetics: Studies in Talk-in-Interaction and Literature Twenty-Five Years after Jefferson*. Edited by Raymond F. Person Jr., Robin Wooffitt, and John P. Rae. Research in Language and Communication. London: Routledge, 2022.

Frog and William Lamb, eds. *Weathered Words: Formulaic Language and Verbal Art*. Publications of the Milman Parry Collection of Oral Literature 6. Washington, DC: Center for Hellenic Studies, 2022.

Frost, Ram, and Shlomo Bentin. "Processing Phonological and Semantic Ambiguity: Evidence from Semantic Priming at Different SOAs." *Journal of Experimental Psychology: Learning, Memory, and Cognition* 18 (1992): 58–68.

Frost, Ram, and Michal Kampf. "Phonetic Recoding of Phonologically Ambiguous Printed Words." *Journal of Experimental Psychology: Learning, Memory, and Cognition* 19 (1993): 23–33.

Garsiel, Moshe. *Biblical Names: A Literary Study of Midrashic Derivations and Puns*. Ramat Gan: Bar-Ilan University Press, 1991.

Gelston, Anthony. "Some Hebrew Misreadings in the Septuagint of Amos." *VT* 52 (2002): 493–500.

———. *The Twelve Minor Prophets*. BHQ 13. Stuttgart: Deutsche Bibelgesellschaft, 2010.

Glanz, Oliver. *Understanding Participant-Reference Shifts in the Book of Jeremiah: A Study of Exegetical Method and Its Consequences for the Interpretation of Referential Incoherence*. SSN 60. Leiden: Brill, 2013.

Glenny, W. Edward. *Finding Meaning in the Text: Translation Technique and Theology in the Septuagint of Amos*. VTSup 126. Leiden: Brill, 2009.

———. "Hebrew Misreadings or Free Translation in the Septuagint of Amos?" *VT* 57 (2007): 524–47.

Glock, A. E. "Taanach." *ABD* 6:287–90.

Goodwin, Charles. "Audience Diversity, Participation, and Interpretation." *Text* 6 (1986): 283–316.

———. *Conversational Organization: Interaction between Speakers and Hearers*. Language, Thought and Culture. New York: Academic Press, 1981.

Gorfein, David S., Stephanie Berger, and Andrea Bubka. "The Selection of Homograph Meaning: Word Association When Context Changes." *Memory & Cognition* 28 (2000): 766–73.

Goshen-Gottstein, Moshe H. "Biblical Philology and the Concordance." *JJS* 8 (1957): 5–12.

Gottlob, Lawrence R., Stephen D. Goldinger, Gregory O. Stone, and Guy V. Van Orden. "Reading Homographs: Orthographic, Phonologic, and Semantic Dynamics." *Journal of Experimental Psychology: Human Perception and Performance* 25 (1999): 561–74.

Graybill, Rhiannon. "'Hear and Give Ear!': The Soundscape of Jeremiah." *JSOT* 40 (2016): 467–90.

Greenberg, Seth N., and Jean Saint-Aubin. "Letter Detection for Homographs with Different Meanings in Different Language Texts." *Bilingualism: Language and Cognition* 7 (2004): 241–53.

Greenspoon, Leonard J. "Iesous." Pages 174–94 in *A New English Translation of the Septuagint and Other Greek Translations Traditionally Included under That Title*. Edited by Albert Pietersma and Benjamin G. Wright. Oxford: Oxford University Press, 2014. http://ccat.sas.upenn.edu/nets/edition/.

Greer, Tim. "Word Search Sequences in Bilingual Interaction: Codeswitching and Embodied Orientation toward Shifting Participant Constellations." *Journal of Pragmatics* 57 (2013): 100–117.

Grossman, Maxine L. "Community Rule or Community Rules: Examining a Supplementary Approach in Light of the Sectarian Dead Sea Scrolls." Pages 303–30 in *Empirical Models Challenging Biblical Criticism*. Edited by Raymond F. Person Jr. and Robert Rezetko. AIL 25. Atlanta: SBL Press, 2016.

Hamilton, Jeffries M. "Ashan." *ABD* 1:476–77.

Hanks, William F. "Person Reference in Yucatec Maya Conversation." Pages 149–71 in *Person Reference in Interaction: Linguistic, Cultural, and Social Perspectives*. Edited by N. J. Enfield and Tanya Stivers. Language, Culture, and Cognition 7. Cambridge: Cambridge University Press, 2007.

Hayashi, Makoto. "Language and the Body as Resources for Collaborative Action: A Study of Word Searches in Japanese Conversation." *Research on Language and Social Interaction* 36 (2003): 109–41.

Heath, Christian, and Paul Luff. "Embodied Actions and Organizational Activity." Pages 281–307 in *The Handbook of Conversation Analysis*. Edited by Jack Sidnell and Tanya Stivers. BHL. Oxford: Wiley-Blackwell, 2013.

Helasvuo, Marja-Liisa, Minna Laakso, and Marja-Leena Sorjonen. "Searching for Words: Syntactic and Sequential Construction of Word Search in Conversations of Finnish Speakers with Aphasia." *Research on Language and Social Interaction* 37 (2004): 1–37.

Hempel, Charlotte. "Pluralism and Authoritativeness: The Case of the S Tradition." Pages 193–208 in *Authoritative Scriptures in Ancient Judaism*. Edited by Mladen Popović. JSJSup 141. Leiden: Brill, 2010.

———. "The Social Matrix That Shaped the Hebrew Bible and Gave Us the Dead Sea Scrolls." Pages 221–37 in *Studies on the Text and Versions of the Hebrew Bible in Honour of Robert Gordon*. Edited by Geoffrey Khan and Diana Lipton. VTSup 149. Leiden: Brill, 2012.

Hendel, Ronald. "The Oxford Hebrew Bible: Prologue to a New Critical Edition." *VT* 58 (2008): 324–51.

———. *Steps to a New Edition of the Hebrew Bible*. TCS 10. Atlanta: SBL Press, 2016.

———. "What Is a Biblical Book?" Pages 282–302 in *From Author to Copyist: Essays on the Composition, Redaction, and Transmission of the Hebrew Bible in Honor of Zipi Talshir*. Edited by Cana Werman. Winona Lake, IN: Eisenbrauns, 2015.

Hengel, Martin. 2010. "The Four Gospels and the One Gospel of Jesus Christ." Pages 12–26 in *The Earliest Gospels: The Origins and Transmission of the Earliest Christian Gospels—The Contribution of the Chester Beatty Gospel Codex P45*. Edited by Charles Horton. JSNTSup 258. London: T&T Clark, 2010.

Heritage, John. "A Change-of-State Token and Aspects of Its Sequential Placement." Pages 299–345 in *Structures of Social Action: Studies in Conversation Analysis*. Edited by J. Maxwell Atkinson and John Heritage. Studies in Emotion and Social Interaction. Cambridge: Cambridge University Press, 1984.

———. "Epistemics in Action: Action Formation and Territories of Knowledge." *Research on Language and Social Interaction* 45 (2012): 1–29.

———. "The Epistemic Engine: Sequence Organization and Territories of Knowledge." *Research on Language and Social Interaction* 45 (2012): 30–52.

———. "*Oh*-Prefaced Responses to Inquiry." *Language in Society* 27 (1998): 291–334.

———. "*Oh*-Prefaced Responses to Assessments: A Method of Modifying Agreement/Disagreement." Pages 196–224 in *The Language of Turn and Sequence*. Edited by Cecilia E. Ford, Barbara A. Fox, and Sandra A. Thompson. Oxford Studies in Sociolinguistics. Oxford: Oxford University Press, 2002.

Holladay, William L. "Form and Word-Play in David's Lament over Saul and Jonathan." *VT* 20 (1970): 153–89.

———. *Jeremiah 2: A Commentary on the Book of the Prophet Jeremiah Chapters 26–52*. Hermeneia. Minneapolis: Fortress, 1989.

Holmes, Janet. "Functions of *You Know* in Women's and Men's Speech." *Language in Society* 15 (1986): 1–21.
Honko, Lauri. *Textualizing the Siri Epic*. Helsinki: Suomalainen Tiedeakatemia, Academia Scientiarum Fennica, 1998.
Hornkohl, Aaron D. "Diachronic Exceptions in the Comparison of Tiberian and Qumran Hebrew: The Preservation of Early Linguistic Features in Dead Sea Scrolls Biblical Hebrew." Pages 61–92 in *The Reconfiguration of Hebrew in the Hellenistic Period*. Edited Jan Joosten, Daniel Machiela, and Jean-Sébastien Rey. STDJ 124. Leiden: Brill, 2018.
Horsley, Richard A. "Oral and Written Aspects of the Emergence of the Gospel of Mark as Scripture." *Oral Tradition* 25 (2010): 93–114.
Hunt, Melvin. "Aner (Place)." *ABD* 1:248.
———. "Ibleam." *ABD* 3:355.
Hutchby, Ian. "Poetics and Performativity in the Management of Delicacy and Affiliation." Pages 31–51 in *Bridging the Gap between Conversation Analysis and Poetics: Studies in Talk-in-Interaction and Literature Twenty-Five Years after Jefferson*. Edited by Raymond F. Person Jr., Robin Wooffitt, and John P. Rae. Research in Language and Communication. London: Routledge, 2022.
Hutchby, Ian, and Robin Wooffitt. *Conversation Analysis: Principles, Practices and Applications*. Cambridge: Polity, 1998.
Jefferson, Gail. "List-Construction as a Task and Resource." Pages 63–92 in *Interaction Competence*. Edited by George Psathas. Studies in Ethnomethodology and Conversation Analysis. Washington, DC: University Press of America, 1990.
———. "On the Poetics of Ordinary Talk." *Text and Performance Quarterly* 16 (1996): 1–61.
Jurić, Dorian. "Back in the Foundation: Chauvinistic Scholarship and the Building Sacrifice Story-Pattern." *Oral Tradition* 34 (2020): 3–44.
Kabergs, Valérie, and Hans Ausloos. "Paronomasia or Wordplay? A Babel-Like Confusion: Towards a Definition of Hebrew Wordplay." *Bib* 93 (2012): 1–20.
Kallai, Zecharia. "Simeon's Town List: Scribal Rules and Geographical Patterns." *VT* 53 (2003): 81–96.
Kawamoto, Alan H., and John H. Zemblidge. "Pronunciation of Homographs." *Journal of Memory and Language* 31 (1992): 349–74.
Kelber, Werner H. "The 'Gutenberg Galaxy' and the Historical Study of the New Testament." *Oral History Journal of South Africa* 5 (2017): 1–16.

———. *Imprints, Voiceprints, and Footprints of Memory: Collected Essays of Werner Kelber*. RBS 74. Atlanta: Society of Biblical Literature, 2013.

———. "The Work of Marcel Jousse in Context." Pages 1–53 in *The Forgotten Compass: Marcel Jousse and the Exploration of the Oral World*. Edited by Werner H. Kelber and Bruce D. Chilton. Eugene, OR: Cascade, 2022.

Kirk, Alan. "Manuscript Tradition as a Tertium Quid: Orality and Memory in Scribal Practices." Pages 215–34 in *Jesus, the Voice, and the Text: Beyond the Oral and the Written Gospel*. Edited by Tom Thatcher. Waco, TX: Baylor University Press, 2008.

———. *Memory and the Jesus Tradition*. London: T&T Clark, 2018.

———. *Q in Matthew: Ancient Media, Memory, and Early Scribal Transmission of the Jesus Tradition*. LNTS. London: T&T Clark, 2016.

Kitzinger, Celia, Rebecca Shaw, and Merran Toerien. "Referring to Persons without Using a Full-Form Reference: Locally Initial Indexicals in Action." *Research on Language and Social Interaction* 45 (2012): 116–36.

Kline, Jonathan G. *Allusive Soundplay in the Hebrew Bible*. AIL 28. Atlanta: SBL Press, 2016.

Knoppers, Gary N. "Projected Age Comparisons of the Levitical Townlists: Divergent Theories and Their Significance." *Textus* 22 (2005): 21–63.

Krašovec, Jože. *Transformation of Biblical Proper Names*. LHBOTS 418. London: T&T Clark, 2010.

Kratz, Reinhard G. "Nahash, King of the Ammonites, in the Deuteronomistic History." Pages 163–88 in *Insights into Editing in the Hebrew Bible and the Ancient Near East: What Does Documented Evidence Tell Us about the Transmission of Authoritative Texts?* Edited by Reinhard Müller and Juha Pakkala. CBET 84. Leuven: Peeters, 2017.

———. "Textual Supplementation in Poetry: The Song of Hannah as a Test Case." Pages 21–50 in *Supplementation and the Study of the Hebrew Bible*. Edited by Saul M. Olyan and Jacob L. Wright. BJS 361. Providence, RI: Brown University, 2018.

Kwon, JiSeong James. *Scribal Culture and Intertextuality: Literary and Historical Relationships between Job and Deutero-Isaiah*. FAT 2/85. Tübingen: Mohr Siebeck, 2016.

Laakso, Minna. "Collaborative Participation in Aphasic Word Searching: Comparison between Significant Others and Speech and Language Therapists." *Aphasiology* 29 (2015): 269–90.

Lange, Armin, and Matthias Weigold. "The Text of the Shema Yisrael in Qumran Literature and Elsewhere." Pages 147–77 in *Textual Criticism and Dead Sea Scrolls Studies in Honour of Julio Trebolle Barrera: Florilegium Complutense*. Edited by Andrés Piquer Otero and Pablo A. Torijano Morales. JSJSup 157. Leiden: Brill, 2012.

Lee, Margaret E., ed. *Sound Matters: New Testament Studies in Sound Mapping*. Biblical Performance Criticism 16. Eugene, OR: Cascade, 2018.

Lemmelijn, Bénédicte. "Text-Critically Studying the Biblical Manuscript Evidence: An 'Empirical' Entry to the Literary Composition of the Text." Pages 129–64 in *Empirical Models Challenging Biblical Criticism*. Edited by Raymond F. Person Jr. and Robert Rezetko. AIL 25. Atlanta: SBL Press, 2016.

Lenzi, Alan. "Scribal Revision and Textual Variation in Akkadian *Šuila*-Prayers: Two Case Studies in Ritual Adaptation." Pages 63–108 in *Empirical Models Challenging Biblical Criticism*. Edited by Raymond F. Person Jr. and Robert Rezetko. AIL 25. Atlanta: SBL Press, 2016.

Lerner, Gene H. "Responsive List Construction: A Conversational Resource for Accomplishing Multifaceted Social Action." *Journal of Language and Social Psychology* 13 (1994): 20–33.

Lerner, Gene H., and Celia Kitzinger. "Introduction: Person-Reference in Conversation Analytic Research." *Discourse Studies* 9 (2007): 427–32.

Levin, Yigal. "From Lists to History: Chronological Aspects of the Chronicler's Genealogies." *JBL* 123 (2004): 601–36.

Lionarons, Joyce Tally, ed. *Old English Literature in Its Manuscript Context*. Morgantown: West Virginia University Press, 2004.

Lord, Albert B. *The Singer of Tales*. Harvard Studies in Comparative Literature 24. Cambridge: Harvard University Press, 1960.

Lundbom, Jack R. *Jeremiah 21–36: A New Translation with Introduction and Commentary*. AB 21B. New York: Doubleday, 2004.

McCarter, P. Kyle, Jr. *I Samuel: A New Translation with Introduction, Notes, and Commentary*. AB 8. Garden City, NY: Doubleday, 1980.

McCreesh, Thomas P. *Biblical Sound and Sense: Poetic Patterns in Proverbs 10–29*. JSOTSup 128. Sheffield: JSOT Press, 1991.

McKane, William. *A Critical and Exegetical Commentary on Jeremiah 1: Introduction and Commentary of Jeremiah I–XXV*. ICC. Edinburgh: T&T Clark, 1986.

McLay, R. Timothy, trans. and ed. "Daniel." Pages 991–1022 in *A New English Translation of the Septuagint and Other Greek Translations Traditionally Included under That Title*. Edited by Albert Pietersma and

Benjamin G. Wright. Oxford: Oxford University Press, 2014. http://ccat.sas.upenn.edu/nets/edition/.

Makri-Tsilipakou, Marianthi. "The Category (Greek) 'Woman,' 'Lady,' or 'Girl,' or 'Lass,' or...." *Gender and Language* 9 (2015): 33–58.

Martin, Gary D. *Multiple Originals: New Approaches to Hebrew Bible Textual Criticism*. TCS 7. Atlanta: Society of Biblical Literature, 2010.

Martone, Corrado. "Textual Plurality and Textual Reconstructions: A Cautionary Tale." *RevQ* 30 (2018): 131–41.

Meer, Michaël N. van der. "Exclusion and Expansion: Harmonisations in the Samaritan Pentateuch, Pre-Samaritan Pentateuchal Manuscripts and Non-Pentateuchal Manuscripts." Pages 41–76 in *The Samaritan Pentateuch and the Dead Sea Scrolls*. Edited by Michael Langlois. CBET 94. Leuven: Peeters, 2019.

Meredith, Joanne, and Elisabeth Stokoe. "Repair: Comparing Facebook 'Chat' with Spoken Interaction." *Discourse & Communication* 8 (2014): 181–207.

Metso, Sarianna. 2019. *The Community Rule: A Critical Edition with Translation*. EJL 51. Atlanta: SBL Press, 2019.

———. *The Textual Development of the Qumran Community Rule*. STDJ 21. Leiden: Brill, 1997.

Metzger, Bruce M. "St. Jerome's Explicit References to Variant Readings in Manuscripts of the New Testament." Pages 179–90 in *Text and Interpretation: Studies in the New Testament Presented to Matthew Black*. Edited by Ernest Best and R. McLachan Wilson. Cambridge: Cambridge University Press, 1979.

Milik, J. T. "Tefillin, Mezuzot et Targums (4Q128–4Q157)." Pages 31–93 in *Qumran Grotte 4.II*. Edited by Roland de Vaux and J. T. Milik. DJD VI. Oxford: Clarendon, 1977.

Miller, Marvin. *Performances of Ancient Jewish Letters: From Elephantine to MMT*. JAJSup 20. Göttingen: Vandenhoeck & Ruprecht, 2015.

Miller, Shem. *Dead Sea Media: Orality, Textuality, and Memory in the Scrolls from the Judean Desert*. STDJ 129. Leiden: Brill, 2019.

———. "The Oral-Written Textuality of Stichographic Poetry in the Dead Sea Scrolls." *DSD* 22 (2015): 162–88.

Milstein, Sara. *Tracking the Master Scribe: Revision through Introduction in Biblical and Mesopotamian Literature*. Oxford: Oxford University Press, 2016.

Moshavi, Adina. "Conversation Analysis." In *Linguistics for Hebraists and Biblical Scholars*. Edited by John A. Cook and Robert D. Holmstedt. University Park, PA: Eisenbrauns, forthcoming.

Mroczek, Eva. *The Literary Imagination in Jewish Antiquity*. Oxford: Oxford University Press, 2016.

Mulkay, Michael. "Agreement and Disagreement in Conversations and Letters." *Text* 5 (1985): 201–28.

———. "Conversations and Texts." *Human Studies* 9 (1986): 303–21.

Müller, Reinhard, and Juha Pakkala, eds. *Insights into Editing in the Hebrew Bible and the Ancient Near East: What Does Documented Evidence Tell Us about the Transmission of Authoritative Texts?* CBET 84. Leuven: Peeters, 2017.

Müller, Reinhard, Juha Pakkala, and Bas Ter Haar Romeny. *Evidence of Editing: Growth and Change of Texts in the Hebrew Bible*. RBS 75. Atlanta: Society of Biblical Literature, 2014.

Murphy, Roland E. *The Song of Songs: A Commentary on the Book of Canticles or The Song of Songs*. Hermeneia. Minneapolis: Fortress, 1990.

Mylonas, Natalie, Stephen Llewelyn, and Gareth Wearne. "Speaking to One's Heart: דבר and Its Semantic Extension." *JHebS* 16 (2016). https://doi.org/10.5508/jhs.2016.v16.a7.

Newsom, Carol A., with Brennan W. Breed. *Daniel: A Commentary*. OTL. Louisville: Westminster John Knox, 2014.

Niditch, Susan. *Oral World and Written Word: Ancient Israelite Literature*. LAI. Louisville: Westminster John Knox, 1996.

Noegel, Scott B. *Janus Parallelism in the Book of Job*. JSOTSup 223. Sheffield: Sheffield Academic, 1996.

———, ed. *Puns and Pundits: Word Play in the Hebrew Bible and Ancient Near Eastern Literature*. Bethesda, MD: CDL, 2000.

———. "'Word Play' in Qoheleth." *JHebS* 7 (2007). https://doi.org/10.5508/jhs.2007.v7.a4.

Noegel, Scott B., and Gary A. Rendsburg. *Solomon's Vineyard: Literary and Linguistic Studies in the Song of Songs*. AIL 1. Atlanta: Society of Biblical Literature, 2009.

Nõmmik, Urmas. "The Idea of Ancient Hebrew Verse." *ZAW* 124 (2012): 400–408.

O'Connell, Kevin G. "The List of Seven Peoples in Canaan: A Fresh Analysis." Pages 221–41 in *The Answers Lie Below: Essays in Honor of Lawrence Edmund Toombs*. Edited by Henry O. Thompson. Lanham, MD: University Press of America, 1984.

O'Keeffe, Katherine O'Brien. *Visible Song: Transitional Literacy in Old English Verse*. Cambridge Studies in Anglo-Saxon England. Cambridge: Cambridge University Press, 1990.

Oelschlaeger, Mary L., and Jack S. Damico. "Word Searches in Aphasia: A Study of Collaborative Responses of Communicative Partners." Pages 211–30 in *Conversation and Brain Damage*. Edited by Charles Goodwin. Oxford: Oxford University Press, 2003.

Pakkala, Juha. *God's Omitted Word: Omissions in the Transmission of the Hebrew Bible*. Göttingen: Vandenhoeck & Ruprecht, 2013.

Pakkala, Juha, and Reinhard Müller. *Editorial Techniques in the Hebrew Bible: Toward a Refined Literary Criticism*. RBS 97. Atlanta: SBL Press, 2022.

Pardee, Cambry G. *Scribal Harmonization in the Synoptic Gospels*. NTTSD 60. Leiden: Brill, 2019.

Parry, Donald W. "'How Many Vessels'? An Examination of MT 1 Sam 2:14/4QSam[a] 1 Sam 2:16." Pages 84–95 in *Studies in the Hebrew Bible, Qumran, and the Septuagint Presented to Eugene Ulrich*. Edited by Peter W. Flint, Emanuel Tov, and James C. VanderKam. VTSup 101. Leiden: Brill, 2006.

Paul, Shalom M. *Amos: A Commentary on the Book of Amos*. Hermeneia. Minneapolis: Fortress, 1991.

———. "Polysemous Pivotal Punctuation: More Janus Double Entendres." Pages 369–74 in *Texts, Temples, and Traditions: A Tribute to Menahem Haran*. Edited by Michael V. Fox, Victor Avigdor Hurowitz, Avi Hurvitz, Michael L. Klein, Baruch H. Schwartz, and Nili Shupak. Winona Lake, IN: Eisenbrauns, 1996.

———. "Polysensuous Polyvalency in Poetic Parallelism." Pages 147–63 in *Sha'arei Talmon: Studies in the Bible, Qumran, and the Ancient Near East Presented to Shemaryahu Talmon*. Edited by Michael Fishbane, Emanuel Tov, and Weston W. Fields. Winona Lake, IN: Eisenbrauns, 1992.

Perdue, Leo G., ed. *Scribes, Sages, and Seers: The Sage in the Eastern Mediterranean World*. FRLANT 219. Göttingen: Vandenhoeck & Ruprecht, 2008.

Perrin, Nicolas. "Hermeneutical Factors in the Harmonization of the Gospels and the Question of Textual Authority." Pages 599–605 in *The Biblical Canons*. Edited by Jean-Marie Auwers and H. J. de Jonge. BETL 163. Leuven: Peeters, 2003.

Person, Raymond F., Jr. "The Ancient Israelite Scribe as Performer." *JBL* 117 (1998): 601–9.

———. "Biblical Historiography as Traditional History." Pages 73–83 in *Oxford Handbook of Biblical Narrative*. Edited by Danna Nolan Fewell. Oxford: Oxford University Press, 2016.

———. "Character in Narrative Depictions of Composing Oral Epics and Reading Historiographies." Pages 277–94 in *Voice and Voices in Antiquity*. Vol. 11 of *Orality and Literacy in the Ancient World*. Edited by Niall W. Slater. MnSup 396. Leiden: Brill, 2016.

———. *The Deuteronomic History and the Book of Chronicles: Scribal Works in an Oral World*. AIL 6. Atlanta: Society of Biblical Literature, 2010.

———. *Deuteronomy and Environmental Amnesia*. Earth Bible Commentary 3. Sheffield: Sheffield Phoenix, 2014.

———. "Education and the Transmission of Tradition." Pages 366–78 in *Wiley-Blackwell Companion to Ancient Israel*. Edited Susan Niditch. Oxford: Blackwell, 2016.

———. "Formulas and Scribal Memory: A Case Study of Text-Critical Variants as Examples of Category-Triggering." Pages 147–72 in *Weathered Words: Formulaic Language and Verbal Art*. Edited by Frog and William Lamb. Publications of the Milman Parry Collection of Oral Literature 6. Washington, DC: Center for Hellenic Studies, 2022.

———. *From Conversation to Oral Tradition: A Simplest Systematics for Oral Traditions*. Routledge Studies in Rhetoric and Stylistics. London: Routledge, 2016.

———. "Harmonization in the Pentateuch and Synoptic Gospels: Repetition and Category-Triggering within Scribal Memory." Pages 318–57 in *Repetition, Communication, and Meaning in the Ancient World*. Edited by Deborah Beck. MnSup 442. Leiden: Brill, 2021.

———. *In Conversation with Jonah: Conversation Analysis, Literary Criticism, and the Book of Jonah*. JSOTSup 220. Sheffield: Sheffield Academic, 1996.

———. "Multimodality and Metonymy: Deuteronomy as a Test Case." In *Orality and Narrative: Performance and Mythic-Ritual Poetics*. Vol. 12 of *Orality and Literacy in the Ancient World*. Edited by Anton Bierl, David Bouvier, and Ombretta Cesca. MnSup. Leiden: Brill, forthcoming.

———. "'Oh' in Shakespeare: A Conversation Analytic Approach." *Journal of Historical Pragmatics* 10 (2009): 84–107.

———. "Poetics and List Formation: A Study of Text-Critical Variants in Lists Found in the New Testament, Homer, and the Hebrew Bible." Pages 218–46 in *Bridging the Gap between Conversation Analysis and Poetics: Studies in Talk-in-Interaction and Literature Twenty-Five Years after Jefferson*. Edited by Raymond F. Person Jr., Robin Wooffitt, and John P. Rae. Research in Language and Communication. London: Routledge, 2022.

———. "The Problem of 'Literary Unity' from the Perspective of the Study of Oral Traditions." Pages 217–37 in *Empirical Models Challenging Biblical Criticism*. Edited by Raymond F. Person Jr. and Robert Rezetko. AIL 25. Atlanta: SBL Press, 2016.

———. "A Reassessment of *Wiederaufnahme* from the Perspective of Conversation Analysis." *BZ* 43 (1999): 239–48.

———. "The Role of Memory in the Tradition Represented by the Deuteronomic History and the Book of Chronicles." *Oral Tradition* 26 (2011): 537–50.

———. "Self-Referential Phrases in Deuteronomy: A Reassessment Based on Recent Studies concerning Scribal Performance and Memory." Pages 217–42 in *Collective Memory and Collective Identity*. Edited by Johannes Unsok Ro and Diana Edelman. BZAW 534. Berlin: de Gruyter, 2021.

———. *Structure and Meaning in Conversation and Literature*. Lanham, MD: University Press of America, 1999.

———. "Text Criticism as a Lens for Understanding the Transmission of Ancient Texts in Their Oral Environments." Pages 197–215 in *Contextualizing Israel's Sacred Writings: Ancient Literary, Orality, and Literary Production*. Edited by Brian Schmidt. AIL 22. Atlanta: SBL Press, 2015.

Person, Raymond F., Jr., and Chris Keith. "Media Studies and Biblical Studies: An Introduction." Pages 1–15 in *The Dictionary of the Bible and Ancient Media*. Edited by Tom Thatcher, Chris Keith, Raymond F. Person Jr., and Elsie Stern. London: Bloomsbury, 2017.

Person, Raymond F., Jr., and Robert Rezetko. "The Importance of Empirical Models to Assess the Efficacy of Source and Redaction Criticism." Pages 1–35 in *Empirical Models Challenging Biblical Criticism*. Edited by Raymond F. Person Jr. and Robert Rezetko. AIL 25. Atlanta: SBL Press, 2016.

Petersen, William L. "The Diatessaron and the Fourfold Gospel." Pages 50–68 in *The Earliest Gospels: The Origins and Transmission of the Earliest Christian Gospels—The Contribution of the Chester Beatty Gospel*

Codex P45. Edited by Charles Horton. JSNTSup 258. London: T&T Clark, 2010.

Peterson, John L. "Aijalon." *ABD* 1:131.

———. "Ain." *ABD* 1:131–32.

———. "Gath-rimmon." *ABD* 2:910–11.

———. "Gibbethon." *ABD* 2:1006–7.

———. "Holon." *ABD* 3:257–58.

———. "Jattir." *ABD* 3:649–50.

———. "Juttah." *ABD* 3:1135.

———. "Kibzaim." *ABD* 4:36–37.

Pioske, Daniel D. *David's Jerusalem: Between Memory and History*. Routledge Studies in Religion. London: Routledge, 2015.

———. "Memory and Its Materiality: The Case of Early Iron Age Khirbet Qeiyafa and Jerusalem." *ZAW* 127 (2015): 78–95.

———. *Memory in a Time of Prose: Studies in Epistemology, Hebrew Scribalism, and the Biblical Past*. Oxford: Oxford University Press, 2018.

———. "Retracing a Remembered Past: Methodological Remarks on Memory, History, and the Hebrew Bible." *BibInt* 23 (2015): 291–315.

Polak, Frank. "Whodunit? Implicit Subject, Discourse Structure, and Pragmatics in the Hebrew and Greek Bibles." Pages 223–48 in *From Author to Copyist: Essays on the Composition, Redaction, and Transmission of the Hebrew Bible in Honor of Zipi Talshir*. Edited by Cana Werman. Winona Lake, IN: Eisenbrauns, 2015.

Propp, William H. C. *Exodus 19–40: A New Translation with Introduction and Commentary*. AB. New York: Doubleday, 2006.

Pulikottil, Paulson. *Transmission of Biblical Texts at Qumran: The Case of the Large Isaiah Scroll 1QIsa^a*. JSPSup 34. Sheffield: Sheffield Academic, 2001.

Rae, John P., Robin Wooffitt, and Raymond F. Person Jr. "Bridging the Gap: Conversation Analysis and Poetics from Jefferson to Now." Pages 1–28 in *Bridging the Gap between Conversation Analysis and Poetics: Studies in Talk-in-Interaction and Literature Twenty-Five Years after Jefferson*. Edited by Raymond F. Person Jr., Robin Wooffitt, and John P. Rae. Research in Language and Communication. London: Routledge, 2022.

Ready, Jonathan. *Homeric Simile in Comparative Perspectives: Oral Traditions from Saudi Arabia to Indonesia*. Oxford: Oxford University Press, 2018.

———. *Orality, Textuality, and the Homeric Epics: An Interdisciplinary Study of Oral Texts, Dictated Texts, and Wild Texts*. Oxford: Oxford University Press, 2019.

Rendle-Short, Johanna. "Dispreferred Responses When Texting: Delaying That 'No' Response." *Discourse & Communication* 9 (2015): 643–61.

Rendsburg, Gary A. *Diglossia in Ancient Hebrew*. AOS 72. New Haven: American Oriental Society, 1990.

———. *How The Bible Is Written*. Peabody, MA: Hendrickson, 2019.

———. "Word Play in Biblical Hebrew: An Eclectic Collection." Pages 137–62 in *Puns and Pundits: Word Play in the Hebrew Bible and Ancient Near Eastern Literature*. Edited by Scott B. Noegel. Bethesda, MD: CDL, 2000.

Rey, Jean-Sébastien. "Reflections on the Critical Edition of the Hebrew Text of Ben Sira: Between Eclecticism and Pragmatism." *Textus* 27 (2018): 187–204.

Rezetko, Robert, and Ian Young. *Historical Linguistics and Biblical Hebrew: Steps Toward an Integrated Approach*. ANEM 9. Atlanta: SBL Press, 2014.

Ringgren, Helmer. "Oral and Written Transmission in the O.T.: Some Observations." *Studia Theologica* 3 (1949): 34–59.

Robinson, Jeffrey D. "The Role of Numbers and Statistics within Conversation Analysis." *Communication Methods and Measures* 1 (2007): 65–75.

Rubin, Aaron D. "Genesis 49:4 in Light of Arabic and Modern South Arabian." *VT* 59 (2009): 499–502.

Rubin, David C. *Memory in Oral Traditions: The Cognitive Psychology of Epic, Ballads, and Counting-Out Rhymes*. Oxford: Oxford University Press, 1995.

Sacks, Harvey, and Emanuel A. Schegloff. "Two Preferences in the Organization of Reference to Persons in Conversation and Their Interaction." Pages 15–21 in *Everyday Language: Studies in Ethnomethodology*. Edited George Psathas. New York: Irvington, 1979.

Sanderson, Judith E. *An Exodus Scroll from Qumran: 4QpaleoExodm and the Samaritan Tradition*. HSS 30. Atlanta: Scholars Press, 1986.

Sarna, Nahum M. *Genesis: The Traditional Hebrew Text with the New JPS Translation*. JPS Torah Commentary. Philadelphia: Jewish Publication Society, 1989.

Sasson, Jack M. "Word-Play in Gen 6:8–9." *CBQ* 37 (1975): 165–66.

Schart, Aaron. "Totenstille und Endknall: Ein Beitrag zur Analyse der Soundscape des Zwölfprophetenbuches." Pages 257–74 in *Sprachen—Bilder—Klänge: Dimensionen der Theologie im Alten Testament und in seinem Umfeld; Festschrift für Rüdiger Bartelmus zum seinem 65. Geburtstag*. Edited by Christiane Karrer-Grube, Jutta Krispenz, Thomas Krüger, Christian Rose, and Annette Schellenberg. AOAT 359. Münster: Ugarit-Verlag, 2009.

Schegloff, Emanuel A.. "Identification and Recognition in Telephone Conversation Openings." Pages 23–78 in *Everyday Language: Studies in Ethnomethodology*. Edited by George Psathas. New York: Irvington, 1979.

———. "Reflections on Quantification in the Study of Conversation." *Research on Language and Social Interaction* 26 (1993): 99–128.

———. "The Relevance of Repair to Syntax-For-Conversation." Pages 261–86 in *Discourse and Syntax*. Edited by Talmy Givon. Syntax and Semantics 12. New York: Academic Press, 1979.

———. "Some Practices of Referring to Persons in Talk-in-Interaction: A Partial Sketch of a Systematics." Pages 437–85 in *Studies in Anaphora*. Edited by Barbara Fox. Typological Studies in Language 33. Amsterdam: Benjamins, 1996.

Schegloff, Emanuel A., Gail Jefferson, and Harvey Sacks. "The Preference for Self-Correction in the Organization of Repair in Conversation." *Language* 53 (1977): 361–82.

Schenker, Adrian. "What Do Scribes, and What Do Editors Do? The Hebrew Text of the Masoretes, the Old Greek Bible and the Alexandrian Philological *Ekdoseis* of the Fourth and Third Centuries B.C., Illustrated by the Example of 2 Kings 1." Pages 275–93 in *After Qumran: Old and Modern Editions of the Biblical Texts—The Historical Books*. Edited by Hans Ausloos, Bénédicte Lemmelijn, and Julio Trebolle Barrera. BETL 246. Leuven: Peeters, 2012.

Schorch, Stefan. "Dissimilatory Reading and the Making of Biblical Texts: The Jewish Pentateuch and the Samaritan Pentateuch." Pages 109–27 in *Empirical Models Challenging Biblical Criticism*. Edited by Raymond F. Person Jr. and Robert Rezetko. AIL 25. Atlanta: SBL Press, 2016.

———. *Das Buch Genesis*. Vol. 1 of *Die Vokale des Gesetzes: Die samaritanische Lesetradition als Textzeugin der Tora*. BZAW 339. Berlin: de Gruyter, 2004.

Scolnic, Benjamin Edidin. *Theme and Context in Biblical Lists*. SFSHJ. Atlanta: Scholars Press, 1995.

Screnock, John. "A New Approach to Using the Old Greek in Hebrew Bible Textual Criticism." *Textus* 27 (2018): 229–57.

Segal, Michael. "Harmonization and Rewriting of Daniel 6 from the Bible to Qumran." Pages 265–79 in *Hā-'îsh Mōshe: Studies in Scriptural Interpretation in the Dead Sea Scrolls and Related Literature in Honor of Moshe J. Bernstein*. Edited by Binyamin Y. Goldstein, Michael Segal, and George J. Brooke. STDJ 122. Leiden: Brill, 2017.

Sidnell, Jack, and Tanya Stivers, eds. *The Handbook of Conversation Analysis*. BHL. Oxford: Wiley-Blackwell, 2013.

Speiser, E. A. *Genesis: Introduction, Translation, and Notes*. AB. Garden City, NY: Doubleday, 1964.

Spencer-Miller, Althea. "Rethinking Orality for Biblical Studies." Pages 35–68 in *Postcolonialism and the Hebrew Bible: The Next Step*. Edited by Roland Boer. SemeiaSt 70. Atlanta: Society of Biblical Literature, 2013.

Stivers, Tanya, N. J. Enfield, and Stephen C. Levinson. "Person Reference in Interaction." Pages 1–20 in *Person Reference in Interaction: Linguistic, Cultural, and Social Perspectives*. Edited by N. J. Enfield and Tanya Stivers. Language, Culture, and Cognition 7. Cambridge: Cambridge University Press, 2007.

Stulman, Louis. *The Prose Sermons of the Book of Jeremiah*. SBLDS 83. Atlanta: Scholars Press, 1986.

Tal, Abraham, and Moshe Florentin, eds. *The Pentateuch: The Samaritan Version and the Masoretic Version*. Tel Aviv: Tel Aviv University Press, 2010.

Talmon, Shemaryahu. "Double Readings in the Masoretic Text." *Textus* 1 (1960): 144–84.

———. "Observations on Variant Readings in the Isaiah Scroll (1QIsa[a])." Pages 117–30 in *The World of Qumran from Within: Collected Studies*. Jerusalem: Magnes; Leiden: Brill, 1989.

———. "Oral Tradition and Written Transmission, or the Heard and the Seen Word in Judaism of the Second Temple Period." Pages 121–58 in *Jesus and the Oral Gospel Tradition*. Edited by Henry Wansbrough. JSNTSup 64. Sheffield: Sheffield Academic, 1991.

———. "Synonymous Readings in the Textual Traditions of the Old Testament." Pages 335–83 in *Studies in the Bible 1*. Edited by Chaim Rabin. ScrHier 8. Jerusalem: Magnes, 1961.

———. "The Textual Study of the Bible: A New Outlook." Pages 321–400 in *Qumran and the History of the Bible Text*. Edited by Frank Moore

Cross and Shemaryahu Talmon. Cambridge: Harvard University Press, 1975.
Teeter, David Andrew. *Scribal Laws: Exegetical Variation in the Textual Transmission of Biblical Law in the Late Second Temple Period*. FAT 92. Tübingen: Mohr Siebeck, 2014.
Thompson, Henry O. "Almon." *ABD* 1:161.
Tigay, Jeffrey H. "Conflation as a Redactional Technique." Pages 53–95 in *Empirical Models for Biblical Criticism*. Edited by Jeffrey H. Tigay. Philadelphia: University of Pennsylvania Press, 1985.
———, ed. *Empirical Models for Biblical Criticism*. Philadelphia: University of Pennsylvania Press, 1985.
Tigchelaar, Eibert J. C. "The Scribes of the Scrolls." Pages 524–32 in *T&T Clark Companion to the Dead Sea Scrolls*. Edited by George J. Brooke and Charlotte Hempel. London: T&T Clark, 2018.
Timpanaro, Sebastiano. *The Genesis of Lachmann's Method*. Edited and translated by Glenn W. Most. Chicago: University of Chicago Press, 2005.
Toews, Wesley I. "Jokmeam." *ABD* 3:933.
Tov, Emanuel. "The Coincidental Textual Nature of the Collections of Ancient Scriptures." Pages 20–35 in *Textual Criticism of the Hebrew Bible, Qumran, Septuagint: Collected Essays, Volume 3*. VTSup 167. Leiden: Brill, 2015.
———. "The Development of the Text of the Torah in Two Major Text Blocks." *Textus* 26 (2016):1–27.
———. "Different Editions of the Song of Hannah and of Its Narrative Framework." Pages 149–70 in *Tehillah le-Moshe: Biblical and Judaic Studies in Honor of Moshe Greenberg*. Edited by Mordechai Cogan, Barry L. Eichler, and Jeffrey H. Tigay. Winona Lake, IN: Eisenbrauns, 1997.
———. "From 4QReworked Pentateuch to 4QPentateuch(?)." Pages 73–91 in *Authoritative Scriptures in Ancient Judaism*. Edited by Mladen Popović. JSJSup 141. Leiden: Brill, 2010.
———. "The Harmonizing Character of the Septuagint of Genesis 1–11." Pages 470–89 in *Textual Criticism of the Hebrew Bible, Qumran, Septuagint: Collected Essays, Volume 3*. VTSup 167. Leiden: Brill, 2015.
———. "Interchanges of Consonants between the Masoretic Text and the Vorlage of the Septuagint." Pages 255–66 in *Sha'arei Talmon: Studies in the Bible, Qumran, and the Ancient Near East Presented to Shemaryahu*

Talmon. Edited by Michael Fishbane and Emanuel Tov. Winona Lake, IN: Eisenbrauns, 1992.

———. "The Literary History of the Book of Jeremiah in the Light of Its Textual History." Pages 211–37 in *Empirical Models for Biblical Criticism*. Edited by Jeffrey Tigay. Philadelphia: University of Pennsylvania Press, 1985.

———. "Loan-Words, Homophony and Transliterations in the Septuagint." *Bib* 60 (1979): 216–36.

———. "The Nature and Background of Harmonizations in Biblical Manuscripts." *JSOT* 10.31 (1985): 3–29.

———. "The Scribal and Textual Transmission of the Torah Analyzed in Light of Its Sanctity." Pages 154–65 in *Textual Criticism of the Hebrew Bible, Qumran, Septuagint: Collected Essays, Volume 3*. VTSup 167. Leiden: Brill, 2015.

———. *Scribal Practices and Approaches Reflected in the Texts Found in the Judean Desert*. STDJ 54. Leiden: Brill, 2004.

———. "Some Aspects of the Textual and Literary History of the Book of Jeremiah." Pages 145–67 in *Le livre de Jérémie: Le prophéte et son milieu, les oracles et leur transmission*. Edited by Pierre-Maurice Bogaert. BETL 54. Leuven: Leuven University Press, 1981.

———. "Some Reflections on Consistency in the Activity of Scribes and Translators." Pages 36–44 in *Textual Criticism of the Hebrew Bible, Qumran, Septuagint: Collected Essays, Volume 3*. VTSup 167. Leiden: Brill, 2015.

———. *Textual Criticism of the Hebrew Bible*. 2nd ed. Minneapolis: Fortress, 2001.

———. *Textual Criticism of the Hebrew Bible*. 3rd ed. Minneapolis: Fortress, 2012.

———. "Textual Harmonization in Exodus 1–24." *TC: A Journal of Biblical Textual Criticism* 22 (2017). https://tinyurl.com/SBL7015a.

———. "Textual Harmonizations in the Ancient Texts of Deuteronomy." Pages 271–82 in *Hebrew Bible, Greek Bible, and Qumran: Collected Essays*. TSAJ 121. Tübingen: Mohr Siebeck, 2008.

———. "Textual Harmonization in the Stories of the Patriarchs." Pages 166–88 in *Textual Criticism of the Hebrew Bible, Qumran, Septuagint: Collected Essays, Volume 3*. VTSup 167. Leiden: Brill, 2015.

Troxel, Ronald L. "What Is the 'Text' in Textual Criticism?" *VT* 66 (2016): 603–26.

———. "Writing Commentary on the Life of a Text." *VT* 67 (2017): 105–28.

Tsumura, David Toshio. "Scribal Errors or Phonetic Spellings? Samuel as an Aural Text." *VT* 49 (1999): 390–411.
Ulrich, Eugene. *The Biblical Qumran Scrolls: Transcriptions and Textual Variants*. VTSup 134. Leiden: Brill, 2010.
———. "The Canonical Process, Textual Criticism and Latter Stages in the Composition of the Bible." Pages 267–91 in *Sha'arei Talmon: Studies in the Bible, Qumran, and the Ancient Near East Presented to Shemaryahu Talmon*. Edited by Michael Fishbane and Emanuel Tov. Winona Lake, IN: Eisenbrauns, 1992.
———. "The Evolutionary Production and Transmission of the Scriptural Books." Pages 47–64 in *Changes in Scripture: Rewriting and Interpreting Authoritative Traditions in the Second Temple Period*. Edited by Hanne von Weissenberg, Juha Pakkala, and Marko Marttila. BZAW 419. Berlin: de Gruyter, 2011.
Vayntrub, Jacquline. *Beyond Orality: Biblical Poetry on Its Own Terms*. London: Routledge, 2019.
Vermeulen, Karolien. "To See or Not To See: The Polysemy of the Word עין in the Isaac Narratives (Gen 17–35)." *JHebS* 9 (2009). https://doi.org/10.5508/jhs.2009.v9.a22.
———. "Two of a Kind: Twin Language in the Hebrew Bible." *JSOT* 37 (2012): 135–50.
Vroom, Jonathan. "A Cognitive Approach to Copying Errors: Haplography and Textual Transmission of the Hebrew Bible." *JSOT* 40 (2016): 259–79.
———. "The Role of Memory in *Vorlage*-Based Transmission: Evidence from Erasures and Corrections." *Textus* 27 (2018): 258–73.
Waard, Jan de. "'Homophony' in the Septuagint." *Bib* 62 (1981): 551–61.
Wagner, Andreas. "Der Parallelismus Membrorum zwischen Poetischer Form und Denkfigur." Pages 1–26 in *Parallelismus Membrorum*. Edited by Andreas Wagner. OBO 224. Fribourg: Presses Universitaires; Göttingen: Vandenhoeck & Ruprecht, 2007.
Watts, James W. "Narratives, Lists, Rhetoric, Ritual, and the Pentateuch as a Scripture." Pages 1135–45 in *The Formation of the Pentateuch: Bridging the Academic Cultures of Europe, Israel, and North America*. Edited by Jan C. Gertz, Bernard M. Levinson, Dalit Rom-Shiloni, and Konrad Schmid. FAT 111. Tübingen: Mohr Siebeck, 2016.
Wenger, Rachelle. "Redundancy Is Information: The Literary Function of Participant Reference in Biblical Hebrew Narrative." *BT* 63 (2012): 179–84.

West, Stephanie, ed. *The Ptolemaic Papyri of Homer*. Cologne: Westdeutscher, 1967.

Westermann, Claus. *Isaiah 40–66: A Commentary*. OTL. Philadelphia: Westminster, 1969.

Wevers, John William. *Exodus*. SVTG 2. Göttingen: Vandenhoeck & Ruprecht, 1991.

———. *Genesis*. SVTG 1. Göttingen: Vandenhoeck & Ruprecht, 1974.

Wolff, Hans Walter. *Dodekapropheten: Joel–Amos*. BKAT 14.2. Neukirchen-Vluyn: Neukirchener Verlag, 1963.

———. *Joel and Amos: A Commentary on the Books of the Prophets Joel and Amos*. Hermeneia. Philadelphia: Fortress, 1977.

Wollenberg, Rebecca Scharbach. "The Book That Changed: Narratives of Ezran Authorship as Late Antique Biblical Criticism." *JBL* 138 (2019): 143–60.

———. "A King and a Scribe like Moses: The Reception of Deuteronomy 34:10 and a Rabbinic Theory of Collective Biblical Authorship." *HUCA* 90 (2019): 209–26.

Woods, William L. "Language Study in Schizophrenia." *Journal of Nervous and Mental Disease* 87 (1939): 290–316.

Wooffitt, Robin, Darren Reed, Jessica A. Young, and Claire Jackson. "The Poetics in Jefferson's Poetics Lecture." Pages 97–116 in *Bridging the Gap between Conversation Analysis and Poetics: Studies in Talk-in-Interaction and Literature Twenty-Five Years after Jefferson*. Edited by Raymond F. Person Jr., Robin Wooffitt, and John P. Rae. Research in Language and Communication. London: Routledge, 2022.

Wolters, Al. "*ṢÔPIYYÂ* (Prov 31:27) as Hymnic Participle and Play on Sophia." *JBL* 104 (1985): 577–87.

Yogev, Jonathan, and Shamir Yona. "Opening Alliteration in Biblical and Ugaritic Poetry." *ZAW* 127 (2015): 108–13.

Young, Ian. "Ancient Hebrew without Authors." *JSem* 25 (2016): 972–1003.

———. "The Dead Sea Scrolls and the Bible: The View from Qumran Samuel." *ABR* 62 (2014): 14–30.

———. "Manuscripts and Authors of the Psalms." *Studia Biblica Slovaca* 8 (2016): 123–36.

———. "The Original Problem: The Old Greek and the Masoretic Text of Daniel 5." Pages 271–301 in *Empirical Models Challenging Biblical Criticism*. Edited by Raymond F. Person Jr. and Robert Rezetko. AIL 25. Atlanta: SBL Press, 2016.

———. "Starting at the Beginning with Archaic Biblical Hebrew." *HS* 58 (2017): 99–118.

Young, Ian, Robert Rezetko, and Martin Ehrensvärd. *Linguistic Dating of Biblical Texts*. 2 vols. London: Equinox, 2008.

Zahn, Molly M. *Genres of Rewriting in Second Temple Judaism: Scribal Composition and Transmission*. Cambridge: Cambridge University Press, 2020.

———. *Rethinking Rewritten Scripture: Composition and Exegesis in the 4QReworked Pentateuch Manuscripts*. STDJ 95. Leiden: Brill, 2011.

Zakovitch, Yair. "Implied Synonyms and Antonyms: Textual Criticism vs. The Literary Approach." Pages 833–49 in *Emanuel: Studies in Hebrew Bible, Septuagint, and the Dead Sea Scrolls in Honor of Emanuel Tov*. Edited by Shalom M. Paul, Robert A. Kraft, Lawrence H. Schiffman, and Weston W. Fields. VTSup 94. Leiden: Brill, 2003.

Ancient Sources Index

Hebrew Bible

Genesis
5:29	216, 220–21
12:16	165
14:13	119
14:24	119
15:19–21	106, 123, 127
24:35	165
25:24	279, 282
30:43	165
32:5	165
32:15	165
32:28	79
34:28	165
37:1	244
38:25	244, 282
38:26	279
45:2	243
46:21	105
47:17	165
47:31	245

Exodus
1–24	184–85
2:3	185
2:6	185
2:17	165
2:22	185
3:8	106, 123–24, 127–28
3:10	178, 185, 192, 194
3:11	178, 185, 192, 194
3:17	106, 123–24, 127
3:18	178, 185–86, 192, 194
3:19	178, 185, 192, 194
4:13	185
4:31	186
7:14–11:10	158
7:26	76
9:1	76
9:3	165
10:6	185
11:7	84
11:8	185
12:31	186
14:28	161
14:28–29	136
14:29	159–62
15:16–20	266–70
15:16–21	267–70
15:18	160
15:19	136
15:25	185
16:23	185
18:21–27	136, 154–58
20:10	163–64
20:10–12	132, 136, 147–50
20:10–17	147
22:2	165
22:4	165, 261–62
22:9	165
22:10	165
23:23	106, 123–24, 127–28
23:28	106, 123–24, 127–28
24:4	185
26:1	282
26:10	79
26:19	282
26:21	282
26:24	277–79, 281–84, 298

Exodus (cont.)		33:5–37	229
26:31	282	34:1–15	103
26:36	282	34:1–29	103, 116
32:11	88–90	34:11	116
33:2	106, 123, 125, 127–28		
34:11	106, 123, 125, 127–28	Deuteronomy	
36–37	283	1–9	154
36:8	282	1:9–18	136, 154–58
36:24	282	1:27–32	136, 151–53
36:26	282	5:14	147, 150, 163–65
36:29	277–79, 282–84, 298	5:14–16	132, 136, 147–50
36:30	282	5:16	147
36:35	282	5:21	165
36:37	282	5:27	77
		6:1	78
Leviticus		6:4–5	18
1:2	76	6:4–9	18
11:1–37	104	6:6–9	18
15:3	262, 263–65	7:1	127–28, 130
16:29	132, 147–50, 163	9:26	88–91
		9:29	88–91
Numbers		12:32	129
1:20–46	103	19:14	228
3:14–39	103	20:17	106, 123, 126–28
7	104	22:1	165
10:11–28	103	22:4	165
11:1–3	229	26:1–11	237
11:3	216, 229–30	28:31	165
11:34	230	28:43	244
13:23	230	33:20	84
13:29	106, 123, 125–27		
13:33	150–51, 153	Joshua	
13:33–14:1	136, 150–53	6:21	165
20:13	230	7:24	165
21:3	230	11:3	106, 122–23, 126–28
23:24	84	12–19	121
26:38–40	105	12:21	119
27:14	230	15:32	116
31:28	165	15:48	115
31:30	165	15:51	116
31:32–40	104	15:55	117
31:33	165	17:11	119–20
31:38	165	18:24	117
31:44	165	19:1	116
33:1–49	103	19:7	116

19:41	117	15:27	119
19:44	119	16:15	119
19:45	120	16:17	119
21:1–43	112–13, 120–21	18:31–34	183
21:13–26	106, 109–22, 130	18:36	184

Ruth
		2 Kings	
2:21	184	9:27	120
4:18–22	103	18–20	85
		19:9	85–86

1 Samuel
		23:13	136
2:1–7	289	24:18–25:30	86
2:1–10	297	25:30	87
2:3–10	289–98		
2:12–17	129	1 Chronicles	
10:27–11:2	284–89, 298	1–9	105
11	277	4:31	116
12:3	165	4:32	116
12:12	288	6:39–66	112
12:12–17	107	6:42–55	113–22
12:14	104–8	6:57–60	106, 113–22
12:16	104–8	6:67–70	106, 113–22
13:3	117	7:6–12	105
13:16	117	7:8	118
14:5	117	8:1–40	103, 105
17:34	84	12:24–39	103
22:19	165	15:25–16:3	145
27:8	165, 254	16:8–36	
27:9	165		
30:27	115	2 Chronicles	
		11:10	116

2 Samuel
		Ezra	
3:6–39	189	1:8–11	104
3:23–25	184, 189–92, 197	2	103
6:12–19a	145		
12:16	86	Nehemiah	
15:28	254	11:3–19	105
20:14	254–55		
22	2	Job	
23:8–39	103	1:3	165

1 Kings
		Psalms	
4:12	118	18	2
11:1–8	138	22:21	84
11:7	136–39		

Psalms (cont.)
24:3 — 72
37:34 — 223–25
73:3 — 224–25
74:13 — 252
78:13 — 252
91:8 — 216, 223–25, 234

Proverbs
2:8 — 296
3:1 — 69
3:8 — 216, 225–26, 234
3:10 — 204
5:1 — 69
5:3 — 69
6:16 — 204
8:3 — 204
8:19 — 210
10–29 — 204
10:20 — 210
12:21 — 255
12:23 — 257–58
13:14 — 252–53
14:34 — 247–48
15:4 — 204
15:30 — 256–57
15:32 — 203–5
19:27 — 204
22:17–23:11 — 228
22:28 — 228
23:10 — 227–28, 234
23:27 — 69
25:16 — 251
25:27 — 249–51
26:17 — 203, 215–16
30:15b–16 — 106, 108–9, 130
31:10–31 — 222
31:21–22 — 216, 221–23, 234

Song of Songs
1:2 — 216, 226–27, 234
4:3–6 — 278–82, 298
4:4–7 — 280
4:5 — 277
7:3 — 225

7:3–5a — 278–82, 298
7:4 — 277

Isaiah
10:29 — 117
30:20 — 215
33:20 — 203, 213–14
34:8 — 224
35 — 136
35:10 — 145–46
36–38 — 85
37:9 — 85–86
40:12 — 252
40:27 — 76
43:16 — 252
47:1 — 203, 211–13
47:10 — 248–49
47:11 — 249
48:7 — 203, 208–9
48:9–11 — 203, 209–11
49:6 — 79–80
49:15 — 228
51 — 136
51:3 — 145
51:10 — 252
51:11 — 145–46
69:20 — 228

Jeremiah (MT)
9:21 — 77
9:22–23 — 296–97
10:10–13 — 296
26:1 — 136, 139–40, 166
27:1 — 136, 139–40, 166
27:1–10 — 139
27:3 — 139
27:6 — 188
27:10 — 188
27:12 — 139
29:21 — 184, 187–89
29:21–22 — 216–20
33:12 — 188
37:3 — 188–89
48:21 — 116
48:21–24 — 103

Ancient Sources Index

52	86	1QSa	62
52:34	87, 301		
		1QSb	62
Ezekiel			
7:25	104	4Q1 (4QGen-Exod^a)	124, 128
9:9	244		
48	103	4Q4 (4QGen^d)	17
Daniel		4Q14 (4QExod^c)	266–67, 270
3	136, 140–45		
5	144	4Q22 (4QpaleoExod^m)	78, 154–58
5:2	80		
5:4	81–82	4Q27 (4QNum^b)	154–58
5:20	80		
5:23	81–82	4Q51 (4QSam^a)	190–92
6	136, 140–45		
11:12	80	4Q107 (4QCant^b)	278–81
Hosea		4Q149 (4QMezA)	147–50
9:7	224		
		4Q256 (4QS^b)	82–83,
Amos			
6:4–7	203, 205–7	4Q258 (4QS^d)	83, 91–93, 113
6:7	301		
		4Q261 (4QS^g)	91–93, 95, 113
Zechariah			
13:9	210	4Q364–367 (4QReworked Pentateuch, 4QPentateuch)	159–62

Deuterocanonical Books

		4QDeutⁿ	77
Ben Sira			
4:30	84–85	4QExod^b	185
11:3	87–88		
42:21	129	4QExod^c	266

Dead Sea Scrolls

		11Q1 (11QpaleoLev^a)	262
1QIsa^a	2, 79–80, 85–86, 145–46, 208–12	11Q11 (11QapocrPs)	223–25

New Testament

1QIsa^b	211		
		Hebrews	
1QS (Community Rule)	62, 82–83, 91–93, 95	11:21	245

Rabbinic Literature

Genesis Rabbah
    25:2   220

m. Peah
    5:6   228
    7:3   228

Modern Authors Index

Aejmelaeus, Anneli	294–96	Cook, Johann	13–14
Albright, William Foxwell	112–13	Crawford, Sidnie White	16–17, 21, 136–40, 154, 157–58, 166
Arnold, Patrick M.	117–18		
Askin, Lindsey A.	20, 22, 25–26	Cross, Frank Moore	182, 284, 286–87
Atkinson, J. Maxwell	238	Czachesz, István	3
Auld, A. Graeme	112–13, 287	Damico, Jack S.	49
Ausloos, Hans	202, 229–30	Davidson, Robert	246
Baltzer, Klaus	210	Dayfani, Hila	247
Barr, James	245	Debel, Hans	4, 7, 299
Ben Zvi, Ehud	112	DeConick, April D.	33
Bentin, Shlomo	241–42	Delnero, Paul	73
Berger, Stephanie	242	Doane, Alger N.	29–30, 32, 35–36
Bird, Graeme D.	10	Dotan, Aron	200, 231
Blenkinsopp, Joseph	145, 210, 212	Driver, S. R.	246
Blumenthal, David R.	199	Dunkle, Roger	179
Boadt, Lawrence	208–9, 212	Ehrensvärd, Martin	208, 306, 308
Bolling, George Melville	162	Eidevall, Göran	206
Bowles, Hugo	216, 301	Enfield, N. J.	170
Breed, Brennan W.	13, 141	Epp, Eldon Jay	6
Brettler, Marc Z.	118	Eshel, Esther	77, 147
Brooke, Alan England	106	Exum, J. Cheryl	280
Brooke, George J.	12, 17, 20, 33, 78	Fitzgerald, Aloysius	200, 210–11
Brouwer, Catherine E.	49	Foley, John Miles	11, 24, 29, 45, 57–59, 63–64, 71, 180, 299–300, 305
Brown, Penelope	173		
Bubka, Andrea	242	Fontaine, Carole R.	180
Carr, David M.	23, 30, 33–36, 59, 68, 74, 82–83, 95, 134, 309	Fox, Michael V.	12, 17, 22, 40, 69–70, 108–9, 204–5, 215, 221–22, 225–28, 247–53, 255–58
Carroll, Robert P.	139–40, 218		
Casanowicz, Immanuel M.	199, 205–6, 215, 220–21, 253	Franke, Chris	210
		Freedman, David Noel	122, 128, 259
Cassuto, Umberto	221, 283	Frog	59, 72
Ceresko, Anthony R.	199	Frost, Ram	241–42
Cerquiglini, Bernard	6	Garsiel, Moshe	181, 218–20, 288–89
Cogan, Mordechai	138	Gelston, Anthony	207
Collins, John J.	141–44	Glanz, Oliver	182–84, 194

Glenny, W. Edward	207	Knoppers, Gary N.	105, 112–13
Glock, A. E.	119	Krašovec, Jože	181–82
Goodwin, Charles	172, 236–37	Kratz, Reinhard G.	287, 289, 294–97
Gorfein, David S.	242	Kwon, JiSeong James	13–14
Goshen-Gottstein, Moshe H.	31–32, 304	Laakso, Minna	49
		Lamb, William	59, 88
Gottlob, Lawrence R.	241–42	Lange, Armin	18
Graybill, Rhiannon	200	Lee, Margaret E.	200
Greenberg, Seth N.	242	Lemmelijn, Bénédicte	158, 166, 309
Greer, Tim	49	Lenzi, Alan	61
Grossman, Maxine L.	61–62	Lerner, Gene H.	56, 97–101, 177
Hamilton, Jeffries M.	117	Levin, Yigal	105
Hanks, William F.	172	Levinson, Stephen C.	170
Hayashi, Makoto	47	Lionarons, Joyce Tally	22
Heath, Christian	237, 240	Llewelyn, Stephen	59
Helasvuo, Marja-Liisa	49	Lord, Albert B.	56, 61, 64, 71, 75, 179, 182,
Hempel, Charlotte	4	Luff, Paul	237, 240
Hendel, Ronald	7–8, 12–13, 15–17, 22–26, 67–70, 247	Lundbom, Jack R.	139–40, 218
Hengel, Martin	132	Makri-Tsilipakou, Marianthi	177
Heritage, John	44, 175–76	Martin, Gary D.	6, 15, 226–27, 283
Holladay, William L.	139, 199, 218–20	Martone, Corrado	40, 191
Holmes, Janet	44	McCarter, P. Kyle, Jr.	286–87, 296
Honko, Lauri	61	McCreesh, Thomas P.	204–5
Hornkohl, Aaron D.	8, 13	McKane, William	187
Horsley, Richard A.	30–31	McLean, Norman	106
Hunt, Melvin	119–20	Meer, Michaël N. van der	162
Hutchby, Ian	43, 238, 298	Meredith, Joanne	239
Jackson, Claire	96	Metso, Sarianna	82–83, 92
Jefferson, Gail	xiii, 39, 45–47, 50–57, 63–64, 69–71, 78, 83–85, 90, 94–102, 105, 135, 166–70, 176–77, 195, 200–202, 216, 218, 231–33, 235–36, 238–39, 275–76, 279, 300–301	Metzger, Bruce M.	131
		Milik, J. T.	147
		Miller, Marvin	30
		Miller, Shem	30–31, 33, 36, 72, 91–95, 159–62, 165, 265–70, 272–73, 277
Joosten, Jan	136–40	Milstein, Sara	18–19
Jurić, Dorian	9	Moshavi, Adina	181
Kabergs, Valérie	199, 202	Mroczek, Eva	31
Kallai, Zecharia	104–5	Mulkay, Michael	238–39
Kampf, Michal	241	Müller, Reinhard	150–53, 287, 309
Kawamoto, Alan H.	241–42	Murphy, Roland E.	281
Keith, Chris	10, 31	Mylonas, Natalie	59
Kelber, Werner H.	8, 10–11, 304	Newsom, Carol A.	140–43
Kirk, Alan	30–31, 33, 35–36	Niditch, Susan	21, 30, 43
Kitzinger, Celia	174–75, 177	Noegel, Scott B.	199, 234
Kline, Jonathan G.	223–25	Nõmmik, Urmas	199

Modern Authors Index

O'Connell, Kevin G. 122–28
O'Keeffe, Katherine O'Brien 10
Overton, Shawna Dolansky 122, 128, 259
Pakkala, Juha 150–53, 258–59, 287, 309
Pardee, Cambry G. 131–32, 134, 163–64
Parry, Donald W. 105–8
Parry, Milman 57, 60, 179–80, 182
Paul, Shalom M. 200, 206
Perdue, Leo G. 20
Perrin, Nicolas 132
Person, Raymond F., Jr. 10, 21, 27, 30–31, 34, 38–39, 43–44, 56, 59, 62, 64, 71, 73–74, 87, 96, 113, 122, 129–30, 132, 135, 145, 158, 161, 187, 237, 259, 304–7
Petersen, William L. 132
Peterson, John L. 115–17, 119–20
Pioske, Daniel D. 15, 30, 121
Polak, Frank 181
Propp, William H. C. 283
Pulikottil, Paulson 79, 145–46, 248–49
Rae, John P. 56
Ramey, Peter 59
Ready, Jonathan 10, 30–31, 36, 60–61
Reed, Darren 96
Rendle-Short, Johanna 239
Rendsburg, Gary A. 199–200, 208, 222
Rey, Jean-Sébastien 84, 87, 94–95
Rezetko, Robert 158, 208, 259, 305–9
Ringgren, Helmer 1–3, 9, 14
Robinson, Jeffrey D. 232
Romeny, Bas Ter Haar 150–53, 287, 309
Rubin, Aaron D. 199
Rubin, David C. 303–4
Sacks, Harvey 46–47, 56, 96, 170–71, 176, 236
Saint-Aubin, Jean 242
Sanderson, Judith E. 79, 88–90
Sarna, Nahum M. 246
Sasson, Jack M. 199
Schart, Aaron 200
Schegloff, Emanuel A. 46–47, 167, 170–71, 173, 176, 178, 232
Schenker, Adrian 19–21, 294

Schorch, Stefan 243–46
Scolnic, Benjamin Edidin 103–4
Screnock, John 192
Segal, Michael 142–44
Shaw, Rebecca 174–75
Sidnell, Jack 43
Sorjonen, Marja-Leena 49
Speiser, E. A. 246
Spencer-Miller, Althea 300
Stivers, Tanya 43, 170
Stokoe, Elisabeth 239
Stulman, Louis 187
Talmon, Shemaryahu 9, 13–15, 32, 34, 69, 72–80, 85, 93–95, 182, 195, 198, 275, 310
Teeter, David Andrew 22
Thackeray, Henry St. John 106
Thompson, Henry O. 118
Tigay, Jeffrey H. 154, 158, 308–9
Tigchelaar, Eibert J. C. 20
Timpanaro, Sebastiano 6
Toerien, Merran 174–75
Toews, Wesley I. 119
Tov, Emanuel 7–8, 12, 28, 87, 131–36, 147, 150, 153, 159, 163, 184–88, 196, 199, 226, 233, 247, 252, 258–59, 265, 287, 292, 294–96
Troxel, Ronald L. 6, 8, 11–13, 15–17, 37, 304–5
Tsumura, David Toshio 253–55, 258, 271, 283–84
Ulrich, Eugene 5, 19, 88, 136–40, 208–9, 223, 278, 284, 290
Vayntrub, Jacqueline 59
Vermeulen, Karolien 199, 234, 278–84
Vroom, Jonathan 22, 24–27, 259–65, 272, 276, 286, 288
Waard, Jan de 214
Wagner, Andreas 72
Watts, James W. 105, 128–29
Wearne, Gareth 59
Weigold, Matthias 18
Wenger, Rachelle 183–84, 194
West, Stephanie 162
Westermann, Claus 210

Wevers, John William 220
Wolff, Hans Walter 206
Wollenberg, Rebecca Scharbach 14, 18–19, 131
Wolters, Al 199
Woods, William L. 54
Wooffitt, Robin 43, 56, 96, 298
Yogev, Jonathan 199
Yona, Shamir 199
Young, Ian 4–5, 9, 31, 80–81, 86, 144, 165, 208, 304, 306, 308
Young, Jessica A. 96
Zahn, Molly M. 1–3, 9, 15, 160, 305
Zakovitch, Yair 225–28
Zemblidge, John H. 241–42

Milton Keynes UK
Ingram Content Group UK Ltd.
UKHW011043231123
433129UK00005B/462